D0781545

The Professional Restaurant Manager

David K. Hayes, Ph.D.
Panda Pros Hospitality Management and Training

Allisha A. Miller
Panda Pros Hospitality Management and Training

Jack D. Ninemeier, Ph.D.
The School of Hospitality Business
Michigan State University

PEARSON

Boston   Columbus   Indianapolis   New York   San Francisco   Upper Saddle River
Amsterdam   Cape Town   Dubai   London   Madrid   Milan   Munich   Paris   Montréal   Toronto
Delhi   Mexico City   São Paulo   Sydney   Hong Kong   Seoul   Singapore   Taipei   Tokyo

Editorial Director: Vernon Anthony
Senior Acquisitions Editor: William Lawrensen
Editorial Assistant: Lara Dimmick
Director of Marketing: David Gesell
Marketing Manager: Stacey Martinez
Senior Marketing Assistant: Les Roberts
Project Manager: Susan Hannahs
Senior Art Director: Jayne Conte

Cover Designer: Suzanne Duda
Cover Art: Fotolia/© Andrew Bayda
Full-Service Project Management: Revathi Viswanathan, PreMediaGlobal
Composition: PreMediaGlobal, Inc.
Printer/Binder: LSC Communications
Cover Printer: LSC Communications
Text Font: MinionPro 10/12

Credits and acknowledgments borrowed from other sources and reproduced, with permission, in this textbook appear on the appropriate page within the text.

Microsoft® and Windows® are registered trademarks of the Microsoft Corporation in the U.S.A. and other countries. Screen shots and icons reprinted with permission from the Microsoft Corporation. This book is not sponsored or endorsed by or affiliated with the Microsoft Corporation.

Copyright © 2014 by Pearson, Inc. All rights reserved. Manufactured in the United States of America. This publication is protected by Copyright, and permission should be obtained from the publisher prior to any prohibited reproduction, storage in a retrieval system, or transmission in any form or by any means, electronic, mechanical, photocopying, recording, or likewise. To obtain permission(s) to use material from this work, please submit a written request to Pearson, Inc., Permissions Department, One Lake Street, Upper Saddle River, New Jersey 07458, or you may fax your request to 201-236-3290.

Many of the designations by manufacturers and sellers to distinguish their products are claimed as trademarks. Where those designations appear in this book, and the publisher was aware of a trademark claim, the designations have been printed in initial caps or all caps.

Library of Congress Cataloging-in-Publication Data

Catalogue in Publication data available from the Library of Congress

5

ISBN 10: 0-13-273992-5
ISBN 13: 978-0-13-273992-4

This book is dedicated to professionals who, in a wide variety of settings, work tirelessly to serve great food to their customers, students, patients, clients, members or guests in the spirit of hospitality . . . as well as to Mary Francis Kennedy (MFK) Fisher.

Fellow Michigander M. F. K. Fisher, the brilliant and prolific author of more than 20 books dedicated to food, shared a fascinating thought with her readers. She believed that sharing food with others was a significant interpersonal activity that should be done with a genuine and caring concern.

The authors completely agree with her.

We would add that the professional restaurant managers to whom this book is dedicated gladly share with others not just food, but also an essential part of themselves.

David K. Hayes, Ph.D.   Allisha A. Miller   Jack D. Ninemeier, Ph.D.

CONTENTS

PREFACE

Professional restaurant managers hold some of the most exciting—and challenging—jobs in the hospitality industry.

There's no doubt that the restaurant business is highly competitive. This is true whether one makes his or her professional career in the commercial or noncommercial segments of food service. This book was written to detail—in an easy-to-read, easy-to-understand and easy-to-remember style—exactly what professional restaurant managers must know and do to be successful in that highly competitive environment.

The authors are well aware that the restaurant business is as multidisciplinary as it is complex. As a result, professional restaurant managers must understand the importance of food science, the culinary arts, accounting, law, marketing, beverage management and cost control—among other subjects! Of course, each of those subjects (and more) is worthy of extensive study. There is also a need, however, for a single resource that shows exactly how restaurant managers draw from each of these key areas to operate their businesses profitably. *The Professional Restaurant Manager* was developed to be that single resource.

INTENDED AUDIENCES

Instructors

Instructors adopting this book for use in class will find a basic yet comprehensive text that addresses, in everyday language, all major aspects of restaurant operations.

From concept to operation, *The Professional Restaurant Manager* tackles the specific topics that food service managers must understand to do their jobs well.

It's appropriate for those just beginning to study the restaurant industry and those currently working in the industry who seek to advance their careers by continuing their education.

The Supplemental Teaching materials developed for this text have been extensively reviewed and allow for easy instructor use. The PowerPoint slides, enhance student learning by making the text easy to understand and easy to remember. To access supplementary materials online, instructors need to request an instructor access code. Go to www.pearsonhighered.com/irc, where you can register for an instructor access code. Within forty-eight hours after registering, you will receive a confirmation email, including your instructor access code. Once you have received your code, go to the site and log on for full instructions on downloading the materials you wish to use.

Students

Serious hospitality students want to understand how an entity as large and complex as a restaurant is planned and managed. *The Professional Restaurant Manager* provides that information in an easy-to-read format.

Regardless of their specific area of interest in the restaurant industry, readers will learn how restaurant managers use a variety of skills to better serve their guests. Students planning careers in both the commercial and the noncommercial segments of the food service industry will find the information in *The Professional Restaurant Manager* highly relevant to their personal success and to the success of their operations.

Industry Professionals

Many people are interested in how restaurant managers do their jobs. Those who own or lend money to restaurants need to understand what restaurant managers can be expected to do to help ensure the quality and growth of their restaurant investments.

Employees look to a restaurant's leaders to make decisions that benefit their short-term personal goals and their long-term employment interests. They expect fair treatment and a safe, pleasant working environment that's professionally managed.

Guests, of course, rely upon professional restaurant managers to ensure that they receive value and quality for the dollars they spend when dining away from home.

Finally, because they *are* professionals, restaurant managers seek to better understand how their own efforts complement those of the entire restaurant staff. In any restaurant, managers, supervisors and hourly employees all benefit when they understand how the work of each meshes with the other. *The Professional Restaurant Manager* is a valuable text for all those who wish to learn more and expand their knowledge of restaurant management.

CHAPTER ORDER AND CONTENT

To truly understand the restaurant industry, one must first understand its history and structure (Chapter 1) as well as how restaurants are developed (Chapter 2). Because the number of legal issues affecting the operation of a restaurant is significant, the legal responsibilities of restaurant managers must also be well known (Chapter 3).

Experienced restaurant managers know that excellent food and service can only be delivered with a well-trained and highly motivated staff (Chapter 4). Many of the key decisions made by the restaurants' employees and managers (e.g., what to buy, what to cook and how much to charge) are based upon the restaurant's menu (Chapter 5) and the facility in which it operates (Chapter 6).

While there is no universal agreement on the best order in which to study restaurant operations, it is agreed that all restaurant managers must get ready for production (Chapter 7), oversee the preparation of quality foods (Chapter 8), serve their guests professionally (Chapter 9) and, if alcoholic beverages are part of a restaurant's menu offerings, serve these products responsibly (Chapter 10).

Restaurant managers are responsible for the financial performance of their operations. As a result, they carefully control costs (Chapter 11) and manage revenue (Chapter 12). Perhaps the ultimate management responsibility is that of managing for profits (Chapter 13).

CHAPTER FUNDAMENTALS

The restaurant industry is an exciting one, and the authors sought to convey its excitement through a text that would be, first and foremost, user-friendly. To that end, each chapter in *The Professional Restaurant Manager* includes the following instructional elements.

Chapter Outline

Each chapter begins with a carefully developed, tiered outline that allows the reader to find important information with the maximum ease.

Learning Objectives

Each chapter addresses specific learning objectives. These clearly written, one-sentence objectives help students know exactly what they should learn by reading the chapter.

In This Chapter

Each chapter includes a short narrative summary that describes what will be presented in the chapter and why it is important.

Restaurant Terms and Concepts

As is true in many professional fields, restaurateurs often speak their own unique language. Restaurant managers refer to the *POS* for current sales data and formulate beverage service policies with an eye toward *dram-shop legislation*. Required *EP weight* and *AP yield* are calculated prior to making *POs* (and those POs may well include *IQF* items!)

Restaurant-specific terms are used extensively in the book; they're defined when they first appear, often with direct-use examples that help to further clarify their meaning. Unique vocabulary is such an important part of the industry—and this book—that the glossary contains over 424 restaurant industry-specific definitions.

Web at Work

In many cases, a restaurant-industry specific website adds significant and particularly useful information to the book. Such websites are presented under the heading "Web at Work." The addition of selected Web resources is intended to enhance the book's content. The Web references in this book are purposely extensive and found in every chapter.

Green at Work

This feature addresses the restaurant industry's increasing use of environmentally friendly business practices. The adoption of sustainable business practices by the restaurant industry isn't just good for the environment, it's good for business. This element, present in each chapter, explores how restaurant managers are addressing an area of ever greater importance to their businesses, to their customers and to future generations.

All in a Day's Work

Food service managers in all segments of the industry routinely face unique problems and situations that require outstanding decision-making skills. The "All in a Day's Work" element of this text poses true-to-life food service problems and challenges and then asks readers to consider their response to the management issues they present. These true-to-life scenarios make for excellent classroom discussion topics and are numbered, within each chapter, for easy identification.

Restaurant Terms and Concepts Glossary

At the end of each chapter, readers will find a complete listing of the industry-specific terms defined in the chapter. As a result, readers can quickly review these terms to make sure that they understand and can use them in their proper context. They'll find this glossary to be a helpful reference as they encounter industry terms and jargon in their other readings and in their careers.

Work in Progress

This feature, consisting of 10 discussion questions per chapter, encourages students to think and talk about specific issues related to the material they've mastered. Many of these questions can serve as excellent homework, writing assignments or in-class discussions.

The authors believe that *The Professional Restaurant Manager* fills an important need in the hospitality industry literature. Its up-to-date and comprehensive but plainly presented coverage of all areas of the restaurant business makes it an essential addition to the professional library of the serious food service student.

It's our hope that students, instructors and industry professionals alike will find *The Professional Restaurant Manager* to be a significant contribution to their study of restaurant management. It has been our honor to work in this exciting field and to contribute, through the publication of learning materials such as this book, to the professional development of our fellow restaurateurs and future industry leaders.

David K. Hayes, Ph.D.
Panda Pros Hospitality
Management and Training
Okemos, MI

Allisha A. Miller
Panda Pros Hospitality
Management and Training
Lansing, MI

Jack D. Ninemeier, Ph.D.
The School of Hospitality Business,
Michigan State University

ACKNOWLEDGMENTS

The production of a book like this one is truly the culmination of the efforts of many. The authors' thanks go to William Lawrensen, our editor, for his outstanding assistance in this text's development; to editorial assistant Lara Dimmick for her prompt and professional dedication to our book; and to the entire production staff at Pearson Education for their tireless efforts.

We'd also like to recognize the support of Vernon Anthony, editorial director at Pearson Education, for his long-standing support of the authors and his belief in our work.

Our text reviewers also provided tremendous assistance: Michael Baldwin, Bellingham Technical College; Daniel Beard, Orange Coast College; Douglas Frey, Sullivan County Community College (SUNY); Susan Gregory, Eastern Michigan University; and Jay Kitterman, Lincoln Land Community College. They greatly improved the structure and content of the text. For their efforts, we are truly grateful.

The Restaurant Business

Learning Objectives

After carefully reading and studying the information in this chapter, you will:

1. Know how segmentation can help you better understand the restaurant industry.

2. Recognize that successful restaurants require careful planning prior to their opening.

IN THIS CHAPTER

This book is about the restaurant industry and is written for those who will work in it. If you plan a career as a restaurant manager, you'll be employed in a very exciting business. Whether you want to own or to manage a fine dining establishment, 100+ pizza shops, a popular pub in a vibrant college town, or a busy neighborhood restaurant serving authentic ethnic cuisine, you and your business will be part of a vast and exciting network of eating and drinking places.

The restaurant industry is large and as a result, the number of professional opportunities in it is large as well. Knowing about the size, history, and various parts of the restaurant industry will give you a better appreciation of the opportunities it can provide you.

One good way to study the vast restaurant industry is to examine its distinct segments. This information can enable you to choose the segment that will best help you be successful in meeting your own career and personal goals. Successful restaurant managers can operate popular and profitable businesses in all of the various industry segments, so choosing the one that is best for you makes good career sense.

Just as successful restaurant managers are found in all segments of the industry, successful restaurants are found in all of the segments. One thing all successful restaurants have in common is that they meet the needs of their customers. Doing a good job meeting customer needs and expectations is the result of careful management planning. A restaurant's location, its exterior design and interior décor, menu, and required financing are just some of areas that require careful planning prior to opening a restaurant. In this chapter, you will learn about all of the areas thoughtful managers must consider when they make plans to open a new restaurant.

THE RESTAURANT INDUSTRY

If you're reading this book, it's most likely because you want to open or manage a restaurant. When you do, you'll be joining one of the world's largest industries. Restaurants are big business both in the United States and internationally. In fact, nearly 1 of every 10 U.S. workers is employed in the restaurant industry.[1] Current employment estimates suggest that by the year 2020, over 14 million Americans will be working in the restaurant industry.

The restaurant business is the second largest nongovernment employer in the United States, so the employment opportunities in restaurants are vast no matter who you are or where you come from. Did you know that restaurants in the United States employ more minority managers than any other industry? In fact, 59% of all food service managers are female, 15% are Hispanic, and 18% are African American.[2] This makes the restaurant business one of the country's most diverse. It's easy to understand this diversity when you recognize that nearly half of all adults will work in a restaurant at some point in their lives. Many of those, of course, choose to stay in the industry and many of those restaurant workers go on to become professional restaurant managers.

National Restaurant Association (NRA)

A professional trade and lobbying group representing nearly 400,000 restaurant locations.

As large as it is today, the restaurant industry is still growing. According to the **National Restaurant Association (NRA)**, consumers in 1955 spent 25 cents of every food dollar on foods eaten away from home. By 2010, that number had grown to 47 cents of every food dollar—an increase of nearly 100%![3]

Because the industry continues to grow, the number of food service managers needed is projected to increase another 8% from 2010 to 2020.[4] The industry's growth means that an ever increasing number of exciting job opportunities will be available for those who want to manage restaurants as well as those who wish to start their own restaurants.

A Brief History of Eating Out

The restaurant business is often considered the "food eaten away from home" business. In fact, earlier in this chapter, you learned that one important measurement used by the NRA to monitor the size of the restaurant industry is the percentage of their food dollar consumers spend at home and the percentage they spend on food eaten away from home. Today, with the large increase in restaurant drive-through, take-out, and home-delivered meals, the industry actually provides busy consumers with many meals eaten away from home and with many meals eaten at their

---

WEB AT WORK!

The National Restaurant Association (NRA) is the world's largest food service industry trade association. It members are the owners of food, beverage, and lodging operations as well as those who manage and work in them. It also operates the National Restaurant Association Educational Foundation (NRAEF). Founded in 1919, the NRA is headquartered in Washington, DC. Each May, it holds its annual conference in Chicago, IL.

The NRA provides recent industry statistics on an annual basis. To see current data on the size and scope of the restaurant business, go to:

www.restaurant.org

Click on "Research and Insights" and then on "Industry Forecast" to see up-to-date information about the size and growth of the restaurant business.

---

[1]http://www.restaurant.org/research/facts/ (retrieved April 22, 2013).

[2]http://www.restaurant.org/research/facts/ (retrieved April 22, 2013).

[3]http://www.restaurant.org/research/facts/ (retrieved April 22, 2013).

[4]http://www.bls.gov/opub/ted/2005/dec/wk3/art04.htm (retrieved January 15, 2011).

homes! As consumers spend more money on food prepared or served away from their homes, the restaurant industry continues to grow.

While there are a variety of ways to examine the origin of restaurants, one of the best is to consider the reasons why people initially needed to buy foods prepared away from home. From a historical perspective, there were three main groups of people that had a need for food purchased or eaten away from where they lived: 1) merchants involved in the trading of goods from one area of the world to another, 2) those traveling for religious purposes, and 3) those that ate out to entertain others or simply themselves.

TRADE   Throughout recorded history, there have been references to commerce and trading among peoples living in different parts of the world. Archeologists have found evidence of established trading routes that operated as early as the 5th century B.C. At that time, caravans traveling in what today are Turkey, Afghanistan, and northern India would stop for rest at a caravansary.

The typical caravansary was simply an elaborate, walled-in area that was either square or rectangular. Travelers and their animals entered through a single gate built into the wall that could be heavily defended against thieves by the caravansary operator. Typically located one day's travel apart on a trade route, caravansaries provided a place for the caravan's animals to be corralled, fed, and watered. They also provided safe lodging, food, and beverages for the caravan's merchants and traders.

The expansion of the Roman Empire meant the operation of caravansary rest stops eventually passed into Roman hands. The result was that today's hospitality industry terminology owes much of its origin to Latin: the language of the Romans. In fact, the word *hospitality* is taken from the Latin word *hospitium*. Variations of that Latin term are today's words *host*, *hostess*, and *hotel* as well as *hospital* and *hospice*, all of which relate to the concept of caring for and feeding, those who are away from their homes.

RELIGION   The second large group of travelers requiring foods eaten away from home consisted of religious pilgrims traveling to holy sites or on church-related business. As a result, church-operated monasteries regularly took in religious travelers and provided them with food and shelter during their journeys.

As people found more reasons to travel, public inns operated by private innkeepers were developed. Like the church-operated havens for rest, these inns provided food and shelter to large numbers of travelers. Until about 1765, those seeking food were most often offered only what the innkeepers chose to serve. But in 1765, a Paris chef named Boulanger began offering a choice of nourishing soups to passersby. On a board hanging over the door to his business, Boulanger painted a phrase to advertise his establishment; he included the French word *restaurant*, meaning "to restore."[5] Boulanger was so successful that dining rooms throughout the world still display his original wording, and a restaurant owner or manager is now referred to as a **restaurateur**.

Restaurateur
The owner or operator of a restaurant.

While it's difficult to write a definition of "restaurant" that would please all food industry professionals, this book takes the reasonable position that all professionals responsible for providing food to those eating away from home can legitimately be considered restaurateurs.

ENTERTAINMENT   Eating out is fun today. It was also fun in the past. As a result, eating out has historically been seen by many as a form of or integral part of entertainment.

An Ancient Roman seeking entertainment might have chosen to eat out at a *thermopolium*: a small, pub-like shop selling warm wines and the ancient equivalent of snack foods. Rome also had many hot food shops and taverns (*tavernas*), where meals could be purchased and consumed with friends and family. The menus offered at these establishments included the normal Roman fare of hot sausages, bread, cheese, dates, and, of course, wine. Ancient Romans also ate out at the baths, which often had food shops as well as libraries, hair-cutting facilities, and other services.[6]

From simple shared meals to elaborate banquets, mankind has consistently combined its love for food and drink with entertainment activities. Evidence of this today can be seen in the

[5]http://en.wikipedia.org/wiki/Restaurant (retrieved January 5, 2011).
[6]http://www.hadrians.com/rome/romans/food/roman_eating_out.html (retrieved January 5, 2011).

many food operations located in tourist areas, ski resorts, casinos, golf courses, beaches, sports stadiums, and amusement parks.

Modern Restaurant Industry Segments

The types of customers served in restaurants today go far beyond those who are traveling away from home for business, religious, or entertainment reasons. This is easily seen by examining some examples of the many reasons people eat meals at restaurants very far from or near their homes, including:

- The couple who go out to share a romantic dinner
- The family whose mother or father decide that dining *out* with the family is faster and more convenient than cooking at home
- Patients and visitors in a hospital
- Office workers who leave their offices for a lunch break
- Factory workers who don't have time to go home and prepare food to be eaten during assigned meal breaks
- Armed forces serving their country in locations across the world
- Businessmen and women entertaining important clients
- College students temporarily living in residence halls away from home
- Tourists traveling for pleasure or education
- Large family gatherings celebrating birthdays, anniversaries, and holidays
- Friends who meet to socialize over good food and drinks

Of course, there are many other reasons many people must or prefer *eating out* to cooking their own food and eating it at home. In fact, why people eat out, and the goals of those who feed them, is one good way to better understand how operations in the restaurant industry are classified. (see Figure 1.1).

While there are no legally mandated definitions of various restaurant types, one very popular method used by food industry professionals to categorize meals served away from home is by considering whether the food is served in a **commercial** or **noncommercial** setting.

Figure 1.2 lists some examples of food service operations that are commonly classified as either commercial (for profit) or noncommercial (not for profit). When defined as a location serving food to those away from home, it's easy to see that professional restaurant managers will be found in both settings. It's also true, however, that most food service professionals use the term *restaurant* to indicate those profit-seeking businesses open to the general public.

Despite the fact that some noncommercial food service operations—such as those located in the student union on a college campus or a hospital cafeteria—may indeed be open to the general public, in this book we will focus primarily on commercial eating and drinking places. We will do so because, in nearly all cases, the management techniques and principles required to successfully operate a for-profit commercial food service facility can be readily applied to the operation of successful noncommercial facilities.

The commercial restaurant industry is vast, but there are numerous ways that these operations can be segmented, including price (for example low, medium, or high priced) or location (for example, by a restaurant's location in a city, suburb, or shopping center). Other classification systems could be based on the type of **cuisine** offered by the restaurant (for example, Italian, Chinese, Mexican, or American) or whether the food served is typically eaten in the restaurant's designated dining area or taken away from the restaurant to be eaten elsewhere.

Commercial

Food service operations that are typically open to the general public. These operations most often seek to make a profit by providing food and beverages to as wide an audience of customers as possible.

Noncommercial

Food service operations that are not typically open to the general public. The goal of these units is to provide meals for a specially targeted audience in a cost-effective way. This segment is also commonly referred to as "not for profit," "nonprofit," or "institutional" food service.

Cuisine

A specific group of cooking traditions and practices associated with a specific culture. Most often named after the cooking style or the region where the culture is found. Examples include French, Italian, Creole, German, and Asian cuisines.

FIGURE 1.1

Major Restaurant Industry Divisions

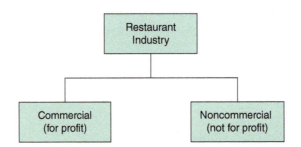

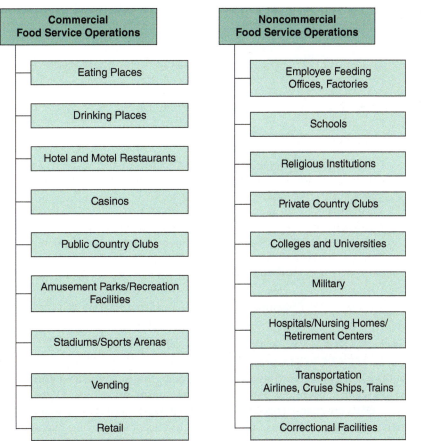

FIGURE 1.2

Examples of Commercial and Noncommercial Food Service Operations

Although there is inevitable overlap when attempting to classify restaurants by any single operating characteristic, Figures 1.3 and 1.4 lists some of the cuisines and menu options many observers find useful when analyzing the commercial restaurant industry. The segments presented are classified in two different ways. The first is by price and service level (Figure 1.3), the second by the type of menu options (Figure 1.4).

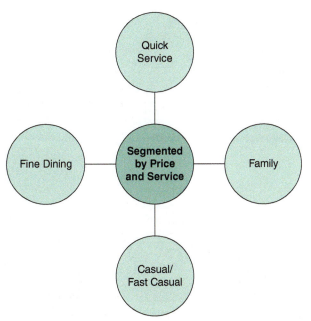

FIGURE 1.3

Commercial Restaurants Segmented by Price and Service

FIGURE 1.4

Commercial Restaurants Segmented by Menu Option

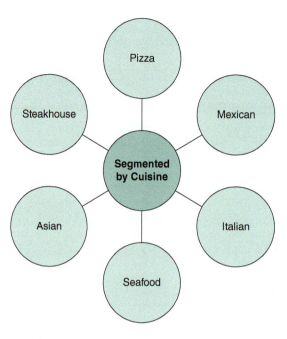

RESTAURANT SEGMENTS BY PRICE AND SERVICE LEVEL

QUICK-SERVICE RESTAURANTS (QSRs) The quick-service restaurant (QSR) segment is one of the largest and most visible of all restaurant groups. Although a great number of restaurants in this segment operate as part of a **chain restaurant**, many other QSRs operate independently.

QSRs are characterized by their limited menus, fast service, and modest prices. QSRs are extremely popular with customers who are in a hurry and/or on a budget.

In the United States, well-known examples of successful QSRs include McDonald's, Burger King, Whataburger, and Wendy's. While hamburgers represent the single most popular menu item in the United States, a large group of QSRs feature different menu items very successfully. Examples include chains such as Chick-fil-A (chicken sandwiches), Subway (submarine sandwiches), Arby's (roast beef sandwiches), KFC (fried chicken), and Long John Silver's (seafood).

QSRs typically provide a dining area for their customers. Many QSRs, however, sell as much or more of their food to **drive-through customers** as they do to those who eat in their restaurants.

Chain restaurant

A restaurant that shares the name, menu and operating practices with other restaurants that are part of the same organization. Well-known examples include McDonald's, Wendy's, Subway, Panda Express, and Qdoba Mexican Grill.

Drive-through customers

Restaurant guests who place and receive their carry out food orders without leaving their car.

Many customers buy their food from QSRs but take it away to eat in their car, office, or home.

© Ministr-84 / Shutterstock

WEB AT WORK!

QSR Magazine is written for professionals in the quick-service restaurant industry and is available online or in print. To see examples of the industry coverage provided by *QSR Magazine*, go to:

www.qsrmagazine.com

Click on "News" to read recent articles about current issues in this very large restaurant segment.

While some observers outside the food service industry disparage working in QSR management, those within the industry recognize the tremendous financial opportunities that can result from the ownership of a successful operation. George Will, a popular columnist for *The Washington Post* was correct when he wrote:

"McDonald's has made more millionaires, and especially black and Hispanic millionaires, than any other economic entity ever, anywhere."[7]

While owning a successful QSR is no guarantee you will become a millionaire, owning such a restaurant can definitely increase your chances of becoming one!

Restaurant managers working in the QSR segment are among the industry's most technologically advanced. They are also noted for their ability to ensure consistency and cleanliness in their operations. These are traits that serve them well if they stay within the QSR segment or if they move on to other segments.

FAMILY   The family restaurant segment is an interesting one because families are, of course, also welcome at each of the restaurant segments identified in this chapter. Thus, it would seem that the term *family* when discussing restaurants would not be of great value. However, the family restaurant category is widely recognized in the restaurant industry for two reasons:

- Unique menu and serving periods
- Segment size

Unique Menu and Serving Periods

Restaurants that fall into the family category tend to have wide-ranging menus. As a result, they may have ethnic dishes, selected menu items from a wide variety of cuisines, and standard American favorites. Unlike many other restaurant types, family-style restaurants are typically open for breakfast, lunch, and dinner. So it's not surprising that some family restaurants are best known for their breakfasts, while others may do the majority of their business at lunch or dinner. This restaurant category includes many different types of restaurants that are open 24 hours a day, seven days a week (24/7).

Segment Size

The family restaurant segment is large. It consists of many locally owned, locally managed, non-chain-affiliated restaurants. It also includes some of the country's largest chains. The 1,500-unit Denny's family restaurant group is a good example of a major chain in this restaurant category. Other major chains include the 1,500+-unit Waffle House chain, the nearly 1,500-unit International House of Pancakes (IHOP) chain, and the 600-unit Cracker Barrel chain.

Other well-known restaurant groups in this category include Bob Evans, Perkins, and Big Boy. Family-style restaurants are typically characterized by their moderate menu prices, wide menu variety, and emphasis on friendly service.

CASUAL/FAST CASUAL   Many industry observers utilize the term *casual*, and more recently *fast casual*, when referring to a distinct classification of restaurants. While no universally accepted

---

[7]http://www.washingtonpost.com/wp-dyn/content/article/2007/12/26/AR2007122601485.html (retrieved January 10, 2011).

definition exists for a casual restaurant, it's generally considered to provide table service to guests and serve moderately priced food in an informal atmosphere. Casual restaurants usually have a full bar with separate bar staff and a rather large beer and wine menu. They are frequently part of a chain, but many are independently owned and operated. In the United States, examples of casual restaurant chains include Applebee's, the Tex-Mex-themed Chili's group, Ruby Tuesdays, Red Lobster, and Olive Garden.

The *fast casual* segment is a relatively new type of operation. Falling somewhere between the QSR and casual restaurant, a fast casual operation doesn't provide its guests with table service, but its food quality is intended to be higher than that typically found in a QSR. Panera Bread, Chipotle Mexican Grill, Five Guys Burger and Fries, and Noodles & Company are examples of popular operations that would fit the broadly accepted definition of a fast casual restaurant.

FINE DINING   A *fine dining* operation is what comes to mind for many hospitality professionals when they think about owning or managing their own restaurants. Like the other restaurant classifications, there is no universally accepted definition for fine dining; however, most industry professionals would likely agree that a fine dining restaurant differs from other restaurant segments in three critical areas:

- Menu
- Service levels
- Ambiance

Menu
The type of cuisine offered in fine dining restaurants varies greatly; however, in all cases these operations serve masterfully prepared foods of extremely high quality. For many guests, a fine dining restaurant is selected to celebrate a birthday, an anniversary, or other special occasion. Because that is true, fine dining restaurants of all types offer the best in ingredients, food quality, and preparation methods.

Many fine dining restaurants are either owned by a chef or employ a talented chef who develops the operation's menu. He or she may creatively vary it with the changing seasons to take advantage of locally produced fresh ingredients.

The number of menu items offered in a fine dining restaurant may be large or rather limited; however, each item must be outstanding. Fine dining restaurants also offer their guests an extensive and high-quality beverage menu to complement the foods they serve.

Service levels
Fine dining restaurants provide their guests with exceptionally high levels of personal service. All restaurants seek to provide good guest service; however, in most cases, a fine dining restaurant's well-trained staff would also likely:

- Escort guests to the table, holding the chair for women
- Explain complex menu items in detail
- Recommend appropriate beverages to accompany menu selections
- Clean the table between courses
- Replace napkins and/or glassware, dishes, and eating utensils between courses
- Be exceptionally knowledgeable about upscale dining room service procedures

Ambience
Some of the most beautifully designed interiors in the world are found in fine dining restaurants. These upscale atmospheres are fitting, given the higher menu prices typically charged by fine dining restaurants. Not only will the restaurant's walls, flooring, and artwork reflect the operation's upmarket ambience, but the staff's uniforms and the china, glassware, and other table top items used are also carefully chosen. In all cases, the intent of the restaurateur is to create a prestigious environment that is as memorable as the food and beverages served.

RESTAURANT SEGMENTS BY MENU OPTION   Restaurants are operated in a variety of physical settings. In addition to traditional locations, food service facilities are found on cruise ships, in airports, at country clubs, and in health clubs, to name just a few varied locations. In addition, mobile food carts and food trucks now offer "flexible location" food services to a variety of customers.

Many fine dining restaurants are operated by chef-owners who directly supervise food production in their restaurant kitchens.

Today, farmers markets, grocery stores, and a variety of nontraditional operations offer guest menu options ranging from limited to extensive. While the location and style of service can be useful ways to segment restaurants, one of the most prevalent methods is by the menu items offered to guests.

PIZZA   If hamburgers are the single most popular item on restaurant menus in the United States, pizza comes in at No. 2. But unlike the hamburger, the characteristics of a "quality" pizza vary widely and are widely debated.

In some parts of the country, thick-crusted, heavily tomato-sauced pizza is considered to be best. In other areas, diners prefer stuffed or thin-as-a-cracker crusts with fresh vegetables and tomatoes in place of a heavy tomato sauce.

Despite some disagreement about the best way to make (and even to eat!) pizza, it's clear that pizzerias (pizza restaurants) are extremely popular worldwide. Americans eat more than 4 billion pizzas every year; 93% of all Americans eat pizza at least once a month.

Pizzerias represent approximately 17% of all U.S. restaurants. Many of these restaurants specialize in carryout or delivery of their products.

Large and very popular chains that emphasize takeout or delivery pizza include Domino's, Papa John's, and Little Caesars. The largest pizza chain is YUM Brand's Pizza Hut. Pizza Hut has more than 7,500 restaurants in the United States and 5,600-plus worldwide. Most Pizza Hut restaurants offer customers takeout, delivery, and dine-in options. Despite the popularity of the nationwide chains, smaller chains or independent pizza restaurants thrive in many communities.

WEB AT WORK!

Pizza Today is published by MacFadden Protech, LLC, International Pizza Expo, and the National Association of Pizzeria Operators.

Pizza Today addresses issues of interest to those working in the pizzeria segment of the restaurant industry and is available online or in print. To see examples of the industry coverage provided by *Pizza Today*, go to:

www.pizzatoday.com

Click on "News and Views" to see recent articles about current issues in this unique restaurant segment.

MEXICAN The Mexican restaurant category is broad and generally considered to include a wide range of cuisines originating in Central and South America as well as Tex-Mex foods— a blend of the cuisines found in Mexico and Texas. While it's extremely popular in California and the southwestern part of the United States, the Mexican-style restaurant can be found in all parts of the country and the world.

The cuisine of Mexico includes an extensive use of cilantro, chilies, cumin, grilled meats and seafood, tortillas, rice, and beans. Menu items offered in Mexican-style restaurants range from those that can be made quickly and inexpensively to those that require very high levels of culinary skill.

Mexican restaurants are an excellent example of the overlap that often occurs when restaurants are classified by any one of their operating characteristics. In the United States, YUM Brand's Taco Bell is an extremely popular QSR chain, with over 5,500 operating restaurants. It has thousands more units operating internationally. However, many mid-priced Mexican-style restaurants are very popular with families and could easily be classified as family-style restaurants. Finally, fine dining Mexican-style restaurants thrive in most major metropolitan areas. Despite their range of operating characteristics, the Mexican-style restaurant is considered by many to be a unique restaurant segment.

ITALIAN Italian-style restaurants are popular throughout the world—of course, that includes the United States. While many offer pizza on their menus, a great number also specialize in pasta dishes, meats, and seafood and may emphasize wine as a meal accompaniment.

Italian restaurants of all types can vary greatly in the menu items they offer their guests. This is due to the differences inherent in the cuisines of northern and southern Italy. Northern Italian cuisine is heavily influenced by French cooking and liberally uses butter, cream, and fresh egg pastas. Southern Italian cuisine has more of a Mediterranean influence and is characterized by the heavy use of olive oil and dried pastas as well as the extensive use of tomatoes.

As is true with Mexican restaurants, Italian-style restaurants can be found in the QSR segment (e.g., the Fazoli's chain); in the mid-priced range of restaurants appealing to families (e.g., the popular Olive Garden and Romano's Macaroni Grill chains) and in higher priced segments (the Maggiano's Little Italy chain).

WEB AT WORK!

Maiden Name Press publishes *El Restaurante Mexicano*, a bilingual (Spanish and English) magazine for hospitality professionals in Mexican, Tex-Mex, Southwest and Latin restaurants. It's available online or in print.

To see examples of the specialized coverage provided by *El Restaurante Mexicano*, go to:

www.restmex.com

El Restaurante Mexicano publishes a monthly e-mail newsletter and is on Facebook and Twitter.

GREEN AT WORK!

Green practices are those activities that responsible restaurant operators undertake to protect the environment and to minimize damage to the planet that could result from the restaurant's operation. There are many practices that ensure that restaurants operate in an environmentally friendly manner. The seafood items that restaurateurs and chefs choose to offer on their menus provide one excellent example.

Many different seafood items are served in restaurants because they are very popular. But for future generations of seafood lovers to enjoy the same fish species served in restaurants today, it's critical that restaurateurs take an active role in helping prevent the overfishing of these fish species. Overfishing occurs when the harvesting of fish from oceans, lakes, rivers, or ponds reduce fish populations below an acceptable or sustainable level.

The goal of **sustainable fishing** is to maintain fish populations at levels that ensure these species will not become extinct due to overharvesting. Restaurateurs of all types demonstrate their commitment to preventing environmentally destructive fishing methods when they chose to offer their customers only seafood products that have been responsibly obtained and in ways that ensure the long-term sustainability of the species they are buying. This means carefully choosing the seafood items they offer and the suppliers who provide those items.

It's important to recognize that the overwhelming majority of restaurant customers care about eco-friendly practices. When a restaurateur publicly demonstrates his or her commitment to "green at work" practices such those related to helping ensure the long-term viability of fish species, the reputations of the restaurant and the restaurateur are positively affected. It's good for business, and it's the right thing to do for the planet!

Green practices

Activities that protect the environment and minimize damage to the planet that may result from the operation of restaurants.

Sustainable fishing

Fish harvesting methods that help ensure the long-term viability of a fish species.

Non-chain-affiliated Italian restaurants are extremely prevalent in most urban and suburban areas of the United States. Often family-owned for many generations, menu prices can vary from the very modest to the highest prices charged in their areas.

SEAFOOD Seafood restaurants are always popular near coastal shores, where fish are plentiful. In the United States, seafood restaurants are abundant along the coastlines from Maine to Florida, from Florida to Texas, and from California to Washington.

Seafood restaurants from Main to Florida place their menu emphasis on the oysters, lobster, cod, and other fish species for which the Atlantic coast is famous. Gulf Coast restaurants stretch from Florida through Louisiana and Texas. The Gulf area is noted for its shrimp, crawfish, oysters, and catfish. The influence of **Cajun cuisine** and **Creole cuisine** cuisines in New Orleans, Louisiana, and its surrounding areas makes seafood restaurants in this region among the most famous in the world.

From Southern California to Washington State and beyond, the Pacific Ocean provides area restaurants with popular local seafood, including salmon, trout, rockfish, snapper, and crab.

Of course, coastal residents aren't the only ones who love seafood. As a result, seafood restaurants are popular throughout the United States and the world. Restaurants serving seafood range from the 1000+-unit Long John Silver's chain, where menu prices are relatively low, to the 700+-unit mid-priced Red Lobster chain. Other regional chains and non-chain-affiliated seafood restaurants are numerous; many charge menu prices that are among the highest in their areas.

Cajun cuisine

A style of cooking named for the French-speaking Acadian (Cajun) immigrants deported by the British from the area that is now Nova Scotia (Canada) to the area around New Orleans, Louisiana, in the late 1700s and early 1800s.

Creole cuisine

A style of cooking named for the European aristocrats who moved to New Orleans, Louisiana, in the late 1600s. The word *Creole* comes from the Spanish word *criollo*. a native or inhabitant of Latin America who is of European descent. The various cultures that contributed to the creation of Creole cuisine include Native American, Caribbean, African, French, Spanish, English, German and Italian.

WEB AT WORK!

In 2010, Marriott International became the first large global hotel company to launch a sustainable seafood program. Named *Future Fish*, the program calls for all Marriott hotels to source at least 50% of their seafood from certified sustainable, responsible fisheries and aquaculture farms.

To learn more about this innovative program, go to:

www.chefblog.marriott.com

Type "future fish" into the search bar found on this site.

FIGURE 1.6

Considerations in Restaurant Site Selection

Population Center	Area Classification	Zoning Issues
Large city	Residential	Restaurant use allowed
Medium-sized city	Industrial	Building visibility adequate
Small city/town	Downtown	Needed signage permitted
Rural community	Shopping center/mall	Adequate parking available
Interstate highway exchange	Other	Liquor license available

Site Issues	Traffic-Related Issues	Cost-Related Issues
Building purchase or lease	Daily traffic counts	Total site selling price or lease cost
Lot size and shape adequate	Curbs/sidewalks adequate	Cost per square foot
Landscaping appropriate	Site ingress and egress	Mandatory site renovation or improvement costs
Availability of municipal utilities (water/power/sewage)	Signage height and size adequate	Design/décor-related site improvement costs
Adequate police/fire protection	Presence of potential hazards	Appraisal/property taxes

restaurant must be located in an area that provides a readily available target market large enough to support the restaurant. In some large metropolitan areas, this target market may be drawn from only a few city blocks; in more suburban or rural areas, the target market may be drawn from many miles away.

It's important to remember that today's restaurant customers have a wide range of dining choices. Thus, it's not realistic to assume they will walk or drive long distances to one restaurant when other, closer alternatives are equally desirable. For that reason, the site of a new restaurant must be carefully chosen. Figure 1.6 lists some of the many factors that must be considered prior to choosing the site. These factors are also important when considering the purchase of an existing restaurant.

In some cases, the fact that multiple restaurants are located in close proximity will actually help each individual restaurant increase its sales.

CONCEPT   Some industry professionals might maintain that the development of a restaurant's concept must actually be known *before* the site selection. They would state, for example, that the decision to create a casual-style pizzeria restaurant should be made before an appropriate site for a pizzeria is selected. In fact, in many cases, this is how the decisions unfold.

Alternatively, the site itself may suggest the concept that would or would not be appropriate. For example, a building suitable for a pizzeria located near a college campus may be an excellent site; however, a similar building located far from campus may be a poor location for a restaurant whose target market is college students.

In a similar manner, a good concept for a small site located within a shopping mall's food court would likely include inexpensive foods served to shoppers fairly quickly. A restaurant serving expensive foods that take a long time to prepare would likely be a poor choice for that same mall space.

It's important to understand that a popular restaurant concept can help attract large numbers of the target market, but the concept alone will not be enough to ensure a new restaurant's success. For example, QSRs serving hamburgers are very popular. However, not every restaurant designed to serve hamburgers in a QSR format will be successful.

The restaurant business can be very challenging. Studies conducted by a number of universities and professional research teams indicate that, on average, about 25% of all restaurants fail within their first year of operation. Nearly half (44%) of all new restaurant start-ups are closed within the first four years of operation.[8] While these numbers show the challenge of creating successful restaurant, they also show that *more* than half of all new restaurant start-ups are still in business after four years!

There are a number of differences between restaurants that close quickly and those that remain open, including location, management, popularity of the concept, proper financing, and operational profitability. For professional restaurateurs, perhaps the most important concept-related factor is profitability. To understand why, consider that QSRs are the single most profitable restaurant segment. Despite that, many professional restaurateurs (and hospitality management students!) envision something very different from a QSR when they picture their ideal restaurant. Why? For many restaurateurs, their businesses are an extension of their personalities, desire and creativity.

While profitable, QSRs may be viewed by some hospitality professionals as lacking the variety, glamour, and opportunity for the self-expression and creativity they seek when developing their own restaurant concept. While such a self-oriented approach to concept development can be very satisfying personally, it's a very different approach from that taken by the professional restaurant investor whose desire is a significantly large **return on investment (ROI)** rather than individual expression.

For example, with $150,000 annual profit achieved from a $1,000,000 investment, the return on investment would be calculated as $150,000/$1,000,000 = 15% ROI.

In the final analysis, the best restaurant concepts are popular with guests, allow the restaurant owner to achieve his or her own goals of self-expression, *and* can be operated profitably.

MENU   For most guests, the items sold by a restaurant are the single most important factor in deciding whether to eat there. As a result, the items chosen and prices charged to guests are exceptionally important in the development of a restaurant concept. In fact, a restaurant's menu is critical to its success. The word, "**menu**," like many others in the culinary world, is French; its literal translation is "detailed list."

The items appearing on a menu are important for many reasons, including their large impact on a restaurant's ability to attract and retain customers. (How restaurateurs and chefs decide what to include on their menus is addressed in Chapter 5.)

Commercial restaurants typically produce one of two menu types. The most common is the **à la carte menu**. Here, guests order items individually, and each item is separately priced. A **table d'hôte menu** is composed of a grouping of menu items that may include an appetizer, entree, dessert, and beverage. The group of items is then offered for sale at one price. Because there is one fixed price, these menus are often referred to as *prix fixe* menus.

Return on investment (ROI)

A ratio of profits achieved to money invested.

Menu

A term meaning "detailed list." In common restaurant industry usage, a menu is 1) the items offered for sale and 2) the way the items offered for sale are made known to guests.

À la carte menu

A meal chosen item-by-item; each item is priced separately.

Table d'hôte menu

A meal composed of a grouping of menu items offered at one fixed price. Such a menu may also be called *prix fixe* (English pronunciation: pree-fiks).

---

[8]http://www.restaurantowner.com/downloads/failure_rate_study.pdf.

Effective advertising attracts restaurant customers the first time; quality menu items and outstanding service cause those customers to return.

The role of a menu as a communication device is as important as the food that the menu presents. Today's menus are delivered to guests in an increasingly large number of ways. They are printed and handed to seated guests; they appear online on restaurant websites; and they are sent by mass e-mail, fax, phone app, Facebook, or Twitter (just to name but a few of the many methods!).

DESIGN   Guests begin forming their impressions of a restaurant long before they order and eat their food. The restaurant's building, signage, landscaping, parking lot, entrance area, lobby, dining room, bar, tables, and chairs are all design-related items that have a powerful impact on guests' perceptions of a business before they ever place a food order. Thus, restaurateurs must carefully consider **décor** as well as the layout of their interior dining spaces when developing their restaurant concepts.

Décor

The decoration of a room and the arrangement of the objects in it.

Successful restaurants may have casual or formal interiors. Different design and décor combinations can make the interior of a restaurant casual or romantic, high energy, or cozy.

Just as the physical presentation of a menu item can affect how guests think the item will taste, the design of a restaurant will affect guests' perceptions of an operation's food and service quality. In most cases, restaurants' guests seek much more than food; they're looking for a total dining experience. The way the interior of a restaurant makes guests feel is an incredibly important part of their experience. Room layout, furnishings, art work, colors, shapes, and textures all add to the total ambiance of a restaurant and must be carefully planned. When a restaurant is newly built, these planning concerns may be easier to address than if the building had housed a different type of restaurant.

Marketing

Activities designed to attract and expand a restaurant's target market.

Advertising

The distribution of information about a business that is paid for by the business.

Publicity

Newsworthy information about a business that is distributed for free.

MARKETING   The long-term economic health of a restaurant depends upon securing its proper share of the available target market. Ultimately, a well-run restaurant must attract, maintain, and expand a strong customer base. This is the goal of the **marketing** effort.

Marketing occurs both inside and outside a restaurant. Within the restaurant, management directs an internal sales effort. For example, restaurant servers and creative menu design or signage can help to market specific menu items that the restaurant wishes to sell. (This will be further explained in Chapter 5.)

Externally, managers must effectively market and promote the image, products and services offered by the restaurant. They do this through a combination of **advertising** and **publicity**.

When both internal and external marketing activities are done well, the restaurant has a good chance of succeeding. Both types of marketing are critical management tasks because, without an adequate customer base, the restaurant will simply not reach the sales numbers it needs to pay its expenses and remain a viable business entity.

FINANCING   If location is the single most important ingredient in a restaurant's success, proper financing could be considered the second most important. It's a well-known fact that a new restaurant's expenses begin to accrue long before it opens and begins to make a profit. Financing provides the income that the restaurant needs during this period of unprofitability. In nearly every case, a restaurant that lacks start-up funding simply would not be able to pay its bills until it becomes profitable enough to do so. Start-up costs incurred by a restaurant vary based on its location and concept, but all restaurants will incur pre-opening costs related to:

- Land and building acquisition or lease
- Legal fees
- Required licenses
- Required insurance
- Utility deposits and prepayments
- Kitchen equipment and tools
- Dining room furnishings
- China/flatware/glassware
- Employee uniforms
- Initial food and beverage inventories
- Pre-opening marketing costs
- Pre-opening payroll costs

Even after a new restaurant opens, it may take many months or even years before it reaches targeted levels of profitability. A restaurant must have access to enough cash or credit to pay its bills in a timely manner starting from the very first day it opens. Chapter 2 discusses different methods restaurateurs use to secure adequate start-up financing.

Savings, short-term and long-term loans, and grants are some of the most common sources of restaurant financing. Operators determine the amount of money they need, and how it can be obtained, before they create the business plan. Realistic estimates of how quickly the restaurant

© Dimitry Shironosov/Shutterstock

Creating a formal business plan is a critical step in the process of seeking project funding from outside investors or lenders.

will reach its targeted level of profitability must also be made: these estimates are an integral part of the formal business plan.

Creating a well-developed business plan takes time. Typically, however, the more time devoted to the process, the better the final plan. Recall that a quality business plan serves three distinct purposes:

1. Be a communication device that provides readers with a clear understanding of the restaurant's concept and location.
2. Function as an operating tool that establishes a time line for the restaurant's development and financial targets for its ongoing operation.
3. Assist in fund-raising by describing the restaurant's need for financing and how borrowed start-up money will be repaid by the business.

Because cities, states, and potential lenders may have different requirements, the information that a business plan must include may vary somewhat. Figure 1.7 is an example of a typical restaurant business plan.

FIGURE 1.7
Sample Business Plan Content Checklist

- ☐ Cover sheet with restaurant's name and plan preparer's contact information
- ☐ Date of plan preparation
- ☐ One- to two-page executive summary
- ☐ Table of contents
- ☐ Legal description of the organization developing the restaurant
- ☐ Description of the restaurant's concept
- ☐ Market analysis
    - ☐ Target market
    - ☐ Competitive analysis
    - ☐ Advertising and marketing plan
- ☐ Financial projections
    - ☐ Pre-opening financing
        - ☐ Required amount
        - ☐ Use of funds
        - ☐ Source of funds
        - ☐ Funds repayment plan
    - ☐ Three-year balance sheet
        - ☐ For the legal entity developing the restaurant
        - ☐ For the new restaurant
    - ☐ Three-year income and expense (P&L) statement with assumptions
        - ☐ Years 1–2: Monthly projections and assumptions
        - ☐ Years 1–3 Annual projections
    - ☐ Three-year statement of cash flow
        - ☐ Years 1–2: Monthly projections
        - ☐ Years 1–3 Annual projections
- ☐ Recommended appendices
    - ☐ Organizational chart
        - ☐ Resumes of owners
        - ☐ Resumes of managers
    - ☐ Sample menu
    - ☐ Copy of leases
    - ☐ Copy of licenses
        - ☐ Business license
        - ☐ Liquor license
        - ☐ Food license
    - ☐ Copy of fire permits
    - ☐ Copy of insurance policies
    - ☐ Copies of staff job descriptions
    - ☐ Blueprints or floor plans
        - ☐ Furniture/fixtures/equipment list
        - ☐ Décor-related price quotations
        - ☐ Artist's renderings of interior space

WEB AT WORK!

PlanMagic is a company that offers a wide range of business, financial, marketing, and media plan software designed to help create a business plan. To see an example of the restaurant business plan templates this and other companies offer, go to:

www.planmagic.com

Click on "Products" and then on "PlanMagic Restaurant."

ALL IN A DAY'S WORK: 1.2

"I can envision the restaurant in my head, I just have a hard time putting it into words. I'm not a writer, I'm a chef. That's where I'm hoping you can help me," said Dan.

Dan Fleet was talking with Shingi Rakuni. Shingi had graduated from the hospitality management program at State University two years earlier and had just started her first job with a large national restaurant chain. There she met Dan, who was the sous chef at the restaurant Shingi helped manage.

"I've been in the business for 20 years," continued Dan. "I know this market and I know my restaurant will be a big success. I've saved some money, but not enough. When I talked to my bank, they said they would be glad to consider me for a loan *after* they see my business plan. Well I don't have a written business plan. I don't even know where to start. That's where I need your help, Shingi!"

1. Why do you think Dan's bank wants to see his business plan before they would be willing to consider making a loan to him?
2. Assume Dan wanted to seek start-up finding from members of his own family or his friends instead of a bank. Would he still need a business plan? Explain your answer.

Restaurant Terms and Concepts

National Restaurant Association (NRA) *2*	Drive-through customers *6*	Sashimi *12*	Menu *15*
Restaurateur *3*	Cajun cuisine *11*	Ambiance *12*	À la carte menu *15*
Commercial *4*	Creole cuisine *11*	Concept *13*	Table d'hôte menu *15*
Noncommercial *4*	Green practices *11*	Target market *13*	Décor *16*
Cuisine *4*	Sustainable fishing *11*	Business plan *13*	Marketing *16*
Chain restaurant *6*	Sushi *12*	Start-up funding *13*	Advertising *16*
		Return on investment (ROI) *15*	Publicity *16*

Work in Progress

1. Consider the last three times you ate in a restaurant. Why did you choose to eat out rather than at your home? Do you think the people you ate with chose to eat out for the same reasons?
2. Consider your own community. Do you think more restaurant managers are employed in the commercial or noncommercial segments of the restaurant industry?
3. What industry segment includes the restaurant that you enjoy the most? What specific characteristics make that restaurant your favorite?
4. What industry segment would interest you most as a professional restaurant *manager*? Why?
5. What industry segment would interest you most as a restaurant *owner*? Why?
6. If you wanted to own your own restaurant, would you rather purchase an existing operation or develop a new one? Explain your answer.
7. Do you think there will always be a market for new restaurants? Why?
8. Why do you think the marketing section is such an important part of the overall business plan for a new restaurant?
9. Which part of a restaurant business plan do you think would be of most interest to potential investors? Why?
10. Assume you wanted to start your own restaurant. Would you write your own business plan or hire someone to write it for you? Why?

2

Developing a Restaurant

Chapter Outline

The Rise of the Restaurant Chain

Costs of Franchise and Independent Restaurants
  The Initial Franchise Fee
  Royalty Fees
  Marketing Fees
  The Cost of Independence

Operating Franchised and Independent Restaurants
  Advantages of Franchised Restaurants
  Disadvantages of Franchised Restaurants
  Advantages of Independent Restaurants
  Disadvantages of Independent Restaurants

Securing Needed Capital
  Equity Funding
  Debt Financing
  Leasing

The Impact on ROI

Learning Objectives

After carefully reading and studying the information in this chapter, you will:

1. Know the advantages and disadvantages of opening franchised and independent restaurants.

2. Be able to identify the key factors to consider when arranging financing for a start-up restaurant.

IN THIS CHAPTER

In Chapter 1, you learned that managers who choose to develop new restaurants must be careful planners. The restaurant industry is competitive and challenging. Starting a new restaurant is challenging, too.

In general, the restaurateur who wishes to open and operate his or her own restaurant must first address two significant issues: affiliation and financing.

In the planning stages, the restaurateur must decide if a new restaurant will be part of a chain or be operated independently. Both have distinct advantages and potential drawbacks. In this chapter, you will learn about these plusses and minuses.

The second significant issue facing most new restaurant owners and managers is how the business will be financed. It most often takes weeks or months after a restaurant's opening for it to generate enough revenue to pay its bills and earn a profit. Significant expenses are incurred in developing a restaurant; many of these must be paid prior to the opening of the business. The amount of start-up money that is required, how the money will be obtained, and how it will be paid back over time are major concerns to anyone developing a restaurant.

THE RISE OF THE RESTAURANT CHAIN

A chain restaurant shares the name, menu, and operating practices of other restaurants that are part of the same chain (see Chapter 1). To join a chain, a restaurateur must purchase a **franchise**.

A franchise relationship is one in which, for a fee, a **franchisor** allows a **franchisee** to copy a successful business model.

The first restaurant franchises in the United States were granted in 1932 by Howard Deering Johnson. At that time, Johnson operated a single—and very successful—Howard Johnson's restaurant in Quincy, Massachusetts. Johnson originally thought to expand by opening more restaurants himself, but the stock market crash of 1929 prevented him from doing so. His new idea was to let other restaurant operators use the Howard Johnson's name, recipes, logo and even building design in exchange for a fee.

In 1932, Johnson granted an acquaintance the right to open the first franchised Howard Johnson's restaurant in Orleans, Massachusetts. By 1954, the Howard Johnson's chain consisted of 400 restaurants operating in 32 states.

McDonald's founder Ray Kroc opened his first McDonald's restaurant on April 15, 1955. On that same day, he formed a corporate entity named "McDonald's Corporation" and began selling franchises. As of 2014, McDonald's is the world's largest restaurant chain in terms of food revenue. The McDonald's Corporation originally formed by Kroc now operates some of its own McDonald's restaurants and grants franchises to thousands of other operators worldwide.

Today, hundreds of different restaurant franchises are granted to thousands of franchisees around the globe. In some cases the franchisor will operate a significant number of units; in other cases a franchisor may not actually operate any restaurants. The number of units a chain restaurant franchisor operates or franchises to others varies. Figure 2.1 lists ten of the most popular chain restaurants in the 2010s, their franchisor, the percentage of the units that are operated by the franchisor, and the percentage of the units that are operated by their franchisees.

Franchise

A relationship through which a business is run using the same name and operating system of another business.

Franchisor

A person or business entity that sells a franchise.

Franchisee

A person or business entity that buys a franchise.

Company	Franchisor	% Franchisor Operated	% Franchisee Operated
McDonald's	McDonald's Corp.	19%	81%
KFC	Yum! Brands, Inc.	29%	71%
Burger King	Burger King Holdings	11%	89%
Subway	Doctor's Associates, Inc.	0%	100%
Pizza Hut	Yum! Brands, Inc.	16%	84%
Wendy's	Wendy's/Arby's Group	21%	79%
Taco Bell	Yum! Brands, Inc.	22%	78%
Dunkin Donuts	Dunkin Brands, Inc.	0%	100%
Domino's Pizza	Domino's Pizza, Inc.	5%	95%
Tim Hortons	Tim Hortons Inc.	1%	99%
Courtesy of Panda Pros.			

FIGURE 2.1

Ten Popular U.S.-Based Restaurant Franchise Companies

| WEB AT WORK! |

Some industry observers feel the size of a chain restaurant company is best measured by the number of units operated under its name. Other observers feel total revenue generated is the best measure of a restaurant chain's true popularity. Nation's Restaurant News (NRN) produces an online publication that annually ranks the top 100 U.S.-based restaurant chains using a variety of measures including sales growth, total U.S. units, and total sales.

To stay abreast of the biggest and fastest growing U.S.-based restaurant chains go to:

www.nrn.com

Choose "Industry Data" then choose "U.S. Top 100".

COSTS OF FRANCHISED AND INDEPENDENT RESTAURANTS

If you wish to start a restaurant, the decision to purchase a franchise versus opening an independent unit is important for many reasons. Restaurant owners and managers who elect to purchase a franchise typically do so because they're impressed with the **business model** created and marketed by a franchisor to potential franchisees.

Business model

The plan implemented by a company to generate revenue and make a profit from operations.

A restaurant franchisor's business model includes much more than the determination of what will be served on the menu. The terms of the formal agreement between the franchisor and franchisee, the costs of the franchise, the degree to which operating standards will be enforced, and the amount of discretionary on-property decision making permitted are among the key issues that must be carefully assessed prior to purchasing a franchise.

Generally, there are three major costs incurred when purchasing a franchise. These are:

1. Initial franchise fee
2. Royalty fees
3. Marketing fees

The Initial Franchise Fee

Franchisors charge a one-time fee to those who buy their franchises. This fee is usually directly related to the restaurant chain's history of success. Thus, for example, the fee charged by McDonald's, a chain with a long track record of popularity and profitability, will be larger than the fee charged by a newer, less established restaurant group. Initial franchise fees also tend to be higher for restaurant concepts that generate higher annual revenues. As a result, the initial franchise fee for a steakhouse restaurant in a chain where the average annual unit sales exceed $2,000,000 will usually be higher than the initial franchise fee charged for restaurants in a small sandwich shop chain with average unit sales of less than $500,000 per year.

Sellers in many businesses reduce prices for in-quantity purchases. The same is true of those selling franchises: they often offer a lower per-unit initial franchise fee to a buyer purchasing the right to open multiple units rather than a single unit. Initial franchise fees can be considered as "right to join the chain" fees and these fees must be paid *prior* to the opening of the franchised restaurant.

The initial franchise fee grants the restaurateur the right to use the franchisor's name and logos as well as other assets such as recipes, training and operating materials, and computer software systems. It also typically includes franchisor support and assistance prior to the opening of the restaurant, including help with site selection, building construction and layout, equipment selection, interior design, and signage. In some **franchise agreements**, the franchisor will be granted some or even complete control over these items and others, including the required completion of pre-opening manager and employee training programs.

Franchise agreement

The legal contract detailing the terms of the relationship between a franchisor and a franchisee.

In the restaurant industry, initial franchise fees typically range from $10,000 to $50,000 or more per unit to be opened.

Royalty Fees

Royalty fees are a second franchisor-mandated charge. The name given to these fees may vary somewhat and include royalty fees, continuing fees, or sales-based fees; these fees are paid over the life of the franchise agreement. The amount of these fees is established in the franchise agreement and is typically expressed as a percentage of total revenue achieved by the restaurant.

For example, if a franchised restaurant is obligated by the franchise agreement to pay a 4% royalty fee on monthly sales, and in a given month the franchisee's restaurant achieved $100,000 in sales, then the royalty fee to be paid to the franchisor would be $4,000.

$$\$100,000 \text{ sales achieved } (\times) \text{ .04 royalty rate } = \$4,000 \text{ royalty fee}$$

While the most common case is to establish royalty fees as a percentage of restaurant revenue, a minimum royalty fee may also established. Royalty fee payments may be due to the franchisor on a weekly, monthly, or quarterly basis. While the initial franchise fee can be considered "right to join the chain" fees, royalty fees can be considered "right to stay in the chain" fees. Royalty fees typically pay for franchisor services such as ongoing training, updates to operating manuals and procedures, ongoing consulting, and mandated inspections.

In the restaurant industry, royalty fees typically range from 4% to 10% of unit revenues.

Marketing Fees

Marketing fees are mandatory franchisee contributions used to finance chain-wide advertising and marketing programs initiated by the franchisor. As you will learn in Chapter 9, effective marketing is essential to the success of a restaurant. While there is no requirement to do so, many restaurant professionals believe the average restaurant should allocate 3% to 6% of its revenue to marketing.

In a chain, the marketing fees paid by franchisees are used to purchase advertising designed to benefit all members of the chain. For large chains, these advertising programs can be targeted at regional, national, or even international audiences. Smaller chains may produce advertising programs designed to reach smaller, more regional audiences.

The marketing fees paid to franchisors are intended to supplement the marketing efforts undertaken by the chain's individual franchisees. The franchise agreement may call for a payment of marketing fees as well as establish a franchisee's mandated spending levels for local advertising.

The Cost of Independence

Some restaurateurs feel franchise fees are too high and, as a result, decide to open restaurants that aren't part of a chain. While such operators won't pay franchise fees, it would be a mistake to assume that their restaurants will avoid paying for many of the services provided by franchisors to their franchisees.

For example, while an independent restaurateur does not pay an initial franchisee fee, that same restaurateur would likely incur the expense of paying for needed architectural drawings or blueprints that a franchisor would normally provide to its franchisees when they pay their initial franchise fees. In a similar manner, while independent restaurants won't pay a marketing fee to a franchisor, these same operations will spend money for advertising. Independent restaurateurs will also incur the expense and time of planning their own advertising campaign, negotiating prices for the ads, and monitoring their placement. These activities are services routinely provided by franchisors to their franchisees.

It's incorrect to conclude that restaurateurs who operate franchised restaurants are any less skilled or less creative than those who operate independent restaurants. Both franchised and independent restaurant operators must use their planning, organizing, supervising, and financial control skills to be successful. In most cases, just as those who purchase a franchise are impressed with the franchisor's business model, those who elect to operate their own restaurants as independents have faith in the business model they themselves have developed. Because the advantages and disadvantages associated with franchised versus independent restaurant operations are so significant, it's important that they're well understood by any restaurateur planning to open a new business.

OPERATING FRANCHISED AND INDEPENDENT RESTAURANTS

To succeed in the restaurant industry, it's important to understand the pros and cons of opening and operating a franchised or independent restaurant.

WEB AT WORK!

The International Franchise Association (IFA) is the oldest and largest organization representing franchising worldwide. IFA's mission is to protect, enhance, and promote franchising through government relations, public relations, and educational programs. Many of its members are restaurateurs. To see the educational services IFA offers its members, go to:

www.franchise.org

Click on "Professional Development."

Advantages of Franchised Restaurants

Restaurateurs who elect to purchase a franchise typically do so because quality franchised restaurants offer these advantages:

1. They have demonstrated success in the market.

Restaurant concepts that provide good franchising opportunities have a record of being popular with guests over an extended period of time. This reduces the risk of the new restaurant failing to attract sufficient volume levels to generate a profit.

2. Can be opened at a lower cost.

Because most franchisors have already incurred the expense associated with their buildings' interior and exterior design and blueprints, individual franchisees can benefit from using these critical and lower-cost building tools. Some franchisors have developed partially pre-fabricated units to make construction even faster. As a result, and construction of new restaurant is faster and less expensive than if these important tools had to be developed and paid for individually. Signage, logos, menus, and uniforms may also cost franchisees less due to efforts previously undertaken by franchisors.

3. They can be operated at a lower cost.

A restaurateur's operating costs may often be lowered because of his or her affiliation with a chain. For example, a chain may be able to negotiate reduced costs from food suppliers due to the large quantity of products its franchisees may buy. The per-unit costs of advertising and marketing for each operator may also be significantly reduced when they're spread over many restaurants units.

4. They have proven training systems in place.

Successful restaurateurs know that a well-trained staff is an essential key to operational profitability. When franchisees pay initial royalty fees, they avail themselves of the franchisor's

Franchisors offer critical support before and after their franchisee's restaurants have opened.

> ## GREEN AT WORK!
>
> Increasingly, quick-service restaurant customers want to feel good about their food choices. So healthier menu options, such as salads, wraps, and fruit, have become popular fixtures on QSR menus in recent years. And many QSR customers care just as much about a healthy Earth as they do about a healthy menu choice.
>
> Some QSR franchisors have responded to this increased interest by making eco-friendliness a significant part of their marketing efforts. For example, Fort Lauderdale–based Pizza Fusion displays the tagline *"Saving the Earth, one pizza at a time"* in its advertising and on its website. An entire section of the Pizza Fusion website explains many of the company's strategies for being greener than the average restaurant: They use hybrid cars as delivery vehicles, recycle their pizza boxes and offer customers discounts for bringing them back to be recycled, and use the heat from their ovens to warm their restaurants.
>
> As restaurant customers become more aware of green practices, expect them to pay more attention to the green practices of the restaurants they choose to frequent.

existing training programs and systems. In fact, one of the most important criteria to be used when selecting a franchise company is the quality of its employee and management training programs.

5. They can enhance the owners' ability to secure start-up funding.

Lenders and investors are often more willing to provide funding for a restaurant operating with a market-proven concept than for one that does not have a track record of success. Potential sources of funding also know that franchisors will offer their franchisees experienced and readily available operational support if they experience difficulties before or after their restaurants open.

Disadvantages of Franchised Restaurants

Experienced restaurateurs know there can be distinct challenges and drawbacks to opening a franchised restaurant. Disadvantages include:

1. The fees charged by franchisors make it too difficult to achieve desired profit levels.

Purchasing a franchise can be very expensive. Initial franchise fees may run as high as $50,000 or more. Additional franchisor-mandated purchases related to the building, signage, equipment, and inventory can easily add thousands more to the start-up costs. After the restaurant is open, royalty and marketing fees can cost operators 5 to 15% (or more) of their restaurant's total annual sales.

Of course, franchisees do receive services for the fees they pay. However, when operators calculate the total price of affiliating with a franchisor, some conclude that the financial costs are simply too high to allow them to make the profits they desire.

2. The potential for expansion may be limited.

Franchisors usually allow their franchisees the rights to operate only in a tightly defined and restricted geographic location. These territorial restrictions ensure that one franchised restaurant does not unfairly encroach upon the territory of another. The end result, however, can be significant limits to a successful restaurant's growth or expansion in a specific location or geographic area.

3. The restaurant may suffer from guilt by association.

The use of a shared name by all of the restaurants in a chain is widely viewed as one of the major benefits of franchise ownership. However, name recognition can also be a weakness. A customer may receive inferior service or poor-quality food in one franchised restaurant and consequently form a negative opinion about all of the units in the chain.

Name recognition can also be a distinct disadvantage if another franchised unit or the franchise company itself receives bad press or suffers from a less-than-stellar image. For example, if a case of **foodborne illness** in one unit in the chain is widely reported, customers who hear about it may avoid eating at any of the restaurants in that chain.

Foodborne illness

Sickness that results from eating contaminated food.

4. Operational control is too restricted.

Experienced restaurateurs know that franchisors place a large number of operational restrictions on their franchisees. They may limit the menu items that may be sold, the cooking methods to be used, pricing, employment-related policies, marketing, and other operational areas that are critical to the success of a restaurant. These restrictions are usually designed to enhance uniformity across the chain and to benefit all franchisees.

Some operating mandates—such as the requirement of offering value-priced menu items sold at or near an operator's cost—may appear to be for the franchisor's own benefit, and perhaps even at the expense of their franchisees. These policies or procedures must be followed, or the franchisee can be subject to franchisor-imposed fines or even loss of the franchise. The inability to control their own businesses decision making is one significant reason why some restaurateurs prefer not to become part of a franchise group.

5. The term of the franchise agreement is too long.

The decision to enter into a franchise agreement cannot be taken lightly. Most franchise agreements are written for 10 or more years. Generally, a franchisee that seeks an early termination of the franchise agreement will still be held legally responsible for payment of all the franchisee fees that would have been collected by the franchisor over the entire length of the agreement.

Advantages of Independent Restaurants

Restaurateurs who elect to open an independent (nonfranchised) restaurant recognize that doing so will require a significant amount of research and money. Unlike the restaurateurs who affiliate with a franchise support system, those who open an independent restaurant must create every part of the business, including concept development, site selection, building design, logo development, training, operations, and marketing.

Despite the extra work involved, thousands of new independent restaurants open each year. Restaurateurs who open an independent operation typically do so because:

1. Their concept is unique.

Every successful restaurant group started with a single independent restaurant that ultimately became popular enough to launch a chain of similar units. The lesson here is twofold. First, the restaurant concept conceived of by an individual restaurateur may be so unique that no existing franchisor currently offers a similar tested model. So choosing a franchisor offering a similar concept is simply not possible.

© Simone van den Berg/Shutterstock

Signature menu items can greatly enhance the reputation of independently operated restaurants.

Second, while many successful restaurant concepts can be readily franchised, some cannot. It could be that the successful implementation of the concept heavily depends on the location of the restaurant, the special skills of the restaurant's operators or the uniqueness of the operation's **signature menu items**.

2. They want total control of their operations.

Perhaps the reason independent restaurateurs give most often for choosing to "go it alone" is the complete control they will have over their operation. Because most independent restaurateurs are experienced operators, many prefer to make their own decisions about how their businesses will be developed and managed.

For people who like the idea of not having to answer to anyone else, becoming an independent restaurant operator has great appeal. The success or failure of their business is completely in their own hands. Many **entrepreneurs** relish that arrangement and challenge.

3. They can avoid the financial requirements imposed by the franchisor.

Franchisors who grant others the franchise rights to a successful restaurant concept are understandably careful about whom they choose as partners. As a result, they may place considerable financial and related requirements on potential franchisees. For example, franchisors typically establish minimum standards related to:

- The financial net worth of the individual or company seeking the franchise
- The amount of un-borrowed cash that must be available for immediate investment
- The credit history of the individual seeking the franchise

It's not unusual for the financial requirements of opening a franchised restaurant to exceed $500,000 or more. When a restaurateur does not have the required level of financial resources, or has a poor credit history, an independent operation may be the most viable option.

4. The opportunity to maximize profits is greater.

Most restaurateurs recognize that the risk of failure is reduced when a franchisor opens a restaurant that has a proven concept. However, in *equally* successful restaurants, those restaurants that aren't required to pay a franchisor's initial franchise fee, as well as ongoing royalty and marketing fees, may return more profits to their owners than those restaurants that must pay those fees.

It's also important to recognize that the relationship between a franchisor and a franchisee isn't a true partnership in terms of shared risk: Franchisors aren't responsible for the operating losses of their franchisees. Franchisors don't collect their fees as a percentage of operating profits, but rather base their fees on predetermined percentages of achieved *revenue*. As a result, it's the franchisee who bears all of the financial risk of poor operating performance.

5. The opportunity to expand and grow is greater.

Most often, a franchisor grants a franchisee the right to operate in a single location or in a tightly restricted geographic area. Thus, extremely successful operators may face significant restrictions on their ability to expand and open additional units. Independent restaurateurs face no such restrictions.

In fact, the owners of an independent restaurant that becomes highly successful can grow their business as quickly as they choose—or even become franchisors.

Disadvantages of Independent Restaurants

There are significant drawbacks to opening a restaurant as an independent. These include:

1. A lack of name recognition.

Perhaps the greatest hurdle that independent restaurateurs face is simply making their presence known to their target markets. Customers readily understand the menu offerings and pricing structure of chain restaurants with large marketing budgets. Independent restaurants must educate their customers about who they are and what they serve if they're to capture their fair share of their target markets. This can be costly, and those costs cannot be shared among several units as they can be when a restaurant is part of a multiunit chain.

2. Higher operating costs.

When chain restaurants negotiate with suppliers, they can often secure prices (for the exact same items) that are 10 to 15% below the prices charged to independent restaurant operators. The combined purchasing power of large chain operations can put independent operators at a significant disadvantage when it comes to paying the lowest price possible for needed products and supplies.

Signature menu item

A food or beverage item that guests associate with a specific food service operation. Examples may include a "one-pound pork chop" or an "oyster boat" (a loaf of French bread hollowed out and filled with deep-fried oysters).

Entrepreneur

A person who organizes and manages a private business, usually with considerable initiative and risk.

Large chain restaurants can often negotiate lower prices for food products—a great benefit for the chain's franchisees.

3. Limited access to specialized restaurant experts.

When restaurateurs buy a quality franchise, they're also buying access to the services of experts employed by the franchisor. As a result, specialists in restaurant design, advanced technology systems, and employee training are often readily available to assist franchisees. Independent restaurateurs may not have such access to experts—they may be required to find and pay a premium for these specialists' services when they need them.

4. Inability to learn from and share with others.

Successful franchisees often point to their ability to share ideas, issues, and solutions with other franchisees in their chain as one of the great advantages they enjoy as operators. Independent restaurateurs, are "on-their-own" when it comes to addressing new operational issues or problems. For experienced restaurateurs, this may not be a problem; however, lack of peer support can be a significant disadvantage for those with fewer years in the business.

5. A reduced ability to secure external financing.

Studies of new restaurants that quickly go out of business typically identify poor management and insufficient start-up funding as the two most common reasons for failure.

One reason why it's more difficult for an independent restaurateur to secure start-up finding is the hesitancy on the part of most lenders and investors to finance an unknown restaurant concept. As a result, the funds needed to start an independent restaurant may be harder to secure or may be given only with strict loan conditions and high costs.

WEB AT WORK!

Independent restaurant operators can voluntarily join forces to provide advice and support to each other when they share goals and objectives.

While many such support groups exist, the Springfield (MO) Independent Restaurant Association is a good example of independent operators coming together to gain many of the benefits enjoyed by chain restaurant owners. To learn more about this group, go to:

www.dinelocally.com

Click on "About Us."

> ### ALL IN A DAY'S WORK: 2.1
>
> "I'm thinking about starting my own pizza place," said Sara to her friend Sofia. "I think I have just about enough money to do it. If I can get a loan for the rest, I know I can make it work."
>
> "A pizza place," said Sofia. "That's so exciting! Are you thinking about a Dominos, a Papa Johns, or a Little Caesars?"
>
> "No," replied Sofia. "They're great, but I want to open a sit-down place and serve more than just pizza."
>
> "Oh, I get it. Like a Pizza Hut, or a Sbarros?" asked Sofia.
>
> "No... like a Sara's," replied her friend with a smile.
>
> "Never heard of it!" replied Sofia, also smiling. "It better be good!"
>
> **1.** What are some key challenges Sara will face if she opens her own restaurant?
> **2.** What are some advantages Sara's new restaurant may have over better-known competitors that may operate in her target market area?

In this chapter, you will learn more about the specific methods used to finance new restaurants. The process is usually more complex for independent restaurateurs than for those seeking funding to open a franchise that has a proven history of success.

SECURING NEEDED CAPITAL

In Chapter 1, you learned that securing **capital** financing is a critical aspect of the overall business plan for a new restaurant and a key to its success.

Very few entrepreneurs have enough of their own money to fully fund a new restaurant. Even those who have sufficient personal funds may still find it advantageous to borrow money when opening a new business.

In this section, you'll learn why a combination of **equity funding** and **debt financing** is often the most desirable way to secure the total amount of capital needed to open a new restaurant.

Some restaurateurs choose to **lease**, rather than buy, some of the items they need to start their restaurants. In this section, you'll learn why leasing can be a valuable capital-saving tool when developing a restaurant's overall financing plan.

Equity Funding

We've addressed the fact that the way a new restaurant is financed will be a vital part its business plan. After the costs of starting a new restaurant have been determined, a plan for financing those costs must be developed. In general, if you plan to open a new restaurant, you do so to maximize your return on investment (ROI). The way your restaurant is financed has a direct impact on your eventual ROI.

To illustrate this point, assume that you have decided to open a new franchised or independent restaurant. One of your first tasks is to find the location that makes the most sense to you and to determine the total cost required to construct and furnish a building in that location. Let's say that the total cost is $1,000,000.

In simplified financing terms, you have two very different options. The first is to pay the $1,000,000 in cash. This money may come from your savings, from family members, as gifts from friends, from the sale of your other investments, from one or more partners in your business, or from a **venture capitalist**. The partner may wish only to contribute funds. Or, the partner may take on a role in the actual administration and/or operation of the business. When an owner requires partners to assist with start-up funding, it's important that the roles of the owner and all the partners be well defined and well understood by all.

Regardless of the source of money, if you paid for 100% of a restaurant's construction costs without borrowing money, you would be contributing only **equity** (owner's) funds to start your business.

A second option is to borrow the entire $1,000,000 and agree to make regular payments to the lender until the loan is repaid.

Considered somewhat differently, with equity funding, you raise capital by selling part of the ownership in your restaurant. For example, if you find one or more partners who agree to

Capital

The investment cash used to start a new restaurant.

Equity funding

The personal money used to finance a new restaurant.

Debt financing

The borrowed money used to finance a new restaurant.

Lease

An arrangement that allows a restaurant to use items such as land, buildings, or equipment without purchasing them.

Venture capitalist

A person or organization that invests in a business venture by providing capital for start-up or expansion. Venture capitalists typically seek higher rates of return or ownership than they would receive in more traditional investments.

Equity

The amount of personal money owners contribute to purchase an asset. Also, the value of an asset minus the amount of money owners borrow to purchase the asset.

invest $500,000 in your new restaurant, you might give them 50% ownership of the business in return. In a similar manner, partners who invest 10% of the costs might receive 10% ownership. If you use only your own money for your equity financing, you will, in effect, sell 100% ownership in the business to yourself. With an equity funding arrangement, you can personally own anywhere from 1 to 100% of your new business.

Debt Financing

In many cases, restaurateurs don't have all the money they need to start their new businesses. So they may seek debt financing to make up the difference. Debt financing providers can include banks, finance companies, credit unions, credit card companies, and private companies. A business loan, for example, is a common type of debt financing.

Depending upon the credit history of the restaurateur, securing a business loan may be faster, easier, and more desirable than searching for additional equity investors. Remember that in most projects, each additional owner who contributes equity funding to a project reduces the amount of ownership retained by the project's initial owner. For example, if a restaurateur needs $1,000,000 to start a new business, but has only $500,000 in personal funds, he or she may have to give up 50% ownership in the new business in exchange for securing the additional $500,000 in equity funds needed to open the restaurant. That may not be desirable.

With debt financing (rather than equity funding), lenders don't own a share of the business, but do secure the right to be repaid prior to any repayments made to those who have provided equity funding. In addition to ownership-related advantages, borrowers know that as they pay down their loans, they also build creditworthiness. This usually makes them even more attractive to potential lenders and increases their chances of securing additional loans in the future.

© Goodluz/Shutterstock

Banks and other lending institutions will carefully review a restaurant's revenue and expense forecast prior to lending money to its owners.

WEB AT WORK!

The Small Business Administration (SBA) can be of great assistance to restaurateurs seeking start-up funding. The SBA's mission is "to maintain and strengthen the nation's economy by enabling the establishment and viability of small businesses and by assisting in the economic recovery of communities after disasters."

To learn more the SBA's efforts to fulfill this mission by helping small businesses secure loans, go to:

www.sba.gov

Click on "Loans and Grants."

With a 100% debt financing option, borrowers retain 100% ownership of their businesses; however, they also assume the **liability** of repaying all of the borrowed money plus all interest charges for the loan.

Despite its advantages, many potential restaurateurs are surprised to discover how difficult it is to secure debt financing. As one wise entrepreneur stated:

"It's harder than it looks, and it doesn't look all that easy!"

Many lenders are understandably hesitant to risk their existing loan funds by making them available to unproven business ventures. It's important to understand that there are no rules in the United States (and in most other countries) about the parties to whom a bank must lend (with the exception of laws related to illegal discrimination).

Because potential lenders often place varying requirements on businesses that are requesting loans, the information lenders require when considering making a loan may differ somewhat. However, the lender usually asks the potential borrower to include a three-year financial **pro forma**: a detailed estimate of the revenue, expenses and profits to be achieved by the business.

Pro forma financial documents include other vital information about a business's estimated assets, liabilities, and available cash over a particular time period. If money is borrowed, the pro forma statements will indicate how and when the business will pay back those funds.

Banks are free to lend as little or as much as they like depending on their own assessment of the risks and rewards of lending. Historically, traditional banks have been hesitant to lend to small start-up businesses such as restaurants unless the creditworthiness of the borrower is extremely well established or if loan repayment is guaranteed by the **Small Business Administration (SBA)**.

Figure 2.2 lists some of the most important factors banks and other lending institutions typically consider when assessing an application for a business loan.

Liability

A debt that is owed and must be repaid.

Pro forma

A financial statement prepared on the basis of assumed, future events and activities.

Pro forma statements indicate management's best estimate of a business's future revenue, expense, and profits as well as its assets and liabilities, over a specified time period.

Small Business Administration (SBA)

A U.S. government agency that does not make loans but rather helps educate and prepare business owners to apply for loans through a financial institution or bank. If the loan is initially granted by the bank, the SBA then guarantees that it will be repaid as promised.

- ☐ Total project cost
- ☐ Total loan amount requested
- ☐ Percentage of the total project cost to be contributed by equity funds
- ☐ Amount of equity funding personally contributed by the potential borrower
- ☐ Percentage of total project cost to be contributed by debt financing
- ☐ Reasonability of the assumptions made in the business's estimates of its future financial performance
- ☐ Quality of assets pledged as loan collateral (security)
- ☐ The ability to readily convert secured assets to cash in the event that the borrower stops loan repayments
- ☐ The work experience of those who will run the business
- ☐ The quality of the business idea as presented in the business plan
- ☐ The financial worth of the borrower
- ☐ The willingness of the borrower to personally guarantee the loan
- ☐ The personal credit rating/history of the borrower

FIGURE 2.2

The Factors That Lenders Consider When Making a Small Business Loan

FIGURE 2.3

Equity Funding vs. Debt
Financing

Differences Related To:	Equity Funding	Debt Financing
Amount of total funding available	Up to 100%	Typically limited to 50 to 75% of total project costs
Funds secured	Contributed by owners of the business	Provided by lenders
Ownership of the business	May be shared with contributors of the funds	Retained by borrower
Repayment	Made from business profits after fulfilling all loan repayment requirements	Interest on loan repayments are considered a business expense; the amount and timing of repayment is established when the loan is granted
Difficulty of securing needed capital	Moderate to high	High to very high

Because of their proven history of success and reduced risk, it's not surprising that lenders are often more inclined to lend money to support the opening of a new and successful *franchised* restaurant concept than they are to an independent operation with an unproven concept.

Loans from family members or friends are a common source of business start-up money; these funds may not be subject to the same conditions as loans obtained from financial institutions. Figure 2.3 summarizes some key differences between using equity funds and borrowed funds (debt) when securing the capital needed to develop a new restaurant.

Leasing

While a detailed examination of the tax and cash flow advantages and disadvantages of leasing versus buying is well beyond the scope of this book, as a professional restaurant manager, you should know that leasing can be an effective way to reduce the amount of start-up capital needed to open a restaurant.

A lease is simply a formal arrangement that allows a restaurant to use items such as land, buildings, or equipment without purchasing them. The amount of cash needed to secure the items via leasing is usually less than that required to purchase the items, because the items are rented rather than bought. Of course, in a lease arrangement, actual ownership of the item remains with the **lessor**, not the **lessee**; thus, the lessee may use the leased item only in the manner and time called for in the lease.

Figure 2.4 lists some important differences between leasing and buying property with regards to a restaurant.

Lessor

A person or organization that leases property to another.

Lessee

A person or organization that leases property from another.

THE IMPACT ON ROI

Chapter 1 states that financing details are an important part a restaurant's business plan. After the costs of starting a new restaurant have been determined, a plan for financing those costs must be developed. If you plan to open a new restaurant, you usually do so in a quest to maximize your ROI. The choices you make about how to finance your restaurant have a direct impact on your eventual ROI.

To illustrate, recall that the definition of ROI is the ratio of annual profits achieved to money invested. ROI is calculated as:

$$\frac{\text{Annual profits}}{\text{Investment}} = \text{ROI}$$

For example, if a restaurateur invests equity of $500,000 in a new restaurant and achieves $50,000 in annual profits, the ROI is:

$$\frac{\$\,50,000}{\$\,500,000} = 10\%$$

FIGURE 2.4

Key Differences between Leasing and Buying Property

Differences Related To:	Buying	Leasing
Immediate effect on start-up cash needed	Typically results in an increased usage of start-up cash	Typically results in a decreased usage of start-up cash
Ability to use the property as security for a loan	The property can be used by its owner as collateral to secure a loan	The property cannot typically be used as collateral to secure a loan sought by its lessee
Long-term ownership rights	Ownership of property passes to the owner's beneficiary	Rights to use property are ended upon termination of lease
Violation (nonpayment) of lease terms	Owner reclaims property	Rights to use property are forfeited
Depreciation rights	Property is depreciated for tax purposes	Property is not depreciated for tax purposes
The right to use the property	Property may be used in any manner the owner sees fit	Property use is limited to specific terms of the lease

Alternatively, if the restaurateur invests equity of $250,000 in a new restaurant and achieves $50,000 in annual profits, the ROI for that investment is:

$$\frac{\$\,50,000}{\$\,250,000} = 20\%$$

As these examples show, reduced amounts of equity investment resulting in equal profit returns yield higher returns on the investment. So it's not surprising that many investors seek to minimize the amount of equity funding they must provide to start a business and seek to maximize their **leverage** by utilizing increased amounts of borrowed money.

It's essential to understand that regardless of whether a restaurateur funds an investment with his or her own equity, or with equity funds obtained from others, ROI on equity funds is achieved only *after* those who have supplied debt financing have earned their own ROIs. Stated another way, equity ROIs are **subordinate** to debt ROIs because the repayment of borrowed funds must take place before an investment's profit generation is determined.

To illustrate the impact of equity and debt on ROI, consider this scenario. Noel wants to develop her own restaurant. She will be the major investor. The total project is estimated to cost $1,700,000. According to her business plan, profits (**net operating income (NOI)**) from her restaurant are estimated at $340,000 per year.

Assume Noel invests $1,700,000 of her own money to open the restaurant. Her ROI is calculated as follows:

$$\frac{\$\,340,000}{\$\,1,700,000} = 20\%$$

While many investors would consider 20% an excellent ROI, Noel feels she can do better.

To achieve a higher level of ROI, Noel is considering applying for debt financing. Because of her excellent background, strong business plan and personal credit history, Noel feels she can secure one or more loans at an annual interest rate of 8%. Figure 2.5 illustrates the effect that funding her investment with varying levels of debt and equity will have on her ROI.

In most cases, the greater the financial leverage (funding supplied by debt), the greater the ROI will be on equity funds supplied by an equity investor.

As you can see from the data in Figure 2.5, if Noel funds 75% (rather than 100%) of her project's cost with equity and 25% with debt, the ROI she will receive on her equity funds is 24%, a higher ROI than the 20% she will achieve if she doesn't leverage her investment at all.

Leverage

The use of borrowed money to fund an investment.

Increased leverage results in *decreased* amounts of equity funding needed in an investment, thus *increasing* the investment's equity return.

Subordinate financing

Money to be repaid only after all other financing debts are resolved.

For example, in terms of investments, the repayment to owners of invested equity funds is subordinate to the repayment of externally secured debt.

Net operating income (NOI)

Operating income after operating expenses are deducted but before interest on debts and income taxes are paid.

Also known as "earnings before interest and taxes" (EBIT).

FIGURE 2.5

Effect of Debt on Equity Returns: $1,700,000 Project

With 75% Equity and 25% Debt

Percentage Source of funds	Amount Contributed	Returns and Repayments (NOI)	Percentage Return	Debt Coverage Ratio
Equity 75%	$ 1,275,000	$ 306,000	24%	
Debt 25%	$ 425,000	$ 34,000	8%	10.0
Total 100%	**$1,700,000**	**$340,000**	**20%**	

With 50% Equity and 50% Debt

Percentage Source of funds	Amount Contributed	Returns and Repayments (NOI)	Percentage Return	Debt Coverage Ratio
Equity 50%	$ 850,000	$ 272,000	32%	
Debt 50%	$ 850,000	$ 68,000	8%	5.0
Total 100%	**$1,700,000**	**$340,000**	**20%**	

With 25% Equity and 75% Debt

Percentage Source of funds	Amount Contributed	Returns and Repayments (NOI)	Percentage Return	Debt Coverage Ratio
Equity 25%	$ 425,000	$ 238,000	56%	
Debt 75%	$ 1,275,000	$102,000	8%	3.3
Total 100%	**$1,700,000**	**$340,000**	**20%**	

With even greater leverage (for example, 50% debt financing and 50% equity financing), Noel can achieve even greater returns (32% ROI) on her equity investment. With 75% debt financing and 25% equity financing, Noel will achieve a 56% return on her equity investment.

To maximize ROIs, restaurants must be popular and profitable.

© Diego Cervo/Shutterstock

Given the data presented in Figure 2.5, a restaurateur seeking to open a new restaurant may ask, "Why not fund nearly 100% of every investment using debt?" The answer to this question lies in the Figure 2.5 column titled "Debt Coverage Ratio."

Debt coverage ratio is a measure of how much risk is involved in making a loan to a business. The formula for debt coverage ratio is:

$$\frac{\text{Annual profit (NOI) generated*}}{\text{Required debt service}} = \text{Debt coverage ratio}$$

In this formula, **debt service** is the annual amount that must be repaid to those who have lent money to the business.

As shown in Figure 2.5, when 25% of the project's cost is supplied by debt, the debt coverage ratio is 10 ($340,000 ÷ $34,000 = 10). When 50% of the project's cost is supplied by debt, the debt coverage ratio is reduced to 5 ($340,000 ÷ $68,000 = 5). When 75% of the project's cost is supplied by debt, the debt coverage ratio is 3.3 ($340,000 ÷ $102,000 = 3.3).

Recall that those who supply loans to a business must be repaid before the business pays those who supply equity funding. The debt coverage ratio then, is a measure of how likely the business is to actually have the funds necessary to repay the loans. The higher the debt coverage ratio, the more likely the business will generate the funds needed to repay its loans. The lower the debt coverage ratio, the greater the risk of the investment.

Just as investors evaluate a potential ROI to determine if an investment is a "good" one, lenders analyze debt coverage ratios and their own willingness to assume risk when deciding whether to lend money to an investor. It's also important to note that as any investor's risk increases, the returns expected from that investment should also increase. So those who seek debt funding for projects that show lower-than-desirable debt coverage ratios, often find that the only loans they receive come at a higher cost. Consequently, the interest rates lenders charge on the loans they supply are higher, and payback times may also be reduced. Because many lending institutions consider businesses in the hospitality industry to be high risk, most normally provide debt financing for no more than 50 to 75% of a project's total cost.

Debt service

The annual amount that must be repaid to those who have lent money to a business.

Debt service is determined by the amount of a loan, the interest rate charged for it, and the length of time allowed for the loan's repayment.

---

*Net operating income

ALL IN A DAY'S WORK: 2.2

"So you see," said Roscoe, "I need a loan for $800,000."

Roscoe Lefever was talking to Nancy Berger, the business loan officer at Local Community Bank.

Roscoe and Nancy were reviewing Roscoe's business plan for a new restaurant he wanted to open.

"Yes," replied Nancy. "I see the total project cost is $850,000. And you have $50,000 of that."

"That's right," said Roscoe. "$40,000 from my savings and $10,000 that I borrowed from my folks."

"I see that," said Nancy. "And your financial projections are that the restaurant will have annual sales of $1,000,000 with an after-expense NOI of $100,000. With $70,000 of that designated for debt repayment."

"That's right," replied Roscoe. "Is that a problem?"

"It's not a problem if you hit those numbers," replied Nancy, "but have you thought about what you'll do if you don't hit them?"

1. What factors do you think are most important to Nancy as she considers whether to grant Roscoe's loan request?
2. Assume Roscoe's projections are accurate. What would be the debt coverage ratio resulting from an $800,000 loan that required repayments of $70,000 per year? What would be Roscoe's equity rate of return? If you were Nancy, would you make the loan? Explain your answer.

Restaurant Terms and Concepts

Work in Progress

1. Is your favorite restaurant an independent or is it franchised? Why is it your favorite?

2. Why do you think so many experienced restaurateurs choose to open franchised restaurants?

3. Consider your favorite restaurant chain. Would owning one or more restaurants in that chain appeal to you? Explain your answer.

4. Assume you wanted to open a takeout pizzeria near your school. Would you want it to be part of a franchise group or an independent operation? Explain your answer.

5. Consider a very successful independent restaurant in your area. Is its success the result of its location, the skill of one or more of the restaurant's operators, the unique cooking methods for its signature menu items, or something else? Do you believe the restaurant could be successfully franchised?

6. What likely challenges do entrepreneurs seeking to start businesses utilizing 100% equity funding face?

7. What likely challenges do entrepreneurs seeking to start businesses utilizing 100% debt financing face?

8. Assume you were the loan officer at a bank. What information would you want from potential borrowers before you agreed to lend money for a start-up restaurant? For a franchised restaurant?

9. Some restaurateurs elect to lease, rather than buy, some types of advanced equipment such as point-of-sale (cashiering) systems and office computers. Why do you think leasing these items may make more sense than buying them outright?

10. Assume your start-up restaurant had the option of either equity funding or borrowing the money you need to open it. Which option would you choose? Explain your answer.

3

The Legal Aspects of Restaurant Management

Chapter Outline

Restaurant Organizational Structures
Sole Proprietorships
Partnerships
Corporations

Restaurant Laws and Regulations
Laws Related to Restaurant Operations
Laws Related to Employees
Laws Related to Guests

Learning Objectives

After carefully reading and studying the information in this chapter, you will:

1. Know the distinguishing characteristics of the most common legal entities used to operate restaurants.

2. Understand and know the importance of properly managing legal issues related to restaurant operations, employees and guests.

IN THIS CHAPTER

If you choose to start your own restaurant, you must make a number of important decisions, including whether to buy a franchise or to operate independently and how to secure start-up funding for your business. You must also decide where the business will be located, what you'll serve, your operating hours, and the prices you'll charge. One crucial decision to be made early in the process, however, is the form of business structure you'll choose. Structure, in this case, refers to the legal formation of your restaurant business.

In the United States, there is a large body of regulations and laws that govern how business structures are taxed, the liability these businesses assume, and the legal rights their owners enjoy. Courts and governments treat these diverse business structures differently. So the decision about which business structure will best meet the needs of a specific restaurant is a crucial one. In this chapter, you'll learn about the most common business structures used in the restaurant industry. You'll also learn how these different structures can directly affect the business and your role as its owner or manager.

Regardless of the organizational structure chosen by a restaurant owner, the actual management of a restaurant is subject to a large number of federal, state, and local laws and ordinances. As a result, restaurateurs have a lawful duty to adhere to these legal requirements.

Some laws related to restaurant operation are very straightforward and easily understood. The requirement, for example, that restaurants of all types maintain accurate financial records that will permit a fair assessment of the taxes they must pay is easily understood. Similarly, the legal requirement that a restaurant should serve only food that is safe to eat is a sound one that protects both customers and the restaurant.

Other laws are less well known yet must still be followed. One example is the legal requirement that all restaurateurs must allow authorized health inspectors reasonable entry to perform required inspections. While there are nuances in many local laws that can affect restaurant operations (for example, the prohibition or restrictions in some communities related to the Sunday sale of alcoholic beverages), all restaurant managers should be familiar with those laws that directly affect their restaurants. In this chapter, you'll learn about many of those restaurant-related laws and how they directly impact a restaurant's operation, its employees and its guests.

RESTAURANT ORGANIZATIONAL STRUCTURES

One of the most appealing aspects of the restaurant business is the chance to own one restaurant, dozens of restaurants, or even a several-hundred-unit chain of restaurants. Regardless of their long-term goals, when restaurateurs initially form a business, they must select a legally recognized organizational **business structure** for it.

Business structure

A legally recognized business entity.

The organizational structure of a business matters for many reasons. Perhaps one of the most significant is that the government and the courts treat business owners differently based on the organizational structures they have chosen for their businesses.

For example, the taxes that will be owed by a business are based, in large part, on its organizational structure. In addition, the limits of an owner's personal liability for the debts of a business are affected by the business's organizational structure. Lending institutions and investors most often consider the structure of a business prior to making decisions about the wisdom of supplying funds to it. Moreover, the costs of starting a business are directly impacted by the structure chosen for it. Even an owner's ability to sell or transfer ownership of his or her business will be affected by its organizational structure.

A number of different organizational structures are available to restaurateurs. The most common of these are the:

- Sole proprietorship
- Partnership
- Corporation

Sole Proprietorships

Sole proprietorship

A form of business structure in which one individual owns, and frequently operates, the business.

Many restaurants are operated as a **sole proprietorship**.

A sole proprietorship is the least complex business structure available to restaurateurs. In this structure, the proprietor (owner) of the business will own all of it and be held personally responsible for all of its debts.

A sole proprietorship can be legally used as the operating structure of any size restaurant. In this structure, both the **assets** of the business and of its owner must be used to pay any debts, expenses, and taxes due from the operation of the business.

Asset

Property, including cash, that is owned by an individual or a business.

When the business is structured as a sole proprietorship, its owner is required by law to pay all costs incurred by operating the restaurant. So if the restaurant fails, all personal assets held by the owner of the business must be made available to satisfy the debts incurred by the business. This includes cash, savings, and other personal property—even if that property was not used to operate the business. Thus, the owner's liability for any debts incurred by the business is considered to be unlimited.

In the sole proprietor structure, if the restaurant is successful, any profits made from its operation will be taxed at the same rate as the owner's personal income tax. At the end of each tax year, the sole proprietor simply lists the income achieved, and expense incurred, by the business and then reports any profits (or losses) on his or her own income tax return.

If, at any time, the owner of the business wants to sell it to someone else, he or she is able to do so without seeking approval from any other person or entity. The owners of a sole

Sole proprietors often both own their restaurant and serve as its manager.

proprietorship are also free to pass on their business to anyone they want, simply by stating that wish in their wills.

A sole proprietor's business may be operated under a different name. If so, the name of the business and the individual owning it must be legally registered with the appropriate governmental agency (usually the state in which the business is operated), to let those who will do business with the restaurant know the true identity of its owner.

For example, if Bill Lawrensen started a restaurant, selected the sole proprietorship business structure, and called his restaurant "Bill's Bar-B-Q," the legal name of the business would be "Bill Lawrensen, **DBA** Bill's Bar-B-Q."

Starting a sole proprietorship is easy and inexpensive. The owner of the business simply opens a bank account and then develops an accounting system designed to keep track of the business's revenue and expenses. Those who choose to do business with the restaurant (for example, vendors and suppliers) and those who may be asked to invest in, or lend to, the restaurant do so based on their assessment of the restaurant owner's personal financial integrity. Unless the owner of the business is financially very well off, this can sometimes have a negative effect on a vendor's willingness to extend credit to the operator and of lenders to lend to the business. These are financial realities often faced by sole proprietors and by those who are employed to manage their restaurants for them.

DBA

An abbreviation of "doing business as." Most often used when sole proprietors operate a business under a name different from their own.

Partnerships

A **general partnership** is very similar to a sole proprietorship except that with this type of organizational structure, two or more individuals or entities agree to share in the ownership of a business.

A partnership may be formed orally, but is best formed by a written contract. The terms of the contract (also called a **partnership agreement**) detail the rights and responsibilities of each co-owner of the business.

Items that a partnership agreement should address include how much time and money each owner will contribute to the business, who will operate the business, how profits will be split among the owners, and who is responsible for any losses that may be incurred by the business. The issue of who is responsible for losses is especially important because, as is true in a sole proprietorship, the partners in a general partnership are held personally responsible for any debts incurred by their business. Responsibility for debt in a general partnership is of special concern because the co-owners in a general partnership legally assume both personal and **joint liability** for the debts of the business.

General partnership

A business structure consisting of two or more owners or entities that share in the profits and losses of a business.

Partnership agreement

A formal contract outlining the financial and operational arrangement agreed to by the co-owners of a business.

Joint liability

Co-responsibility to repay all of an obligation.

© Michael Jung/Shutterstock

Limited partnerships consist of two distinct classes of partner: general partners (GPs) and limited partners (LPs).

Thus, for example, if two owners in a general partnership agree that they will share 50–50 in the profits and expenses of a business, but one owner dies, disappears, or declares bankruptcy, *all* of the debts of the business operated by their partnership will become the responsibility of the other owner. Any profits earned by the business are usually distributed to the individual partners in the business and will be taxed at the same rate as these owners' personal income.

Many restaurants are operated under the general partnership structure; however, as the risk of potential liability increases, some owners choose instead to form a **limited partnership**.

A limited partnership consists of two distinct types, or classes, of partner: the limited partner (LP) and the general partner (GP).

The LP, in most cases, is simply someone who invests money in the partnership. LPs in a limited partnership are responsible for debts equal only to the amount they have actually invested in the company. In exchange for these limits on their liability, they aren't permitted to engage in the management of the business. In fact, in most states, if an LP becomes actively involved in the management of the business, the state may revoke the LP's protection and thus make the LP jointly liable for the debts of the business.

In a limited partnership, the general partners (who may also be referred to as managing partners) have the same legal standing as the partners in a general partnership. They may share in control of the business and profits. However, they're also jointly responsible for the debts of the business. General partners may or may not be investors, but they serve as the business's operating and financial managers.

Profits earned in a limited partnership are distributed to the partners in accordance with their partnership agreement. Profits are then taxed at the same rate as each partner's personal income.

In most states, the rules related to the formation of a limited partnership are very specific. Typically, forms must be filed with the secretary of state or another governmental agency. Usually, the partnership's operating agreement must also be submitted for review before the state will grant a business the legal right to form and to operate under a limited partnership structure.

Limited partnership

A form of partnership similar to a general partnership except that in addition to one or more general partners (GPs), there is one or more limited partners (LPs).

Corporations

Often, a restaurant is operated as a **corporation**.

When a corporation is formed, its owners are called **shareholders**. The most common type of corporation is the **C corporation** (C Corp).

A C Corp is formed anytime a group of owners choose it as their business structure. Like all corporations, a C Corp has a legal identity separate from that of its owners. A C Corp can legally borrow money, own property, hire employees, sue, and be sued. C Corps are different from sole proprietorships and partnerships because the corporation itself, not its shareholders, is responsible for all of its debts. This is a great advantage to shareholders because it removes them from individual liability for the debts of a business operated by the corporation.

A C Corp gets its name from Chapter C of the U.S. Internal Revenue Code. While the great advantage of a C Corp is the elimination of its owner's individual liability, a C Corp has a significant disadvantage. It is simply this: *Profits from a C Corp are taxed twice.*

The first tax is imposed on the profits that are earned by the corporation. After these corporate taxes are paid, any remaining profits can be distributed to the shareholders of the corporation in the form of **dividends**.

The individual shareholders are then required to pay taxes on the dividends they receive. Note that shareholders aren't required to pay individual income taxes on profits unless the profits have been distributed to them in the form of dividends.

While their profits are taxed twice, and while corporation are more expensive to form and operate than sole proprietorships and partnerships, the limits corporations place on personal liability make them a popular choice for restaurateurs choosing a business structure. The rules required to form a corporation vary from state to state, but most require documents to be filed with the state agency specifically responsible for approving corporate formations.

A **Subchapter S Corporation**, or more commonly referred to as an S Corp, also gets its name from the U.S. Internal Revenue Code.

An S Corp business structure limits the liability of its owners while avoiding the double taxation that applies to C Corps.

The federal requirements for forming an S Corp are quite specific. Restrictions on S Corps relate to the number of allowable shareholders, the citizenship of shareholders, and a prohibition against shares being owned by corporations; as well as requirements related to the annual, and mandatory, filing of the corporation's financial information.

In an S Corp, the profits earned by the business are distributed to shareholders in proportion to their ownership of the company. These profits must then be reported on the shareholder's personal income tax form and are taxed at the rate applicable to that shareholder. Unlike a C Corp, however, taxes must be paid on income from an S Corp even if the profits have not been distributed to its owners. S Corps are often a good choice for small or family-operated restaurant companies with few individual owners.

A **limited liability company (LLC)** is a fairly new type of corporate business structure created by some states.

An LLC combines some of the most important advantages of a corporation with the simplicity and advantages of a partnership. In most states, LLC owners (also called members) are protected from personal liability for the debts of the business operated by the LLC. As a result, any member can serve as the company's owner or manager, and still protect his or her personal assets from liability for debts incurred by the company. From that perspective, an LLC operates much like a corporation.

If formed according to specific rules, the Internal Revenue Service (IRS) allows an LLC's profits to be taxed only once, thus, from a taxation perspective, LLCs operate in a manner most similar to a sole proprietorship or a partnership.

An LLC is governed by an **operating agreement** that establishes the rules for operating the LLC.

Depending on the state in which it's formed, an LLC may be required to pay an annual filing fee or an annual registration fee to keep its legal status in effect.

As you have learned, the specific business structure chosen for a business can affect ownership rules, personal liability, and taxation. Other aspects of a business's operation can also be affected by an owner's choice of business structure. For that reason, restaurateurs seeking to

Corporation

A formal business structure recognized as a legal entity, with privileges and liabilities separate from those of its owners.

Shareholder

An individual or other entity that owns one or more shares (portions) of a corporation. Also referred to as a "stockholder."

C corporation

A corporation that may be formed without restriction on the number of foreign or domestic shareholders. Also known as a "C Corp."

Dividend

The portion of its profits paid by a corporation to its shareholders.

Subchapter S corporation

A corporation that offers liability protection to its owners but is exempt from paying corporate taxes on its profits.

Also known as an "S Corp" or "Sub S Corp."

Limited liability company (LLC)

A form of corporation created under state law rather than federal law.

Operating agreement

The legal document outlining the manner in which an LLC is formed and how it will be managed.

FIGURE 3.1

Comparison of Business
Structures

Business Structure	Owner(s)	Liability for Company Debts	Income Taxes on Business Profits
Sole Proprietorship	Single owner	Unlimited personal liability for company debt	Paid once at the owner's personal tax rate
General Partnership	Two or more owners (partners)	Unlimited personal liability for company debt for all partners	Paid once at each partner's personal tax rate
Limited Partnership	Two or more owners (general partners and limited partners)	Unlimited personal liability for general partners (GPs); personal liability limited to the amount of the partner's investment for limited partners (LPs)	Paid once at each general partner or limited partner's personal tax rate
C Corporation	Unlimited number of owners (shareholders)	Personal liability limited to the amount of the shareholder's investment	Paid twice, once at the corporate tax rate and once at the individual shareholder's personal tax rate if distributed as a dividend
S Corporation	Limited number of owners (shareholders)	Personal liability limited to the amount of the shareholder's investment	Paid once in proportion to ownership in the S Corp and at the shareholder's personal tax rate whether the profits are or aren't distributed
Limited Liability Company	Unlimited number of owners (members)	Personal liability limited to the amount of the member's investment	Paid once at the member's personal tax rate

determine the best business structure for a new restaurant should seek the legal advice from an attorney and tax advisor who well understand the advantages and disadvantages of operating under each of the different business structures available in their state.

Figure 3.1 details some of distinguishing characteristics of the different business structures most commonly chosen by restaurateurs for their businesses.

ALL IN A DAY'S WORK: 3.1

"Trust me. This will be great," said Allen. "We'll both make a fortune."

Allen Brennan was talking to Scott Larson. Both were hospitality professionals and had been friends for more than 15 years. Allen had an idea for starting a new restaurant and wanted Scott to partner with him in its development and operation.

Scott was already the sole proprietor of a popular and profitable restaurant. Allen had recently quit his job as a district manager in a quick-service restaurant chain.

"I don't know," replied Scott. "I'm pretty busy just managing my current shop."

"That's no problem," replied Allen, "I'll manage the new place for us. We'll split the profits 50/50 since you'll be the one putting up all the money for our start-up. You won't have to do anything except cash your monthly checks from all the money we'll make!"

1. Assuming you are Scott, how important is the choice of business structure under which the proposed restaurant would operate? Explain your answer.
2. What affect could the choice of business structure chosen for the start-up restaurant have on Scott's current restaurant?

RESTAURANT LAWS AND REGULATIONS

You've learned that laws can directly affect how a restaurateur makes decisions about ownership requirements, taxation and personal liability limits. While they need not become attorneys, there are many other laws and regulations restaurateurs must become familiar with in order to operate their restaurants legally. They include:

- Required business licenses, including liquor licenses
- Health and fire permits
- Zoning requirements
- Building/construction inspections
- Sales tax permits
- Federal employee I.D. numbers
- Employment-related issues, including those involving:
  - Recruitment
  - Selection and hiring
  - Harassment prevention
  - Unions
  - Wage payments
  - Overtime
  - Payroll taxes
  - Required insurance contributions
- Restaurant operations–related issues, including:
  - OSHA
  - Food safety
  - Fairness in providing customer service
- Insurance requirements, including:
  - Workers' compensation
  - Liquor liability
  - Building insurance
  - Personal liability
- Tax accounting and tax payments made to:
  - Federal taxing authorities
  - State taxing authorities
  - Local taxing authorities

Figure 3.2 lists some of the most important governmental agencies you're likely to encounter as a restaurant manager as well as the purpose of each entity. While it's not realistic to assume that you'll know about every law or regulation that could possibly affect your business, you need to become familiar with the major federal-, state-, or local-level regulatory concerns that enforce laws affecting all restaurateurs in the areas of:

- Operations
- Employees
- Guests

Laws Related to Restaurant Operations

From a legal perspective, restaurant operators owe a **duty of care** to every person entering their businesses.

Duty of care

A legal obligation that requires a specific type of conduct.

A duty of care simply refers to the way things should be done. For all restaurateurs, important duties of care include:

- *Buying and serving only food and beverages that are safe to eat*

To this end, restaurateurs must make sure that their vendors sell foods that are safe and that the storage and preparation methods used in the restaurant will keep the food safe to eat until they are properly served to guests.

- *Providing a safe and secure environment*

This includes the interior of the restaurant, its exterior, and even its parking areas.

FIGURE 3.2

Legal Entities Affecting Restaurant Operators

Jurisdiction	Agency/Entity	Purpose
Federal	Internal Revenue Service (IRS)	Monitors collection of taxes (e.g., employee withholding tax) and payment of taxes (e.g., federal income tax)
	Environmental Protection Agency (EPA)	Serves as a regulator of pesticide use as well as water and air pollution
	Occupational Safety and Health Administration (OSHA)	Ensures, as far as possible, the safe and healthful working conditions of all employees
	Equal Employment Opportunity Commission (EEOC)	Enforces laws against discrimination in employment
	Department of Justice (DOJ)	Responsible for the enforcement of immigration laws and employment verification requirements as well as the Americans with Disabilities Act (ADA)
	Bureau of Alcohol, Tobacco, and Firearms (ATF)	Enforces federal law related to the manufacture and sale of alcohol and tobacco products
	Department of Labor (DOL)	Enforces federal laws related to employee rights, including health insurance requirements related to the Affordable Care Act (ACA), minimum wages, child labor laws, overtime wage payments, pensions, family medical leave, and unionization
	Food and Drug Administration (FDA)	Ensures the proper labeling of foods as well as the safety of the food supply
State	Alcohol Beverage Commission (ABC)	Monitors alcoholic beverage sales, hours of operation, licensing, and reporting of sales for tax purposes as well as administering any revocation of licenses
	Employment Security/Wage and Hour	Administers pay disputes, child labor laws, worker-related unemployment benefits, worker safety issues, and injury compensation
	Treasury/Controller	Responsible for the collection of state-imposed taxes as well as administering any state-sanctioned lottery or gaming activities
	Public Health Department	Responsible for the standards, inspection, and licensing of facilities that serve food and beverages
	Attorney General	Monitors state regulations related to franchisors and franchising
Local	Health and Sanitation	Responsible for the local inspection and licensing of food facilities, ensures compliance with any state- or municipality-imposed health and sanitation codes
	Building/Zoning	Regulates land use, issues permits for building and renovation projects as well as parking requirements
	Fire Department	Conducts facility inspections to ensure emergency lighting and sprinklers are installed and operating properly; establishes and enforces limits on the maximum number of guests that can be legally served in food and beverage facilities
	Local Law Enforcement	Enforces laws related to underage drinking and illegal parking; responds to reported guest disturbances
	Assessor	Responsible for assessing the value of property and collecting property-related taxes

> ### WEB AT WORK!
>
> The law related to the hospitality industry is an important and growing legal field. The first and a very often-quoted reference work related to hospitality law is the classic book *Hotel, Restaurant and Travel Law*, written by Cournoyer, Marshall and Morris.
>
> To review the most recent edition of this excellent resource, go to
>
> www.amazon.com
>
> Select "Books" in the drop-down search bar and then enter the author's name(s) or the book's title.

- *Serving alcohol in a responsible manner*

A variety of specific beverage-service-related laws (**dram shop laws**) describe in great detail the manner in which alcohol can be legally sold to help ensure that this important standard of care is met.

Dram shop laws

A variety of state and local regulations specifying the rules that must be followed by those who hold licenses to sell alcohol.

- *Hiring qualified employees and training them properly*

For example, if certain employees must have knowledge about food sanitation to do a job properly, the people chosen for that job must possess the required knowledge or learn it from their employer.

- *Warning those who could be injured about the presence of any potentially unsafe conditions*

This duty of care relates to informing others of potential danger. For example, if large numbers of customers are known to be allergic to a particular recipe ingredient, the presence of that ingredient in a dish should be made known to customers before they buy it.

- *Terminating employees who pose a threat to others*

If an employee is known to pose a threat to customers or other employees, the duty of **reasonable care** requires that such an employee be terminated.

Reasonable care

The amount of care a reasonably prudent person would use in a similar situation.

Reasonable care means that you must correct potentially harmful conditions that you know about or that you should have known about.

Sometimes it's difficult to determine the amount of reasonable care that should be exercised in a specific situation. For example, the standard would be quite clear for clearing sidewalks of ice and snow that have resulted from a winter storm. However, removing all chances of slipping on a sidewalk during a winter storm requires guests to be reasonably careful as well. The legal doctrine

As a place of public accommodation, a restaurant is required to welcome and serve every type of guest.

© MN Studio/Shutterstock

> ### GREEN AT WORK!
>
> Governmental regulations related to the environmental practices of restaurants aren't the wave of the future. They're already here. In fact, restaurant managers need to look no further than the increasing number of cities and states outlawing smoking in restaurants to see the impact that governmental regulations related to the environment can have on a business.
>
> Regardless of one's position on the environmental issues that may be addressed by local, state, and even federal law related to such diverse areas as air quality, mandatory recycling, waste disposal, and energy usage, it's clear that restaurant managers should know about legislative actions that can affect their businesses.
>
> One good way to stay informed is to become an active member of the Green Restaurant Association (GRA). The GRA (www.dinegreen.com) was founded with the mission of creating an ecologically sustainable restaurant industry. Among its many services (including certification) is ensuring that its members are regularly informed about the most cost-effective ways to be "Green at Work."
>
> Environmental legislation affecting restaurants is sweeping across the United States and the rest of the world. From plastic bag and Styrofoam cup bans, to recycling mandates, more and more cities are in the process of either considering or passing legislation relating to matters of restaurants and the environment.
>
> Because GRA members already know about these important environmental issues and have generally adopted best practices voluntarily, when legislation is enacted, the GRA's restaurants are able to continue running their businesses while their competitors are often left scrambling to comply with the latest mandates.

Negligent

Guilty of the failure to exercise reasonable care.

of reasonable care places a significant burden on restaurant managers. It requires that they use all of their knowledge and experience to operate restaurants in a way that's consistent with that of a "reasonable" manager who faces a similar set of circumstances. If managers fail to do so, they may be found to have been **negligent** in their duty to provide reasonable care.

Restaurant managers are responsible for their own actions, but they can also be held accountable for the acts of their employees. In some cases, managers can even be held responsible for the acts of their guests and their suppliers. If a threatening situation is foreseeable, restaurant managers have a duty to address and correct that situation.

Laws Related to Employees

The number of laws, rules, and regulations directly related to a restaurant's employees is large. These laws have been enacted at the federal, state, and local levels to ensure fairness to all workers. Among the many worker-related laws restaurant managers must know about are those laws related to:

- Workplace discrimination
- Worker pay
- Worker evaluation

Discrimination

Unfair treatment to another person based on his or her religion, race, age, national origin, gender, or the condition of pregnancy.

WORKPLACE DISCRIMINATION The Equal Employment Opportunity Commission (EEOC) is a federal agency that was established by Title VII of the Civil Rights Act of 1964 and is responsible for enforcing workplace laws prohibiting **discrimination** related to:

- Religion
- Race/color/ethnicity
- Age
- National origin
- Gender
- Pregnancy

Harassment

Threatening and illegal verbal, physical, or visual conduct.

The EEOC also enforces laws related to sexual and other forms of **harassment** as well as portions of the Americans with Disabilities Act (ADA).

The impact of the EEOC on a restaurant's management can be significant. The types of complex questions that can only be properly addressed by a thorough understanding of the role of the EEOC and current federal law include:

- Can a manger legally schedule a worker to work on one of that worker's most important religious holidays?
- May a manager prohibit a worker from wearing a religious artifact (e.g., a cross or other religious symbol) while at work?

WEB AT WORK!

The EEOC enforces federal laws that make it illegal to discriminate against a job applicant or an employee because of the person's race, color, religion, sex (including pregnancy), national origin, age (40 or older), disability, or genetic information. Most employers with at least 15 employees are covered by EEOC.

To stay up-to-date on current laws and to learn more about the role of the EEOC, go to:

www.eeoc.gov

Click on "About EEOC."

- May a restaurant prohibit a worker from wearing clothing that expresses a religious sentiment (such as a hijab worn by Muslim women or a yarmulke worn by Orthodox Jewish men)?
- May an Asian restaurant hire employees exclusively from ethnic groups viewed by its customers as "Asian"?
- Can a manager require all of his or her restaurant employees to speak English?
- May a cocktail lounge hire exclusively young and attractive female waitstaff?

In these and other examples, it's essential to understand the importance of respecting **diversity** and to grasp the role of the EEOC in prohibiting discrimination.

It's the role of the EEOC to investigate employee complaints of discrimination. If a restaurant is found guilty of discrimination, it can be forced to pay **damages** and to reimburse the affected employee(s) for lost wages and benefits as well as attorney fees.

Another area related to discrimination in hiring concerns those who can be legally hired. It's illegal to hire any person who is not authorized to work in the United States. Laws and regulations regarding who is authorized to work in the United States and the proof they must present to verify their identities are subject to modification on a continual basis. So managers should regularly check with a human resources expert or their legal counsel to ensure that they're in full compliance with all federal and state laws regarding the documents currently required for legal employment status verification and how the documents must be maintained.

While the federal government prohibits discrimination in employment practices, many states and even some towns and cities, have enacted their own anti-discrimination laws, too. Some of these laws prohibit discrimination against those not protected under federal law. These currently include prohibitions against discrimination based on sexual orientation, marital status, body weight, and arrest record.

The EEOC is also responsible for enforcing laws that prohibit all forms of worker harassment, including **sexual harassment**.

Restaurants and their employees must be especially knowledgeable about **quid pro quo** and **hostile environment** harassment; the two types of sexual harassment prohibited by federal and state law.

Title VII of the federal Civil Rights Act, as amended in 1972, prohibits sexual harassment in the workplace. As a result, many forms of behavior that were long ago tolerated at work are no longer permitted. This includes uninvited and offensive touching, lewd comments, speaking in a derogatory or offensive manner, and the display of offensive pictures or other materials. To prevent and defend against charges of having allowed harassment to occur, restaurant managers should:

1. Adopt a **zero tolerance** policy for sexual and other forms of harassment.
2. Exercise reasonable care to prevent and promptly correct any sexually harassing behavior.
3. Develop a system encouraging employees to report instances of harassment to management.

Restaurant managers must be aware that they and their businesses can also be held liable for **third-party harassment**. This occurs when a restaurant guest or other nonemployee harasses a restaurant employee.

In the restaurant business, where friendly interactions between guests and employees are often a critical component of the business, the risks of third-party harassment are significant. Flirting and mild-to-even-blatant suggestive comments by customers aren't uncommon in some hospitality settings. However, that the old saying, "The customer is always right" does *not* extend to harassment.

The law clearly states that employees should not be subjected to offensive behavior of a sexual nature. Thus, all employers have a responsibility to protect all employees from third-party harassment.

Diversity

Ethnic, socioeconomic, and gender variety in a group, society, or business.

Damages

Payments made to compensate another for harm, loss, or injury.

Sexual harassment

Threatening and illegal verbal, physical, or visual conduct of a sex-related nature (e.g., touching or making suggestive remarks or gestures.)

Quid pro quo

The asking or demanding of sexual favors *in exchange* for maintaining employment.

Hostile environment

The presence of a verbally, physically or, visually offensive workplace.

Zero tolerance

A policy that takes seriously even the slightest violation of rules prohibiting harassment.

Third-party harassment

Harassment of a business's employee by someone other than that business's paid employees (e.g., harassment by a customer, vendor, or service provider).

Employees must understand the procedures used to report harassing behavior and should be carefully instructed in how to initiate complaints and how and when the complaints will be investigated. Important information to communicate to employees includes:

- To whom should the employee report the complaint?
- In what form should the complaint be initiated (i.e., verbally or in writing)?
- What actions will be taken to investigate?
- When can the employee expect a resolution of his or her complaint?
- What should employees do if their complaints aren't resolved to their satisfaction?

As a restaurant manager, it's your job to prevent harassing behavior by management, fellow employees and visitors to your restaurant. To limit a restaurant's potential liability for harassment, the best approach is for restaurant managers to a) create policies that clearly prohibit sexual harassment in the workplace, b) conduct all-employee training to ensure that every worker understands the restaurant's harassment policies, c) investigate harassment complaints promptly, and d) discipline or dismiss offending workers when appropriate or immediately take the steps necessary to prevent harassment by nonemployees.

In addition to the Civil Rights Act of 1964 and the EEOC, restaurant managers should be very familiar with two other discrimination-related laws, the ADA and the Age Discrimination in Employment Act (ADEA).

The Americans with Disabilities Act (ADA)

The Americans with Disabilities Act (ADA) prohibits discrimination against people with disabilities. Title I of this federal law focuses primarily on employment. Groups protected by the ADA include those with a qualified physical or mental disability, including acquired immune deficiency syndrome/human immunodeficiency virus (AIDS/HIV), cerebral palsy, hearing or visual impairments, and alcoholism (as well as some other identified disabilities).

Three groups of individuals are protected under the ADA:

1. An individual with a physical or mental impairment that substantially limits a major life activity. Examples of a "major life activity" under the Act are: seeing, hearing, talking, walking, reading, learning, breathing, taking care of oneself, lifting, sitting, and standing.
2. A person who has a record of a disability.
3. A person who is "regarded as" having a disability.

The ADA helps ensure that employers consider job applicants fairly, as long as the person seeking the job has the capability of doing it or if he or she could do it with a **reasonable accommodation** from the employer.

Reasonable accommodation

Any modification or adjustment to a job or the work environment that will enable a *qualified* person with a disability to participate in the application process or to perform essential job functions.

Not all accommodations are reasonable, and thus required. For example, an employer doesn't have to eliminate a primary job responsibility to accommodate an employee with a disability. Nor is an employer required to lower productivity standards. An employer isn't required to make a reasonable accommodation if the accommodation would cause an undue hardship on the employer.

In order to be a *qualified* individual with a disability under the ADA, a person must meet the legitimate skill, experience, education, or other requirements of an employment position that he or she wants to fill and be able to perform the essential functions of the position with or without reasonable accommodation.

It's not the intent of the ADA to require employers to hire unqualified staff. Rather, it's intended to ensure that only those skills, experience, and education—**bona fide occupational qualifications (BOQs)**—that an applicant actually must possess to perform a job are what is considered in the hiring process.

Bona fide occupational qualifications (BOQs)

Employment qualifications that employers are allowed to consider when making decisions about hiring and retaining employees.

BOQs that address necessary education requirements, language skills, experience, minimum age (for example, in order to operate a meat slicer or serve alcoholic beverages), and physical attributes (such as the amount to be lifted or the ability to work in a very small production area) are acceptable. However, BOQs cannot be used to deny employment to candidates who otherwise would be able to perform necessary tasks. For example, a requirement that a dishwasher must speak English fluently is probably not truly necessary to perform that job. This is especially true if multi-language training videos and/or visually informative safety posters that can effectively communicate needed information to non-English speakers are available, and if the kitchen's manager can easily learn and use "basic" kitchen terms in the applicant's native language.

> ## WEB AT WORK!
>
> The ADA affects the way all restaurants operate as well as how employees can be legally selected, retained and promoted.
>
> To stay up-to-date on current laws and to learn more about the ADA, go to:
>
> www.ada.gov
>
> Click on "ADA Questions and Answers" (located in the right-hand column under "ADA Publications").

The Age Discrimination in Employment Act (ADEA)

The Age Discrimination in Employment Act (ADEA) applies to employers with 20 or more employees. It protects individuals who are 40 years of age or older from employment discrimination based on age. Under the ADEA, it's illegal to discriminate against a person because of his or her age with regard to hiring, firing, layoffs, pay, benefits, or training.

The ADEA also makes it unlawful to retaliate against an individual for opposing employment practices that discriminate based on age or for filing an age discrimination charge, testifying or participating in any way in an investigation, proceeding, or litigation under the ADEA. The ADEA generally makes it unlawful to include age preferences, limitations, or specifications in job descriptions or advertisements. A job advertisement may specify an age limit only in the rare circumstances where age is shown to be a BOQ needed for the normal operation of the business. A job description can list the training, education, and experience necessary to perform a job if these factors are truly important.

The Older Workers Benefit Protection Act of 1990 (OWBPA) amended the ADEA to specifically prohibit employers from denying benefits to older employees. In some cases it costs more to provide benefits such as health and life insurance to older workers than to younger workers (even when the benefits are the same) and that can create a disincentive to hire older workers. Therefore, in limited circumstances, an employer may be permitted to reduce benefits based on age, as long as the cost of providing the reduced benefits to older workers is the same as the cost of providing benefits to younger workers.

The ADEA does not apply in those cases where another law (for example, the minimum age required to legally serve alcohol) prohibits a worker from performing a job because of age.

WORKER PAY   Restaurant managers have a great deal of leeway in determining how much to pay employees. However, there are pay-related legal restrictions you must know about and follow. For example, the Federal Equal Pay Act (passed in 1963) requires that you must provide

> ## ALL IN A DAY'S WORK: 3.2
>
> "Yes, it's true," said Tom Ellis, "I do have AIDS."
>
> Tom was talking to Shondra Jackson, the manager of Le Petite, a coffee shop that had recently opened.
>
> Shondra had hired Tom because of his many years of experience as a waiter, his friendly personality, and his willingness to work the busy rush hours, when Shondra needed her best people on the floor.
>
> But recently, there had been open grumbling and rampant rumors from some of the other employees about Tom's sexual orientation and, because of his rumored illness, whether it was appropriate for him to even work in the restaurant.
>
> Tom had taken it upon himself to talk openly with Shondra about the gossip and to ask if there were anything he could do to help her refocus the staff on the job at hand and not his illness.
>
> 1. Do you think Tom is working in a "hostile environment" as defined by the EEOC? Why?
> 2. What specific actions should Shondra take in this situation to refocus her staff's efforts on food quality and guest service standards?

equal pay to men and women for equal work if the work they do is equal in required skill, effort, and responsibility. An employee's gender, his or her personal situation (e.g., married or single), or financial status cannot be allowed to serve as a basis for making worker pay or wages determinations. In addition to equal pay for equal work, there are other laws that impact worker pay.

For example, the IRS enforces regulations related to mandatory taxes due on wages. These include regulations related to income taxes, Social Security and Medicare payments, and regulations about taxation and tax withholding requirements for tipped employees. While the laws related to employment are many, one of the most important pay-related pieces of federal legislation restaurant managers must understand is the Fair Labor Standards Act (FLSA).

Minimum wage

The least amount of money employers covered by the FLSA or state law may pay their employees.

The FLSA established the rules about employing children. In addition, it requires employers to pay their workers a federally mandated **minimum wage**. It also mandates overtime pay for work performed in excess of 40 hours per week. In some (but not all) states, there are also state-mandated overtime pay regulations that apply to those who work more than eight hours in one day.

While nearly all employees are covered by the FLSA's minimum wage rules, there are some important exceptions. For example, the FLSA currently allows an employer to pay an employee who is under 20 years old a less-than-minimum training wage for the first 90 calendar days after the employee has been hired.

The FLSA also makes an exception for tipped employees, but only if the tips reported by the employees plus the wages received from their employers equal or exceed the minimum hourly wage rate mandated by the federal government. However, some states prohibit employers from claiming all or part of federally allowed tip credit for workers in their states.

Note that only tips given directly to employees (not those given directly to employers) may be considered as tipped income. In fact, if an employer takes direct control of the tips employees receive, that employer will not generally be allowed to count the tips toward the tip credit provisions of the FLSA.

The FLSA does allow a manager whose employees are tipped on a credit card to reduce the employees' credit card tips by an amount equal to the processing charges levied by the credit card company on the tipped amount.

Restaurant managers must make sure that the compensation systems they use are fair and don't illegally discriminate among their employees.

> **WEB AT WORK!**
>
> The FLSA is continually modified as minimum wage rates change and alterations to laws (including child labor laws) and tip pooling arrangements are made.
>
> To learn more and to monitor important changes to the FLSA, managers should regularly visit the Department of Labor website, at:
>
> http://www.dol.gov/whd/flsa/

In addition to federal legislation, some states have also implemented minimum wage laws. Where state laws and federal law regarding minimum wages conflict, restaurant managers must always pay their employees the higher of the two mandated wage rates.

While the FSLA doesn't limit the number of hours employers can require employees over age 16 to work, it does require that employees covered by the act must be paid at least 1.5 times their regular rate of pay for any hours worked in excess of 40 hours per week (a week is defined as seven consecutive 24-hour periods).

In general, salaried employees are exempt for the overtime provision of the FLSA; however, there are some exceptions to this. Restaurant managers should carefully evaluate their own operations and the law to determine if the exceptions apply to their businesses.

In addition to the FLSA, the Family and Medical Leave Act of 1993 (FMLA) directly affects worker pay. The FMLA allows eligible employees to take up to 12 weeks of *unpaid* leave each year for specified family and medical reasons. The FMLA applies to all restaurants that employ 50 or more employees at one or more locations within a 75-mile radius.

To be granted FMLA benefits, an employee must have worked for the employer for at least 12 months and have worked at least 1,250 hours in the previous 12 months. Unpaid leave must be granted for

- The birth of a child
- The care of an immediate family member who is ill
- The employee's own illness

Upon returning from leave, the employee must be returned to his or her original job (or a similar one) with no penalty.

WORKER EVALUATION   Two important areas in which the law directly affects restaurants are **employee discipline** and performance appraisal.

When employees believe that disciplinary actions are intended to help identify areas for improvement, fewer accusations of unfairness or discrimination in the use of discipline are likely to arise. When there is a good relationship between restaurant managers and their employees, effective disciplinary actions can lead to improved worker performance. When disciplining employees, restaurant managers should make sure that:

- Reprimands are carried out in private
- The discipline is based on what the employee did, not who he or she is
- The disciplinary action is undertaken as promptly as possible
- The disciplinary actions are uniformly applied to all employees
- The severity of the punishment is in keeping with the seriousness of the problem
- A **progressive disciplinary program** is used

Employees naturally react unfavorably to disciplinary actions they perceive to be unfair. They may even file employment-related lawsuits as a result. For example, when an employee is disciplined for an action that other employees do but aren't disciplined for, the disciplined employee may bring charges of discrimination or bias. Thus, any performance appraisal system put in place by a restaurant manager that results in employee pay increases or promotions should be designed in such a way as to ensure fairness and to minimize any employee-initiated EEOC charges of bias or discrimination in its implementation.

Ideally, an effective performance appraisal process answers two central questions:

1. How well does the staff member being evaluated perform the job?
2. What corrective actions can be taken to improve the employee's performance?

Employee discipline

Corrective actions uniformly applied and designed to encourage employees to follow established policies, rules and regulations.

Progressive disciplinary program

A carefully planned series of corrective actions—each increasing in its severity—designed to encourage employees to follow established policies, rules, and regulations.

Remember that performance appraisals don't need to be carried out only when formally required by a restaurant's written policies. Instead, some appraisal systems allow for informal conversations that can occur at any time and that are designed to give managers an opportunity to improve employee performance on a continual basis. Regardless of the specific characteristics of their appraisal programs, effective restaurant managers must design fair appraisal systems, explain them fully to the restaurant's employees and then apply them justly every time.

Laws Related to Guests

In addition to laws related to general restaurant operations and employees, restaurant managers have specific legal responsibilities to their guests. One good way to examine these legal obligations is to consider the responsibilities that a manager has regarding:

- All guests
- Serving food
- Serving alcoholic beverages

RESPONSIBILITIES TO ALL GUESTS   A restaurant that doesn't satisfy its guests won't stay in business. In fact, guests are so important that one good description of the purpose of a restaurant manager is to obtain, and then retain, enough guests to make sure that the business is profitable. Despite the importance of guests, there are specific legal challenges that arise anytime guests are served.

From a legal perspective, a restaurant **guest** is anyone using a restaurant's services.

Restaurant guests include all diners, whether or not they're paying the bill for any purchases made in the restaurant.

Because a restaurant has always been considered a **public accommodation** business, it has also been required to admit everyone who wanted to come in.

More recently, laws have been established that require restaurant managers to use reasonable care in determining who is to be served.

It's illegal to deny service to anyone on the basis of race, color, religion, or national origin. It's also a violation of the law to admit any type of customer and to then segregate him or her (for example, by restricting seating only to predesignated sections of a restaurant) based on those same characteristics. In addition, many towns and cities prohibit such discriminatory practices even in privately owned and operated facilities, such as country clubs and private city clubs.

While restaurant managers may not discriminate against guests, they can and should refuse to admit or serve guests in certain situations. These include refusing:

- To serve guests if they cannot demonstrate the ability to pay for items purchased
- To serve alcohol to underage customers
- To serve alcohol to visibly intoxicated guests
- Service to those with a highly contagious disease
- Service to guests who have an item prohibited by local law (such as a concealed gun or knife)
- Service to any person who poses a real threat to other guests or employees by their actions or their words
- To allow entrance to guests with animals (except approved guide/assistance animals used by the physically impaired)
- To allow entrance if the restaurant is full

However, although they have the right to refuse service in special cases, managers aren't permitted to "pick and choose" those guests who will be affected when they exercise that right. For example, if a manager requires guests to demonstrate that they can pay prior to ordering food, that same policy must apply to all of the restaurant's guests, not just to a pre-selected group.

Restaurant managers are legally obligated to ensure that their facility meets all applicable local building codes as well as comply with access requirements mandated by Title III of the ADA. Title III requires public accommodations to provide access to people with disabilities on a basis that is equal to that of the general public. Specifically, Title III requires all restaurants to:

1. Remove barriers that prevent people with mobility impairments to use their facilities. Examples include providing parking spaces for the disabled, wheelchair ramps or lifts, and accessible restroom facilities.

Guest

Any customer lawfully utilizing the services of a restaurant.

Public accommodation

A facility that provides eating, sleeping, or entertainment services to the general public.

2. Provide auxiliary hearing and visual aids. Examples include menus produced in Braille or large print. (Menus in Braille are not required, however, if waiters are trained to read the menu to customers with sight impairments.)

3. Modify any operating policies that could be considered to discriminate against people with disabilities. This may include prohibiting all animals (including guide or service animals) from the restaurant or requiring a driver's license prior to serving a guest alcohol. (Some people with disabilities may not drive; they would not have a license but would likely have another form of identification.)

RESPONSIBILITIES RELATED TO SERVING FOOD

As a restaurant manager, you have a legal obligation to sell only food that is wholesome and to deliver it to your guests in a way that is safe. This responsibility is mandated by the Uniform Commercial Code (UCC) as well as other state and local laws. The UCC states that when you sell food and beverages, there is an implied warranty that your products are **merchantable**.

Restaurant managers are legally obligated to handle and serve menu items in a way that protects guests from foodborne illnesses or other harm. To help restaurateurs do so, local health departments conduct routine and mandatory inspections of kitchens and may offer training or certification classes for restaurant employees. While restaurants can be held responsible for food-related illnesses they cause their guests, they can also help minimize this liability when they demonstrate reasonable care by providing food safety training to all employees who handle or serve food.

(See Chapter 5 for a discussion of how to serve food safely.)

Merchantable
Fit for an intended use (in the case of food and beverages, "fit" for human consumption).

RESPONSIBILITIES RELATED TO SERVING ALCOHOLIC BEVERAGES

Throughout history, alcoholic beverages have been manufactured, served and enjoyed in nearly every society, including the colonial Americas. In fact, it was Founding Father Benjamin Franklin who famously said; "Beer is proof that God loves us and wants us to be happy."[1] But in 1920, the U.S. Congress passed the Eighteenth Amendment to the Constitution, prohibiting the manufacture, sale and transport of all alcoholic beverages in the United States.

Not surprisingly, the law only put a stop to the legal manufacture and sale of alcoholic beverages. Many people still drank, but they drank illegally made, poor-tasting and, frequently, alcoholic beverage products that were actually dangerous to drink. In 1933, Congress recognized the failure of prohibition and repealed the Eighteenth Amendment, while expressly allowing local states, county, and towns to pass their own laws restricting or even prohibiting the sale and consumptions of alcohol within their legal **jurisdictions**.

As a result, there are a wide variety of state-sanctioned alcohol-related laws, regulations and codes existing in the United States. Restaurant managers must know which ones apply to their own businesses.

Alcohol is a product that must be handled carefully: some people overindulge in its consumption or become addicted to it. Most societies tightly control the dispensing of drugs and other products that they consider potentially dangerous (which is why pharmacists must go to school in order to earn the right to legally dispense drugs). In many states, any individual over a certain age can serve alcohol—regardless of whether he or she has received mandatory training prior to working as a bartender or beverage server. For that reason, restaurant managers should take their responsibilities for serving alcohol very seriously.

Jurisdiction
The geographic area over which a legal authority extends.

> ### WEB AT WORK!
>
> The ServSafe Food Safety® program offered by the National Restaurant Association (NRA) is the most widely respected and recognized food safety training program available to restaurant managers and their staffs. To learn more about this valuable program, go to:
>
> www.servsafe.com

---

[1] http://thinkexist.com/quotation/beer_is_proof_that_god_loves_us_and_wants_us_to/146025.html retrieved 4/25/2013.

Unlike food items, restaurants don't have an inherent "right" to serve alcohol. In fact, the sale of alcohol is restricted by states in a variety of ways, including:

1. *Who may sell it:* In all states, a state-issued liquor license is required before a business will be permitted to sell alcohol.

2. *When it may be sold:* Most communities have liquor codes that restrict the hours or, in some cases, days on which alcohol may be sold.

3. *Where it may be sold:* In most states, businesses that serve alcohol are prohibited from operating in close proximity to schools or churches. In addition, the terms of a liquor license may restrict the sale of alcohol to limited and very clearly defined areas within a restaurant's building or on its grounds.

4. *Who may serve it:* States commonly impose minimum age requirements for those who serve alcoholic beverages. The majority of states permit adults age 18 or older to "serve" alcoholic beverages in a restaurant. Generally the term "server" refers to a waitperson, whereas "bartender" refers to a person who dispenses alcoholic beverages. The minimum age requirements for bartenders in a state vary between 18 and 21 years old. Some states allow employees under age 21 to tend bar if a manager who is older than 21 is present when the underage person is tending the bar, or if the underage bartender undergoes special alcoholic beverage service training.

In some states, individuals under age 18 or 21 may be allowed to stock coolers with alcohol or to clear alcoholic beverages from tables, but aren't allowed to serve it. Restaurant managers must know the specific age-related requirements for serving alcoholic beverages in their own states.

5. *Who may buy it:* In the United States, guests must be 21 to purchase alcohol. But not all guests over 21 should be served. For example, restaurateurs are prohibited from selling alcohol to:
    a. People who are visibly intoxicated
    b. People without proper identification
    c. People suspected of buying alcohol for the purpose of giving it to a minor

6. *How it can be sold:* Most states and communities have laws that restrict the manner in which alcohol may be served. For example, many localities prohibit the service of more than one alcoholic beverage to a single guest at the same time. Others restrict the manner in which promotions, specials, or discounts on the selling price of alcohol may be offered to a restaurant's guests.

7. *Required records of its sale:* All states require that records of the sale of alcohol be carefully maintained. The purpose of this record keeping may be to help ensure the full payment of taxes due on the sale of alcohol, to monitor alcohol suppliers or to ensure the proper sale and pricing of alcohol in restaurants.

Local communities can exercise a great deal of control over the way in which alcoholic beverages can be marketed and served in restaurants.

© Dmitriy Shironosov/Shutterstock

Most states are very cautious when issuing licenses to sell alcohol and can be very aggressive in revoking the licenses of restaurants that don't adhere to all of the state requirements. In many states, law enforcement officers are allowed to conduct unannounced inspections of the businesses where alcohol is served or will even intentionally send minors into a business to see if the operation will serve them.

In addition to serving alcohol legally, restaurants are required to sell alcohol responsibly. (See Chapter 10 for a discussion on serving alcohol responsibly.)

Restaurant Terms and Concepts

Business structure *38*
Sole proprietorship *38*
Asset *38*
DBA *39*
General partnership *39*
Partnership agreement *39*
Joint liability *39*
Limited partnership *40*
Corporation *41*
Shareholder *41*
C corporation *41*

Dividend *41*
Subchapter S corporation *41*
Limited liability company (LLC) *41*
Operating agreement *41*
Duty of care *43*
Dram shop laws *45*
Reasonable care *45*
Negligent *46*
Discrimination *46*

Harassment *46*
Diversity *47*
Damages *47*
Sexual harassment *47*
Quid pro quo *47*
Hostile environment *47*
Zero tolerance *47*
Third-party harassment *47*
Reasonable accommodation *48*

Bona fide occupational qualifications (BOQs) *48*
Minimum wage *50*
Employee discipline *51*
Progressive disciplinary program *51*
Guest *52*
Public accommodation *52*
Merchantable *53*
Jurisdiction *53*

Work in Progress

1. What are three fundamental differences between a general partnership and a limited partnership?
2. What are three fundamental differences between a C Corporation and an S Corporation?
3. Why is the issue of limited personal liability so important for an independent restaurateur?
4. Assume that restaurants in your state aren't required to provide alcohol server training to those employees who serve alcoholic beverages, so neither do you. How would you defend yourself against a charge of failure to exercise reasonable care if one of your employees served alcohol to an underage person, who then left your restaurant and, while driving home, caused a car accident that killed him as well as two others in the vehicle he hit?
5. Assume an employee at your restaurant wanted to wear a religious symbol on the outside of his or her work uniform. How could you determine if the employee had a protected right to wear the symbol?
6. Many restaurants utilize a "tip pooling" arrangement, in which tips are shared proportionally by the employees (hosts, waiters,

bussers) who collectively serve guests. Assume one of your service employees refuses to share his tips. Who would you contact to determine your right to force his participation in your operation's tip pooling arrangement?

7. Describe the specific steps you would take to make sure that your restaurant exercised reasonable care for guest safety during an ice storm that caused your sidewalks to become slippery.
8. Google "Child labor laws" in your state. Make a list of common restaurant tasks employees under age 16 are prohibited from performing in your state.
9. Because the potential liability for sexual harassment charges can be significant if the relationships end, some restaurants prohibit all of their managers and supervisors from engaging in romantic relationships with current employees outside of work. Would you support and enforce such a policy? Explain your answer.
10. It's always illegal to serve alcohol to an intoxicated guest. Develop a checklist to help your bartenders and servers know the steps they should take when it's clear that a guest is intoxicated but is still demanding to be served more alcoholic beverages.

4

Managing a Professional Staff

Chapter Outline

Securing Professional Staff
    Recruiting Employees
    Selecting Employees
    Orientating Employees

Leading Professional Staff
    Training Employees
    Motivating Employees
    Facilitating Employee Performance

Learning Objectives

After carefully reading and studying the information in this chapter, you will:

1. Know the procedures for recruiting, selecting, and orientating restaurant employees.
2. Understand the manager's role in training, motivating, and facilitating the work of employees.

IN THIS CHAPTER

Restaurant managers have no more significant responsibility than the effective leadership of their employees. Food quality, labor costs, and the work environment itself are among the factors affected by the team members who serve guests and help achieve the restaurant's goals.

The process of managing employees begins at the time of recruitment and selection. Current and accurate job descriptions must be created for all positions so applicants know the work tasks to be done in the positions they're considering. Potential applicants must learn about the job opening; employers today use both traditional and inventive "high-tech" ways to publish work opportunities. Then a formal selection process is used to determine the best applicant for the job.

New employees must learn about their new employer and acquire the knowledge and skills they need to be successful on the job. A properly developed and implemented orientation program provides general information that all employees must know. Then a well-organized and performance-driven training program should be used to teach employees the job skills they will need to perform their jobs well.

Professional restaurant managers can **motivate** and retain their employees. They can create work environments that allow employees to find pride and joy in what they do and, as a result, to seek meaningful, long-term, and successful careers.

Much of a restaurant manager's time is spent facilitating the work of employees and improving productivity. This chapter will review common leadership styles and principles useful in doing so.

SECURING PROFESSIONAL STAFF

As an effective restaurant manager, you'll use basic procedures to recruit, select, and orientate your new employees.

Recruiting Employees

Job descriptions describe what people working in a position must do, so they're useful when new employees are recruited. For example, in some operations dishwashers only wash dishes, while in others they may also bus tables.

Figure 4.1 shows a shortened job description for a restaurant manager. Note that it tells the position to which he/she reports (Part I), indicates job tasks to be done (Part II), and explains basic personal qualifications (Part III).

> **Motivate**
>
> The act of providing an employee with a reason to do something. Employees are motivated when their supervisor offers them something they want (for example, higher pay rates) in return for something the supervisor wants (for example, quality work performance in a higher-level position).
>
> **Job description**
>
> A list of the tasks that must be performed by a person working in a specific position.

Job Description: Restaurant Manager

Part I—Reports to:

District manager

Part II—Position Overview:

- Supervises kitchen manager, dining room manager, and bar manager.
- Develops guidelines to recruit, select, motivate, train, and manage all restaurant employees.
- Achieves stated quality and financial goals.

Part III—Job Tasks:

- Interacts with district manager, kitchen manager, and dining room manager to plan menus.
- Approves purchasing requisitions and works with the kitchen manager and bar manager to streamline the purchasing process.
- Budgets for and manages food, beverage, labor and all other costs; takes corrective actions as needed to control costs.
- Ensures compliance with all legal requirements related to sanitation, fire safety, bar operation, and other areas of potential liability.
- Plans marketing, advertising, and promotion programs in conjunction with campaigns outlined by the district manager.
- Approves the hiring, training and scheduling of restaurant personnel.
- Generates input from guests about food and beverage product and service quality and resolves any complaints.
- Prepares required reports for district manager.
- Arranges for maintenance and repair of equipment and other services as necessary.
- Accounts for all revenues and prepares daily bank deposits.
- Completes end-of-day building inspection.
- Ensures all safety and security procedures are consistently followed.
- Maintains all employee files and ensures that necessary documentation is complete and accurate.

Part III—Qualifications:

Education: Community college or university graduate with hospitality-related degree preferred.

Experience: A minimum of two years as a cook or chef and two years of food service management experience. Basic knowledge of safety/sanitation regulations and food and beverage production techniques. Possesses leadership, financial management, and guest relations skills.

Physical abilities: Must be able to work in fast-paced environment for up to eight hours a day and to lift at least 50 pounds.

Date of last revision: 6/10/XX

Approved by: W. Anthony, District Manager

FIGURE 4.1

Restaurant Manager Job Description

WEB AT WORK!

To review job descriptions for a wide variety of food service positions in properties of all types throughout the United States, go to:

www.careerbuilder.com

Type in the position you wish to study, click on "Find Jobs" and then click on "View Full Job Description" of the featured positions.

WEB AT WORK!

Many potential restaurant employees use the Internet to look for work. Hcareers.com is a leading hospitality recruiting website:

www.hcareers.com

Check out this website and see how you might use it when you're looking for a job as well as how a restaurant manager seeking employees might use it.

Recruiting

Searching for those who are interested in vacant positions.

Internal recruiting

The use of existing employees to help fill position vacancies. Current employees may be promoted from within to fill vacant positions, or they may refer friends, neighbors, and others to the property.

External recruiting

Activities used to inform people who don't work for the restaurant that new staff members are needed to fill vacant positions.

Compensation package

The money and other valuable items (fringe benefits) provided in exchange for the work employees do.

Job descriptions should be reviewed and updated when job tasks change so they consistently provide current information for potential job applicants.

Recruiting involves looking for those who are interested in vacant positions. Finding qualified and motivated staff members is never easy, but can be carried out through **internal recruiting** and **external recruiting**.

Restaurant managers can use a variety of recruitment tactics including:

- Using professional job titles (e.g., "steward" instead of "dishwasher")
- Using a recruitment package with a fact sheet, current job description, write-up of best job features, and an employee **compensation package** worksheet
- Rewarding current employees for their referrals
- Using positive statements from current employees in job ads
- Recruiting guests (some are looking for a position!)

Technology provides modern ways in which potential job applicants learn about vacant positions.

© wavebreakmedia ltd/Shutterstock

- Adding an employment section to the restaurant's website
- Sponsoring work-study programs and talking with career counselors at local schools
- Inviting classes for tours of the property

Selecting Employees

A formal **selection** process provides accurate and useful information about job candidates. Sources of information include:

- *Application form.* Figure 4.2 shows a sample **application form**. There are federal, state, and local laws and regulations about employment discrimination issues that must be considered when the application is developed. An attorney often reviews drafts of the form to ensure it only requests that information necessary to fairly evaluate an applicant's eligibility.
- *Employment interview.* Two basic types of interview questions can be used in an effective employee interview. **Direct interview questions** help restaurant managers learn specific information (e.g., "How long have you worked in restaurants?"). **Open-ended interview questions** provide information about applicants' opinions and attitudes (e.g., "What extra steps can service staff take to make sure guests coming to our restaurant are pleased with their experience?")

Selection

The process by which job applicants are evaluated in order to assess their suitability for a position.

Application form

A document job applicants fill out with employment-related information about themselves when they're applying for a job.

Direct interview questions

Specific questions asked to learn factual information about job applicants.

Open-ended interview questions

Questions asked to learn about an applicant's opinions and attitudes.

FIGURE 4.2

Sample Application Form

VERNON'S RESTAURANT APPLICATION

Print or Type Clearly

Last Name First Middle	Position(s) Desired
Street Address	Wage/Salary Desired Date Available for Work
City State Zip	Social Security Number
Phone: Home Work	Are you presently employed? ☐ Yes ☐ No May we contact your present employer? ☐ Yes ☐ No
To verify previous employment, please indicate if you have worked under another name. ☐ Yes ☐ No If yes, other name used:	

EMPLOYMENT RECORD

List your previous experience, beginning with your most recent position. (Include military experience as a job.)

Employer 1	(Area Code) Phone Number	Employer 2	(Area Code) Phone Number
Address	City, State, Zip Code	Address	City, State, Zip Code
Starting Position	Starting Salary	Starting Position	Starting Salary
Last Position	Final Salary	Last Position	Final Salary
Dates Employed	Immediate Supervisor	Dates Employed	Immediate Supervisor
Duties		Duties	
Reason for Leaving		Reason for Leaving	

(Continued)

EDUCATION AND SKILLS

School	Location	Graduation Date	Major
High School			
College			
Additional Training			

Which languages do you speak fluently?

Are there any hours, shifts, and days of the week that you won't be able to work? Please specify.

I'm able to work (check the following) F/T – P/T – On-Call Evenings – Overnight – Weekends – Holidays – Overtime

Do you have relatives or acquaintances working here? ☐ Yes ☐ No If yes, please indicate their name and relationship.	Have you been convicted of a felony within the last seven years? ☐ Yes ☐ No If yes, please indicate dates and details. _____ _____ Do you have any felony charges currently pending against you? ☐ Yes ☐ No _____ Note: Conviction of a felony will not necessarily disqualify you from employment.
Are you under age 18? ☐ Yes ☐ No	Are you authorized to work in the United States? ☐ Yes ☐ No

Can you perform the essential functions of the job for which you are applying with or without accommodation? Please explain.
_____

_____

PERSONAL REFERENCES *(do not include employers or relatives)*

Name	Position & Company	Current Address	Telephone

CERTIFICATION AND SIGNATURE—PLEASE READ CAREFULLY

I declare that my answers to the questions on this application are true, and I give (company) the right to investigate all references and information given. I agree that any false statement or misrepresentation on this application will be cause for refusal to hire or immediate dismissal.

I agree that my employment will be considered "at will" and may be terminated by (company) at any time without liability for wages or salary except for such as may have been earned at the date of such termination.

I understand that (company) is a drug-free workplace and has a policy against drug and alcohol use and reserves the right to screen applicants and test for cause.

I acknowledge that if I need reasonable accommodation in either the application process or employment, I should bring the request to the attention of _____ .

I authorize you to make such legal investigations and inquiries of my personal employment, criminal history, driving record and other job-related matters as may be necessary in determining an employment decision. I hereby release employers, schools or persons from all liability in responding to inquires in connection with my application.

I understand that an offer of employment and my continued employment are contingent upon satisfactory proof of my authorization to work in the United States of America.

Sign here _____   Date _____
           (applicant's signature)   (month/day/year)

Adapted from Hayes, D., Miller, A., and Ninemeier, J. (2012). *The Professional Kitchen Manager*. Pearson Education, Inc.

An employer should review an application form before the interview to determine the questions he or she wishes to ask the applicant. The employer can use a written list of questions for the interview. He or she should listen more than talk and ask only questions that relate to the applicant's ability to perform the work. For example, don't ask about ethnic background or religion—these are illegal questions; do ask about eligibility to work within the United States—a legally acceptable question.

- *Drug test results.* Employees who use drugs are more likely to have off- and on-the-job accidents and extended absences from work. While legal conditions allowing drug tests differ by state, voluntary testing is legal in every state.
- *Applicable tests.* Knowledge or skill tests can help determine an applicant's job eligibility. For example, someone stating previous cooking experience might be asked about the ingredients needed to make a specific sauce.
- *Reference checks.* Increasingly, the amount of information learned from reference checks is limited because past employers and others may fear legal repercussions if the information they supply prevents an applicant from being hired. Questions about employment dates, **hourly wage** or **salary** levels and, perhaps, whether the job applicant would be re-hired, might be answered.
- *Background checks.* Sometimes employee resumes and applications include some false information, and **background checks** about education, training, and criminal records may be conducted if a consent form signed by the job applicants to authorize a background check is obtained.
- *Physical examination.* A physical examination that includes a tuberculosis test should be considered. State and local health laws in this regard vary and must be followed. Also, managers should not unfairly prevent workers with physical disabilities from gaining employment if their disability will not affect their job performance.
- *Other interviews.* If the new employee will be supervised by another person, the potential supervisor should also interview job candidates and provide input before a hiring decision is made.

After a hiring decision has been made, the **job offer** becomes important. It should be made in writing and contain the terms and conditions of the employment offer. If the job offer made to one applicant is not accepted, it can then be made to another applicant. If no qualified applicant has been identified, then the selection process begins again.

Most food service operations offer **at-will employment**. Note: The sample application form shown above mentions this concept in its "Certification and Signature" section. This means that if the employment contract is for an indefinite time period, it can be terminated by either the employer or the employee at any time for any reason. However, an employee cannot be terminated for reasons that are illegal under state and federal law. For example, most employers

Hourly wage

Money paid to an employee for work performed during a one-hour time period.

Salary

Money paid to an employee for work performed as calculated on a weekly, monthly, or annual basis.

Background check

A review of an applicant's criminal history, credit, driving record, or other information relating to employment qualifications.

Job offer

An invitation to the most qualified job applicant that outlines the terms and conditions under which employment is offered.

At-will employment

An employment contract that can be terminated by either the employer or the employee at any time for any reason.

WEB AT WORK!

If you'd like to learn more about employee drug testing and employment background checks, go to:

www.allbusiness.com

Enter "pre-employment drug tests" and "pre-employment background checks" into the search box to find recent articles on both topics.

cannot fire an employee for reasons including race, religion, or gender or because the employee complained about illegal activities, discrimination or harassment, or workplace health and safety violations. Nor can employees be fired for exercising their legal rights such as taking family and medical leave, serving in the military, or taking time to vote or serve on a jury.

Orientating Employees

Orientation
The process of providing basic information about a restaurant that must be known by all staff members in every department.

Orientation is the process of providing basic information about the restaurant that must be known by all staff members in every department. Implemented effectively, it informs new employees about the restaurant's policies and procedures, helps them become comfortable with the work environment and lets them know clearly where they "fit in."

The goals of an effective orientation program should be:

- To provide an overview of the property
- To review the new staff member's current role and address future promotional opportunities
- To explain policies, rules and other important information
- To outline specific expectations including responsibilities of the restaurant to the staff member and of the staff member to the restaurant
- To motivate new staff members

An effective orientation program eliminates confusion, heightens a new employee's enthusiasm, creates favorable attitudes, and makes a positive first impression. Properly conducted orientation sessions address the normal concerns of most new staff members and answer questions such as "Where do I 'fit in' the organization?" and "What are my duties, rights and limits?"

Figure 4.3 illustrates a checklist that identifies many important orientation concepts.

Employee handbook
A manual that explains employment policies relating to employment issues; compensation, including benefits; operating concerns; and legal and other requirements.

Many restaurant managers provide an **employee handbook** during orientation and review detailed information about important policies and procedures.

It's important to assemble all the materials needed before beginning an orientation session, including copies of the restaurant's mission statement and employee handbooks as well as tax withholding, insurance application and other required forms.

Would you be as anxious as this person on your first day of work? Effective orientation programs help reinforce the decision to join the restaurant's team.

Smirnof/Shutterstock

FIGURE 4.3

Sample Orientation Checklist

Introduction

- ☐ Welcome new staff member(s)
- ☐ Present/explain mission statement
- ☐ Discuss history of organization
- ☐ Review clients served (if applicable)
- ☐ Note products and services provided
- ☐ Review organization chart

Staff Member–Related Policies

- ☐ **Appearance**

Hygiene	Name tags
Uniforms	Jewelry, visible tattoos and piercings

- ☐ **Conduct**

Attendance	Drug-free workplace information
Respectful behavior	Harassment policy and discussion

- ☐ **Job Performance**

Position description	Work schedule
Training program	Breaks
Performance evaluation system	Probationary period

- ☐ **Employee Benefits**

Vacation	Education incentives
Sick leave	Meals/uniform allowances
Insurance programs	Other
Workers' compensation	

- ☐ **Compensation and "Paper Work"**

Salary/wages	Pay periods; pay days
Checking in/out of work shifts	Compensation increase policies
Overtime policies	Withholding tax and insurance forms

- ☐ **Safety Concerns**

Safety training	Emergency situations
Fire evacuation procedures	Food safety training (general, if applicable)
Reporting injuries	

- ☐ **Other Orientation Information**

Smoking	Lockers
Parking	Access to facility during non-working time
Employee restroom(s)	Work permits (minors and non-citizens)
Personal time	

- ☐ Provide staff member handbook
- ☐ Answer questions
- ☐ Review departmental induction and training programs
- ☐ Provide tour of property*
- ☐ Other:

*A detailed tour of the new staff member's department can be provided by the supervisor during the later induction program.

Adapted from Hayes, D., Miller, A., and Ninemeier, J. (2012). *The Professional Kitchen Manager*, Pearson Education, Inc.

WEB AT WORK!

Information to help small businesses such as restaurants comply with federal, state, and local business laws and government regulations is readily available. For example, to learn about legal concerns that should be addressed in employee handbooks, go to:

www.business.gov

Enter "employee handbooks" in the search box.

ALL IN A DAY'S WORK: 4.1

"I can just look at a person and tell whether he or she will be a good employee," said Mario, the kitchen manager. He was talking to Janet, the manager at Baker's Restaurant.

"That's one reason why I can hire a person quickly. Another reason is that we need someone right now to replace the cook who just left," he continued.

"Mario, I know you have a lot of restaurant experience, and I know you need a new cook," replied Janet. "I'm also aware of the stress that is created when we hire a person who leaves after just a few months. We need to take the time to do an effective search and screening before we hire anyone."

"Well, I'll need to work a few extra hours every day until we find somebody, so I say we need a short and simple process to get somebody onboard right away!"

1. How should Janet respond to Mario's desire to hire someone right away?
2. What tactics should Janet use to find the "right" cook for the restaurant?

LEADING PROFESSIONAL STAFF

Employees who complete orientation activities must acquire the knowledge and skills required to be successful in their jobs, while more experienced personnel must remain current with the requirements of an ever-changing workplace. Effective **training** is critical to attain both these goals.

Training

The process of developing an employee's knowledge and skills to improve job performance.

Training Employees

Training must be **cost-effective** and provide benefits that outweigh its costs. It must be performance-based and planned and delivered in a way that helps trainees learn how to perform the tasks required for effective on-the-job performance.

The need for training to be performance-based can create a significant challenge, because to do so:

Cost-effective

A situation in which time and money gained is greater than incurred costs.

- All position tasks must be identified
- The knowledge and skills required to perform each task must be known
- Training that provides the knowledge and skills required for each task must be developed
- Each required **competency** must be known in advance

Competency

A recognized standard level of knowledge, skills, and abilities required for successful job performance.

Typically, performance-based training is best delivered at the jobsite in one-on-one interactions between the **trainer** and **trainee**.

Trainer

A qualified individual who teaches another employee about a specific task or skill in the workplace and how to do it.

TRAINING BENEFITS   Both employers and employees benefit from well-run training programs. Benefits to effective training include:

Trainee

An employee learning about a specific task or skill.

- Improved performance: Trainees learn knowledge and skills to perform required tasks more effectively, improving their on-the-job performance.
- Decreased operating costs: Improved job performance helps to reduce errors and work that must be redone, and this reduces associated costs.

- More satisfied guests: Training can yield restaurant staff who are guest-service-oriented and who want to please customers.
- Decreased work stress: Stress created by interactions with supervisors upset about poor work performance or from frustrated guests about quality defects will be reduced.
- Increased job advancement opportunities: Competent employees are likely to be promoted to more responsible and higher-paying positions.
- Fewer operating problems: Busy restaurant managers can focus on priority concerns and will not need to address routine problems caused by inadequate training.
- Higher levels of work quality: Effective training identifies quality standards that define acceptable products and service levels.

TRAINING PRINCIPLES   It takes time and money to develop and deliver effective training. These basic principles should be incorporated into the training process:

- Trainers must know how to train and be given the time to do it well
- Trainees must want to be trained and recognize its worth
- Training must focus on employee skills that will improve job performance
- Training should consider the trainees' experiences. Effective trainers establish a benchmark of what trainees already know and can do and then emphasize unfamiliar subject-matter

One-on-one training is commonly used to teach food-production techniques to kitchen employees.

© Marin Conic/Fotolia

- Training should be informal, focus on the trainees, and take place in the workplace
- Trainees should be allowed to practice. Skills are typically learned by observing how something is done and then by practicing and demonstrating the activity in a step-by-step sequence
- Tasks should be taught separately and broken into steps taught in proper sequence
- Training should consider the trainee's attention span and learning pace

TRAINERS AND THE TRAINING PROCESS The restaurant manager, other managers or supervisors, and even experienced entry-level employees may be responsible for training in some properties. All effective trainers have the desire to train and share other common characteristics. They have the proper attitude about their employer, peers, and training assignment and possess the necessary knowledge and skills to do the job for which training is provided. They also have effective communication skills and speak in a language that is understandable to the trainee.

Successful trainers have patience and recognize that training must sometimes be repeated several times in several different ways. They show genuine respect for the trainees, treat them as professionals, and celebrate the trainees' successes.

Figure 4.4 lists the steps in an effective training process.

Let's review each step in the training process.

Step 1: Define Training Needs

Tactics to identify training needs include:

- *Observation of work performance:* Restaurant managers who "manage by walking around" may notice work procedures that deviate from the standard operating procedures and that should be addressed and corrected.
- *Input from employees and guests:* Formal and informal methods should be used to receive input to identify areas where training is needed.

FIGURE 4.4

Overview of Training Process
Adapted from Hayes, D., Miller, A., and Ninemeier, J. (2012). *The Professional Kitchen Manager.* Pearson Education, Inc.

*Since restaurant managers primarily use individual on-the-job training procedures, they will be discussed in this chapter.

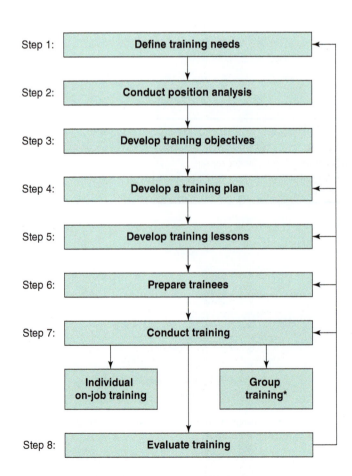

- *Inspections:* Formal inspections such as those related to safety can identify problems. Informal inspections made by managers before, during and after work shifts can also identify training needs.
- *Analysis of data:* Differences between forecasted results and actual results may suggest problems that can be corrected by training.
- ***Exit interviews***: Formal or informal discussions with employees who have resigned from the restaurant may suggest training topics to help reduce **employee turnover** rates and to improve the business.

Step 2: Conduct Position Analysis

A **position analysis** identifies how all tasks in a position should be performed and is helpful when operating procedure changes require employees to do things in new ways.

Figure 4.5 shows the four basic activities in the position analysis process.

PREPARE TASK LIST   A **task list** identifies the duties included within a single position. For example, a cook must know how to follow standard recipes, operate food production equipment, and clean a workstation among many other duties.

Procedures to develop a task list include:

- Asking supervisors and experienced workers in the position being analyzed open-ended questions, such as "What do you do during a normal work shift?"
- Reviewing written information about a position including job descriptions, task lists, and training materials.
- Observing staff members as they work and comparing what they actually do to the tasks identified when they were asked about them.

After an analysis of the information is conducted, the manager can develop an extensive list of position tasks and factors, such as work-shift loads or production volume, that directly impact new tasks being developed. Once developed, training requirements for a specific position are known, and new employees can be taught how to correctly perform each of them.

DEVELOP TASK BREAKDOWNS   A **task breakdown** indicates how each task identified in the task list should be accomplished. For example, one task for a cook may be "to properly operate a deep fryer." This task involves several steps that include safely loading, monitoring and unloading the equipment. Once developed, trainers can review task breakdowns with trainees during the training.

Writing a task breakdown does not need to be complicated or time consuming. For example, a manager can:

- Watch an experienced staff member perform a task
- Record each activity (step) in sequence
- Share the task analysis information with other experienced staff members and supervisors
- Make modifications as needed to produce a uniform work method

CONSIDER PERFORMANCE STANDARDS   Proper performance must be clearly defined so employees know what is expected and managers know when performance is acceptable. The goal

Exit interview

A meeting with a departing employee that is conducted to learn what can be done to improve the restaurant.

Employee turnover rate

The number of employees who leave during a specific period of time. This is calculated by dividing the total number of employees who leave an organization by the total number of employees during a specific period of time.

Total number of employees who leave (÷) Total number of employees = Turnover rate

Position analysis

A process to identify each task in a position and how it should be done.

Task list

A position analysis tool that indicates all duties included within a position.

Task breakdown

A position analysis tool that indicates precisely how each task identified in the task list should be accomplished.

FIGURE 4.5

Position Analysis Activities
Adapted from Hayes, D., Miller, A., and Ninemeier, J. (2012). *The Professional Kitchen Manager.* Pearson Education, Inc.

of training must be to teach a trainee how to correctly perform a task, and the definition of "correct" refers to both the quality and quantity of work performed.

Performance standards should be reasonable (i.e., challenging but achievable) and specific so they can be measured. Staff should be trained in procedures specified by task breakdowns; they must be given the tools and equipment needed to complete the task correctly.

WRITE JOB DESCRIPTION   You've learned that job descriptions are helpful recruitment tools; however, they also identify training needs. A new employee must learn everything required to perform the job as summarized in the job description. The job description can be used for performance evaluation of activities that consider whether staff adequately perform the tasks in their job description.

Step 3: Develop Training Objectives

Training objectives help connect the purpose of a training program with its content and are also used to evaluate training. Effectively developed objectives specify what trainees should know and be able to do when training is successfully completed. Training planners must know what the training is to accomplish, and training objectives help them do this.

To be useful, objectives must be reasonable and attainable, as well as measurable. They're *not* reasonable when they're too difficult or too easy to attain. The following objective for a supervisory training program to reduce turnover is probably not reasonable:

> *"As a result of successful training, there will be no turnover except for* **attrition** *beginning with staff members employed after 1/1/XX."*

By contrast, a reasonable objective may state that:

> *"Turnover for servers will be reduced by 20% within 12 months after completion of the supervisory training program."*

Steps 4 and 5: Develop Training Plans and Training Lessons

Training plans organize training content and provide an overview of the structure and sequence of the training program. They show how individual **training lessons** should be sequenced to best allow trainees to learn the skills and knowledge required for successful performance.

Attrition

A reduction in the workforce caused by voluntary separation.

Training plan

An overview of the content and sequence of a training program.

Training lesson

The information and methods used to present one session in a training plan.

Training activities for serving personnel must include procedures for interacting with food production staff.

© CandyBox Images/Fotolia

A well-organized training plan:

- Provides an introduction that explains why the training is important
- Includes an overview of training content
- Allows training lessons to progress, from simple to complex, so trainees feel at ease and comfortable with the training
- Builds on the trainees' experiences
- Presents basic information before more detailed concepts are discussed
- Uses a logical order. What must first be known before other information is developed or as skills are attained?

Formal training plans allow managers to:

- Plan the dates and times for each training lesson
- Consider the topic to be taught (lesson subject)
- Consider the best training locations
- Decide who will be responsible for the training
- Identify trainees for whom specific training lessons are needed

A training lesson tells the "why, what and how" of a specific training session:

- Why = the training objectives
- What = the training lesson's content
- How = the training methods to be used

Figure 4.6 reviews procedures to develop training lessons.

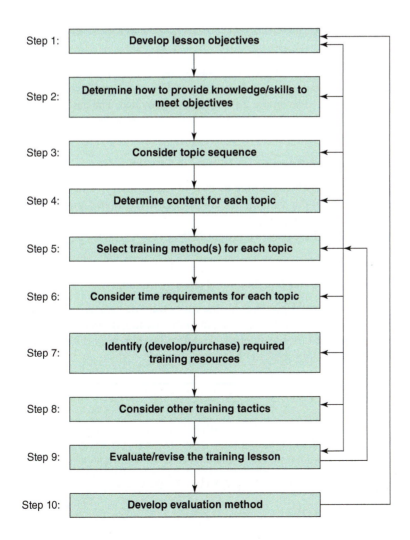

FIGURE 4.6

Steps to Develop a Training Lesson

Adapted from Hayes, D., Miller, A., and Ninemeier, J. (2012). *The Professional Kitchen Manager*. Pearson Education, Inc.

Step 1: Develop lesson objectives

Step 2: Determine how to provide knowledge/skills to meet objectives

Step 3: Consider topic sequence

Step 4: Determine content for each topic

Step 5: Select training method(s) for each topic

Step 6: Consider time requirements for each topic

Step 7: Identify (develop/purchase) required training resources

Step 8: Consider other training tactics

Step 9: Evaluate/revise the training lesson

Step 10: Develop evaluation method

To illustrate, assume a training lesson about handling customer complaints is being developed, and the model in Figure 4.6 is to be applied:

- Step 1: Develop lesson objectives. "Servers will be able to manage customer complaints using a six-step service recovery process."
- Step 2: Determine how to provide knowledge/skills to meet objectives. A training video showing how to handle complaints will provide much of the necessary subject matter.
- Step 3: Consider topic sequence. The lesson will begin with an introduction, continue with the video, and use a discussion to review specific learning points.
- Step 4: Determine content for each topic. There is only one topic (managing complaints), and a review of off-the-shelf training resources reinforces the decision that it will be effective.
- Step 5: Select training method(s) for each topic. A short (15 minute) video followed by a 10 minute discussion will be used.
- Step 6: Consider time requirements for each topic. The session will require 5 minutes for the introduction, 15 minutes for the video, and 10 minutes for a follow-up discussion.
- Step 7: Identify (develop/purchase) required training resources. A training video will be required.
- Step 8: Consider other training tactics. The session will conclude with a discussion.
- Step 9: Evaluate/revise the training lesson. The manager's experience with previous training sessions helps to plan an effective presentation.
- Step 10: Develop evaluation method. The manager will use a 10-question, true/false test to evaluate trainees' knowledge of customer complaint resolution methods.

Figure 4.6 also indicates the cyclical nature of training lesson development: The evaluation/revision (Step 9) can lead to changes in any or all of the earlier steps in lesson development, and the after-lesson evaluation (Step 10) helps to assess whether the lesson objectives (Step 1) were met.

Step 6: Prepare Trainees

The implementation of a training program is always easier when trainees have helped develop the training programs; they may suggest new ways of doing things and areas in which they feel the need to know more. Trainees are best motivated when they're told what to expect and why the training is needed and when ample training time is provided. The best restaurant managers carefully explain that training will directly relate to the trainee's work and then review how the trainee will be evaluated.

Step 7: Conduct On-the-Job Training

On-the-job training

Individualized training in which an experienced and knowledgeable trainer teaches another employee how to perform necessary tasks in the workplace.

On-the-job training is an excellent training method for new and experienced restaurant employees because it uses many of the training principles discussed earlier. Figure 4.7 shows the four phases in effective on-the-job training.

Let's look at each of these phases more carefully.

TRAINING PREPARATION   The basic principles used when preparing for on-the-job training have been noted throughout our examination of effective training:

- State training objectives: Objectives for the entire training program will be available in the training plan and for each training segment in the training lesson.
- Use/revise applicable task breakdowns: Trainers should review the list of applicable task breakdowns because they indicate the training content.

WEB AT WORK!

Professional hospitality associations provide resources that busy managers can use for training programs. For example, check out the websites of the Educational Institute of the American Hotel & Lodging Association and the National Restaurant Association Educational Foundation.

www.ei-ahla.org

www.nraef.org

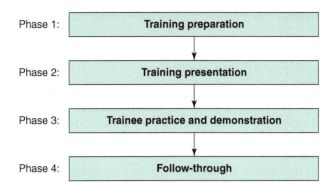

FIGURE 4.7

On-the-Job Training Process
Adapted from Hayes, D., Miller, A., and Ninemeier J. (2012). *The Professional Kitchen Manager.* Pearson Education, Inc.

- Consider the training schedule: The training plan should indicate the length of the training activity and when it should occur.
- Select training location: When practical, training should occur in the workstation where the task will be performed.
- Prepare for training lesson: Assemble training materials/equipment in the training area.
- Prepare the trainee: A new staff member should know that the training will provide the knowledge and skills necessary to perform all job tasks. Experienced staff should understand that the training will provide the knowledge/skills needed to perform a task differently or to learn a new task.
- Determine what the trainee already knows: If, for example, a piece of food service equipment must be operated, the trainee can be asked to demonstrate its proper operation. If this is done correctly, this part of the training is not necessary. If the trainee can't do so, training should address equipment operation.

TRAINING PRESENTATION   During this part of the training, the restaurant manager can make use of the training lesson and task breakdown completed as part of the position analysis process.

For example, how can employees learn to conduct a physical inventory in the storeroom? They can receive a copy of the position description that confirms the inventory task is part of their position. The training should occur in the storeroom and begin with a task overview. The trainer can show trainees how the storage area is organized and review how the inventory worksheet is completed. Trainees can be shown the counting process for inventoried items as well as the procedures used to ensure products are placed on shelves correctly and rotated to reduce spoilage.

The trainer can explain the first step in the task, answer questions and then allow the trainees to repeat, practice and/or demonstrate the step. If necessary, the sequence of steps should be repeated.

TRAINEE PRACTICE AND DEMONSTRATION   Several principles are important during this phase of on-the-job training:

- The trainee should be asked to repeat or explain key points.
- The trainee should demonstrate or practice the task. Typically, steps are taught by the trainer and practiced by the trainee in the sequence demonstrated.
- When the task is difficult, initial progress may be slow. The trainee may require more extensive repetition to build speed while consistently and correctly performing the task.
- Some trainees learn faster than others; the training can be presented at the speed judged "best" for the individual trainee.
- Correct performance should be acknowledged before addressing problems.
- Trainees should be praised for proper post-training performance.

FOLLOW-THROUGH   The final phase of on-the-job training allows the trainer to ensure that the training will be effective. The trainee should be asked to perform, in sequence, each step in the task. The trainer should encourage questions and provide ongoing reinforcement that inspires the trainee's positive attitude. Close supervision immediately after training and occasional supervision after a task has been mastered can help to ensure that the trainee consistently performs the task correctly.

EVALUATING TRAINING   The final step in the training process involves evaluation to:

- Assess whether training objectives were attained
- Identify how the training can be improved
- Determine the success of individual trainees
- Gather information to help justify and improve future programs

Training should be evaluated at its conclusion. However, it may also be helpful to assess training several months (or even longer) after a training lesson is completed to learn if the lesson's content is still being applied on the job correctly.

Training evaluation methods can include objective tests (written, oral, or skill-based), observation of after-training performance, interviews with trainees or trainers and exit interviews. Training records should be maintained in each trainee's personnel file and should include information about training dates and topics as well as notes about the trainee's successful completion of the training.

WEB AT WORK!

To review practical and hospitality industry-related articles about training, go to the Hotel-Online website:

www.hotel-online.com

Enter "training" in the "Search Hotel Online!" box.

GREEN AT WORK!

You've learned that restaurant managers are increasingly concerned about the environment. There are many environmentally conscious procedures that can be implemented; however, "green" practices must first be identified, and then employees must learn about their importance and be trained to apply them.

Where does one start? One excellent source of information is the Green Restaurant Association, at **www.dinegreen.com**. Its website has an education section that provides practical suggestions for "going green."

Restaurant managers can review information about the following topics:

- "The big picture"
- Disposable products
- Chemicals
- Food and beverage
- Energy and water
- Building and construction
- Waste

As you review this information, you'll learn how to implement "green" procedures at a restaurant you manage and obtain excellent information useful for developing training programs on how best to implement these procedures.

ALL IN A DAY'S WORK: 4.2

Aria, the owner/manager of Aria's Steakhouse, has a dilemma. Her dining room manager has given her one week's notice about leaving, and this key position must be quickly filled.

Her first thought is, "Fortunately, Bill is a great food server. He has been here a while and knows the serving procedures. I can promote him to the dining room manager position and train him before the current dining room manager leaves."

"On the other hand," thinks Aria, "Who will replace Bill? I can always rely on him to be here when he's scheduled, take care of our customers, and help some of our other servers."

"What should I do?"

1. Assume Aria will promote Bill to be the new dining room manager. What training priorities will be needed to prepare him for the job?
2. What pre-planning tactics might Aria use in the future to reduce the kind of problem she encounters when key staff members leave?

Motivating Employees

Experienced restaurant managers know that the best way to reduce the need for ongoing employee recruitment, selection, and orientation activities is to reduce turnover rates by keeping the employees they have. However, current employees will only perform well if their **morale** levels are high. The investments to bring staff members onboard and the valuable knowledge, skills, and experience of these employees can be lost when employees quit due to low morale. Fortunately, there are simple and practical ways for restaurant managers to improve morale and their employee **retention rates**.

Contrary to popular belief, a restaurant manager can't motivate employees; rather, motivation is an inner drive to attain desired goals. Therefore, a manager's primary strategy should be to provide a work environment in which employees can fulfill their personal needs, interests and goals while achieving the objectives of the restaurant. Leadership is the ability to accomplish objectives by working with and through people. A restaurant leader creates conditions that motivate employees by establishing goals and influencing employees to attain them.

In today's workplace, an effective manager guides and influences rather than orders employees to undertake specific actions. The manager is a facilitator and coach who assembles resources and provides guidance as opposed to the dictatorial taskmaster of yesterday. The manager who is flexible and can select a style that is comfortable to work with and appropriate for the employee and the situation will likely be better able to provide an environment within which motivation can occur.

Restaurant managers develop a motivated staff by creating a climate in which employees want to work with rather that against the goals of the operation. To help employees become motivated, it's important to understand their needs, interests and goals. What motivates one employee may have little effect on another because needs, interests and goals vary from employee to employee. These motivational factors are a function of each individual's background, personality, intellect, attitudes, and other characteristics. The challenge for managers is to get to know the employees whom they lead.

Successful motivators know what it takes for their employees to become motivated. This is not an easy task, because some employees may not know, or at least can't verbalize, their needs or goals. Much motivation is subconscious. For example, some high-energy employees may be top performers because they fear rejection from co-workers if they don't produce above-average results. These employees may not even be aware that they're seeking approval from their peers.

How can a restaurant manager know when an employee has a motivational problem or whether the general morale level is low? Common-sense observations can help—sophisticated studies aren't always necessary. Begin by investigating a number of factors that indirectly relate to low motivational or morale levels:

- High absenteeism rates
- High turnover rates
- Increases in accidents
- Unusually high number of employee complaints or grievances

Further observation may uncover a general lack of cooperation among employees or increasing conflicts in the work environment. Many common practices, when done correctly, can create the right working environment. For example, effective restaurant managers train their employees properly, provide them with safe and well-maintained tools and equipment and remove obstacles to their success. They also help employees resolve problems and provide them with continuing education opportunities to learn on the job.

Employees who won't perform, don't meet work standards or abuse attendance, vacation and other policies should be eliminated from the restaurant team because they affect the good employees who do most of the work. By the same token, poor performance by managers and supervisors is likely to lower employee morale and increase employee dissatisfaction and turnover.

MAKING FIRST IMPRESSIONS COUNT Restaurant managers should make sure new employees know that their total compensation consists of more than just wages or salary. **Benefits** including meals, uniforms, educational assistance, healthcare, vacation, paid time off and sick leave

Morale

Workers' feelings about their employers, workplace and other aspects of their job.

Retention rate

The number of employees who remain during a specific period of time divided by the number of employees who worked during that same period. One calculation for annual retention rate percentage is:

Number of employees who remain (÷) Total number of employees = Annual retention rate %

Benefits

Indirect financial compensation paid to attract and retain employees or to meet legal requirements. Some benefits are mandatory (Social Security taxes) while others are voluntary (paid time off).

may be offered to employees. Workers should understand that these benefits add value to their overall position packages.

Other ways to create positive first impressions for new employees include:

- Explaining the long-term benefits of staying with the restaurant. These benefits may include pay raises, extended vacation times and other types of financial compensation and recognition.
- Sharing your vision. Effective managers share their thoughts, ask staff members for ideas and work together as a team to meet goals.
- Creating a **career ladder** to explain how employees can be promoted if they remain with the property. The best restaurant managers analyze each entry-level position and consider how a talented staff member in that job might advance. Career ladders can motivate employees because they provide a plan to help employees move forward in their careers.

Career ladder

A plan that shows how one can advance to more responsible positions within a restaurant.

SUPERVISING EFFECTIVELY   Restaurant managers should supervise their employees in the same way they would like to be supervised. Examples include ensuring that they:

- Administer policies fairly and consistently. Employees don't like it when some workers are favored over others. Policies should be fair and reasonably applied.
- Give employees a personal copy of their work schedule. Many managers post employee work schedules on a bulletin board or through the operation's **intranet**. However, some staff members are more likely to follow a schedule if they receive a personal copy, and sending a text or an e-mail message is a fast and easy way to do this.
- Know about employee assistance programs. Some good employees may need professional assistance because of problems such as alcohol or substance abuse and financial or other personal difficulties. These challenges can affect their attendance, their ability to meet required work standards and their personal interactions with other members of the work team. Restaurant managers can show concern by directing them to professional assistance.
- Invite **fast-track employees** to attend selected management meetings. When staff members know their supervisor has important plans for them, they're more likely to remain with the operation and be motivated as they do so.
- Conduct exit interviews with each departing staff member to allow managers to discover potential problems and plan more effective retention strategies.
- Use employee recognition programs to publicly or privately praise good employees. Verbal recognition, personal recognition letters, bulletin board announcements, plaques, and special recognition pins can show employees that their accomplishments are valued.
- Build a great team and praise it and its individual members often.
- Reward employees who have been called into work on their nonscheduled work days. Recognition rewards and extra benefits are among the ways to say "thank you" for these efforts.
- Make the workplace fun. Restaurant managers can simply ask their staff members what they can do to make the workplace more enjoyable.

Intranet

A network consisting of computers for a single restaurant.

Fast-track employees

Those who perform effectively in their existing position and who participate in a planned professional development program designed to quickly promote them.

HELPING EMPLOYEES BE SUCCESSFUL   Satisfaction at work is a powerful motivator. Unfortunately, some restaurant work is routine, and it may be difficult to change the job to add more variety. Good employees demonstrate success, and this provides the key to recognizing them for it. For example, if you have an employee with an excellent attendance record, make sure he or she knows you appreciate the dedication.

> **WEB AT WORK!**
>
> The Web is a great source of information for those wanting to learn more about motivation. For example, check out:
>
> www.about.com
>
> Type "how to motivate employees" into the search box (which is called "What Can I Help You Accomplish Today?").

The best employees can sometimes be unintentionally punished when extra work projects are assigned to them. This is because managers typically delegate projects to their most competent, not their least competent, staff members. And these best employees may come to feel their contributions are being rewarded with extra work that is not required of others. For that reason, managers must ensure they recognize and reward their best employees for their special efforts.

Facilitating Employee Performance

Restaurant managers must direct the work of many employees and supervise other managers who are responsible for selected staff members. Effective leaders consistently use basic, but effective supervisory principles and tactics as they do so. We will examine some of the most important ones in this section.

LEADERSHIP STYLES Those who study effective managers generally agree that they can utilize four common, but very different, leadership styles:

- **Autocratic** managers make decisions and resolve problems without input from their employees. They give specific work instructions and expect them to be followed. They frequently develop a system of rewards and punishments to encourage compliance with their orders, and they discipline employees when orders aren't followed. They're generally unwilling to **delegate** assignments and feel that results are more important than staff morale.
- **Bureaucratic** leaders "manage by the book" and emphasize the enforcement of policies, procedures, and written rules. Problems that can't be resolved by rules are referred to higher management levels.
- **Democratic** leaders involve staff in the decision-making process. They inform employees about matters that affect them and **empower** employees when possible. Their goal is to help employees develop a high sense of job satisfaction.
- **Laissez-faire** leaders use a "hands-off" approach and do as little directing as possible. All or most **authority** is delegated to staff members to develop goals, make decisions and resolve their own problems.

Few managers use one management style 100% of the time. In fact, the most effective restaurant managers continually adapt their leadership styles to the situations they face and the teams they lead. While sometimes difficult to do, they recognize that different employees react differently in the same situation, and they find advantages to addressing the unique needs of their employees.

COMMUNICATION SKILLS Effective restaurant managers use three basic communication skills:

1. *They consider the viewpoints of others.* When they do, they consider how what they say will be perceived by those to whom they are communicating.
2. *They seek to learn what others know.* The best managers communicate in ways that maximize the information they receive from others. For example, a manager could make a request of an employee and then ask, "Do you understand?" even though "yes" or "no" responses may not indicate the full extent of the employee's understanding. It would be better to ask an open-ended question such as, "Why do you think it's important that this be done?"
3. *They make messages meaningful.* Effective managers know the difference between "talking" and truly communicating. Thus, for example, the way a restaurant manager might give instructions to new staff members compared to how the same message would be delivered to their experienced counterparts would likely be very different.

Communication Barriers Several barriers can hinder communication effectiveness. These include:

- Differing perceptions. If one person is not interested in a message, communication will be a challenge. But if the manager suspects this is happening, he or she might pose the message in a way that illustrates the benefits to the person receiving it.

Autocratic

A leadership approach in which decisions are typically made and problems are resolved without input from affected staff members.

Delegate

The process of assigning authority (power) to subordinates to allow them to do the work that a higher-level manager would otherwise need to do.

Bureaucratic

A leadership approach that involves "management by the book" and the enforcement of policies, procedures and written rules.

Democratic

A leadership approach in which employees are encouraged to participate in the decision-making process.

Empower

The act of allowing employees to make decisions within their areas of responsibility.

Laissez-faire

A leadership approach that minimizes directing employees and, instead, maximizes the delegation of tasks and results to affected staff members.

Authority

The power and responsibility to make decisions.

- Conducting negative coaching interviews in private and praising staff members for good performance in public.
- Comparing employees' performance against standards noted in task lists and task break-downs rather than to how staff members work in comparison to others.
- Establishing and agreeing upon corrective action time frames: If performance is not acceptable, the restaurant manager and staff member should agree upon what must be done to improve it. A time schedule for acceptable performance and/or an additional performance review can then be undertaken.
- Asking staff members how their team's work performance can be improved: Giving them the opportunity to give their own suggestions for workplace improvement can be a powerful motivating factor.

The philosophy noted in this coaching discussion is relevant when you think about how you would like to be treated in your interactions with your own boss. As you do so, you'll also likely identify the tactics your staff members would like you to use during interactions with them. Effective coaching is likely to be high on this list.

CONFLICT MANAGEMENT   Even the most quality-focused restaurants can experience conflict. Managers must know how to address it when it occurs. Some conflicts, such as differences in personal opinions, may be small while others may be significant and involve many employees.

Addressing Conflict   Many conflicts can be avoided by improving communication or eliminating a specific obstacle, but there are times when conflict can be beneficial or necessary. For example, servers can compete against a management-determined sales goal to sell additional desserts on a busy Saturday night; all those who exceed the goal receive a specified gift. This management-approved competition is a form of conflict but helps the restaurant increase sales and the servers increase their tips and receive gifts as a prize for their extra efforts.

Common types of conflict that aren't management initiated can include:

- Conflict within a person that occurs when employees experience differing perceptions about another's comments, actions or attitudes
- Conflict between employees that can result from personality conflicts or sincere differences in opinions about work methods or practices
- Conflict between an individual and a group that can arise, for instance, when someone disagrees with policy changes
- Conflict between formal groups such as departments with different ideas about attaining goals or informal groups such as staff members disagreeing about how work is to be divided among team members

Some conflicts can be caused by relationships between restaurant managers and line-level employees, others arise because of how to spend limited funds and other conflicts involve differences of opinion about the restaurant's goals or how to attain them.

Successful restaurant managers address all these types of conflict, and others, in ways ranging from being cooperative to assertive. These managers can state their opinions without being aggressive and request cooperation to yield positive relationships and sustainable solutions. They can provide honest feedback with those involved in a conflict, and they should accept honest criticism and differing opinions without anger or reprisal and while remaining impartial and fair to all involved in the conflict.

Conflict can be reduced by redefining goals to increase agreements between two conflicting groups or individuals. Conflict can also be resolved by compromise with conflicting groups working together to identify an acceptable solution or appealing to a higher level of authority for resolution.

It's important to remain objective and calm when managing stressful situations and to remember that the restaurant manager's goal is to identify the best possible resolution for a situation rather than to target or criticize individuals. This is so because when someone feels directly attacked, threatened or humiliated, the situation is likely to escalate.

Leading Difficult Employees   There are several types of employees you may encounter that may prove difficult to manage. These can include:

- Those who are openly abusive or hostile. If they are, defend your position but remain calm and restate your idea or position in a different way. Remain friendly and avoid being aggressive. Maintain eye contact and, if appropriate, allow the employee a few minutes to calm down.
- Those who "know-it-all." These employees may be competent but are overly self-assured and don't want to fairly consider ideas suggested by other team members. Speak to these employees firmly without engaging in a direct confrontation. Listen carefully to their position, acknowledge what has been said, and be prepared to support your own position with facts and supporting evidence.
- Those who complain and find fault with everything and everyone. In this case, It's best to remain objective and don't discuss your personal feelings. Listen to specific concerns but try to limit these conversations to specific times, locations and facts. Encourage these employees to become engaged in the problem-solving process.
- Those who are continually negative. Express realistic optimism and engage these employees by using the information constructively: "How can we turn this into a positive outcome?"
- Those who are "super-agreeable" but don't express their honest opinions. Remain non-threatening when meeting with these employees, reassure them that you want honest feedback and encourage them to give it.
- Those who defer all major decisions. These employees may not make decisions because of concerns they will disappoint others. Identify why they want to postpone a decision and help them to prioritize what needs to be done.

WORKPLACE ETHICS   **Ethics** can be described as proper behavior toward others. Determining those actions that constitute ethical behavior is an ever present issue in the restaurant industry.

Ethics

Concerns relating to what is right and wrong behavior when dealing with others.

Ethical conduct is required of restaurant managers at all times. However, the difference between what is "right" and what is "wrong" can be viewed from different perspectives. Consider the following:

- A restaurant manager knows that a "favorite" employee regularly arrives late and leaves early but ignores the situation.
- Another restaurant manager consistently emphasizes the need for "quality" but makes many decisions on the basis of cost. In effect, he says "Do what I say—not what I do!"

Are these managers ethical? Furthermore, how does one decide if a proposed action is ethical? When trying to determine if a course of action is ethical, restaurant managers can ask themselves the following questions:

- Is the proposed action legal?
- Does the proposed action hurt anyone?
- Is the proposed action fair?
- Am I being honest as I undertake the proposed action?
- Can I live with myself if I do what I am considering?
- Would I like to publicize my decision?
- What if everyone did it?

Code of ethics

A formal statement that defines how restaurant employees should relate to each other and the persons and groups with whom they interact.

A **code of ethics** identifies how restaurant employees should interact with and relate to each other and the groups with whom they interact.

WEB AT WORK!

The International Business Ethics Institute provides resources that help leaders learn how to practice ethical management. To view the site, go to:

www.business-ethics.org

Click on "Resources" and then "Business Ethics Primer." At the end of that information, you'll find links to other sites that present information about business ethics.

Restaurant Terms and Concepts

Work in Progress

1. How might recruitment and selection processes differ when a restaurant manager is seeking a kitchen or dining room manager compared to an entry-level employee?
2. What are effective ways to recruit young people for entry-level restaurant positions?
3. What, if any, role should selection tests play as hiring decisions are made?
4. How important is it to verify the information on an employment application? How would you do so?
5. What role should the restaurant manager play in a new employee's orientation program? What role should be played by the employee's immediate supervisor?
6. What basic training principles were most frequently ignored or applied inadequately in your past training experiences? How did they impact your training?
7. What should a restaurant manager say to a department manager who indicates he or she is too busy to develop task lists or task breakdowns before training new employees?
8. How would you describe the best boss you ever had? The worst boss? How can answering these questions help you to become a better boss?
9. What type of leadership style would be of ideal use when managing a newly employed young person? An experienced older employee? Explain your answers.
10. What are two things a restaurant manager might do that you would consider to be unethical?

5

It All Starts with the Menu

Learning Objectives

After carefully reading and studying the information in this chapter, you will be able to:

1. Explain how to plan a menu.

2. Use effective procedures to design a menu.

3. Understand basic food safety principles.

4. Explain why standardized recipes are critical for quality control.

5. Describe how to cost standardized recipes.

IN THIS CHAPTER

Experienced restaurant managers know that "It all starts with the menu": The menu serves as the critical link between a restaurant and its guests. It also impacts the financial success and almost every other aspect of the operation, including personnel, equipment, layout and design, space, and storage.

Once planned, a menu must be designed. Done effectively, it doesn't just indicate available food items and selling prices. It also promotes the sale of profitable and popular alternatives. Many restaurants have a wine menu, and managers must apply specialized knowledge to develop it.

Standardized recipes are used to implement the menu. Their consistent use is critical to provide menu items that meet quality and quantity goals. The advantages to using standardized recipes are maximized when ingredient, portion, and plate costs are determined—these procedures help to establish effective selling prices and keep food costs in line with the restaurant's financial goals.

PLANNING THE MENU

The menu drives necessary operating procedures and how they are planned. In this section, you'll learn about the importance of the menu and how to plan it.

The Importance of the Menu

Your potential guests are the most important consideration when planning the menu. Figure 5.1 summarizes their role in a successful restaurant.

It indicates that a successful restaurant is one that is enjoyed by its guests, and their level of enjoyment is directly affected by the menu.

Restaurant managers must know why guests visit their operation. Do they want a fast meal in a quick service property or an elegant dinner to celebrate a special occasion? Regardless of the reason, restaurant guests all seek **value**. They'll also consider their dining experience, which is affected by food and beverage products, service, and the restaurant's overall atmosphere (environment).

Value

A concept addressing the relationship between selling price and quality.

FIGURE 5.1

Menu Planners Consider the Guests

Adapted from Hayes, D., Miller, A., and Ninemeier, J. (2012). *The Professional Kitchen Manager.* Pearson Education, Inc.

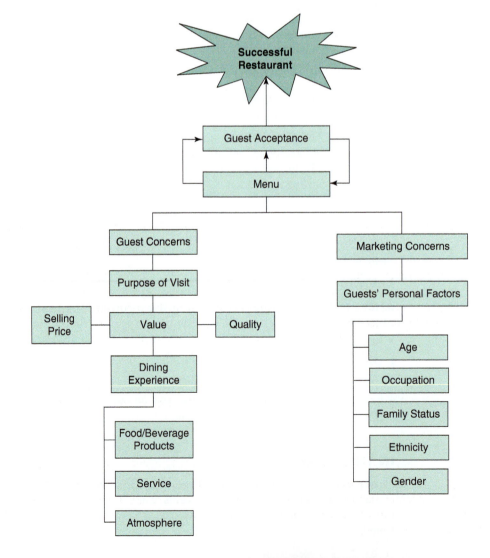

Experienced restaurant managers know it's not possible to offer a menu that will appeal to everyone at all times. Potential guests are influenced by personal factors, including age, occupation, family status, ethnicity (race and culture), and gender.

Restaurants must generate a profit to stay in business. However, "keeping the doors open" is not likely to satisfy those who own or invest in a restaurant. Instead, profits must meet the owner's long-term return on investment (ROI) goals. A menu that offers products targeted to those most likely to visit the property and priced at a level providing value is critical for financial success and for achieving planned ROIs.

Your menu will directly impact the **resources** you need to meet your guest and financial goals. These resources include:

Resources

The assets that restaurant managers use to attain goals, including people, food and beverage products, time, and money.

- Labor (including managers and other employees)
- Food and beverage products
- Equipment for product storage, production, service, and cleanup
- Operating expenses included in the budget
- Space available for storing, production, service, and cleanup
- Standard operating procedures (methods)

Figure 5.2 reviews the positions and responsibilities of those who might be part of a restaurant's menu planning team and discussion of their menu planning role follows the Figure.

FIGURE 5.2
The Menu Planning Team

Position	Menu Planning Concerns
Owner/restaurant manager	Will the menu meet financial goals?
Kitchen manager/chef	Will guests enjoy the items, and can the items be produced to meet necessary quality and quantity standards?
Dining room manager	Will the menu please the guests and build repeat business?
Purchasing agent	Are the ingredients required to produce menu items available at a reasonable price when needed?
Controller (accountant)	Will financial goals be met? Note: Controllers in some restaurants also determine **serving costs** and selling prices.
Bar Manager	Will the menu items complement the wine and other beverage menu available?

Adapted from Hayes, D., Miller, A., and Ninemeier, J. (2012). *The Professional Kitchen Manager.* Pearson Education, Inc.

Serving cost

The cost to produce one serving of a menu item when it's prepared according to the standardized recipe; another phrase for portion cost.

The owner/restaurant manager wants to achieve a financial return that takes into account the risk of losing his or her **investment** and understands the important role that the menu plays in helping to achieve financial goals.

The kitchen manager or chef must produce all the menu items and do so with available equipment, employees, and other resources. The dining room manager has firsthand knowledge about the guests' perceptions of the existing menu and ideas about other potentially popular items.

The purchasing agent has specialized knowledge about product availability, supplier sources, and price trends, while the **controller** will have suggestions about important financial goals and concerns. The bar manager must produce all beverage items and have firsthand knowledge of guests' impressions.

While only high-volume restaurants may employ individuals to hold all of the different positions listed in Figure 5.2, someone in every restaurant must be responsible for the duties of each role.

Investment

The money that an owner has spent to start and run the business.

Controller

The person who records and summarizes a restaurant's business transactions, develops financial statements, and provides suggestions about what "the numbers say"; another word for accountant.

Menu Planning Strategies

The menu in a chef-owned restaurant may feature offerings and/or market-fresh items that change every day. A family-owned operation with an ethnic theme may feature items prepared with traditional family recipes and a menu that never changes. Between these extremes we find a majority of restaurants that revise the items on the menus occasionally as changing guests' preferences are monitored.

FIGURE 5.3

Menu Planning Strategies

Adapted from Hayes, D., Miller, A., and Ninemeier, J. (2012). *The Professional Kitchen Manager.* Pearson Education, Inc.

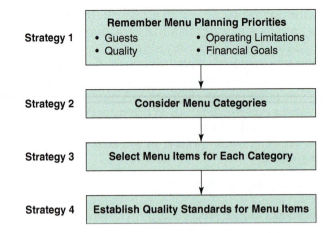

Figure 5.3 reviews helpful planning strategies you will use to develop your own menu. Let's review the strategies in Figure 5.3.

REMEMBER MENU PLANNING PRIORITIES Strategy 1 reminds us to never forget priorities:

- Guests: The menu must reflect the guests' expectations.
- Quality: All menu items must meet the restaurant's quality requirements, which are built into its **standardized recipes**.
- Operating limitations: Factors that limit a restaurant's ability to produce menu items include the knowledge/skill levels of production staff, the availability of ingredients, and volume production requirements. Other concerns include layout and equipment, sanitation issues, and operating costs. Also, service staff must have the knowledge and ability to serve all items required by the menu.
- Financial objectives: Wise restaurant managers consider their operating budget (profit plan) when planning their menu. Product costs must be considered when the menu is planned and prices are set.

CONSIDER MENU CATEGORIES The second strategy requires planners to consider **menu categories** that logically divide all menu items into similar groups of items. For example, guests want to know about available **entrées** and these should not be placed in the same menu category as desserts.

Menu items are typically organized into categories including:

- Entrées: These are usually planned first, taking other categories into consideration.
- House specialties: Some restaurants specialize in barbequed ribs, steaks, or chops and feature them in a separate menu category.
- Appetizers: These are typically served before the meal and are often bite-sized.
- Soups: Some restaurants consider soups a separate category; others include them with appetizers or salads.
- Salads: Some restaurants offer entrée salads and accompaniment (side) salads.
- Sandwiches and wraps: Common sandwiches include hamburgers and those made with deli items such as ham and turkey. Wraps include spring rolls, tacos, and burritos with numerous fillings.
- Vegetables and accompaniments (side dishes): Potatoes, asparagus, broccoli, and other vegetables with varying preparation styles are available on many menus. Accompaniments may be suggested by the operation's theme; for example, beans and rice are served in a restaurant with a Central American theme.
- Desserts: After-dinner items may be listed with other items or on a separate dessert menu.
- Beverages: Coffees, teas, and soft drinks may be listed on the menu, or there may be a separate menu for coffee. Some menus suggest traditional and specialty cocktails, and many include domestic and imported beers. Many restaurants have a wine list, and some feature a water menu.

Some properties offer unique signature menu items, such as a one-pound pork chop. Over time, these become very popular menu items, drawing customers who learn to associate the item with the restaurant.

Standardized recipe

Instructions to produce a food or beverage item that help ensure that the restaurant's quality and quantity standards for the product are consistently met.

Menu category

A group of similar menu items such as entrées or salads.

Entrée

A food served as a meal's main course.

How many menu categories are needed? Effective menu planners consider:

- The number necessary for the variety of menu items guests want.
- Whether a category is needed for unique items.
- How to create a menu that's easy to read. Too few categories create long lists of items within each category, increasing the time that guests will take to order. This is of concern, since maximizing **table turns** is crucial in many restaurants.

When guests' needs are carefully assessed, the number of categories and items offered can often be reduced.

SELECT MENU ITEMS FOR EACH CATEGORY One popular way to plan items for basic menu categories is to do so in the following order:

- Entrees
- Appetizers
- Potatoes, rice and related items
- Soups
- Salads
- Desserts
- Breads
- Beverages

Entrées are often planned first because when guests are dining out, their decisions are often based on their entrée selections. In addition, restaurants with dining themes use specific types of entrées to help "deliver" their cuisines to the guests.

Special menu planning tools can help you and your menu planning team save time and money. These tools include:

- Copies of old and existing menus.
- Copies of competitors' menus.
- Standardized recipes: These are a "must" to ensure that suggested items can be produced according to your restaurant's standards.
- Product inventory and ingredient availability information: Product availability at the right quality and acceptable cost during the time the menu will be available is important.
- Input from managers, employees and those you serve. Be sure to talk with servers who have guest contact and dishwashers who know what items are returned uneaten.

Several factors should be considered when placing items in menu categories, and they are discussed next.

ITEM VARIETY A range of serving temperatures, preparation methods, textures, shapes, and colors should typically be offered by the items available within each category. Menu planners can simplify production and provide guests with wide variety of items when they use **menu rationalization**.

One way to consider the proper menu item variety involves the "3 Ps" of menu planning: product, preparation method, and price:

- Product: A reasonable variety of items are needed within each menu category.
- Preparation: This factor relates to:
  - **Market form**. This addresses how a food item can be purchased. For example, bread can be purchased in a fresh loaf or as a frozen ready-to-bake roll.
  - Preparation/cooking style. Seafood can be steamed, blackened, broiled, or pan-seared and, if several types are available, many different seafood entrees could be made available without excessive production labor. Meats can be cooked with **moist heat** and/or **dry heat**. Vegetables can be boiled, baked, braised, fried, or sautéed and desserts can be served fresh, chilled, cooked, or baked.
  - Serving size/quantity. Consider, for example, a one-half slab of ribs and a full slab of ribs. Also consider the many different serving sizes of steaks or prime rib.
- Price. Items for guests on a budget and/or with higher spending limits can be offered as long as the item offers real value for the diner.

Table turn
The number of times a dining room table is used during a dining period.

Menu rationalization
A menu planning tactic that involves using the same main ingredient in several different menu items.

Market form
Different ways that food products can be purchased. Examples: whole chickens, fresh bone-in chicken breasts or skinless, boneless, and frozen chicken breast portions.

Moist heat
A cooking method in which food is cooked by extended exposure to steam or hot liquids. Examples: stewing and braising.

Dry heat
A cooking method in which the food to be cooked is exposed directly to heat or flame. Examples: broiling and frying.

Organic foods

Foods produced, processed, and packaged without using chemicals including antibiotics or growth hormones in animals and pesticides and fertilizers or radiation while growing fruits and vegetables.

GREEN AT WORK!

The production and sale of **organic foods** is increasing, and many guests want these food items on menus. It's unclear whether organically grown foods actually contain more or better nutrients than food products grown conventionally. However, organic farming also emphasizes soil and water conservation as well as pollution reduction. Those growing these products don't use additional chemicals to fertilize, control weeds or prevent livestock disease. They use natural fertilizers including manure to enrich soil and nourish plants. They also use organic feeds for animals and allow them access to the outdoors rather than giving them antibiotics and confining their movements.

Guests desiring organic foods are often concerned about the environment and are willing to pay higher prices for organically grown foods. While some restaurants plan their menu around these products, many of which are locally grown, other properties provide organic food alternatives to appeal to guests with this concern and to demonstrate an environmental interest.

The U.S. Department of Agriculture (USDA) offers an organic certification program that requires all organic foods to meet specific standards that regulate how foods are grown, handled and processed. Organic foods meeting federal government standards have the following seal to confirm that requirements have been met.

Increasingly, guests have nutrition concerns. It's likely that some menu items can be made more appealing to consumers with nutrition concerns with just minor and very practical changes. For example, a deep-fried chicken breast can also be offered baked and without the skin, which has a higher fat content than the meat.

Food allergy

An abnormal response to a food that has no known cure.

Many guests also have allergy concerns. A **food allergy** is an abnormal response to a food and has no known cure, and the person with the allergy must avoid the food that causes it. Guests with food allergies require the assistance of service employees to provide the correct information about ingredients in and preparation methods for the items they decide to order. They also rely on production employees to handle and prepare food that is safe for them. Restaurants require a written plan that addresses exactly what to do when a guest with a food allergy orders a menu item. The plan should consider who should assist the guest, what cooks must do and what should be done if an allergic reaction occurs.

ITEM TEMPERATURE   Guests typically expect some items to be served hot (such as mashed potatoes) and other items to be served chilled (perhaps tossed salads). Hot and cold items can be offered within the same menu item category.

Texture

A description of how a food feels that is an important factor in food quality.

ITEM TEXTURE, SHAPE AND SIZE   Texture relates to how a food feels and is an important food quality factor. Menu items can be soft or hard, firm or crunchy, liquid or solid, or wet or dry. Many guests like cooked vegetables such as carrots to be "crisp tender" rather than soft, so these menu items should not be overcooked.

Menu items can be round, square, or long and they can be served in a flat or tall portion. Sometimes an item's height can even impact a guest's viewpoint. Consider the slivers of thin and tall fried vegetable strips used in **fusion cuisines**.

Fusion cuisine

Foods that blend the traditions of more than one cuisine.

Umami

A term that describes a savory, brothy, or meaty taste.

ITEM FLAVOR   Common taste sensations are sweet, sour, salty, and bitter. Some consider another taste, **umami**, that refers to savory, brothy, or meaty. Guests also use terms such as hot (think: buffalo wings), spicy (Thai dishes), and smoked (barbecued meats) to describe taste.

The concept of "flavor" is complex and refers to the total experience one has with the food being consumed. A person's sight, taste, touch, smell, and even sound (how about a sizzling steak on a hot platter?) are involved in a food's flavor.

OTHER FACTORS   Color is part of a menu item's appeal, and multiple colors are preferred. Guests expect broccoli to be a shiny, medium-dark green, and they want green beans to be a duller (olive) green. Plate garnishes can help ensure that the plate colors presented to a guest are appealing.

WEB AT WORK!

Menu labeling laws are a current issue; many cities and states are considering legislation that will require nutrition information to appear on a restaurant's menu. To learn more about this topic, go to the website of the Center for Science in the Public Interest:

www.cspinet.org

Type "menu legislation" in the site's search box.

When items are plated for service, menu planners have control over their composition and balance. The **center of the plate** concept can create a pleasing "picture" of the food items that are presented.

ESTABLISH QUALITY STANDARDS FOR MENU ITEMS   Strategy 4 in Figure 5.3 indicates that quality standards must be developed after menu items within each category are identified. Experienced restaurant managers use two tools to develop quality standards: 1) standardized recipes (see the discussion later in this chapter) and 2) purchase specifications (see Chapter 7).

Center of the plate

The concept that the entree should be positioned in the center of the plate with the other items slightly overlapped and moving toward the plate's rim, so that all center-plate areas are covered with food.

DESIGNING THE MENU

This section presents key information about menus and how they're designed.

Basic Menu Information

There are several common types of menus:

- À la carte menu. This menu lists food items that are separately priced. The guest charge is based on the prices of the items that the guest orders.
- Table d'hôte menu. This term means "all at one price"; guest charges don't vary based on what is ordered. A meal may be divided into courses, and guests may select one item from a list of several for each course with no price difference. Many properties also offer a buffet for a specified (fixed) price.
- **Cycle menu**. This menu is planned for a specified time period (example, 28 days) and then repeated. This menu is typically offered by noncommercial food services and in commercial buffet operations.
- **Du jour menu**. The phrase *du jour* means "of the day"; many restaurants offer daily specials in addition to regular menu items.

Cycle menu

A menu in which the food items rotate according to a planned schedule.

Du jour menu

A menu in which some or all food items are changed daily.

Hopefully, the menu being read has been planned and designed with this guest in mind.

© Diego Cervo/Shutterstock

Some restaurants have seasonal menus or feature seasonal menu items on their regular menus. This is often a great idea because foods that are in season are often the freshest and can be purchased at their best prices.

In most table-service restaurants, guests receive a physical, printed menu when they're seated. Figure 5.4 illustrates some common types.

Perhaps every restaurant with a website features a menu or examples of items that are typically offered. This provides potential guests with the opportunity to learn about available items as they consider dining alternatives.

Traditional hardcopy and handheld menus are popular and can be:

- Presented to guests when they're seated
- Sent to potential guests as advertising
- Posted on a sign outside the restaurant to attract passersby
- Left on tables for guests to read when they're seated

However, there are other ways that guests can learn about available food items. Perhaps the most common hardcopy alternative is the menu board at a quick-service restaurant. Word and/or picture descriptions can be provided on simple or electronic menu boards where changes to items, descriptions, graphics, and selling prices can be entered just as you would type words into a Word document.

A restaurant's theme may suggest how the menu is presented. Think about a steak house restaurant with a menu etched into a wooden cutting board. In some operations, wait staff recite or sing the menu.

FIGURE 5.4

Common Types of Menus

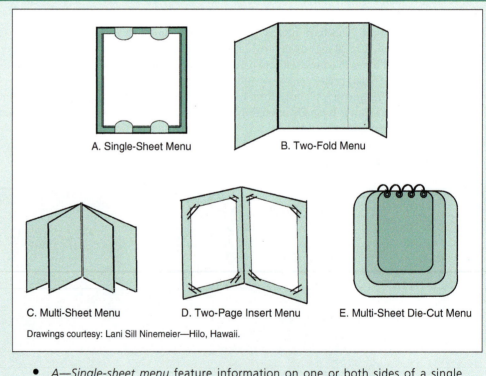

A. Single-Sheet Menu   B. Two-Fold Menu

C. Multi-Sheet Menu   D. Two-Page Insert Menu   E. Multi-Sheet Die-Cut Menu

Drawings courtesy: Lani Sill Ninemeier—Hilo, Hawaii.

- *A—Single-sheet menu* feature information on one or both sides of a single sheet.
- *B—Two-fold menu* opens like a book and often shows the restaurant's name on the cover and menu items on the remaining pages. Note that the example features an opening that is to the right of the menu's center.
- *C—Multi-sheet menu* is similar to the two-page insert menu in (D) except that it has additional inside sheets.
- *D—Two-page insert menu* has two sheets placed into a relatively sturdy and often colorful cover. Inserts can be changed as desired.
- *E—Multi-sheet,* **die-cut menu** allows the menu planners to present an eye-catching design that is often part of a restaurant's theme.

Die-cut menu

A menu that has been punched or cut into a special shape with a metal tool (die).

> ### WEB AT WORK!
>
> International Patterns, Inc. manufactures numerous types of menu boards and other signage for restaurants. Check out the company's website at:
>
> www.internationalpatterns.com

Design Menus to Sell

Today's menus are critical menu **merchandising** tools.

MENU LENGTH   Menus with an excessive number of pages slow the ordering process and reduce the table turn rate. Menus designed to sell items recognize that faster table turns produce more opportunities for additional guests to be seated and greater revenues to be generated.

Very short menus may also create problems because fewer menu items may not appeal to large numbers of guests. Restaurants with short menus are often highly specialized and basically offer only a signature food category along with a few other items.

The number of menu pages is partially determined when your menu is planned, not designed, because the menu must inform your guests about all the food items you want to sell. This reemphasizes the need for restaurant managers to plan with their target market in mind: The menu's design can address factors judged most effective at attracting and re-attracting the guests.

MENU PROMOTION   Always remember that menus should promote the sale of items the restaurant wants to sell: those that are most profitable and popular. Let's assume that Vernon's Restaurant wants to promote its delicious Starry Nights Linguine entrée. Figure 5.5 shows several ways to do so.

Merchandising

Promoting selected menu items to encourage guests to select them.

FIGURE 5.5

Promote Selected Menu Items

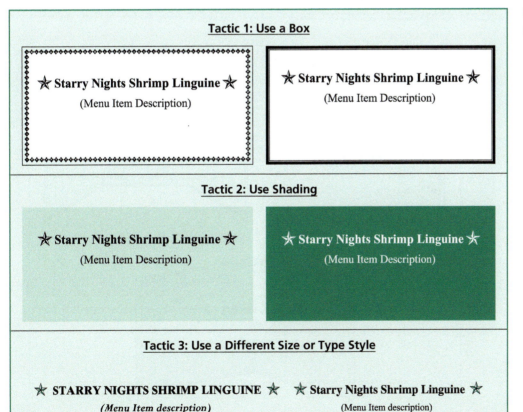

Courtesy of Lani Still Ninemeier, Hilo, Hawaii

Adapted from Hayes, D., Miller, A., and Ninemeier, J. (2012). *The Professional Kitchen Manager.* Pearson Education, Inc.

Color can also be used to promote menu items, but that creates an additional printing expense. Some restaurants use color photos of selected items or color/black-and-white illustrations of concepts in line with the property's theme.

Numerous menu design tactics are important:

- Be sure the menu is attractive and presents a good first impression. Ask yourself, "Am I proud of this menu?"
- Menu type should be easily read
- The menu should not be cluttered
- Make sure that words are correctly spelled and eliminate unnecessary hard-to-read or unfamiliar foreign terms
- The menu should be comfortable to read and handle at the table
- Menus should be durable and easy to clean unless they're disposable (single-use)

Menu layout

A term relating to the placement of menu item categories on the menu.

Prime real estate

The areas on a menu most frequently viewed by guests which should contain the items that menu planners most want to sell.

MENU ITEM LOCATION   The **menu layout** relates to *where* items are placed on the menu. The layout must include space for all menu item categories. Some menu designers place categories on the menu in the sequence of service. However, experienced restaurant managers know that menus have **prime real estate** areas where their most popular and highly profitable items should be placed.

Figure 5.6 shows the prime locations on three common types of menus.

MENU ITEM DESCRIPTIONS   Menu item descriptions answer questions menu readers may have. Consider "Seafood Fettuccine": Will guests know that fettuccine is pasta and what type of seafood and sauce are included? Menu designers should consider what readers must know to make an informed purchase decision and provide this critical information in the menu item's description.

FIGURE 5.6

Prime Locations on Menus

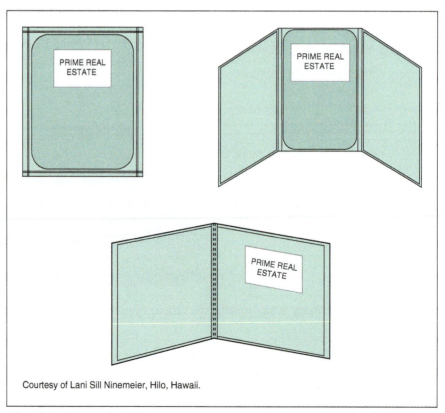

Courtesy of Lani Sill Ninemeier, Hilo, Hawaii.

Adapted from Hayes, D., Miller, A., and Ninemeier, J. (2012). *The Professional Kitchen Manager.* Pearson Education, Inc.

This server is emphasizing menu items that the guest will like and that will be profitable to the restaurant.

Menus designers must write plainly. Avoid technical culinary terms and foreign words that the average guest may not know. Be sure to define menu items correctly. For example, New England clam chowder (white) is not the same as Manhattan clam chowder (red).

Spell words correctly. That means you must carefully check every word! Also, write carefully. For example, only the last description in this list is accurate:

- A delicate seafood fillet served with a baked potato ladled with signature sauce
- A delicate seafood fillet ladled with signature sauce and baked potato
- A delicate seafood fillet ladled with our signature sauce and served with a baked potato

Finally, re-write and re-edit, or retain the services of someone with a solid command of writing and editing skills to do it for you.

WEB AT WORK!

Many companies sell menu design software. To view sites and learn more about this topic, just type "menu design software" into your favorite search engine.

This food presentation is creative and "delivers" the description that was printed in the menu.

Chin Kit Sen/Shutterstock

MENU APPEARANCE   The menu cover provides an early visual impression of the restaurant and the dining experience its guests should expect. Its design must fit with the property's décor and theme. Padded menu covers and backs made from imitation (or genuine!) leather, velvet, or other materials are available. Inexpensive paper covers that change daily are used in properties with **desktop publishing systems**. Menu covers containing see-through "pockets" with the cover on one side and a menu page on the cover's back are also commonly used. Paper menus can be laminated (coated) with a plastic film that makes them easily cleaned.

Other menu appearance concerns include:

- Materials. A menu's construction material affects its durability and ability to be cleaned. If a menu can't be cleaned, it must be discarded regardless of cost.
- Menu shape. An unusual menu shape may help project a particular image. Paper can easily (but not inexpensively!) be cut into shapes other than the typical rectangle.
- Type style. A menu's typeface must be easy to read. Type that is too small or too closely spaced can create confusion. The actual lighting level in the dining area also affects the menu's readability.
- Letter case. Menu copy set primarily in lowercase type is easier to read than type set with all uppercase letters. Variations in type such as italics for emphasis are effective if done sparingly.
- **Cross-selling** opportunities. Information on a dinner menu that promotes a weekend brunch and a description of banquet capabilities or a lunch menu can be useful.
- Property information. Include name, address, telephone and fax numbers, e-mail addresses, and hours of operation on take-home menus.
- Mechanics. The use of color, decorative design details, and **clip-on menus** are important considerations.

Lighter menu colors suggest a warm atmosphere; darker colors on a light background can help emphasize selected items. Decorative details such as pictures, drawings, and designs can add appeal. A menu's graphic design can "bring it all together" and help ensure that the menu is attractive and well-presented.

Desktop publishing system

A personal computer and specific software used to create on-site, high-quality page layouts for menus.

Cross-selling

Tactics to advertise other products or services offered by the restaurant in addition to those on a specific menu.

Clip-on menu

A menu insert or attachment that advertises daily specials or emphasizes other menu items.

WEB AT WORK!

Menu designers can find numerous menu design concepts on the Web. For example:

- Accurate menu descriptions are important. To learn about accuracy in menus, go to:

  www.hotelmule.com

Type "accuracy in menus" in the search box.

- Food allergies create concerns for some guests. To learn about this topic, check out the Food Allergy and Anaphylaxis Network:

  www.foodallergy.org

- Some restaurant guests want nutrition information. Many chain restaurants provide this on their websites (type "restaurant nutrition information" into a search engine) or go to the Dietfacts.com site:

  www.dietfacts.com

FOOD SAFETY

Menu items must be safely prepared. This section reviews basic food handling procedures that should always be followed in every restaurant.

Every year, tens of thousands of cases of foodborne illness are reported. It's likely that many more cases aren't reported. Some of these problems occur in restaurants.

Restaurant managers know that their property's reputation will be affected if foodborne illnesses occur. Outbreaks may make headlines in the newspaper, and local health departments often notify the public about results of their inspections. Furthermore, lawsuits filed by people claiming to have become sick after eating at the property may be successful and can create serious financial problems. Even if they don't, a lot of time and money is typically needed for the legal assistance needed to dispute potential charges of negligence.

Kitchen Sanitation Tour

Let's see how sanitation concerns impact how restaurant managers run their operations.

PURCHASING   Products must be purchased from reliable sources to help ensure they have been produced and handled under sanitary conditions.

Suppliers should use clean delivery vehicles. Refrigerated and frozen products must be kept out of the **temperature danger zone** until they reach the property. There is only a four-hour window of time in which foods can remain in this temperature zone, including the time before the products reach the restaurant. Suppliers' storage facilities must be clean, and products should be properly handled before they reach the receiving area.

Temperature danger zone

The temperature range of 41°F (5°C) to 135°F (57C°) in which harmful germs multiply quickly.

RECEIVING   Employees who receive products must be trained. Fruits and vegetables should be inspected for decay, mold growth, and discoloring; canned items must be checked for bulges and dents along their side seams and rims. Note: Bulges are caused by gas that may have been formed by living germs in the cans, and dents along rims and seams can allow germs to enter the cans.

Frozen foods may have thawed because of improper handling and then refrozen before delivery. Frozen foods that have large ice crystals on their surface and individually quick-frozen (IQF) items (such as peas or corn) that are frozen in clumps instead of in pieces should be rejected.

STORING   Products should be quickly moved from receiving to storage areas. Food should be stored away from walls and at least six inches off the floor, and raw foods should be stored on shelves below cooked and ready-to-eat foods. Items should not be stored under overhead water

The kitchen, which guests generally don't see, must be kept just as clean as the restaurant's public areas.

or sewer lines and should never be located near sanitizing, cleaning, or other chemicals. Proper storage temperatures for food products are:

- Refrigerated food storage: 41°F (5°C) or below
- Frozen food storage: 0°F (−18°C) or below
- Dry storage foods: 50°–70°F (10°–21°C)

Note: Restaurant managers must confirm and always comply with the temperatures cited in applicable food safety codes.

PRODUCTION   Frozen foods should not be thawed at room temperature or left in a sink full of water. Rather, they should be thawed in the refrigerator, as part of the cooking process, or in a sink with cold running water.

Foods in production should remain at room temperature for the shortest time possible. Utensils such as knifes and cutting boards and the work counters upon which they're used should be properly cleaned and sanitized between food preparation tasks to prevent **cross-contamination**. Accurate thermometers must be used to monitor food temperatures.

Frequent hand washing is necessary during food preparation and at all other times during the food handling and serving process.

AFTER-PRODUCTION FOOD HOLDING   Items including casserole dishes and sauces may be held for a long time before service; they must be kept at the proper temperature (above 135°F; 57°C).

Foods held in public areas, including self-service salad or dessert bars or hot food counters, must remain at temperatures of 135°F (57°C) or higher or at 41°F (5°C) or below. These areas must be kept clean, and **sneeze guards** are required by most health codes.

MANAGING LEFTOVERS   Leftover foods to be re-served must be quickly brought to a temperature below 41°F (5°C). This can be done by storing items in shallow containers, using ice baths and frequently stirring products in containers. It's generally best *not* to freeze leftovers for later use because germs can reproduce during the cool-down period. Germs won't die after the product is frozen and will begin to grow and reproduce when the product is thawed.

Cross-contamination

The transfer of harmful germs or bacteria from one surface to another.

Sneeze guards

A see-through barrier to protect foods in self-service counters from guests who might sneeze or cough on them.

> **ALL IN A DAY'S WORK 5.1**
>
> "It's not fair!" said Ned, the kitchen manager at Park Place Bistro. "We were in the middle of our lunch business when the sanitation inspector visited. I admit the kitchen wasn't as clean as it could have been, but we were busier than we should have been!"
>
> "I'm not sure that's a good excuse, Ned," replied Don, the restaurant manager. "The inspector found temperature problems in the refrigerator, no soap in the hand wash area, and ants in the storeroom. Those issues weren't created by a busy shift."
>
> "I'm the manager," Don admitted, "And I'm responsible for the problems and how and when they will be corrected. This must be a priority so we don't harm our guests, employees, or ourselves."
>
> **1.** What should Don do to emphasize the importance of food safety at the restaurant?
> **2.** What tactics should Don and Ned use to ensure that the kitchen remains as clean as possible?

CLEAN-UP **Cleaning** is the removal of soil and pieces of food from items being prepared. After cleaning, some items should be rinsed and sanitized. **Sanitizing** is important for the elimination or the reduction of the number of microorganisms that remain after cleaning.

Plates, knives, and forks along with pots and pans should be cleaned with a detergent or other effective cleaner. They can then be sanitized:

- With heat (typically 180°F [82°C] in mechanical dish or pot/pan washers and 165°F [40°C]) in manual wash sinks; or
- With specially manufactured chemicals; or
- With a combination of heat and chemicals.

Food production and service equipment must be cleaned by following the manufacturer's instructions. Use a clean cloth, brush or scouring pad and warm soapy water. Clean from top-to-bottom or side-to-side and then rinse with fresh water and wipe dry with a clean cloth. An approved chemical sanitizing solution can be spread or sprayed onto food-contact services, and areas should be air-dried before use.

Cleaning chemicals can be dangerous and must be handled carefully. Hand washing sinks must be conveniently located and kept supplied with liquid or powdered (not bar) soap.

Professional waste haulers should frequently remove **refuse** and **garbage**. The areas around dumpsters and other garbage areas must be regularly cleaned and maintained.

Hazard Analysis Critical Control Points

Many restaurant managers implement a system called **hazard analysis critical control points (HACCP)** to continually emphasize sanitation.

Figure 5.7 shows the steps in the HACCP system. It emphasizes anticipating and correcting food safety problems before they occur rather than taking corrective action(s) after a problem arises Identification of **critical control points (CCPs)** focuses attention on the highest priority sanitation concerns, and safe food-handling procedures are incorporated into "how things are done" at the restaurant.

Let's look at the HACCP system steps:

Step 1   *Assess hazards:* Restaurant managers should review their menu items and preparation ingredients and identify those that are the most potentially hazardous. These include foods with high-protein content such as meats, poultry, eggs, and dairy products, and other foods such as beans, pasta and, rice that are frequently contaminated by microorganisms. The HACCP program addresses these biological **hazards** and also emphasizes chemical and/or physical objects that also can contaminate food.

Step 2   *Identify critical control points (CCPs):* Examples of CCPs include cooking, cooling, reheating, and holding hot and cold products at the temperatures which recognize the importance of the danger zone (41° to 135°F; 5° to 57°C). Of these, cooking and reheating relate to efforts to destroy harmful microorganisms. The remaining three (cooling, hot food holding, and cold food holding) involve efforts to prevent or slow bacterial growth.

Cleaning

Removal of soil and food from the items being processed.

Sanitizing

Eliminating or reducing the number of microorganisms on a surface.

Refuse

Solid waste including cardboard and glass that is not removed through the sewage system.

Garbage

Food waste that cannot be recycled.

Hazard analysis critical control points (HACCP)

A practical system using proper food-handling procedures along with monitoring and record keeping to help ensure that food is safe for consumption.

Critical control point (CCP)

Something done in the management of food from receiving to service to helping prevent, eliminate, or reduce hazards.

Hazards

Microorganisms, chemicals, and physical objects that can contaminate food.

FIGURE 5.7

Steps in the HACCP System
Adapted from Hayes, D., Miller, A., and Ninemeier, J. (2012). *The Professional Kitchen Manager.* Pearson Education, Inc.

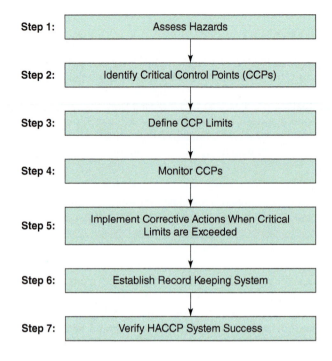

Step 1: Assess Hazards

Step 2: Identify Critical Control Points (CCPs)

Step 3: Define CCP Limits

Step 4: Monitor CCPs

Step 5: Implement Corrective Actions When Critical Limits are Exceeded

Step 6: Establish Record Keeping System

Step 7: Verify HACCP System Success

Critical limit

Maximum/minimum limits that define the extent to which a critical control point must be controlled to minimize foodborne illness risks.

Step 3   *Define CCP limits:* **Critical limits** establish control boundaries. When they're exceeded, hazards may exist or might develop. Each CCP should have a critical limit.

Restaurant managers should establish critical limits based upon food codes, safety experts—including health inspectors—and/or other sources. Critical limits should be easy to measure or observe.

Step 4   *Monitor CCPs:* Some monitoring activities may be continuous (for example, refrigeration units may maintain internal temperature records for later review), and other monitoring may be done at specified intervals. For example, a cook may check the internal temperature of a pasta sauce every 15 minutes when it's being held for service.

Step 5   *Implement corrective actions when critical limits are exceeded:* If the holding temperature of a potentially hazardous food should be below 135°F (57°C), the equipment used to hold it should be checked. Meanwhile, the item should be reheated rapidly. If critical control points are monitored frequently (Step 4), the temperature reduction should be small because ongoing monitoring will have quickly noted that the food was in the temperature. In this situation, the food can be quickly reheated and consumed.

Step 6   *Establish a record-keeping system:* A written HACCP plan should be developed and maintained to provide information about the hazards identified for each menu item/ingredient. The critical control points and their limits should be defined, and procedures and corrective actions taken to address CCPs and their limits should be noted.

HACCP records can be relatively simple to maintain while assuring that information applicable to each HACCP system step is identified for applicable items/ingredients.

Step 7   *Verify HACCP system success:* Verification helps confirm that critical limits established for each CCP will prevent, eliminate, or reduce potential hazards and that the overall HACCP system is working effectively. Review of HACCP plans and CCP records, follow-up on corrective actions, and reviews of procedures to address critical control points are important tactics.

WEB AT WORK!

To learn more about HACCP, check out the following website:

www.allfoodbusiness.com/haacp.php

Other Sanitation Issues

CHEMICAL HAZARDS   Some harmful chemicals occur naturally; one example is the **toxins** (poisons) in shellfish. Others are man-made; examples include food additives and preservatives—such as monosodium glutamate (MSG) or the sulfites in food and wines—that cause illnesses in some persons.

Pesticides are applied to many fruits and vegetables to protect them before harvest. Some of these chemicals can remain on products when they reach the restaurant, so the products must be properly washed. Other chemicals, including those used for facility and equipment cleaning and sanitizing, may get into or onto foods and can cause illness and even death.

Pesticides and other chemicals are used to control insects, rodents, and other pests. These chemicals should be applied by professionals to reduce the chance that residues remain in or on food storage and preparation areas. Chemical poisoning can also occur if foods are stored or processed in some containers such as those made from galvanized metals.

PHYSICAL HAZARDS   Foods can be contaminated with physical hazards such as glassware fragments, metal shavings from can openers, and wood splinters from toothpicks or skewers used in food production. Other contaminants include human hair, food container labels, and stones or rocks in bags of grains.

Food handlers must process foods safely, carefully inspect products being produced and not wear unnecessary jewelry that could be lost during the food production process.

PEST CONTRAL HAZARDS   Rats, mice, flies, and cockroaches carry germs and can contaminate food as they move around preparation areas and onto food ingredients. Restaurant managers must use procedures to prevent their entry into buildings and eliminate food, water, and places where these pests can hide if they enter. An effective pest control program can ensure that preventive actions are working.

Food should be stored properly, and garbage should be kept covered prior to its frequent removal. All areas of the operation should be regularly cleaned, and tight-fitting screens, doors or air curtains help prevent entry of flying insects.

Chemical pest control tactics are needed when the procedures discussed above are ineffective. Signs of rodent infestation include droppings (feces), rub marks along wall baseboards, gnawing marks in wood and tracks in dust.

Rodent control begins with keeping areas free of litter, waste, refuse, unused boxes, crates, and other materials. Traps can also be helpful. A coordinated pest management program is recommended and involves a five-step effort of:

- Inspection
- Identification
- Sanitation
- Use of pest management control procedures
- Evaluation of effectiveness

STANDARDIZED RECIPES: QUALITY CONTROL

Now that you know how to prepare food safely, you're ready to learn how to prepare it consistently. This goal is accomplished by using standard recipes.

All restaurants in every industry segment serving every type of guest need standardized recipes to meet cost and guest expectations. Information in a standardized recipe includes the type and amount of ingredients, preparation procedures including equipment and tools, **yield** and garnishes.

Figure 5.8 shows a sample standardized recipe.

Benefits

The use of standardized recipes helps to ensure consistency, and this benefits the guests and the restaurant. Each time a guest orders the same item it will taste, look, and smell the same. Guests will like this because they can count on receiving consistent value: They'll pay the same amount and will receive the same quality and quantity of the item each time they order it.

Toxin

A poisonous chemical produced by germs or other living things.

Pesticide

A chemical used to kill pests such as rodents or insects.

Yield

The number of servings and the size of each serving produced when a standardized recipe is followed.

FIGURE 5.8

Sample Standardized Recipe

<table>
<tr><td colspan="3" align="center">**Chicken Tetrazzini**</td><td align="right">**No.: 103**</td></tr>
</table>

Chicken Tetrazzini   **No.: 103**

UTENSILS NEEDED: Stock pot, cutting board, French knife, wire whip, mixing bowl, gallon/quart/cup measures, measuring spoons, plastic gloves, clean foodservice cloths, 2 (12″ × 20″ × 2″) steam table pans

YIELD: 48 servings
OVEN TEMP: 350°F (176.6°C)
BAKING TIME: 30 minutes
SERVING SIZE: 1/24 pan
SERVING TOOL: Spatula/spoon

Ingredients	Quantity/Volume	Procedure
Spaghetti	6 lb.	1. Cook spaghetti in salted water. Rinse and drain. *Do not overcook.*
Margarine	2 lb.	2. Cook onions and celery in margarine until transparent.
Celery, cut fine	2 qt.	3. Make roux by adding flour, salt, and pepper to above. Cook 5 minutes.
Onions, cut fine	2 qt.	4. Add chicken stock and cook until thick, stirring as necessary.
Flour, pastry	1 lb., 4 oz.	5. Add cubed chicken (or turkey) and mushrooms; mix.
Salt	1/4 c	6. Add spaghetti; mix well.
Pepper, black	1 tsp	7. Add green peppers just before panning.
Chicken (turkey) stock	2 gal., 2 c	8. Scale 12 lb. into each of 4 (12″ × 20″ × 2″) pans.
Chicken, (turkey) cooked and cubed	12 lb., 8 oz.	9. Mix topping. Top pan with 1 qt. topping.
Mushrooms, fresh/chopped	2 c	10. Bake at 350°F (175°C) for 30 minutes.
Green pepper, chopped	3 c	11. Serving: Divide into servings by cutting pan contents into 6 (length) × 4 (width).
Total weight	48 lb.	*Example:*
Topping		
Bread crumbs, fine	2 qt.	
Sharp cheddar cheese, grated	2 qt.	Holding: Hold prepared product at 140°F until service.

SPECIAL INSTRUCTIONS:

Do not overcook spaghetti. See recipe for chicken stock if none is available.

Adapted from Hayes, D., Miller, A., and Ninemeier, J. (2012). *The Professional Kitchen Manager.* Pearson Education, Inc.

Standardized recipes ensure consistency that the same type and quantity of ingredients are used each time the product is prepared. Also, the yield will be the same, so food costs will be predictable. Thus, the restaurant can best meet its financial goals.

The use of standardized recipes helps the production team prepare the menu items because they indicate:

- Necessary ingredients and their quantity (by weight or volume)
- Required small utensils including measuring tools and pots and pans
- Large equipment, such as ovens, with cooking and baking times and temperatures
- Procedures for pre-preparation, preparation, cooking, holding, and serving
- Yield

The use of standardized recipes helps control labor costs. Since the same preparation activities will be used, it will take approximately the same time to prepare the item, regardless of which employee carries out the work.

> ## WEB AT WORK!
>
> Some restaurant suppliers feature recipes with large quantity yields on their websites. For example, check out those provided by Sysco Corporation:
>
> www.sysco.com/recipes/recipes.htdml

Developing Standardized Recipes

Figure 5.9 shows the steps involved in developing recipes.

Let's review these steps:

Step 1 Observe menu item preparation. The restaurant manager can personally prepare the item or observe employees as they prepare it. What ingredients are used, and in what quantities? How and when are the ingredients weighed and measured? What measuring tools are used, and how is the item portioned after preparation?

Step 2 Consider preparation details. Can some preparation tasks be combined? For example, if smallwares are needed for several preparation steps, a procedure stating, "*Obtain the following items required for preparation*" can be included as an early step.

Step 3 Write recipe draft. A first draft of the recipe that incorporates observations (Step 1) and details (Step 2) now becomes important. A standardized format such as the example in Figure 5.8 can be used.

Step 4 Review and revise recipe draft. The recipe draft (Step 3) should be carefully reviewed and revisions, if necessary, should be made.

Step 5 Use recipe. It should be carefully followed unless obvious production problems are noticed.

Step 6 Evaluate recipe. The recipe used for preparation (Step 5) and the food product it yields should be carefully evaluated to ensure that quality standards are met.

Step 7 Consider further revisions. If Step 6 suggests a problem, further revisions are necessary.

Step 8 Use recipe. After the recipe is finalized, it should be consistently used.

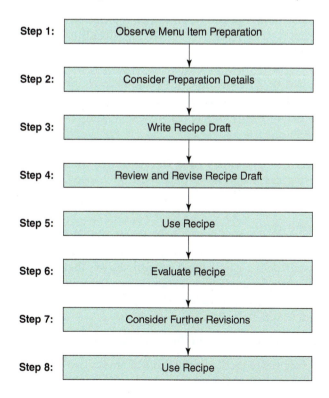

FIGURE 5.9

Standardized Recipe Development
Adapted from Hayes, D., Miller, A., and Ninemeier, J. (2012). *The Professional Kitchen Manager.* Pearson Education, Inc.

FIGURE 5.10

Converting Number of Servings

Recipe conversion factor (RCF)

A factor (number) used to adjust ingredients in a standardized recipe when the number of servings and/or serving size of a current recipe must be changed. To determine this factor:

$$\frac{\text{Desired recipe yield}}{\text{Current recipe yield}} = \text{Recipe conversion factor}$$

Assume the current standardized recipe yields 40 servings (3 ounces each), and 70 servings (3 ounces each) are desired. What quantity of each ingredient is needed for the converted recipe?

Step 1: Calculate the recipe conversion factor (RCF):

$$\frac{\text{Number of desired servings (3 ounces)}}{\text{Number of current servings (3 ounces)}} = \frac{70}{40} = 1.75 \text{ RCF}$$

Step 2: Multiply the quantity of each ingredient in the current recipe by the RCF.

Example: Assume 6 ounces of flour are specified in the current recipe. The amount of flour needed in the revised recipe is 10.5 ounces:

6 ounces of flour (current recipe)	×	1.75 RCF (recipe conversion factor)	=	10.5 ounces of flour (new recipe)

Adapted from Hayes, D., Miller, A., and Ninemeier, J. (2012). *The Professional Kitchen Manager.* Pearson Education, Inc.

Standardized recipes with large quantity yields are readily available in innumerable cookbooks and on the World Wide Web. Many restaurant managers, like other professionals, are connected to a network of people in other organizations who are also excellent sources of potential recipes.

Recipes from external sources should be thoroughly tested before being fully implemented. Careful evaluation, changes, if necessary, and further testing may be in order.

Recipe Conversion Factors

Sometimes recipes with desired yields are available. Frequently, however, recipes must be converted (adjusted) to meet the restaurant's specific needs. Three basic types of recipe conversions may be needed.

CONVERTING NUMBER OF SERVINGS Sometimes, a recipe has the desired serving size (for example, 3 ounces), but it yields more or fewer servings than is needed. What should be done? Let's look at Figure 5.10.

CONVERTING SERVING SIZE Sometimes a standardized recipe yields the required number of servings, but different serving sizes are needed. For example, an existing recipe may yield 70 three-ounce servings of tuna salad but 70 four-ounce servings are desired. Figure 5.11 shows how to make this conversion.

CONVERTING NUMBER OF SERVINGS AND SERVING SIZE Sometimes both the number of servings and the serving sizes in a revised recipe must be changed. This process is illustrated in Figure 5.12.

Recipe Measurements

Recipe ingredients must always be carefully weighed, counted or measured. It's important to express the amounts required for a standardized recipe in the way that's easiest for preparation personnel to weigh or measure the ingredients. Figure 5.13 contains information about the U.S. and metric measurement and weight systems that will help to convert and use standardized recipes.

STANDARDIZED RECIPES: COSTING PROCEDURES

Recipe costing

The process of determining the food cost per portion (serving) and the total food cost to prepare all portions in a standardized recipe.

When standardized recipes are used, menu items will always cost a known amount to prepare because there will be no variation between the amount of ingredients required by the recipe and the amount actually used. It then becomes possible to calculate the menu item's food cost in a process called **recipe costing**.

FIGURE 5.11

Converting the Serving Size

Assume the current recipe yields 70 servings (3 ounces each), and 70 servings (4 ounces each) is needed.

Step 1: Calculate the recipe conversion factor (RCF):

$$\frac{\text{Number of desired servings} \, (\times) \, \text{serving size (4 ounces)}}{\text{Number of current servings} \, (\times) \, \text{serving size (3 ounces)}}$$

$$= \frac{70 \, (\times) \, 4 \, \text{oz.}}{70 \, (\times) \, 3 \, \text{oz.}} = \frac{280 \, \text{oz.}}{210 \, \text{oz.}} = 1.33 \, \text{RCF}$$

Step 2: Multiply the quantity of each ingredient in the current recipe by the RCF.

Example: Assume 12 ounces of chopped onion are specified in the current recipe. The amount of chopped onion needed in the revised recipe is 16 ounces (1 pound):

12 ounces of onion (current amount)	×	1.33 RCF (recipe conversion factor)	=	15.96 ounces of onion (1 pound*) (new recipe)

*Note: There are 16 ounces in 1 pound, so the restaurant manager would round up 15.96 ounces to 1 pound of chopped onion.

Adapted from Hayes, D., Miller, A., and Ninemeier, J. (2012). *The Professional Kitchen Manager.* Pearson Education, Inc.

FIGURE 5.12

Converting Number of Servings and Serving Sizes

Assume the current recipe yields 50 servings (¼ cup each), and 70 servings (¾ cup each) are desired.

Step 1: Calculate the recipe conversion factor:

Desired recipe volume/Current recipe volume

$$= \frac{70 \, (\times) \, \frac{3}{4} \, \text{cup}}{50 \, (\times) \, \frac{1}{4} \, \text{cup}}$$

$$= \frac{52.50 \, \text{cups}}{12.50 \, \text{cups}}$$

$$= 4.20 \, (\text{rounded})$$

Step 2: Multiply the quantity of each ingredient in the current recipe by the RCF.

Example: assume that 3 ounces of flour is specified in the current recipe. The amount of flour needed in the revised recipe is:

3 ounces (current amount)	×	4.2 RCF (recipe conversion factor)	=	12.5 ounces (rounded) (new recipe)

Adapted from Hayes, D., Miller, A., and Ninemeier, J. (2012). *The Professional Kitchen Manager.* Pearson Education, Inc.

Accurate recipe costing also helps restaurant managers because:

- They can evaluate the costs of items being offered on "help yourself" buffets and salad bars. If product costs are excessive, they can replace some higher cost items with lower cost items or consider increasing buffet/salad bar selling prices.
- Managers can use per portion cost information when establishing menu selling prices.

FIGURE 5.13

Common U.S. and Metric Measurements and Weights

Part I: Volume Measure—Gallon to Teaspoons

1 gallon	=	4 quarts	=	128 fluid ounces
1 quart	=	2 pints	=	32 fluid ounces
1 pint	=	2 cups	=	16 fluid ounces
1 cup	=	16 tablespoons	=	8 fluid ounces
1 tablespoon	=	3 teaspoons	=	½ fluid ounces

Part II: Volume Measures—Cup to 1/2 Tablespoon

1 cup	=	16 tablespoons
¾ cup	=	12 tablespoons
⅔ cup	=	10 tablespoons + 2 teaspoons
½ cup	=	8 tablespoons
⅓ cup	=	5 tablespoons + 1 teaspoon
¼ cup	=	4 tablespoons
⅓ cup	=	2 tablespoons
1 tablespoon	=	3 teaspoons
½ tablespoon	=	1½ teaspoons

Part III: Weight-Pounds to Ounces

1 pound	=	16 ounces
¾ pound	=	12 ounces
½ pound	=	8 ounces
¼ pound	=	4 ounces
1 ounce	=	½ fluid ounce

Part IV: Metric Weight and Volume Measurements

1 kilo	=	1000 grams (weight)
1000 milliliters	=	1 liter (volume)

Part V: U.S Measurements and Metric Equivalents

Volume	
U.S	**Metric**
Gallon	3.79 liters
Quart	.95 liters
Pint	473* milliliters
Cups	237* milliliters
Tablespoon	15* milliliters
Teaspoon	5* milliliters
Weight	
Pound	455* grams
¾ pound (12 oz.)	340* grams
½ pound (8 oz.)	228* grams
¼ pound (4 oz.)	114* grams
1 ounce	30* grams

*Indicates rounded amount

Adapted from Hayes, D., Miller, A., and Ninemeier, J. (2012). *The Professional Kitchen Manager.* Pearson Education, Inc.

ALL IN A DAY'S WORK 5.2

"I've been cooking for many years and have never had a problem until now. The new manager has just arrived and has told us we need to write down our recipes and use them all the time!"

Ronnie was talking to his friend, Carl, a bar manager at another restaurant.

"I know what you mean," Carl replied. "We got a new manager about two years ago, and he made us standardize our beverage recipes. It was a lot of work."

"What happened after the new recipe system was in place?" asked Ronnie.

1. Assume that many of the benefits discussed in this chapter were realized at Carl's bar. What are some responses Carl likely made to Ronnie?
2. If you were Carl, what advice would you give to your friend to minimize stress during the recipe development process?

Costing Recipe Ingredients

Recipe costing allows restaurant managers to know the cost of each ingredient used in a recipe. it is easy when the **purchase unit** is the same for the item when it's purchased and used. Consider whole milk that is purchased by the gallon:

Purchase unit

The unit weight, volume, or container size in which a product is purchased.

Purchase unit	Cost per purchase unit	Quantity in recipe	Ingredient (milk) cost
Gallon	$2.80	2 gallons	$5.60

Costing is more difficult when an ingredient is purchased in one purchase unit and used in the recipe in a variation of that purchase unit. To further illustrate this example, consider fluid whole milk:

Purchase unit	Cost per purchase unit	Quantity in recipe	Ingredient (milk) cost
Gallon	$2.80	2 quarts	$1.40*

*There are 4 quarts in one gallon: 4 quarts (one gallon) cost $2.80 so one quart costs $.70 ($2.80 per gallon ÷ 4 quarts = $.70). The cost of milk in the recipe is $1.40 ($.70 per quart x 2 quarts = $1.40).

The ingredient costing process becomes even more challenging when an ingredient is purchased in one purchase unit and used in an entirely different purchase unit:

Celery costs $1.69 per pound, and 1cup of chopped celery is needed in the recipe. To cost this ingredient, two things must be known:

- How to convert pounds (weight) to cups (volume).
- How much celery is lost in cleaning and removing celery leaves and ends. For example, 1pound (16 ounces) of celery as purchased may yield only 14 ounces of chopped celery for the recipe.

Fortunately, guides to **edible food yields** are available. They eliminate the time otherwise needed to conduct yield tests to determine the quantity (weight and number of cups) of cleaned, chopped celery in a pound.

Edible food yield

The useable amount of a food ingredient that can be prepared from a given purchase unit of that ingredient.

WEB AT WORK!

To see numerous charts and tables that provide volume and weight conversions for commonly used ingredients, just type "edible food yields" into your favorite search engine.

Figure 5.14 shows how to cost the recipe originally shown in Figure 5.8.
Let's look at each ingredient in more detail.

- *Item A: Spaghetti.* 6 pounds are needed (column 2), the purchase unit is pound (column 3), and the cost per purchase unit is $1.03 (column 4).

$$6 \text{ pounds} \times \$1.03 = \$6.18$$
$$(\text{col.2}) \times (\text{col.4}) \quad (\text{col.6})$$

FIGURE 5.14

Recipe Costing Worksheet

Recipe: _____ Chicken Tetrazzini _____
Yield: _____ 48 _____ servings   Serving Size: _____ 1/24 (12" × 20" × 2" pan)

Ingredient (1)	Amount (2)	Purchase Unit (3)	Cost Per Purchase Unit (4)	No. of Purchase Units (5)	Ingredient Cost (6)
(A) Spaghetti	6 lb.	(lb)	$1.03	6	$ 6.18
(B) Margarine	2 lb.	(lb)	.89	2	1.78
(C) Celery	2 qt.	Bunch	.99	1.5	1.49
(D) Onions	2 qt.	(lb)	1.69	2.2	3.72
(E) Flour	1 lb., 4 oz.	(lb)	2.10	1.25	2.63
(F) Salt	2.5 oz.	(lb)	.88	.16	.14
(G) Pepper	1 tsp.	(lb)	—	—	—
(H) Chicken stock	2 gal., 2 c	—	—	—	—
(I) Chicken	12 lb., 8 oz.	(lb)	2.35	26	61.10
(J) Mushrooms	2 c	(lb)	4.95	.33	1.63
(K) Green pepper	3 c	(lb)	3.05	1.2	3.66
(L) Bread crumbs	2 qt.	(lb)	1.90	1.75	3.33
(M) Sharp cheese, shredded	2 qt.	(lb)	5.25	2.0	10.50

Total Cost: $96.17

Abbreviations used: lb = pound; qt = quart; oz. = ounce; c = cup; gal = gallon; tsp. = teaspoon

Adapted from Hayes, D., Miller, A., and Ninemeier, J. (2012). *The Professional Kitchen Manager.* Pearson Education, Inc.

- *Item B: Margarine.* 2 pounds are needed (column 2), the purchase unit is pound (column 3), and the cost per purchase unit is .89 (column 4).

$$2 \text{ pounds} \times \$ .89 = \$1.78$$
$$(\text{col.2}) \times (\text{col.4}) \quad (\text{col.6})$$

- *Item C: Celery.* 2 quarts are needed (column 2), the purchase unit is bunch (column 3), and the cost per purchase unit is .99 (column 4). To cost this item, the purchase unit (bunch in column 3) must be converted to the amount needed (quart in column 2). One bunch of celery weighs about 2 pounds (32 ounces; as purchased [AP] weight) and yields 22 ounces after cleaning and trimming. One cup of cleaned/trimmed celery weighs 4 ounces. Therefore, there are 5.5 cleaned/trimmed cups per bunch of celery:

22 oz.		4.0 oz.		5.5 cups
(bunch of cleaned/ trimmedcelery)	÷	(cup of cleaned/ trimmedcelery)	=	(cleaned/timmed celery per bunch)

The recipe requires 2 qts. (col. 2) which is 8 cups:

$$2 \text{ qts.} \times 4 \text{ cups/quart} = 8 \text{ cups}$$

Therefore, 1.5 bunches (as purchased) are needed:

8 cups needed		5.5 cups		1.5 bunches (rounded)
(2 quarts in col.2)	÷	(cups of celery/bunch)	=	(cleaned/timmed)

$$
\underset{\substack{\text{(amount of celery} \\ \text{needed)}}}{1.5 \text{ bunches needed}} \times \underset{\substack{\text{(cost/purchase} \\ \text{unit in col.4)}}}{.99} = \underset{\substack{\text{(celery cost in} \\ \text{recipe [col.6])}}}{\$1.49}
$$

- *Item D: Onions.* 2 quarts are needed (column 2), the purchase unit is pound (column 3) and the cost per purchase unit is $1.69 (column 4).
  One cup of trimmed/cleaned onions weighs 4 ounces. One pound (16 ounces) of onions weighs 14.5 ounces after cleaning and trimming. Therefore, 1 pound of onions (AP) yields 3.6 cups of trimmed/cleaned (EP) onions:

$$
\underset{\substack{\text{(trimmed/deaned} \\ \text{onions/pound}}}{14.5 \text{ oz.}} \div \underset{\substack{\text{(cup of trimmed/} \\ \text{clean onions)}}}{4 \text{ oz.}} = \underset{\substack{\text{(trimmed/deaned} \\ \text{onions/pound)}}}{3.6 \text{ cups}}
$$

The restaurant manager requires 2.2 pounds (as purchased) of onions:

$$
\underset{\text{((2 quarts in col.2)}}{8 \text{ cups}} \div \underset{\substack{\text{(trimmed/deaned} \\ \text{onions/pound)}}}{3.6 \text{ cups}} = 2.2 \text{ pounds}
$$

$$
\underset{\substack{\text{(amount of onion} \\ \text{needed)}}}{2.2 \text{ pounds}} \times \underset{\substack{\text{(cost/purchase} \\ \text{unit in [col.4])}}}{\$1.69} = \underset{\substack{\text{(onion cost} \\ \text{in recipe)}}}{\$3.72}
$$

- *Item E: Flour.* One pound, 4 ounces are needed (column 2). Therefore, 1.25 pounds of flour are required: 1 pound + .25 pound = 1.25 pounds

The total cost of flour required for the recipe is $2.63:

$$
\underset{\substack{\text{(amount of flour} \\ \text{needed)}}}{1.25 \text{ pounds}} \times \underset{\substack{\text{(cost of flour per} \\ \text{pound [col.4])}}}{\$2.10} = \underset{\substack{\text{(cost of flour in} \\ \text{recipe [col.6])}}}{\$2.63}
$$

- *Item F: Salt.* 2.5 ounces of salt are needed (column 2); the purchase unit is pound (column 3) and the cost per purchase unit is .88 (column 4).

$$
\underset{\text{(cost per pound)}}{.88} \div \underset{\text{(ounces in pound)}}{16 \text{ oz.}} = \underset{\text{(cost per ounce)}}{\$0.055}
$$

$$
\underset{\text{(cost per ounce)}}{\$.055} \times \underset{\substack{\text{(amount of salt} \\ \text{needed [col.2])}}}{2.5 \text{ oz.}} = \underset{\substack{\text{(cost of salt in} \\ \text{recipe [col. 6])}}}{\$0.14}
$$

- *Item G: Pepper.* The amount of pepper (1 teaspoon in column 2) is judged to be insignificant; no cost is calculated for this ingredient (column 6).
- *Item H: Chicken stock.* While a large amount of chicken stock is needed for the recipe (2 gallons + 2 cups in column 2), there is no direct cost for this ingredient because it's made in-house from chicken bones and vegetable trimmings. Restaurant managers who buy chicken stock could, of course, include their actual ingredient cost.
- *Item I: Chicken.* 12 pounds + 8 ounces are needed (column 2), the purchase unit is pound (column 3) and the cost per purchase unit is $2.35 (column 4).

The restaurant manager must convert the **as purchased (AP)** yield of one pound of raw chicken to its **edible portion (EP)**.
A table of edible food yields indicates that 1 pound of chicken (whole bird, large fryer) has a 48% yield. The recipe requires 200 ounces of edible chicken: 12 pounds × 16 ounces/pound + 8 oz. = 200 oz.

As purchased (AP)

The weight of a product before it's prepared or cooked; also called "AP weight."

Edible portion (EP)

The amount of a food item that can be served to guests after a product is cooked. For example, a hamburger patty that weighs 4 ounces before cooking may only weigh 3.6 ounces after cooking.

Therefore, 26 pounds of chicken must be purchased to yield 200 oz. for the recipe:

$$\frac{200 \text{ (edible oz. needed)}}{.48 \text{ (percent yield)}} = \frac{417 \text{ oz.}}{\text{(ounces to purchase)}}$$

$$\frac{417 \text{ (edible oz. needed)}}{16 \text{ (ounces/pound)}} = 26 \text{ pounds}$$

$$\begin{array}{c} 26 \text{ pounds} \\ \text{(amount of chicken} \\ \text{to purchase)} \end{array} \times \begin{array}{c} \$2.35 \\ \text{(cost/pound)} \end{array} = \begin{array}{c} \$61.10 \\ \text{(chicken cost in} \\ \text{recipe[col.6])} \end{array}$$

- *Item J: Mushrooms.* 2 cups are needed (col. 2), the purchase unit is pound (column 3) and the cost per purchase unit is \$4.95 (column 4). Mushrooms are purchased by weight but used in a volume measurement in the recipe. A table of edible food yields indicates that 1 pound of mushrooms yields 6.0 cleaned cups of whole mushrooms. Therefore, the recipe requires .33 pounds:

$$\begin{array}{c} 6.0 \\ \text{(cups per pound)} \end{array} \div \begin{array}{c} 2 \\ \text{(cups needed)} \end{array} = 3$$

$$\frac{1.0 \text{ pound}}{3} = .33 \text{ pound needed}$$

$$\begin{array}{c} \$4.95 \\ \text{(cost per pound)} \end{array} \times \begin{array}{c} .33/\text{pound} \\ \text{(amount needed)} \end{array} = \begin{array}{c} \$1.63 \\ \text{(mushroom cost} \\ \text{in recipe [col. 6])} \end{array}$$

- *Item K: Green pepper.* An edible food yield table is required to determine the cost of green peppers:
  1 pound (16 oz. as purchased) yields 81.3% (13 oz.) edible portion:

$$16 \text{ oz.} \times 81.3 = 13 \text{ oz.}$$

1 cup of cleaned green pepper weighs 5.2 oz. so 1 pound (AP) of green peppers yields 2.5 cups:

$$13 \text{ oz.} \div 5.2 \text{ oz.} = 2.5 \text{ cups}$$

Therefore, 1.2 pounds (AP) of green pepper are required:

$$\begin{array}{c} 3.0 \text{ cups} \\ \text{(amount needed)} \end{array} \div \begin{array}{c} 2.5 \text{ cups} \\ \text{(amount/pound)} \end{array} = \begin{array}{c} 1.2 \text{ pounds} \\ \text{(amount to purchase)} \end{array}$$

$$\begin{array}{c} 1.2 \text{ pounds} \\ \text{(amount of green pepper} \\ \text{to purchase)} \end{array} \times \begin{array}{c} \$3.05 \\ \text{(cost per pound)} \end{array} = \begin{array}{c} \$3.66 \\ \text{(green pepper cost} \\ \text{in recipe [col.6])} \end{array}$$

- *Item L: Bread crumbs.* 2 quarts are needed (column 2), the purchase unit is pound (column 3) and the cost per purchase unit is \$1.90 (column 4). A table of edible food yields indicates that there are 4.6 cups of bread crumbs per pound. The recipe requires 8 cups (2 quarts × 4 cups/quart), so 1.75 pounds are needed:

$$\begin{array}{c} 8 \text{ cups} \\ \text{(amount needed)} \end{array} \div \begin{array}{c} 4.6 \text{ cups} \\ \text{(cups/pound)} \end{array} = \begin{array}{c} 1.75 \text{ pounds} \\ \text{(rounded)} \end{array}$$

$$\begin{array}{c} 1.75 \text{ pounds} \\ \text{(amount needed)} \end{array} \times \begin{array}{c} \$1.90 \\ \text{(cost per pound)} \end{array} = \begin{array}{c} \$3.33 \\ \text{(bread crumb cost} \\ \text{in recipe [col.6])} \end{array}$$

- *Item M: Sharp cheese.* 2 quarts are needed (column 2), the purchase unit is pound (column 3), and the cost is $5.25 per pound (column 4).

A table of edible food yields indicates that there are 4.0 cups of shredded (grated) cheddar cheese per pound. The recipe requires 8 cups (2 quarts × 4 cups per quart), so 2 pounds of cheese are required:

8 cups	÷	4 cups	=	2 pounds
(amount needed)		(amount of cheese/pound)		

2 pounds	×	$5.25	=	$10.50
(amount needed)		(cost per pound)		(cheese cost in recipe [col.6])

Each ingredient in the standardized recipe has now been calculated. While the process takes time, the benefits, including knowledge of product costs for menu item pricing decisions, are worth the effort. As you'll learn below, computerized costing is increasingly being used to quicken the process and better ensure accurate calculations.

Other Costing Procedures

After ingredient costs in the standardized recipe shown in Figure 5.14 are known, the total food cost to produce the recipe is known: $96.17 (see the bottom of column 6). Several other recipe costing procedures are then useful.

PORTION COSTS The food cost required to produce one serving of chicken tetrazzini in Figure 5.14 can be calculated:

$97.17	/	48	=	$2.00
(total recipe cost)		(recipe yield − no. of servings)		(per serving cost)

$96.17	÷	48	=	$2.00

Note: The per serving (portion) cost will only be this amount if (a) standardized recipes are carefully followed; (b) if ingredients are carefully weighed, measured and counted; and (c) if the standardized recipe has been costed using prices currently being paid for its ingredients.

PLATE COSTS Some restaurants such as quick service properties price all items such as sandwiches and salads separately. When this pricing plan is used, the food costs for each meal can easily be determined by adding the per-serving cost of each item.

In many other restaurants, however, several food items prepared with different recipes are ordered by the guests. For example, they may order entrée items with **accompaniments** such as salad and choice of potato and vegetable included in the selling price. Then the cost of one serving of a specific food item must be combined with the costs of other food items to determine the total food cost for the guest's meal.

Figure 5.15 shows how to determine the total of all per-serving costs for menu items in a specific meal. It indicates that the total **plate cost** (food cost) for the "fresh white fish dinner" will be $6.89. Note that guests have a choice of three potatoes and four vegetables and may choose between tossed green, Caesar, and spinach salads. Those selecting the tossed green salad have a choice of five dressings.

How were the costs of potato, vegetable, salad, and dressing choices calculated since each item likely has a different food cost, and guests will likely order different items with their entree? One approach is to use the highest-cost choice in each category. For example, if a serving of twice-baked potatoes costs more than other potato choices, its cost would be used in the plate cost calculation.

Accompaniment

An item such as a salad or potato offered with and included within an entree's selling price.

Plate cost

The total of all per-serving costs for menu items included in a specific meal.

FIGURE 5.15

Calculation of Plate Cost

Entrée:	Fresh White Fish Dinner	
Costing Date:	8/03/20XX	

Item	Menu Item	Cost Per Serving
Entrée	Fresh white fish	$ 4.23
Potato	Three choices daily	0.37
Vegetable	Four choices daily	0.42
Salad	Tossed green, Caesar, or spinach	1.12
Dressing	5 choices daily	0.37
Garnish	Lemon wheels	0.02
Bread Loaf		0.27
Butter	Butter/margarine	0.06
Condiment(s)		0.03
	Total Entrée and Accompaniments Cost	$6.89

Adapted from Hayes, D., Miller, A., and Ninemeier, J. (2012). *The Professional Kitchen Manager.* Pearson Education, Inc.

You have several alternatives when the purchase cost of an accompaniment choice increases significantly. You may choose to:

- Replace it with another within the food cost limits for the accompaniment's cost
- Retain it on the menu but price it on an à la carte basis and supplement the item with another choice within cost limitations
- Serve guests a smaller portion size
- Raise the food cost limit allowed for the choice

COSTING "HELP YOURSELF" ITEMS How are food costs determined when guests serve themselves at a "help yourself" buffet or salad bar? Figure 5.16 illustrates a useful worksheet for calculating these costs.

Note that the chicken tetrazzini prepared according to the standardized recipe illustrated in Figure 5.8 is available on the buffet (column 1). A pan containing 24 servings is issued at the beginning of the service (column 2). During the meal period, 60 additional servings were brought to the buffet line (see columns 3 to 5), and 84 servings were available during the meal period (column 6). When buffet service ended, 8 servings of chicken tetrazzini remained (column 7) so 76 portions were served (84 servings – 8 servings). Since each serving costs $2.01 (column 9), the total food cost for all servings of chicken tetrazzini is $152.76 (76 servings × $2.01 = $152.76). The process just described is repeated for all other buffet items.

The total item food cost (column 10) for all items is calculated and divided by the number of buffet guests to calculate the average per-serving cost. In Figure 5.16, the total item food cost is $1386.75. There were 142 guests, so the per-serving food cost was $9.77 ($1,386.75 ÷ 142 = $9.77).

The process of determining per-serving costs on buffet or salad bars does not need to be ongoing. For example, the worksheet in Figure 5.16 could be used for several meal periods, and the results could be averaged to calculate the average per serving costs. As product costs change over time and/or as the variety of self-service items change, the costing process should be repeated to determine current costs.

Food costing is increasingly done with computers using off-the-shelf **recipe management software** that maintains three food cost-related files: **ingredient file**, **standardized recipe file,** and **menu item file**. This software typically includes applications for inventory and purchasing (ordering).

Let's look at each of these files more closely:

- Ingredient file: With some computerized systems, the ingredient file is available through inventory software that maintains information about the quantity and cost of items in

Recipe management software

Written programs, procedures, instructions, or rules relating to computer system operation that involves standardized recipes.

Ingredient file

A computerized record with information about each ingredient purchased including purchase unit size and cost, issue unit size and cost and recipe unit size and cost.

Standardized recipe file

A computerized record containing recipes for the menu items produced including each recipe's ingredients, preparation method, yield, ingredient costs, and each item's selling price and food cost percentage.

Menu item file

A computerized record with information about each menu item's sales as recorded by the restaurant's point-of-sale (POS) system.

FIGURE 5.16

Costing Sheet for Self-Service Items

Self-Serve Item	No. Servings (Beginning)	No. of Serving Refills			Total Servings	Leftover Servings	Total Servings	Per Serving Cost	Item Cost
(1)	(2)	(3)	(4)	(5)	(6)	(7)	(8)	(9)	(10)
Chicken Tetrazzini	24	24	24	12	84	8	76	2.01	152.76

Total: $1,386.75

$1386.75	÷	142	=	$9.77 (rounded)
Food cost (column 10)	÷	number of guests	=	Per-serving cost

Adapted from Hayes, D., Miller, A., and Ninemeier, J. (2012). *The Professional Kitchen Manager.* Pearson Education, Inc.

current inventory and which have been issued. Ingredient file information must be current and accurate because it drives the standardized recipe and menu item files.

- Standardized recipe file: Electronic systems can determine recipe yields based upon estimated yields and then print a recipe converted for the desired amount. Recipe conversion software can convert recipe ingredients from weight to volume measurements or vice-versa and then calculate the ingredient costs for the recipe.
- Menu item file: This record contains POS data including the menu item's selling price, ingredient quantities and unit sales totals.

Some time is needed for the on-going task of up-dating ingredient files when, for example, purchase prices change. However, significantly less time is needed to maintain current ingredient

Managers at this restaurant know what the food on this buffet costs and use the information to establish its selling price.

© Nigel Blythe/Alamy

WEB AT WORK!

Want to learn more about recipe management software? If so, go to any of the following sites:

CostGuard Foodservice Software
www.costguard.com

Eatec Corporation
www.eatec.com

FOOD-TRAK Software
www.foodtrak.com

costs in standardized recipes when electronic rather than manual calculations are made. For example, if five recipes use canned tomato sauce and its cost increases, the restaurant manager need only to change the price once in the ingredient file, and the new cost will carry over to and adjust each affected standardized recipe.

Restaurant Terms and Concepts

Value 82
Resources 83
Controller 83
Serving cost 83
Investment 83
Standardized recipe 84
Menu category 84
Entrée 84
Table turn 85
Menu rationalization 85
Market form 85
Moist heat 85
Dry heat 85
Food allergy 86
Organic foods 86

Texture 86
Fusion cuisine 86
Umami 86
Center of the plate 87
Cycle menu 87
Du jour menu 87
Die-cut menu 88
Merchandising 89
Menu layout 90
Prime real estate 90
Desktop publishing
    system 92
Cross-selling 92
Clip-on menu 92
Temperature danger zone 93

Cross-contamination 94
Sneeze guards 94
Cleaning 95
Sanitizing 95
Refuse 95
Garbage 95
Hazard analysis critical
    control points
    (HACCP) 95
Critical control point
    (CCP) 95
Hazards 95
Critical limit 96
Toxin 97
Pesticide 97

Yield 97
Recipe conversion factor
    (RCF) 100
Recipe costing 100
Purchase unit 103
Edible food yield 103
As purchased (AP) 105
Edible portion (EP) 105
Accompaniment 107
Plate cost 107
Recipe management
    software 108
Ingredient file 108
Standardized recipe file 108
Menu item file 108

Work in Progress

1. This chapter points out that it's important to learn as much as possible about the concerns and personal factors of those in a restaurant's targeted market (see Figure 5.1). What are practical ways to do this?

2. What are some ways that you as a menu planner could consider your restaurant's financial objectives as you plan the menu?

3. This chapter mentioned mailing menus to potential guests as an advertising technique. What are other ways that a restaurant can use a menu to advertise?

4. What are some things that you personally like and dislike about menu design that you notice when you read a printed menu or look at a menu board?

5. What do you think if you're seated in a restaurant and receive a menu that is dirty, wrinkled or just plain unattractive? How, if at all, does this influence your thoughts about the property?

6. If you as a restaurant manager were asked to provide information to service staff about wine, what topics would you discuss?

7. What can you do as a restaurant manager in a busy work environment to develop and deliver high-quality sanitation training for your employees?

8. Assume you are the owner of a small restaurant, and only you and some of your close family members prepare the food. Do you think standardized recipes would be necessary for your operation? Why or why not?

9. What are some common reasons why you think some restaurant managers may not want to use standardized recipes? If you were their boss, how would you counter these reasons?

10. Do you think it's important to cost ingredients in recipes that are required in very small quantities, such as 1 or 2 teaspoons or ounces in a recipe yielding 50 or more servings? Why or why not?

6
The Restaurant Facility

Learning Objectives

After carefully reading and studying the information in this chapter, you will be able to:

1. Understand basic procedures to plan restaurant layouts that promote employee productivity and please guests.

2. Describe equipment used for food storage, production, holding, and serving.

3. Explain design basics for drive-through and carryout food services.

IN THIS CHAPTER

Ideally, restaurant managers would develop a menu and then determine the type of equipment needed to produce the required items. They could then design the kitchen to incorporate the equipment in a way that maximizes worker productivity. There is, however, only one opportunity to do this: when the building is originally built. After that, equipment and **layout** concerns are typically addressed with time-consuming and expensive remodeling. Therefore, an existing kitchen can create challenges as menus evolve to better please guests or as the building serves as "host" to successive restaurants through ownership changes.

Changes in dining areas are also impacted by previous layout and equipment selection decisions. An ill-designed dining room requiring service personnel to make unnecessary trips between point-of-sale equipment and beverage and food pickup areas creates higher-than-necessary service costs and guest complaints.

Layout

A sketch often drawn to scale showing the relationship of workstations to each other.

Pantry

The workstation in which servers pick up items including desserts and pre-made salads that aren't portioned by production staff.

Workstation

An area with necessary equipment in which closely related work activities are done by employees working in similar positions; for example, dishwashers perform tasks in a dishwashing workstation.

Entrances unnecessarily far from parking areas and restrooms accessed by passage through bar areas can also create problems. In addition, inadequate dining space reduces seating capacity and can reduce revenue potential.

Our study of restaurant design and equipment concerns begins as we consider back-of-house receiving, storage, food pickup and **pantry** areas, and pot/pan and dishwashing stations. We'll address design and equipment issues affecting the bar and lounge **workstations**, reception, dining and banquet areas, and food server stations. Finally, we'll "put it all together" and illustrate a possible restaurant layout that incorporates the principles that were discussed.

Many quick-service restaurants generate significant revenues from drive-through sales and, increasingly, restaurants in the casual service and other segments serve customers who place carryout orders. The chapter concludes with a discussion of design considerations for these services.

RESTAURANT LAYOUT AND DESIGN

Planning a restaurant is not easy. With the exception of some chain restaurant companies that offer the same menu in buildings of similar size, one does not take a building plan for one restaurant and use it for another. Instead, restaurant planners must consider the guests who will be served and the employees who will provide the products and services that are offered. Every decision is important because, after a building is constructed, it may not be possible or, at the least, it can be expensive to make structural and/or design changes. Then the building's layout and the equipment will impact menu planning alternates. For example, if the kitchen doesn't have deep frying equipment and proper ventilation, it will be expensive to install it later even if space is available. Future menu planners may need to create menus that don't feature deep-fried items.

Therefore, it's important for architects, designers, and restaurant managers who provide planning input to "get it right the first time." While they must consider the initial menu, they must also allow flexibility to accommodate changing guest preferences. Their task is made challenging because of the need to have a production operation at the same location where a pleasant environment must be available for guests who enjoy their meals onsite.

Members of the restaurant's planning team must work together cooperatively during construction. It's best to employ experienced personnel who will be able to "deliver" the restaurant project within budget and on time. Team members should include:

- *The owner.* The owner invests significant financial resources in the business and wants to attain financial goals, so the owner's input is critical. This individual, or a personal representative, will be a key decision-maker because he or she has the responsibility of paying for the services of all the other team members.
- *The architect.* This specialist should have restaurant and other food service operation design experience. He or she receives abstract ideas from the owner and then develops them into defined plans. Additional information, including basic building design concerns will likely need to be obtained from this professional before the "go ahead" decision to build the restaurant is even made.
- *The restaurant manager.* This person with knowledge and experience in day-to-day operations should be an integral member of the team and provide input about "how the restaurant should work."
- *The chef.* This food production specialist will have useful ideas about equipment and workflow design useful for the opening menu and general ideas about features that will provide flexibility as menus change.
- *The designer.* Sometimes a kitchen or restaurant designer is employed to work with the architect because this individual will be aware of new equipment alternatives and have significant and specific experience in restaurant layout and construction.
- *The builder.* The builder must use the architect's and designer's plans to build the building.

Layout Factors

Three constituencies must be considered when restaurants are designed. They are introduced in Figure 6.1.

Let's look at each of these groups:

- *Guests.* Guests want the products they order to be of a quality, portion size, and price that represent value. When they consume food and beverages on-site, they also consider the dining experience, which is a function of the environment and the service. Front-of-house

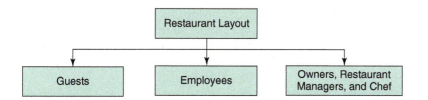

FIGURE 6.1

Restaurant Constituencies Affected by Layout

Adapted from Ninemeier, J., and Hayes, D. (2006). *Restaurant Operations Management*, Pearson Education, Inc.

design must be consistent with the menu and what guests desire and promote employee efficiency so service is not unnecessarily slowed.

- *Employees.* Employees will, hopefully, enjoy their jobs; as a result, their perception of the workplace will be affected by its design. If you consider an "unfriendly" design one that requires employees to work unnecessarily hard or walk unnecessarily long distances, it's easy to see why an efficient layout is good for all workers in a restaurant.
- *Owners and restaurant managers.* Restaurant owners and managers want the operation to be financially successful. This requires a facility design and layout that promote productivity and, in turn, reduce labor costs. They also want to minimize operating problems created by, for example, inadequate food storage areas or inadequate workspaces that could hinder productivity.

CONSIDER ON-SITE PRODUCTION REQUIREMENTS   You know that the menu determines the foods that must be purchased, stored, prepared and served to guests, and this information provides restaurant designers with a great start in planning work flow, equipment placement, and space requirements. However, decisions about the amount of on-site food preparation and production to be undertaken must still be made.

Figure 6.2 illustrates the role of make or buy analysis in helping to determine on-site production requirements.

As noted in Figure 6.2, a **make or buy analysis** determines the market form of products to be purchased. This, in turn, influences the amount of on-site preparation and equipment that is needed. Assume, for example, that beef stew will be on the menu and that carrots are ingredients in this item. Carrots can be purchased fresh by the bunch or peeled and/or chopped/sliced. If they're purchased fresh, refrigerated storage space will be required. If they're purchased by the bunch (whole), a vegetable preparation area will be needed to process them. Carrots can also be purchased canned or frozen. This changes the storage requirements (dry storage for a canned product; frozen storage for frozen items), and a vegetable processing area won't be required for either canned or frozen items.

Beef is the primary ingredient in the stew. Should it be purchased fresh for on-site processing? If so, what cut of beef should be purchased? Should fresh beef be purchased in cubes? Should it be purchased in frozen cubes? Answers to these and related questions affect storage and processing requirements and, in turn, the layout and space needed for production.

Ideally, the make or buy analysis process is an integral part of the menu planning task and will be considered when decisions about needed recipe ingredients are made. However, you've learned that the restaurant should also be designed with flexibility in mind, so some dry, frozen

Make or buy analysis

The process of deciding whether all or part of a menu item should be prepared on-site or purchased as a convenience food.

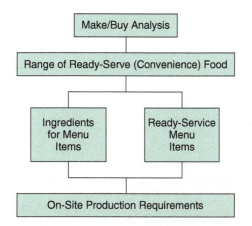

FIGURE 6.2

Food Processing Requirements and Design/Layout Concerns

Adapted from Ninemeier, J., and Hayes, D. (2006). *Restaurant Operations Management*, Pearson Education, Inc.

and refrigerated storage space will likely be provided regardless of the menu items currently being served. In addition, some space with a water source for vegetable preparation is often provided as is some counter space for other preparation tasks including nominal processing of entrées such as cutting sirloin into cubes and breading items to be deep fried. With many menus, this plan provides flexibility to accommodate future menus.

There are, however, some times when decisions must be made that have a significant impact on kitchen layout. Consider the use of fresh-baked bread as an integral part of the restaurant's theme and menu offerings. Specialized equipment including a mixer, roll divider/rounder, proofing cabinets and, perhaps, specialty bake ovens will be necessary. Workstation space to accommodate this equipment will also be needed. If, in the future, a different theme or menu is featured and on-site baked bread is not required, a significant amount of high-cost space and equipment in a prime area of the kitchen will go unused because it is no longer needed to support the new menu.

DINING ROOM OPERATION CONCERNS   Operating concerns in the dining room must be addressed when these areas are planned. For example, will the restaurant accommodate large groups in a banquet room or small groups in a small semi-private dining area? What about the possibility of moving tables together for large groups? Different seating levels, the use of booths, the amount of primary aisle space, the number and locations of emergency exits and the width of aisles to accommodate tableside food preparation must be considered. What about space, if any, for "help yourself" salad bars or buffets? It's important to think about operating concerns applicable to dining areas as the property is designed.

EMPLOYEE-RELATED FACTORS   You've learned that design impacts employee productivity, and improper design can also cause employee fatigue from repetitive tasks done in workstations which don't incorporate **ergonomic** principles. Noise, lighting and temperature affect the comfort, safety and accuracy of each employee's work and should be addressed as buildings are constructed.

Ergonomics

Analysis and studies to better fit a job to the employee who does it and to reduce work-related musculoskeletal disorders.

SANITATION FACTORS   Sanitation is a priority concern of restaurant managers, and layout and equipment planning can make it easy or difficult to comply with safe food handling practices. Consider the availability of undercounter refrigerated units to hold potentially hazardous foods until necessary on serving lines versus work areas that don't have these units.

Will production personnel make frequent trips to a refrigerator to retrieve items during busy shifts, or will they remove large quantities of items to reduce trips and leave them at room temperature in warm workstations until used? Here's a second example: How will dishwashers wash their hands after racking soiled dishes before they remove clean dishes from the machine? If there is no handwashing sink in the area will they rinse their hands under a spray attachment at the soiled dish counter and recontaminate their hands as they grasp the faucet lever? Will they wipe their hands on their aprons?

The restaurant's facility and the equipment must be easy-to-clean. Equipment meeting **National Sanitation Foundation (NSF) International** standards for construction help ensure that the equipment is easy cleaned. Floors, walls and other surfaces can be easy or difficult to clean and maintain based upon their original construction.

National Sanitation Foundation (NSF) International

An organization that develops voluntary standards for the manufacture and installation of food service equipment.

SAFETY AND RELATED FACTORS   Regulatory agencies within every community will have concerns about building construction, compliance with plumbing, electrical and other codes, and

---

WEB AT WORK!

The Americans with Disabilities Act (ADA) regulates accessibility to buildings by individuals with disabilities. Requirements must be adhered to during the design, construction, and alteration of many types of buildings, including access for the general public. To learn more about its accessibility guidelines, go to:

www.access-board.gov/adaag/html/adaag.htm

Review general information and then go to Section 5 "Restaurants and Cafeterias."

with fire safety. Agency representatives will likely visit the site during and after construction and before the building can be occupied.

The concerns of these agencies include factors such as:

- The total number of parking spaces provided including their length and width
- Parking lot access to public thoroughfares adjoining a parking lot
- The number, location, and size of handicapped-accessible parking spaces
- The amount of landscaped area on the restaurant's site
- Restaurant signage (number of allowable square feet relative to the building's exterior) and location of the signs
- Location of emergency building exits
- Number of handicapped-accessible entrance doors
- Number, size, and handicapped accessibility of restroom facilities
- Fire department access points
- Specifications for areas where trash and garbage are contained until removed

Requirements about the above and related concerns dramatically impact how the restaurant can be planned. Many months (even years!) can be spent in obtaining necessary approvals from applicable regulatory agencies for safety, aesthetic and other requirements. Approval times can be extended still further when, for example, concerns of neighboring property owners about road congestion and Americans with Disabilities Act (ADA) provisions for equal access must be considered. These codes and regulations can create significant but very necessary restraints on what restaurant designers and builders can and cannot do.

GREEN AT WORK!

Restaurants can reduce future energy and water costs and practice social responsibility when they construct new facilities in ways that encourage resource conservation. For example, Chipotle Mexican Grill has installed an energy-producing wind turbine outside of a unit, and some McDonalds restaurants reuses its kitchen equipment's exhaust air for heating purposes.

McDonald's opened its first LEED-certified restaurant in 2008.* It features high-efficiency appliances, chairs and tables constructed from recycled materials and even a garden on the roof.

The property's parking lot uses permeable pavers that reduce the cost of the drainage system, clean surface storm water, and minimize storm water run-off.

The McDonald's site also uses sensors to determine the amount of energy used for indoor lighting and the quantity of water used in restrooms. Exterior signage uses **light-emitting diodes** that reduce energy usage by 50%. Interior paint doesn't produce chemical odors and nontoxic chemicals are used for cleaning. Special mats are installed at the unit's entrance to remove dust and particles from customers' shoes that would otherwise circulate through the air.

Light-emitting diode

A semi-conductor that emits visible light when an electric current passes through it.

The property has a system to collect rainwater from the roof and heating, ventilation and air conditioning (HVAC) condensation into an underground cistern that recirculates the water for irrigation.

There are numerous other green "practices" that restaurant planners can incorporate into new construction and, in many cases, remodeling projects. Examples include:

- A "fire-up tool" that identifies the optimal time to turn kitchen equipment and lighting systems on and off.
- "Power factor correction" equipment that reduces transmission losses and ensures that all energy consumed produces useful work.
- High-efficiency rating HVAC systems and **low-proximity exhaust systems** for kitchen equipment.
- Occupancy sensors for lighting control.

Low-proximity exhaust system

A ventilation system for kitchen equipment with a low minimum exhaust (cubic feet per minute) requirement.

To learn more about reducing energy costs in restaurants, go to:

www.energystar.gov

Enter "restaurants" in the search box and then click on "energy star guide restaurants."

*"LEED" stands for leadership in energy and environmental design. This program has been developed by the U.S. Green Building Council. LEED certification is based on standards for sustainable design, water and energy savings, materials selection and other factors.

Workstations

In this section, we will consider planning needs for each area in the restaurant.

RECEIVING AND STORING AREAS   Typical components in a large-volume restaurant's receiving and storing area often include:

- A walk-in freezer
- A walk-in refrigerator
- An office for the general manager with windows to enable observation of the receiving and work preparation areas
- A dry storage area
- Employee locker and rest rooms
- Spaces for mobile racks, a receiving scale and, perhaps, a garbage can or cart-washing area

Production employees will likely need access to the dry storage area at least several times during a shift. It should be located as close to the pre-preparation and production areas as practical. Production employees typically need refrigerator access more frequently than freezer access so refrigerated storage should be located closer to the production area. Note: Some restaurants utilize a walk-in freezer unit on the exterior of the building to save space. Products may then be issued from the central freezer area to a smaller reach-in freezer unit within the kitchen on an as-needed basis.

Adequate space is needed to accommodate effective receiving practices. All incoming products can then be assembled in the receiving area for proper inspection before the delivery invoice is signed and products are moved to the appropriate storage area.

Dry storage areas can be designed to accommodate case and shelving storage. Cases of canned goods, disposable supplies and other boxed goods can be stored on these platforms without the need to open cases. By contrast, other products such as those from broken cases can be placed on shelving. If adjustable shelving units are used, the cubic footage of storage areas can be maximized because space won't be wasted between the top of an item on a shelf and the bottom of the shelf above it.

The dry storage area should be designed with pallets closest to the door to minimize the extra steps otherwise required to carry or cart the heaviest cases to their storage sites.

ENTRÉE PREPARATION AREA   A preparation table with a sink can be helpful when pre-preparing entrée items. For example, fresh steaks can be portioned and trimmed before their transfer to the **cooks' line**. Similarly, frozen headless shrimp could be thawed under running water and then be peeled, de-veined, and further processed on an adjacent preparation table.

Ideally, the entrée preparation area will be close to needed refrigerated/frozen storage areas and the cooks' line.

Cooks' line

The workstation containing the major food production and food holding equipment used to prepare items for plating and pickup by service personnel.

GENERAL FOOD PREPARATION AREA   Many kitchens lack the counter space necessary for adequate food production. Properly-designed food preparation counters have one or more drawers to store small equipment items and, perhaps, an under- or over-counter shelf for pot and pan storage. Mobile units provide flexibility because they can be moved to other areas as needed. Counter space may also be needed to locate mixers, slicers and other equipment.

VEGETABLE PREPARATION AREA   Consider the activities required to prepare fresh produce for a salad bar: fresh carrots, tomatoes and other produce must be prepared (peeled, sliced, and/or chopped). Fresh lettuce must be washed, outer leaves must be removed and the cores must be discarded. A sink (water source and drain) is required for these activities as are cutting boards, French knives, tubs or other pans to store clean produce, a garbage can, and numerous other items.

PANTRY AREA   The pantry area is used by service staff to pick-up items that don't require immediate pre-service production assistance by the food production staff. Examples include tossed and chef's salads, bread/rolls, sliced cakes and pies and other desserts. Coffee and/or tea may be brewed in this area with pots or pitchers used to transport the beverages to server station areas. An under- or over-counter refrigerated unit may be necessary. An ice machine may also be located in the pantry area for server and/or bartender use.

> **WEB AT WORK!**
>
> The Ansul company manufactures a variety of fire suppression systems for restaurants of all sizes. To view its website, go to:
>
> www.ansul.com
>
> Click on "Products" and then "Restaurant Suppression Systems."

POT/PAN AND DISHWASHING AREAS   Sanitation concerns are at the forefront of the design of this area. A three- (or four-) compartment sink of a size to accommodate the pots and pans to be washed is needed. Automated dispensing systems for washing and sanitizing chemicals may be located on the wall above the unit, on a shelf or on the floor under the unit. Special nonslip floor materials, slip-resistant strips or other surfaces should be used in the sink area to reduce employee slips and falls caused by wet floors. The soiled and clean pot/pan counters should be long enough to accommodate the number of soiled/cleaned pots and pans that will be washed at one time. A pot/pan rack to hold clean utensils can be located next to the clean counter. Shelves above and/or below the soiled and clean counters provide other storage possibilities.

A nonslip floor in the dishwashing station area is important. There must be a clean dish counter of adequate length for racks of dishes to air-dry before being removed from the dish counter. This typically requires 60–80 linear inches of space (to accommodate three or four dish racks, each 20" × 20" in size). Space will be needed on the wall and/or under the unit for the dispensing equipment needed for soap/detergents, **sheeting agents** and any other chemicals A hand sink in this area is a "must," and floor space to accommodate mobile dish racks may be needed.

COOKS' LINE AREA   A cooks' line typically houses several items of large food production equipment. This space will be, on a per-square foot basis, one of the most expensive workstations in your restaurant because of the need for a ventilation hood and fire suppression system above the production equipment. The ventilation system removes heat, steam and odors and provides fresh air exchanges. Fire suppression systems are needed to quickly extinguish fires, if any, which began in/on the equipment within the area.

Ample counter space is required on the cooks' line to store items before cooking and to hold and/or plate them after production. Equipment to maintain the temperature of hot foods before server pickup and space for **remote printers**, dishes, and production smallware (pots, pans, and utensils) may be needed.

SERVER PICKUP AREA   Food production personnel pre-plate and place hot foods on a counter in the server pickup area. Service employees then retrieve the items, place them on trays and take them to guest tables. Hot food-warming equipment may be used, and a system of effective communication between production and service staff is necessary to minimize the time between food plating and pickup.

Service staff must have easy access to the front of this pickup counter, and there may be under-counter shelving to store plates and bowls, napkins, serving trays, and other service items. Units may also be designed with warming units built or set into the counter to allow service staff to portion soups or other items.

SERVER STATION AREAS   One or more small workstations may be located around the restaurant's dining areas to house tray stands, server trays, **condiments**, disposable supplies, coffee cups/saucers, water glasses, and other service wares.

Point-of-sale equipment, coffee brewing machines, and space for water pitchers and other items may also be located in these areas.

BAR AREA   A bar used to produce alcoholic beverages is a complex workstation typically contained in a very small space. If the space is well designed, bartenders will have easy access to liquors, beers and wines, and to other ingredients and the small equipment needed to prepare drinks ordered by guests.

Space to locate point-of-sale equipment, to store barware and to place glasses of beverages awaiting pickup by service staff will be needed. Frequently, the bar's design must allow the

Sheeting agent

A chemical used in dish machines to help prevent water spotting and streaking on plates, flatware and other items cleaned by the unit.

Remote printer

An electronic unit in the cooks' line that prints food orders entered into point-of-sale (POS) equipment by service personnel.

Condiment

Salt, pepper, mustard, ketchup, or a similar flavoring substance added in small amounts to food (usually at the table) to improve its taste.

Point-of-sale equipment

A computerized device used by servers and bartenders to record orders. The system tallies revenue, sales and numerous other types of data; abbreviated "POS."

Space in and around bars is typically very limited and must be carefully designed to allow bartenders to efficiently prepare and provide drinks to beverage servers.

© CandyBox Images/Shutterstock

bartender to prepare drinks for guests at the bar and in the lounge and for service staff who then transport the drinks to guests in the lounge or to à la carte dining areas.

Layout Basics

Figure 6.3 illustrates a five-step process for planning a restaurant's layout.

Let's use the five-step process to illustrate the design process for Vernon's Restaurant and Banquet Hall. Assume a properly-zoned site has been selected and purchased. The owner has hired an experienced restaurant manager and, based on the business plan, has developed a mid-scale restaurant theme appealing to single and married couples, businesspersons (for lunch) and others looking for a basic menu of steak and seafood entrées, "signature" pasta dishes, and a full

FIGURE 6.3

Steps in Restaurant Layout Planning

Adapted from Ninemeier, J., and Hayes, D. (2006). *Restaurant Operations Management,* Pearson Education, Inc.

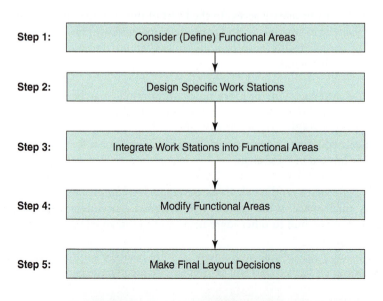

Step 1: Consider (Define) Functional Areas

Step 2: Design Specific Work Stations

Step 3: Integrate Work Stations into Functional Areas

Step 4: Modify Functional Areas

Step 5: Make Final Layout Decisions

line of burgers and other sandwiches. A great weekend brunch business is expected, and the property will serve small to moderate-size banquets for guests at weddings, anniversaries, retirement parties, and other special occasion events.

STEP 1: CONSIDER (DEFINE) FUNCTIONAL AREAS The restaurant is located in a large suburban area, so the availability of most food and beverage products should not be a problem. Most items will be made on-site, but others will not. Make–buy analyses will be used to make these production decisions.

The planning team determines that a relatively small amount of square footage will be required for storage. The team will design the kitchen with maximum flexibility to allow for production of numerous food items along the scale of "made-from scratch" to "full convenience" (see Figure 6.2).

The restaurant will have a license to sell alcoholic beverages. A bar will be planned, but its primary purpose will be to complement the à la carte dining and banquet business. The full à la carte dining menu will be available in the bar area. There may also be some additional appetizers or "bar snacks" offered and some (minimal) seating for guests who only wish to enjoy a beverage will be provided.

The à la carte dining area will also be designed for maximum flexibility. It will allow space for a portable buffet line for weekend brunches, provide ample seating for groups of one to six people, and accommodate larger groups with tables that can be easily rearranged. A "private" dining room with limited public access will also be available for groups of up to (approximately) 20 people.

The planning team anticipates significant revenues to be generated from its banquet business with functions for up to one 100 people. The sole kitchen will be shared between à la carte and banquet production, so only one banquet will be "sold" during each lunch and dinner and banquet size will be limited on busy nights.

In review, the restaurant will be planned with four major functional areas:

- Kitchen
- Bar
- À la carte dining area
- Banquet area

This well-designed workstation makes it convenient for guests to pickup the food they have ordered and allows the restaurant employee to productively handle other tasks.

WEB AT WORK!

Numerous restaurant design and layout consulting organizations have websites. To see one that illustrates actual restaurant layouts, go to:

www.nationalrd.com

Click on "Restaurant Projects" and select the restaurant design that interests you.

STEP 2: DESIGN SPECIFIC WORKSTATIONS   Several workstations are required in each functional area. Figure 6.4 diagrams a basic draft layout for each one:

- Figure 6.4 (A) Receiving and Storing. Frozen, refrigerated, and dry food products are received and stored. Alcoholic beverages are kept in an area that can be locked within the dry storeroom. Chilled wines and expensive pre-portioned entrées are kept in a secured part of the walk-in refrigerator.
- Figure 6.4 (B) Kitchen: Entrée Preparation. Meat, poultry, and seafood entrées are pre-prepared.
- Figure 6.4 (C) Kitchen: Multi-purpose Table. This mobile counter is used for miscellaneous preparation activities and banquet plate assembly.
- Figure 6.4 (D) Kitchen: Vegetable Preparation. Fresh fruits and vegetables are pre-prepared.
- Figure 6.4 (E) Kitchen: Pantry. Servers prepare and retrieve pre-portioned salads, desserts, and other items.
- Figure 6.4 (F) Kitchen: Pot/Pan Sink. Pots and pans are washed, rinsed, and sanitized.
- Figure 6.4 (G) Kitchen: Cooks' Line. Cooks prepare hot food items and à la carte dining room and lounge service staff retrieve them.
- Figure 6.4 (H) Kitchen: Dishwashing Area. Dishes/flatware and related items are washed.
- Figure 6.4 (I) Bar. All alcoholic beverages served in the à la carte dining and banquet rooms and to guests seated at the bar and in the bar area are produced here.
- Figure 6.4 (J) Dining Room: Server Station. Servers retrieve hot/cold beverages and other items and place food/beverage orders with cooks and bartenders.
- Figure 6.4 (K) Dining Room: Reception Counter. Dining room guests are met, greeted and seated.
- Figure 6.4 (L). Other Functional Areas. These include employee locker rooms, public restrooms, and the manager's office.

STEP 3: INTEGRATE WORKSTATIONS INTO FUNCTIONAL AREAS   To this point, we have not directly addressed the layout's size. The planning team will want to maximize "front-of-house" space because a larger guest capacity will typically allow the restaurant to serve more guests and generate more revenue.

To achieve this goal, the team must ensure that the kitchen space is no larger than necessary. Workstations should be designed to accommodate flexible work activities, so multifunctional equipment should be selected. Careful thought must be given to whether convenience foods of appropriate quality can be used to reduce the space required for storage needs and production tasks.

Production personnel generally like a small kitchen to reduce steps between workstations, but typically there is little that can be done to increase productivity when space is too large. By contrast, a small space can be "managed," at least to some extent, by menu planning (a reduction in menu variety) and/or increased use of convenience food. In today's highly competitive restaurant business, it's imperative that every square foot be **cost-justified** to help ensure that costs are minimized and revenue is maximized.

Cost-justification

The process of ensuring that the decisions made attain the highest-possible purpose and that resulting costs are worthwhile.

FIGURE 6.4

Vernon's Restaurant and Banquet Hall

(A) Receiving and Storing[1]

Primary Activities

- Products are received.
- Products are kept in frozen, refrigerated, and dry storage areas; certain areas are locked.

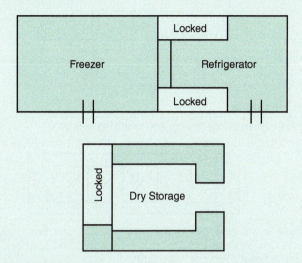

(B) Kitchen: Entree Preparation

Primary Activity: Pre-preparation of meat, poultry, and seafood entrées.

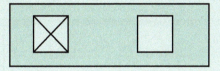

Note: A sink and a meat slicer may be needed as well as under-counter shelving for pan storage.

(C) Kitchen: Multipurpose Mobile Table

Primary Activity: Miscellaneous preparation activities and banquet plate assembly.

Note: A drawer and undercounter shelving provides storage.

(D) Kitchen: Vegetable Preparation

Primary Work Activity: Pre-preparation of fresh fruits and vegetables.

Note: Storage for knives/other small utensils (in drawer) and for cutting boards and pots/pans (on an undercounter shelf) help to reduce the time needed for preparation and production of menu items.

(continued)

---

[1]Note: Drawings are not to scale.

FIGURE 6.4
(continued)

(E) Kitchen: Pantry
Primary Work Activity: Preparation and/or retrieval of pre-prepared salads and desserts.

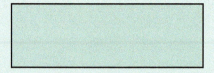

Note: Undercounter refrigerator (for prepared salads), shelving units (for fresh desserts), and a warming device (for fresh breads) are ideal. Water may be necessary depending upon the pantry's location to other workstations. A small freezer is needed for ice creams.

(F) Kitchen: Pot/Pan Sink
Primary Work Activity: Washing, rinsing, and sanitizing pots/pans.

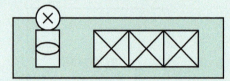

Note: The trough has a spray attachment and disposer to remove food from soiled pots/pans. Wash/rinse/sanitize sinks; ample soiled/ clean counters for accumulated pots/pans. Cleaning chemicals and supplies are stored on shelves under the counter.

(G) Kitchen: Cooks' Line/Server PickUp Area
Primary Work Activity: Cooks heat/cook all items; servers retrieve all hot food items.

Legend
1. Deep Fryer
2. Work Counter
3. Range Oven
4. Grill
5. Broiler
6. Under-counter refrigerator (cooks)
7. Under-counter refrigerator (servers)
8. Under-counter shelving (cooks)
9. Under-counter shelving (servers)

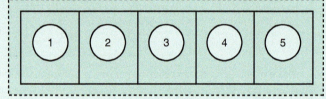

Note: Production equipment must be beneath a ventilation/fire-suspension system. A warming unit and remote printer are needed.

(H) Kitchen: Dishwashing Area
Primary Work Activity: Washing of dishes/flatware and related items.

Legend
1. Soiled dish counter, spray attachment and disposer
2. Dish Machine (rack-type)
3. Clean dish counter (booster heater below)

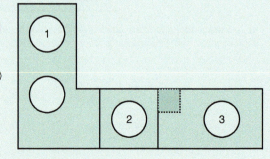

FIGURE 6.4
(continued)

(I) Bar

Primary Work Activity: Alcoholic beverages are served in the à la carte dining and banquet room (when a portable bar is not used) and to guests seated at the bar and in the bar area.

Legend

1. Two-door, reach-in refrigerator
2. POS system
3. POS system on shelf above counter
4. "Step-up" back bar display
5. Ice bin
6. Soiled glass drain board
7. Clean glass drain board
8. Four-compartment sink (used to empty, wash, rinse, and sanitize glassware)
9. Bar stool
10. Speed rail
11. Soda gun (draft beer in this area also; lines run to remote refrigerated storage)
12. Undercounter storage area
13. Hinged counter (for bartender exit)
14. Beverage server pickup area

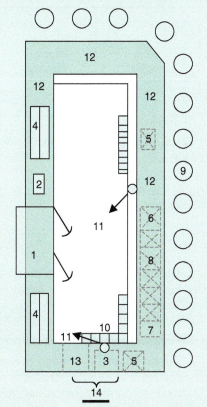

Note: Some bars also have small undercounter glass washing machines.

(J) Dining Room: Server Area Work Station

Primary Work Activity: Servers pick up hot and cold beverages, retrieve products/service supplies, and place food/beverage orders on point-of-sale system.

Note: Counter space is needed for coffee maker and point-of-sale system. Under-and/or over-counter shelving for napkins, flatware, paper supplies, payment card authorizer, and table condiments. Under-counter bun warmer. (Assume a server banking system: Servers collect/retain guest payments until end of shift.)

(K) Dining Room: Reception Counter

Primary Work Activity: Dining room guests are met, greeted, and seated.

Note: Includes a counter area for electronic reservation/table status system and undercounter storage for menus and children's novelties. Requires telephone access.

(continued)

FIGURE 6.4
(continued)

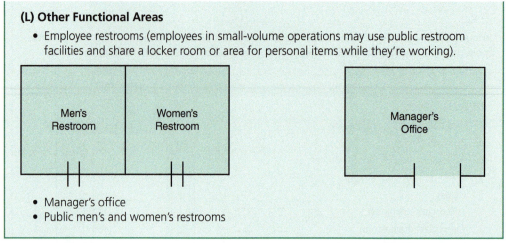

(L) Other Functional Areas

- Employee restrooms (employees in small-volume operations may use public restroom facilities and share a locker room or area for personal items while they're working).

- Manager's office
- Public men's and women's restrooms

Adapted from Ninemeier, J., and Hayes, D. (2006). *Restaurant Operations Management,* Pearson Education, Inc.

After specific workstations are tentatively designed (step 2 above), planners can integrate individual workstations into the functional areas. Figure 6.5 shows a first draft of the layout for the property being planned.

As you continue to review Figure 6.5, note that it shows the functional areas with workstations identified in Figure 6.4. Also note that:

Straight-line flow

The concept that products move, to the extent possible, in a straight-line from receiving, storing, and issuing to pre-preparation, production, and service without the need for unproductive "back tracking."

- The overall kitchen design incorporates a **straight-line flow** for à la carte food production and service. Products flow in a straight line from receiving and storage areas, to pre-preparation and production areas, and then to the server pickup area (Figure 6.5, #13).
- The straight-line flow is slightly modified to accommodate banquet operations: After production, there will be "back tracking" to the multipurpose mobile counter (which may be relocated for pre-plating) and then straight-line flow into the banquet area.
- The dishwashing area is located to accommodate dish return from both the à la carte and banquet dining area. (Figure 6.5, H)

Legend

1. Can/cart wash
2. Employee locker room (men)
3. Employee locker room (women)
4. Manager's office (with windows)
5. Entrée prep table with sink
6. Walk-in freezer
7. Walk-in refrigerator
8. Dry storeroom
9. Prep table
10. Receiving scale
11. Hand sink
12. Cook's production line
13. Server pickup line
14. Vegetable prep table with sink
15. Pantry area
16. Ice machine
17. Three-compartment pot/pan sink with disposer and spray rinse in soiled pot/pan counter
18. Dish wash area (soiled dish counter with disposer/spray rinse, dish machine and clean dish counter (booster heater below)
19. Server station

20. Public restroom (women)
21. Public restroom (men)
22. Bar area
23. Dining area (with room divider for semi-privacy)
24. Reception area with benches
25. Portable bar

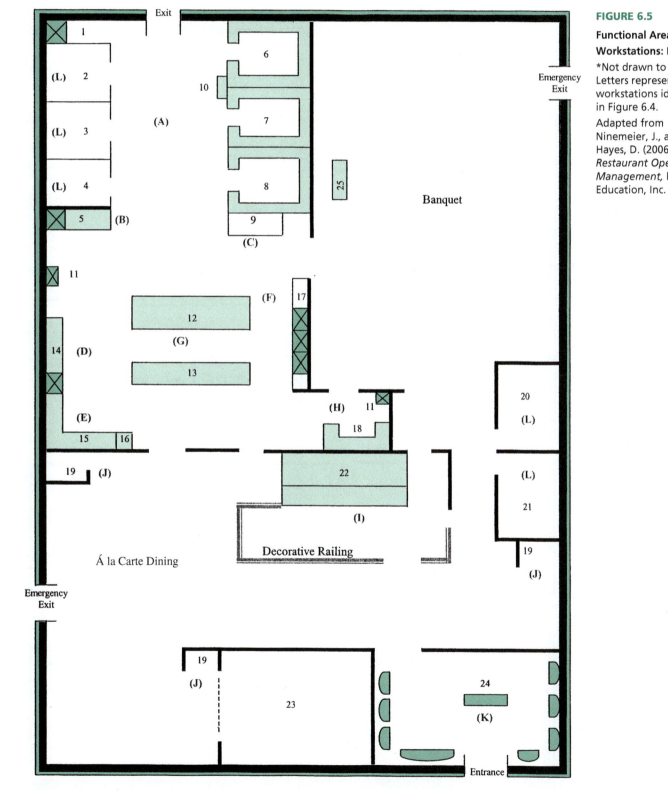

FIGURE 6.5

Functional Areas with Workstations: Draft 1*

*Not drawn to scale. Letters represent workstations identified in Figure 6.4.

Adapted from Ninemeier, J., and Hayes, D. (2006). *Restaurant Operations Management,* Pearson Education, Inc.

Computer-assisted design (CAD) software

Used to draw (develop) sketches of building plans/layouts.

STEP 4: MODIFY FUNCTIONAL AREAS   As a result of their efforts in step 3 above, the planning team has developed a schematic of the restaurant upon which to build improvements. Note: With today's **computer-assisted design (CAD) software**, layout changes can be made quickly and can evolve through ongoing changes with little wasted time/effort. After review and discussion, the planning team decides to make the numerous changes incorporated into the final layout shown Figure 6.6.

FIGURE 6.6

Functional Areas with Workstations: Final Layout*

*Not drawn to scale.

Adapted from Ninemeier, J., and Hayes, D. (2006). *Restaurant Operations Management,* Pearson Education, Inc.

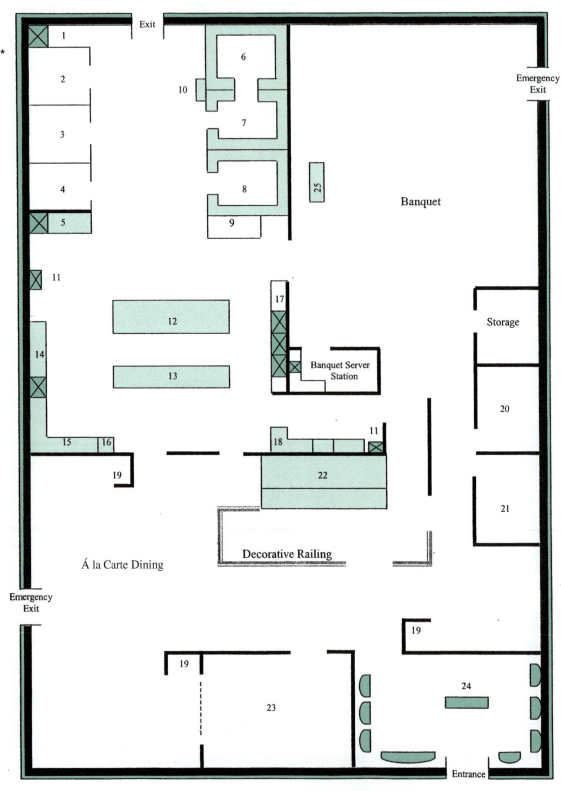

When reviewing the final layout in Figure. 6.6, you'll note the following changes from Figure 6.5:

- The entrance to the walk-in freezer is now through the refrigerator rather than through the freezer's exterior wall to allow more linear space outside of both units for a receiving scale.
- A server station with a water source will be added in the banquet room. Plumbing costs should not be significantly higher because there's a water source (three-compartment sink) on the other side of the partial wall.
- The dish machine area has been reconfigured to an "L"- rather than "U"-shape to allow the soiled dish counter to be located closer to where servers will return dishes from the à la carte dining room.
- The "private" dining room (bottom center of the figure) now has an entry that allows more convenient access for guests entering from the reception area.
- A banquet storage area has been provided for tables, carts, a portable dance floor and other equipment.

This kitchen designer is working on plans for a commercial restaurant that will operate on the lobby level of this high-rise apartment complex.

STEP 5: MAKE FINAL LAYOUT DECISIONS   The draft of the restaurant layout shown in Figure 6.6 may now be shared with officials of the community's regulatory agencies concerned with building codes, fire/emergency exits and other issues. The layout will likely evolve still further but, hopefully, be finalized before construction begins to eliminate costly **change orders**.

Change order

Revisions to building plans after construction has begun.

Exterior Design Concerns

While most of a manager's focus revolves around the restaurant's interior, its exterior is also important. Some owners purchase property and build their restaurants on it. The property's location is a primary concern: it must be accessible for its intended customer market. Many other owners buy or lease a building or space, and these same location concerns are important to them.

Those purchasing property and planning new construction have much more flexibility with exterior design than do those establishing a restaurant in an existing building. Owners leasing space in a food court in a shopping mall probably have few, if any, exterior design options. Others constructing or buying an existing building will likely be confronted with numerous community building code and zoning requirements including those for signage.

Owners of franchised restaurants will likely need to incorporate requirements of the franchisors into exterior building design when permitted by local ordinances. Franchisors and franchisees know that many potential guests recognize their restaurants by the exterior features and signage.

In all cases, the exterior of the restaurant and the grounds, if any, which it occupies must be maintained. Owners know that failure to keep their restaurant in good condition can detract from its overall appearance and curb appeal.

GROUNDS (LANDSCAPING)   Effective landscaping sets a positive visual tone for arriving guests. Poorly maintained grounds, however, can detract from the restaurant's visual attractiveness and result in reduced revenues. In most cases, those who build restaurants understand the need for appropriate and well-designed landscaping. Factors such as the location of driveways, direction of the sun, elevation of the land, existing trees, visual utility lines, and appropriate lawns and plantings are all important concerns.

Ground areas require regular watering, trimming, mowing, fertilization, and pruning by knowledgeable and experienced workers during growing seasons. This can help ensure lush, healthy plant growth and excellent curb appeal.

PARKING AREAS   Many restaurants offer on-site parking; their parking lots must be properly constructed and maintained. Parking surfaces can be damaged from age, cracking (which results from ground erosion or freeze/thaw cycles), deicing salts, and standing water. Owners must routinely address these issues to provide hassle-free parking for their guests.

Many parking lots have individual parking spaces marked by lines painted on the parking surfaces. These can fade or become soiled and should be kept freshly painted. Local building codes and the ADA may mandate special, easily seen markings for some parking spaces.

RESTAURANT EQUIPMENT

Regardless of their size, most restaurants require a variety of food storage, preparation, production, service, dining, and cleanup equipment. Fortunately, there is a wide range of equipment available for almost any purpose so that restaurant managers can purchase **stock equipment** rather than **custom equipment** to save money and reduce delivery times.

In this section, we'll review important factors to consider when purchasing basic types of equipment, including many of the items needed for Vernon's Restaurant and Banquet Hall.

Equipment Purchase Factors

You must carefully consider lots of factors before you make equipment purchase decisions. These include:

- *Function (need).* Because of cost and space requirements, function is a primary concern. However, some restaurant managers violate this basic rule and buy equipment that is rarely used or underused. You may observe this when, for example, you see only the top burner of a **range oven** in use because a **convection oven** is available elsewhere in the kitchen. In this case, one equipment item (a range with a built-in convection oven beneath) would have been a more suitable choice.
- *Capacity.* The number of meals or portions to be produced is an important equipment consideration. However, equipment need not necessarily produce 100 portions of a popular item, for example, because **batch cooking** can reduce necessary equipment capacity. However, if 50 steaks must be charbroiled at about the same time, the equipment to do so must be available.

Stock equipment

Equipment manufactured in large quantities according to standard plans that is often available in dealer inventories or which can be quickly obtained from the manufacturer or distributor.

Custom equipment

Equipment designed according to unique plans or drawings that requires special construction.

Range oven

Food production equipment featuring electric or gas-fueled burners for a top cooking surface with an oven underneath.

Convection oven

An oven that heats by circulating air (convection currents) rather than using a conventional heating process (conduction currents).

Batch cooking

The preparation of food needed in large quantities in small volumes (batches) rather than at one time; this maximizes food quality by reducing holding times until service.

WEB AT WORK!
Many restaurant equipment suppliers have websites showcasing their products and services. To see a website with a variety of equipment and educational information, go to:
www.zesco.com

- *Total cost.* The equipment's function and capacity will influence its costs. However, the purchase price of a piece of equipment is often only part of the total expense and may not even be the largest component of total cost! Installation expenses can be significant especially when, for example, a dish machine requiring power, a water source, and drain must be installed in an area without these features.
- *Design/appearance.* Equipment in nonpublic spaces can generally emphasize function more than appearance. However, equipment in public areas must be functional and appropriately attractive when seen by guests in the restaurant.
- *Size (dimension).* Available square/cubic footage is often an important factor when making equipment purchases. Consider, for example, a new piece of food production equipment that must fit between two existing and stationary pieces of production equipment.
- *Safety/sanitation.* Equipment must be safe to operate, be easy to clean and maintain and keep food safe while in use. Fortunately, restaurant managers in the United States have allies in regulatory and voluntary agencies and associations that provide manufacturing standards that help ensure that safety and sanitation concerns are addressed. These include the U.S. Department of Labor Occupational Safety and Health Administration (general equipment safety concerns); the NSF International (general construction standards related to sanitation); Underwriters Laboratories (safety of electrical equipment); and the American Gas Association (safety of gas-fueled equipment).
- *Flexibility.* We have emphasized the use of multipurpose equipment. Perhaps it's possible to purchase one ice machine with the capacity to meet food production, dining room (salad bar) and bar requirements rather than multiple units. Can a range oven that has an overhead broiler attachment be purchased to eliminate the need for expanding the expensive-to-build space located under the ventilation system?
- Other factors Other issues that buyers must consider include the ease and cost of maintenance, the purchaser's experience with different equipment manufacturers and suppliers; need for mobility; concerns about availability; frequency of use; and cost of repairs.

Common Food Service Equipment

In this section, we'll review many types of equipment commonly found in restaurant operations. The equipment needed for a specific operation will depend upon a restaurant's menu and standard recipes, which will determine the food preparation, cooking, and serving equipment required. In addition, nearly every restaurant will have unique needs for refrigeration, cleaning, and other operation-specific equipment.

FOOD PREPARATION EQUIPMENT   Commonly purchased food preparation equipment includes:

- *Food mixers.* Mixers are used to stir (sugar into whole eggs), knead (in bread production), and whip (as in whipped cream). Many mixers include attachments so cooks can chop, grind, shred, dice, and slice food. Capacities range from just a few cups or quarts (mobile cart or counter models) to 30 gallons or more (floor units).
- *Cutters/mixers (also called vertical cutter mixers or VCMs).* Their uses include quickly preparing salad dressings, kneading bread/pizza dough, making bread crumbs, chopping foods, and mixing cake batters and pie dough.
- *Food cutters/choppers (commonly called "Buffalo" choppers).* Food is placed in a bowl that revolves through blades that cut/chop the food to the desired size.
- *Food processors.* These machines (similar to the home kitchen variety but of larger capacity) are used to emulsify, chop, puree, slice/dice, shred, grate, julienne, and mix foods.
- *Slicers.* These use a rotating knife blade to cut products that are pushed through it. With manual models, cooks push a carriage containing the product back and forth across the knife blade. Automatic models eliminate this step.

WEB AT WORK!

Hobart Corporation is a large manufacturer of a wide variety of food service equipment. To reach its website, go to:

www.hobartcorp.com

On this site, you can learn about numerous items for baking, cooking, deli, food preparation, refrigeration, ware washing, and weighing equipment.

COOKING EQUIPMENT   Special food production equipment is used to cook (apply heat) to food items, including:

- *Ovens.* Common restaurant ovens include range ovens, deck ovens (which have oven units positioned on top of each other), cook-and-hold ovens (which cook meats at low temperature and then hold them at the proper temperature until serving), combination ovens (which can cook with steam, hot air, or both), and microwave ovens (used primarily to heat/reheat convenience foods).
- *Ranges.* A range has a cooking top with heating units under solid tops, open tops (similar to gas/electric tops on home-style ranges) and/or griddle plates.
- *Tilting skillets.* This multipurpose piece of equipment serves as a griddle, deep fryer, and range top among other uses.
- *Broilers and salamanders.* Broilers can have heating units that apply heat to the top, bottom or both surfaces of the item being cooked. Salamanders are small overhead broilers typically mounted on a shelf over a range top. They're also called back-shelf broilers and are used for melting or browning cheese on top of dishes and for other light broiling work.
- *Deep fryers.* Small fryers (table-top models) and larger (free-standing) fryers are heated with gas or electricity. Infra-red models that heat ceramic plates next to the fry pot and then transfer heat to the pot are also available. Pressure fryers seal the frying pot to shorten cooking time.

Restaurant Planners Must Consider the Dining Room Environment—Including Furniture and Fixtures—When Designing a Restaurant.

© Luckyraccoon/Shutterstock

- *Compartment steamers and steam-jacketed kettles.* These typically incorporate a self-contained boiler to generate steam. Most restaurant units use a fan to propel steam throughout the cabinet. Small counter-top models are available as are larger floor units that can hold up to 24 steam-table pans. Steam-jacketed kettles are available in numerous sizes and utilize steam that circulates within the hollow wall of the bowl surrounding the food. Steamers are commonly used to heat canned and frozen vegetables and to re-heat pre-cooked items. Steam-jacketed kettles are used to brown meats and to cook sauces, stews and soups.

SERVING EQUIPMENT   Restaurant production personnel typically prepare some foods that must be held at proper serving temperatures until they're served to guests. Hot food serving carts may be used to transport pre-plated foods from the kitchen to banquet serving areas. Bread/bun warmers may be available in kitchen, pantry and/or server stations. Infrared heating lamps are used on serving counters to help keep food hot until it's picked up by servers for delivery to guests. **Bain maries** use an open hot water bath or double-boiler system to keep hot foods hot. Heated **pass-through equipment** allows food to be placed on shelves or in carts in the kitchen and hold foods at the appropriate temperatures before retrieval by service personnel in dining areas.

Coffee brewers are sized to make 12 cups or less to urns brewing 500 cups or more. Manual (pour-over) units are similar to those used in the home; there is not a direct water line hook-up. Automatic brewers require a water hook-up and don't need to be manually filled with water. Specialized brewing equipment for flavored coffees, **espresso** and **cappuccino** beverages, among others, are increasingly used in restaurants.

REFRIGERATION EQUIPMENT   Refrigerators and freezers are available in reach-in units that may be adequate for the storage needs of a small restaurant and used for workstation storage in larger properties. Walk-in units ranging from 36 sq. ft. (or less) to 400 sq. ft. (or larger) are available. Undercounter units are frequently used in serving lines; cooks' stations and pantry, bakeshop and other workstations. Pass-through units similar to the hot-food pass-through units discussed above are sometimes used.

Ice-making units make cubed ice of numerous sizes and shapes and flaked (shaved) ice. They require water hook-up and drain access and may be water- or air-cooled. Ice bins must be appropriately insulated to hold the ice until it's used.

CLEANING AND MISCELLANEOUS EQUIPMENT   Dishes and other utensils can be washed manually in a three-compartment sink or, alternatively, cleaned in an automatic dish machine. Small undercounter dish machines may be used in low-volume restaurant operations or to clean glasses in bars or pantry areas in larger properties.

Larger dish machines are available, which accommodate dish racks. Single-rack units may require that dishes be cleaned, placed in racks, and then pushed into a dish machine that operates after doors are manually lowered. Larger rack-type units without doors allow operators to push racks onto a conveyor within the machine which then pulls the racks through the unit. Still larger machines (conveyor-type washers) allow dishwashing employees to load dishes onto a conveyor with upright prongs to hold dishes as they go through the machine. After cleaning, dishwashing employees on the unloading (clean) end of the unit remove the dishes from the conveyor and place them into dish racks or other storage or transport equipment. These convey machines also accommodate racks for glasses, cups, and similar items so they can be washed by the machine.

Bain marie

A cooking utensil containing hot water into which another container is placed to keep food warm or to cook it gently.

Pass-through equipment

Refrigerated or hot food compartments separating two work areas that allow food to be placed by production personnel onto a shelf or cart on one side of a wall and then retrieved by serving personnel on the other side of the wall.

Espresso

Coffee produced by forcing hot water under high pressure through finely ground coffee, typically in very small volumes.

Cappuccino

A classic recipe uses typically equal portions of espresso, steamed milk, and whipped cream foam (often sprinkled with powdered cinnamon).

WEB AT WORK!

Do you want to learn more about the NSF International and its role in developing standards for foods service equipment? Or to review standards for food equipment, commercial ware washing and cooking equipment and a wide range of other products? If so, go to:

www.nsf.org

Some restaurants use pot-washing machines to clean and sanitize these utensils after cooked on food and other soil is removed. In many restaurants, however, pots and pans are manually washed in a three-compartment sink or, after initial pre-washing, are moved to the dish machine for final cleaning.

Most restaurants use a garbage disposer into which food waste from plates is scraped before dishes are washed. Other restaurants use these units in three-compartment sink areas. These are most convenient when used in companion with a spray/rinse attachment. The operator activates a lever and then water under slight pressure is sprayed onto the utensil to release food from the dishes, pots, pans, or other items being washed.

OTHER EQUIPMENT   Fire safety codes require that a ventilation hood with fire suppression system units be placed above most items of production equipment used to cook food. The hood and units help remove heat, grease, moisture, steam, and odors from the kitchen and provide an effective means to eliminate fires in or on the equipment placed under the ventilation system.

Racks may be used to store pots and pans kept on undercounter shelving. Areas for case storage and units with adjustable shelving maximize space and are typically required in dry, refrigerated, and frozen storage areas.

Preparation sinks should be located in areas including produce workstations and in other locations where other food items are prepared. Some restaurants use water sources on/ near cook production lines. Preparation sinks should not be used for employee hand washing. Sinks designated for hand washing must be available in preparation and dish/pot/pan washing areas.

Food preparation tables can be stationary or mobile. With flexibility in mind, mobile tables should be used whenever appropriate. If stationary tables are used, they should have legs to raise them off the floor to ease cleaning tasks. Even these units will be more flexible over the longer term than will their counterparts placed on bases attached to the floor.

Elevators/dumbwaiters may be necessary to transport products from storage to preparation areas and/or products from preparation areas to service areas. Hopefully, food storage, preparation and service areas are on the same level to avoid these transportation tasks.

Mobile equipment is useful for moving dishes and glassware from areas where they're cleaned to where they're utilized. Some restaurants use small carts to assist servers with table busing duties. In other operations, personnel use trays or bus tubs for this purpose and then place these items on carts for transport to cleaning areas. Two-wheel carts are useful in receiving/ storage areas to easily and safely move case goods. Restaurants also require a wide variety of utensils and tableware for back-and-front-of-house use.

ALL IN A DAY'S WORK 6.1

"This project is way over budget," said the owner of Vernon's Restaurant and Banquet Hall, speaking to the kitchen designer. "I wonder if we can rethink our equipment needs," he continued. "We're planning to use top-of-the-line equipment, but maybe we can back off from that standard. Is there some equipment we can buy now, and some later? Can we lease or buy used equipment to save money? Can you work out some deals with your equipment suppliers? Maybe if we purchase all or most equipment from the same vendor, they'll lower their costs."

"There may be good ways to reduce costs," said the designer. "However, you're making money on the production of food, and that's not the place to cut corners."

1. What advice would you give the restaurant's planning team about ways to reduce kitchen equipment acquisition costs?
2. Is it a good idea to assume that the restaurant will be a success "from the day the door opens" so profits can be used to pay the equipment and other opening costs? Why or why not?

DESIGNING RESTAURANTS FOR TAKE-AWAY FOOD SERVICES

This chapter has primarily focused on table service restaurants. It concludes with a review of design issues related to drive-through and carryout food services.

Drive-Through Food Services

Many quick-service restaurants offer drive-through service; in some of these restaurants, 60% or more of the total **revenue** generated may be from these sales. In fact, the ability to offer a drive-through alternative is a primary site selection factor for many quick-service restaurants.

Drive-through customers want convenience, fast and accurate service, and high quality food, and these concerns must be considered when you make design and layout decisions related to take-away service.

Not surprisingly, numerous zoning and traffic safety concerns must be addressed during the early stage of drive-through-related construction planning. Local communities will likely have requirements about drive-through lane size and parking lot design, including entrances and exits, the impact of traffic flows around the property and, perhaps, traffic signage; any cost for roadway changes will likely need to be paid by the restaurant owner. Another concern is that governmental reviews, public hearings and other requirements leading to approval can involve a significant time, during which limited additional planning can be done and, as noted above, property purchase/lease may hinge on approval of the drive-through request.

The design of parking lots must accommodate traffic flow through drive-through lanes with additional noncompeting space required for customers who are parking vehicles. There will also be special concerns about pedestrian flow through the parking lot in ways that don't conflict with drive-through traffic. Drive-through and other vehicles must be able to safely merge when entering and exiting the property. Another parking lot concern is that planners often provide space close to the order pickup window for cars to wait for a large or special order to be brought out by an employee.

Parking lot menu boards must be designed and set up to minimize the time required to place orders. There may be a menu board in the drive-through lane for use by customers waiting in line and a second menu board where orders are placed.

Proper lighting in the drive-through lane is critical to ensure customer safety and to illuminate the menu board and ordering station. Some designers specify twice the lighting level of that in the parking lot itself.

Drive-through design concerns that typically must be addressed are the needs for:

- A menu board with speaker and microphone or a window for customers to place orders
- A speaker and microphone or wireless headset system for employees to hear the order if a customer speaker is used
- One or more windows where employees take the order and payment and/or hand the order to the customer

Newer drive-through restaurants feature an electric display within the menu board system to show the full order and total cost. Some restaurants use a secondary display featuring the total order and cost at the payment window.

Orders placed by customers are electronically transmitted by the employee taking the order to preparation areas and entered onto a video screen that monitors preparation. Typically, the same preparation workstations are used for both drive-through and counter services. However, some equipment items, such as additional beverage machines and deep fryers, may be available in the window service area, and POS systems are needed in both window and counter areas.

Drive-through restaurants must have one wall of the kitchen exposed to an outside wall. The typical straight-line flow from production to service may need to be modified to include a turn to the order window about the same distance from the kitchen; in some properties, the window is placed slightly closer to the preparation area. Service employee work flows must be carefully planned because employees must carry food to both service windows and counter areas.

Technology plays a significant role in numerous aspects of quick-service drive-through operations. Some organizations use a remote ordering system in which drive-through customers' orders are routed hundreds or even thousands of miles to a central point and then are relayed back to the specific restaurant for order preparation. Advantages include freeing restaurant employees to focus on production tasks. Off-site order personnel can be trained to up-sell and to know about restaurant-specific issues such as unavailable items.

Revenue

The amount of money generated from the sale of food and beverage products.

WEB AT WORK!

To learn more about how technology can provide a real-time report of drive-through activities so bottlenecks can be corrected, go to:

www.hme.com

Click on "Drive-thru Headsets and Timer Systems."

Systems are available that capture data about the length of time vehicles spend at several points in the drive-through process. This information can identify delay problems that the restaurant's management team can then address.

Surveillance systems must also be considered during design planning. Restaurant managers may wish to monitor activities at the menu board, exterior order window, and the order payment station to view POS operation. Some systems even use cameras to capture license plate data. Other systems perform video tracking of cars as they arrive to fine-tune production estimates about the type and quantity of food that should be prepared.

Carryout Food Services

Quick-service restaurants typically offer carryout food options for guests ("Is your order for here or to go?"), and many table service restaurants have historically prepared foods for guest carryout if they were requested to do so. Today, however, many properties, especially those in the casual service segment, are discovering a new market for carryout services. Revenues from these sales often represent 10% or more of total revenues, and these are generally **incremental sales**.

Incremental sales

Sales that are in addition to, not a replacement of, existing sales.

Carryout orders can be received either by walking into the restaurant or by using curbservice.

WALK-IN FOOD SERVICES   Designing a restaurant for effective carryout service is more complex than it initially seems. Answers to the following questions will drive much of the planning process for this aspect of the restaurant.

Many quick-service restaurants generate 60% or more of their total revenue from drive-through service.

© Scott Nodine/Alamy

- Will orders be received by telephone, fax, through the restaurant's website, and/or when guests arrive at the property?
- Is a separate workstation required in the reception area to accommodate a dedicated employee to take orders, transmit them to production personnel and bring the order to the customer?
- Will a carryout customer wait in line with guests waiting to speak to a receptionist during busy times?
- Where are customers to wait if the order isn't ready when they arrive, and where are prepared orders to be kept until carryout customers arrive?

While managers of many restaurants have recognized the revenue potential for carryout service after their building is constructed, you can begin to see the layout design challenges that must be addressed. The effectiveness of the carryout system is affected by the employees' ability to assist carryout customers.

When restaurants are designed to accommodate carryout services, most potential problems can be minimized. For example, there may be a special entrance, a small area adjacent to the drive-in reception/waiting area, or even a pickup window to make it easier for carryout customers to receive and pay for their meals. A small but comfortable waiting area may also be available.

Many properties offering carryout service provide marked parking spaces for carryout customers to park their vehicles while going into the restaurant for their orders. While this is an excellent idea, carryout customers could still be inconvenienced during busy times by dine-in guests who ignore or miss the signage.

Another design challenge related to carryout involves procedures to increase employee productivity during slow dining periods when, for example, one employee may be able to seat guests desiring table service and assist other customers placing or picking up their carryout orders. Then, planners can consider how to minimize service difficulties when guests must be seated at the same time another customer wants to place or pick up a carryout order. This issue is sometimes addressed by using two employees who have additional work tasks that can be done in the reception and carryout workstations, but these tasks are best considered when the workstations are planned.

CURBSIDE FOOD SERVICES   Some restaurants offering carryout food services allow customers to place their orders away from the property and then pick them up at the curbside. Customers placing orders provide information about vehicle type and color, and an employee brings the order to the car when it arrives at a designated location close to a restaurant entrance.

As with the carryout food services discussed above, the operation of a curbside service is made more or less convenient for the guest and more or less productive for employees based on layout and design planning decisions. Also, like carryout services, these issues are best addressed at the time of building construction rather than figuring out "what will work" in a property not designed for this service alternative.

Customer service will be much more efficient if the curbside employee does not need to use the primary entryway for table service guests.

Restaurants located in cold-weather areas need to address employee comfort issues, and planners of all properties must consider wet floor (safety) issues in indoor areas used to support curbside service. One or more workstations to accommodate the order taker and POS unit and other necessary equipment/materials and/or employees delivering curbside foods will likely be needed.

Technology can assist with almost all aspects of curb side food services as seen in the following example:

- The customer makes menu selection decisions by looking at the restaurant's website. He or she places an electronic order through an online ordering system. Many properties are also equipped to accept orders placed by customers using Web-enabled cell phones—e.g., tweets or text messaging—after supplying an online user name. No employee time is needed for this process.
- The order is transmitted to the property's POS system.

- The order is prepared and packed. Note: Temperature, spills, attractiveness, and ecological concerns require careful analysis of packaging alternatives.
- A notification system can alert the curb-service employee by pager when the customer arrives at the designated curb location. These systems can be interfaced with a computer to track the length of greet and service times.
- The order is taken to the customer, and handheld technology is used to process the payment card transaction. Note: In some properties, the customer uses a payment card to pay for the meal at the time it's ordered.

Note: Typically, all menu items are available through curbside service. With careful planning, an employee can even make salad bar selections for customers, or curbside service customers can be given containers to make a salad bar visit when they arrive.

Restaurant Terms and Concepts

Work in Progress

1. Should restaurant planners consider the menu and the standardized recipes required to produce menu items when food storage, preparation, and production areas are planned? Why or why not?

2. How might technology help in managing purchasing activities to minimize required storage space without an increased risk of running out of stock?

3. Typical restaurant space can be classified by three functions: food storage and production, dining room and beverage production/service. How would you allocate space between these functions?

4. What are some things you could do when designing a dining room to make it flexible for future menu themes?

5. Building codes and other legal requirements can create major cost implications for restaurant construction and remodeling. What are some examples?

6. What are some common food production problems that can occur when kitchens aren't properly planned?

7. What are some common service-related problems that can occur when dining areas aren't properly planned?

8. What are some common operating problems that can occur when bar areas aren't properly planned?

9. What types of problems can occur at Vernon's Restaurant and Banquet Hall if there is busy à la carte service at the same time that an even moderately-sized banquet is being held? What can be done to reduce these problems?

10. What are common problems that can occur when casual-service restaurants offer guests carryout service? How can these problems be minimized?

7
Getting Ready for Production

Learning Objectives

After carefully reading and studying the information in this chapter, you will:

1. Know the information restaurant managers must review prior to making accurate production forecasts.
2. Be able to identify the processes used to purchase needed menu item ingredients in a cost-effective way.
3. Understand the methods used by restaurant operators to prepare purchase orders and manage product inventories.

IN THIS CHAPTER

After a menu has been established and the physical facility readied for operation, restaurant managers turn their attention to the production of the menu items they'll sell.

Preparing for production involves three key areas of management responsibility: 1) production forecasting, 2) purchasing, and 3) inventory management. This chapter addresses each of these important topics.

Production forecasting is an estimate of the number of guest that will be served and what those guests will order from the menu. Without this key step, restaurant managers may have too little food on hand to make the items guests want to buy, which may translate into disappointed guests and reduced sales—or too much food on hand, which can mean increased costs and reduced profits.

After the menu has been planned and estimates made for how many of each menu item will be sold in the future, the food and beverage products needed to make the menu items must be purchased. In this chapter, you'll learn about the importance of effective purchasing techniques and review the critical elements in the purchasing process. This includes thinking carefully about *what* must be purchased, the *quality* and *quantity* of products to purchase, *when* to purchase and just as importantly, from *whom* products should be purchased.

Restaurant managers take several critical steps when determining what they need to buy. First, they calculate how much of a needed ingredient will be used. Next, they establish the amount of product they currently have on hand. An inventory assessment is necessary for several reasons; most importantly, it directly affects the amount of product to be listed on the purchase orders the managers will prepare for their various product suppliers.

A restaurant manager's preproduction activities don't end with the purchasing of products. Every item must be properly checked for quality when it's received, stored properly and finally, issued when needed to the food production workers who will prepare it for guests. In this chapter, you'll learn about all of these essential preproduction activities.

PRODUCTION FORECASTING

A restaurant manager can estimate, or forecast, the number of guests to be served, the number of each menu item that should be produced for sale, or the revenue anticipated for a specific time period.

Production forecast

A list of items to be prepared based on sales estimates for selected menu items.

A **production forecast** is important because it tells restaurant managers how many of each menu item is likely be sold and how much of each menu ingredient must be on hand to serve the number of guests anticipated to be served during a specific time period.

Managers are responsible for production forecasting. In fact, learning to make accurate production forecasts is one of the most critical management skills you can acquire. The importance of an accurate production forecast can be illustrated by answering this question: "Would you like to know how many guests you'll serve next week and what those guests will likely order from the menu when they arrive?" The answer is, of course; yes!

If you knew the answer, you could have the right amount of food on hand to serve all of your guests what they want to be served.

Of course you can't predict your exact sales for any future period. But you can do the next best thing: accurately predict the menu items you'll sell. This is your production forecast. To create an accurate production forecast, restaurant managers use information from the past, present, and future.

Historical Sales Trends

In many areas of business, the past is one of the best indicators of the future. The farther back you can track sales of menu items, the better your future forecasts will be. For example, knowing the number of fish dinners sold in your restaurant on the past 50 Fridays gives you a better forecast of this Friday's fish dinner sales than if you review only the data from last Friday's fish sales.

Modern POS systems allow managers to keep excellent historical records of the sales of past menu items. Some sales data that restaurant managers have found valuable in forecasting the sales of future menu item include:

- The prior day's sales
- Average sales for the prior five *same* days (for example, Sundays or Tuesdays)
- The prior week's average daily sales
- The prior two weeks' average daily sales
- The prior month's average daily sales
- Actual sales on the same day (for the prior month or year)

Figure 7.1 illustrates a typical historical menu item sales report that restaurant managers may retrieve from their POS systems to help them in estimate the number of individual menu items they would forecast to be sold on Monday, January 2.

Historical Menu Item Sales				
Menu Item	Last Monday's Sales	Average Prior 5 Mondays' Sales	Average Daily Sales Last week	Average Daily Sales Last Month
Strip steak	24	21	18	19
Salmon	8	9	10	9
Whitefish	11	14	10	12
Grilled chicken	35	30	32	29
Filet mignon	45	47	42	49

Current Sales Trends

Historical data should always be considered in conjunction with the most recent data available. Assume that a restaurant manager knows that revenues have, on an annual average, increased 5% each month from the same period in the previous year. However, in the last two months, the increase has been closer to zero. This may mean that the increase trend has slowed or stopped completely. Good managers always modify historical trends by closely examining current conditions.

Other factors that can sometimes have an effect on current sales trends include the presence of unusual and adverse weather conditions (which could reduce volume forecast) or concerts, sporting events, festivals, or other activities in the restaurant's market area (which could increase volume forecasts).

Future Sales Trends

For longer-term production forecasts, evaluating future conditions is necessary to estimate the impact that future events will have on revenue. Examples include the opening of new competitive restaurants, specially featured menu items and planned promotions, or even significant changes in your own operating hours.

Local newspapers, trade or business associations, and your chamber of commerce are sources of helpful information about events or circumstances that may affect future sales levels in your restaurant.

When all available historical, current, and future sales trends have been evaluated and considered, restaurant managers can make accurate production forecasts that lead to effective purchasing. Figure 7.2 is an example of a form used for production forecasting.

Note that in Figure 7.2, the restaurant manager reviews all available data and then determines the amount of each item to be prepared for sale on January 2. The production forecast enables the manger to know how much of each menu ingredient or item to have available for sale that day.

FIGURE 7.2

Production Forecast for: Monday, January 2

Menu Item	Last Monday's Sales	Prior 5 Mondays' Sales	Average Daily Sales Last week	Average Daily Sales Last Month	Production Forecast For: Monday, January 2
Strip steak	24	21	18	19	**25**
Salmon	8	9	10	9	**10**
Whitefish	11	14	10	12	**15**
Grilled chicken	35	30	32	29	**40**
Filet mignon	45	47	42	49	**50**

ALL IN A DAY'S WORK: 7.1

"Seriously?" asked the guest. "You're telling me you guys have already run out of the prime rib . . . and baked potatoes?

"I'm sorry sir," replied Justin, the restaurant server. The cooks had just informed him that the kitchen had run out of the two items. "We've been very busy tonight," he continued, apologetically.

"Well, here's the problem," replied the guest. "We only came here because we saw your ad for the Friday night special: prime rib, salad, and baked potato, all for one special price. But now that we're here—and it's only at 8 o'clock—you say you don't have any left? Just what kind of scam are you guys running here?"

1. Do you think the manager of this restaurant manager was actually trying to "scam" customers?
2. What do you think will be the long-term impact on this customer of the restaurant's failure to forecast its sales volume properly?

PURCHASING

Menus dictate the food items to be offered, and standardized recipes indicate the ingredients required to produce the items listed on the menu. A critical process involving several steps will ensure that needed menu ingredients of the right quality will be secured at the right price.

Some very large restaurants and food service operations have a purchasing department with personnel who are specialists in purchasing. Multiunit restaurants and their managers may receive some help from a **centralized purchasing** department.

In smaller-volume restaurants, the manager may order all needed food and beverages, or a kitchen manager may purchase the food, a bar manager may purchase the beverages, and the dining room manager may work with the restaurant manager to determine front-of-house linen, table decoration, and related needs.

Regardless of who bears the responsibilities of buying, it's important to note that the same basic principles are needed to achieve the basic purchasing goal: To obtain the *right* quality of product, in the *right* quantity, from the *right* supplier, at the *right* price, and at the *right* time. Figure 7.3 demonstrates that when that happens, both guests and the restaurant benefit.

Each objective helps explain why effective purchasing is so important.

RIGHT QUALITY The products or ingredients used in a restaurant's standardized recipes will ensure that the menu items served are of consistent quality (which makes guests happy) and served at a known cost (which makes restaurant managers happy).

Consider, for example, the menu description for an 8-ounce (as purchased) the United States Department of Agriculture (USDA) "choice" sirloin steak, which has been pre-costed to help determine its selling price. If an 8-ounce USDA "select" steak is purchased instead, guests won't receive the proper value for their dining dollars. On the other hand, if an 8-ounce USDA "prime" steak is purchased and served, the restaurant manager will spend more than anticipated and higher food costs will result in decreased profits.

Centralized purchasing

A system in which purchasing is the responsibility of a specialist in the purchasing department in a large restaurant or is coordinated with purchasing specialists outside the restaurant in a multi-unit operation.

FIGURE 7.3

Objectives of Effective Purchasing

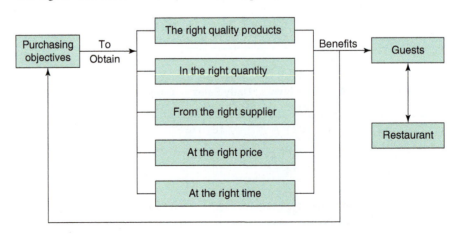

RIGHT QUANTITY   If too little product is purchased, **stockouts** can occur, the restaurant may run out of popular menu items, guests will be disappointed and food production workers may be challenged to produce substitute menu items on short notice. If, however, too much product is purchased, excess money is tied up in inventory, losses due to internal theft of products may increase and there is a greater likelihood of product spoilage.

    Restaurant managers strive to make accurate production forecasts and buy the right amount of ingredients so they can serve the menu items their guests want to buy.

RIGHT SUPPLIER   Restaurant managers in most locations have several sources of supply for many of the products they buy. More than just a product is purchased, however, when a purchase decision is made. Information and service are also very important, and some suppliers do a better job of providing this assistance than others. Furthermore, a supplier offering a "good" price who fails to deliver the promised product on time or of an appropriate quality isn't helping the food service operation achieve its goals.

RIGHT PRICE   Some restaurant managers think that the lowest price means the best price. But experienced restaurant managers know that the value received for the money spent is more important than the lowest price.

    Guests look for value when they purchase menu items. In the same way, restaurant managers want value in the product purchase decisions they make. Price is important, but quality, dependability, and service are also important.

RIGHT TIME   Products ordered for a Saturday night menu special must be delivered on a timely basis. If they're received several days before the Saturday evening special, they may not be fresh when needed. If they're received on the Monday after the event, they're of no use. Food and beverage buyers know that having the right ingredients on hand when they need them is of critical importance to their restaurants' success.

Purchasing Specifications

The question, "What should be purchased?" appears easy to answer: A restaurant manager should purchase ingredients specified by the standardized recipes used to make the restaurant's menu items. However, this question is really more difficult to answer because the exact type of needed ingredients must be identified.

    To do that properly, restaurant managers must understand that the best ingredient to buy is the one with the highest level of quality. The best quality for an item doesn't relate to its cost,

Stockout

The situation that exists when food or beverage products required for production aren't available for service.

Restaurant managers know quality menu items start with quality ingredients.

ifong/Shutterstock

The best purchase specifications make it easy to determine if the product delivered conforms to the specification.

Purchase specification

A tool that details the product characteristics of a specific food or beverage item purchased for a restaurant. Also known as a "spec."

Competitive bidding

A tactic used by purchasers who compare suppliers' prices for those products meeting specifications to determine which supplier is offering the best price.

but rather to its intended use. The closer an item comes to being suitable for its actual use, the better its quality. For example, fresh whole tomatoes will likely be necessary for a chef's salad, while canned tomato pieces may be "best" for use in making a vegetable soup.

Purchase specifications describe the quality requirements of a specific food or beverage product.

Effective purchase specifications have several key characteristics, including:

- Simple (short) as possible while still providing an accurate description of the product.
- Capable of being met, whenever possible, by several suppliers to encourage **competitive bidding**.
- Reasonable to meet and include tolerances (variances) that can consistently be provided by qualified suppliers. For example, a 5-ounce pre-cut steak may have a tolerance of ¼ ounce. Thus, an acceptable steak could weigh between 4⅞ and 5⅛ ounces and still meet specifications.
- Capable of being easily verified upon delivery to ensure that proper quality is received.

Purchase specifications must be carefully developed and should be updated when a restaurant's needs change, its customers preferences evolve, or when new product alternatives become available.

WEB AT WORK!

USDA's Institutional Meat Purchasing Specifications (IMPS) are widely used as a standard for quality descriptions of products as government agencies, schools, restaurants, hotels, and other food service users specify quality requirements to suppliers. To review these specifications, go to:

www.usda.gov

Enter "*IMPS*" in the search field to review general requirements and quality assurance provisions of grading systems; review details for beef, lamb and mutton, veal and calf, pork, and a variety of processed meat items.

Many hospitality organizations use a template of basic information for all (or most) of the products for which specifications are developed.

The information typically contained in a product specification includes:

- Product name or specification number
- Pricing unit
- Standard or grade
- Count/weight/range/size
- Tolerance allowed
- Color
- Geographic origin
- Processing and/or packaging
- Intended use

When restaurant managers carefully detail what they wish to purchase, their suppliers will better understand the context in which the product is needed. They may also be able to provide suggestions about alternative products that were not considered, or which were not available when the purchase specification was initially developed.

Detailed purchase specifications are important to use, but restaurant managers must also remember that information included in the specification must be measurable. Specifying, "corn-fed beef" and the minimum butter fat content of ice cream is very easy to write into a specification, but these quality requirements are difficult to verify upon delivery. If these concerns are important, it may be best to order, in the first instance, from a reputable supplier and, in the second example, by brand of ice cream. Sometimes, hard-to-measure quality information, such as the fat content of ground beef is very important. Large-volume purchasers of this product should, on a routine but random basis, have incoming samples analyzed by a qualified laboratory to confirm that the fat content requirement is met.

It's important to recognize that restaurants will pay for the quality of items identified by their purchase specifications even if they don't receive that quality. In other words, if an item of specified quality is ordered, the product must be inspected when it's received to ensure that the quality is correct. For that reason, professional receiving practices will be addressed later in this chapter. In all cases, however, restaurant managers should ensure that they're buying from qualified food service suppliers, who:

- Consistently provide the quality of products listed in the specification
- Offer products at a reasonable price
- Meet product delivery schedules
- Understand the importance of food safety and proper food handling procedures
- Provide useful support services
- Offer useful product information to the restaurant's manager
- Take ownership of problems that occur and correct them promptly
- Inform the restaurant manager in a timely way about order or delivery problems
- Enjoy a stable financial position
- Are mutually interested in providing value to guests and suggest how costs can be reduced without sacrificing quality
- Have similar values about the importance of maintaining ethical business relationships
- Employ a highly motivated workforce
- Have a genuine interest in helping restaurant managers achieve their goals

WEB AT WORK!

Detailed information about the development of food service purchasing specifications is available in a variety of hospitality industry textbooks. To choose one, go to:

www.amazon.com

Enter "Hospitality Purchasing" or "Hospitality Procurement" in the search field. The authors recommend *Purchasing: A Guide for Hospitality Professionals* written by Hayes and Ninemeier and published by Pearson Education.

Product Yield Percentage

Knowing what to buy and who to buy from are important, but equally important to restaurant managers is knowing *how much* to buy. This purchasing task would be much easier if all products purchased had a 100% product yield. Some products do, but many don't.

For example, a gallon of soy sauce purchased for use in recipes will have a 100% yield because there's no product loss when the soy sauce is used. A pound of fresh onions, however, will most often yield much less than 16 ounces of **recipe-ready** ingredients after the onions have been peeled, trimmed, and chopped for use.

In Chapter 5, you learned that the yield of an ingredient has a direct impact on the recipe-costing process. Thus, for example, if an item is purchased for $3.00 per pound, but its yield is only 50%, the recipe-ready cost of the ingredient is actually $6.00 per pound ($3.00 as purchased cost ($\div$) .50 product yield = $6.00 recipe-ready cost).

Just as a product's yield affects the process of recipe costing, it also affects the purchasing process. For example, assume a restaurant manager wished to serve a 2-ounce mixed green salad to 80 guests. This manager would need 160 ounces, or 10 lbs. of ready-to-serve salad greens (80 guests ($\times$) 2 oz. serving =160 oz. or 10 lbs. of prepared salad greens).

If this manager purchased only 10 pounds of unprocessed fresh salad ingredients, and if loss resulting from the trimming, cleaning, or chopping process occurred, less than 10 pounds of salad would actually be available for service to guests. As a result, 80 2-oz. salads couldn't be prepared. To avoid this problem, buyers who know how much of a recipe-ready ingredient is needed can calculate the ingredient's yield percentage to help determine how much of it they should purchase.

To do that, kitchen managers must know how much of the ingredient they begin with and how much of it remains after it has been fully processed. For example, if a kitchen manager begins with 10 pounds of an ingredient and, after processing, only 9 pounds of the ingredient remain, that ingredient has a 90% yield.

To calculate the **product yield percentage** of any ingredient, restaurant managers use the following product yield percentage formula:

$$\frac{\text{Ending product amount}}{\text{Beginning product amount}} = \text{Product yield percentage}$$

To illustrate, assume that a restaurant manager purchases 10 pounds of fresh carrots (beginning product amount). If after peeling, trimming, and chopping, 8 pounds of recipe-ready carrots remain (ending product amount), the product yield percentage would be computed as:

$$\frac{8 \text{ lbs. ending product amount}}{10 \text{ lbs. beginning product amount}} = 80\% \text{ product yield percentage}$$

Or

$$\frac{8 \text{ lbs.}}{10 \text{ lbs.}} = 80\% \text{ product yield}$$

Restaurant managers who must know product yield percentages on the many different products they buy can readily secure estimates published by a variety of sources (simply Google "edible yields of foods"). However, experienced managers know the actual product yield percentage achieved in their kitchens will depend upon a variety of factors, including:

- The quality of the product originally purchased
- The length of time the product has been in storage
- The skill of the kitchen's employees
- The quality of tools available for product processing
- The actual recipe-ready form of the product required (e.g., sliced, diced, or chopped)

For that reason, many managers prefer to regularly perform their own **yield tests**.

It is critical that restaurant managers know the product yield percentages for each of the products they buy. They can ensure that they'll always purchase the *right quantity* of ingredients to make the menu items they want to serve their guests.

Recipe-ready

The form of an ingredient when it's fully prepared to be added to a recipe. For example, leaf lettuce that has been washed, trimmed, and chopped would be considered, "recipe-ready" for making a leaf lettuce salad.

Product yield percentage

The ratio of a recipe-ready ingredient to its original purchase form.
For example, if the original purchase amount of an ingredient is 10 pounds, but after processing, only 7 pounds of recipe-ready ingredient remain, that product has a 70% product yield (7 lbs. ($\div$) 10 lbs. = 70% product yield).

Yield test

A carefully controlled process to determine the amount (in weight or percentage) of a product that remains after it has been processed into its recipe-ready state.

Edible Portion (EP) Amounts

Because many food products don't have a 100% yield, restaurant managers must calculate the edible portion (EP) amount of these items to determine the as-purchased (AP) weight, count, or volume they must buy to serve their guests. Knowing how to do that properly is an important restaurant management skill.

To illustrate, consider Sasha, the manager for an upscale restaurant. After carefully reviewing her historic and future forecast sales data, Sasha has created a production forecast that estimates that 100 6-oz. beef tenderloin fillets will be sold this coming Saturday night.

Sasha has performed extensive yield tests on the whole beef tenderloins she purchases for this menu item. The tests reveal that there's an approximate 60% yield for this item; thus, the **production loss** is 40%.

An ingredient's production loss percentage is calculated as:

$$\text{AP amount (100\%)} - \text{Yield \%} = \text{Product loss \%}$$

Thus, when Sasha buys the tenderloins in this example, her calculation would be:

$$\text{100\% AP amount} - \text{60\% yield} = \text{40\% product loss}$$

If each tenderloin weighed 10 pounds, the calculation would be

$$\text{10 lbs. AP amount} - \text{6 lbs. EP yield} = \text{4 lbs. product loss}$$

Sasha could also rearrange her formula to calculate the EP yield as follows:

$$\text{10 lbs. AP amount} - \text{4 lbs. product loss} = \text{6 lbs. EP yield}$$

Using what she knows about this item's yield percentages, Sasha now knows that only 60% of the amount of whole tenderloins she buys can be served on Saturday night. Therefore, the amount she needs to buy can be easily calculated using the following formula:

$$\frac{\text{EP amount needed}}{\text{Yield \%}} = \text{Amount to purchase}$$

In this example,

$$\frac{\text{100 portions needed } (\times) \text{ 6 oz. per portion}}{\text{60\% yield}} = \frac{600 \; oz.}{.60} = 1{,}000 \; oz.$$

Converted to pounds, the amount she must purchase is:

$$\frac{1{,}000}{16 \; oz.} = 62.5 \text{ pounds}$$

Production loss

The amount of a product's AP weight that is not servable; this may be due to loss from trimming (for example, removing fat and bones), processing, or cooking.

When managers purchase whole poultry products, or wholesale cuts of fresh beef, pork, or lamb, the production losses incurred to make these items recipe-ready can be significant.

WEB AT WORK!

In the past, EP and AP yield data for common foods have been available for free only in a printed format from the USDA.

Today, yields for many common foods are available on the Internet. To access this yield data, go to:

http://www.nal.usda.gov/fnic/foodcomp/Data/

Since each tenderloin weighs approximately 10 pounds, Sasha must buy seven loins (62.5 lbs. ÷ 10-lb. loin = 6.25 pieces; rounded to 7 pieces) if she is to have enough on hand to serve 100 steaks on Saturday night.

The preparation of many fresh foods, including fruits, vegetables, and meats will result in production loss. Understanding yield percentage and EP amounts needed is important for restaurant managers to accurately determine the AP ingredient amounts they must order to produce the number of items called for in their production forecasts.

As Purchased (AP) Amounts

You've learned that the AP amount of a product multiplied by its yield percentage equals its EP amount as shown in the following formula:

$$\text{AP amount} \ (\times) \ \text{Yield \%} = \text{EP amount}$$

By using algebra and rearranging the parts of this formula, you can easily calculate an AP amount:

$$\frac{\text{EP amount}}{\text{Yield \%}} = \text{AP amount}$$

The ability to calculate an AP amount is important because it helps you know how much of an ingredient you must buy or have on hand to make a recipe. For example, if you have a standardized recipe that calls for 10 pounds of diced carrots and you have calculated that carrots have an 80% yield, the AP amount formula lets you know how many whole carrots you need to prepare the recipe. In this example, the calculation would be:

$$\frac{10 \text{ lbs.}}{80\% \text{ yield}} = \text{AP amount needed}$$

Or

$$\frac{10 \text{ lbs.}}{.80} = 12.5 \text{ lbs.}$$

Restaurant managers can use the AP amount formula to calculate the quantity of an item they must buy or have on hand anytime they know the EP amount needed for a recipe as well as the yield or loss percentage of the ingredient to be used.

INVENTORY MANAGEMENT

After restaurant managers calculate the amount of ingredients needed to produce the menu items they forecast they will sell, they must assess the ingredient amounts they have in **inventory**.

When they know the amounts of ingredients needed, as well as the amounts in inventory, they can use subtraction to determine the amounts they need to purchase by using the following formula:

Inventory

The list of the food and beverages used in a restaurant and the amount of those items currently on hand.

Product amount needed − Product amount in inventory = Amount to buy

Product inventories may be held in a number of different kitchen locations, including:

- Dry storage areas: located throughout the facility
- Freezers: including walk-ins and reach-ins

1. Ingredient	2. Purchase Unit (PU)	3. In Storage	4. In Production	5. Total Inventory
Block cheddar cheese	Pound	5 lbs.	2 lbs.	7 lbs.
Grated cheddar cheese	Pound	1.5 lbs.	3.5 lbs.	5 lbs.

FIGURE 7.4

Restaurant Inventory Worksheet

- Refrigerators: including walk-ins and reach-ins
- Production areas: including dry, refrigerated, and freezer areas within production stations

To determine the amount of an ingredient in inventory, kitchen managers must know five things about it.

1. *The name of the ingredient*: Or its product specification precisely identifies the ingredient on hand.
2. *The purchase unit*: Ingredients may be purchased and stored in a variety of containers, including cases, cans, boxes, bags, cartons, gallons, and pounds. Regardless of how it's received, the purchase unit (PU) represents the measurement in which the item is purchased. Generally, the PU will be the same unit in which the item is counted in inventory. However, the PU and inventory unit may sometimes vary. Examples include flour purchased by the bag and inventoried by the pound, and steak sauce purchased by the 48-bottle case but inventoried by the single bottle.
3. *The amount in storage*: This is the amount or number of units in all of the operation's storage areas, including refrigerators, freezers, and dry goods storage.
4. *The amount in production*: This is the amount or number of units already prepared or held in preparation and postproduction areas such as cooks lines and pantries.
5. *The total amount in inventory*: This is the sum of the amounts held in storage and in production.

To calculate the amount of inventory on hand, restaurant managers use a form similar to the one shown in Figure 7.4.

Purchase Orders

When restaurant managers know the amounts of ingredients needed to service their guests (from their production forecasts) and the amounts they have on hand (in inventory), they prepare a **purchase order (PO)** to inform suppliers about what must be delivered to the restaurant to ensure that all of the ingredients they need will be on hand the day they're needed. Figure 7.5 is an example of a typical PO used in a restaurant.

Note that (upper right-hand corner) the PO number and date are included, as are the preferred delivery date and property contact information in case the supplier has questions.

The purchase order also indicates that the "terms" are "net 30." This means that the buyer will pay the total amount of the invoice ($783.17) within 30 days of the delivery date. Sometimes buyers negotiate a discounted price for faster payment. For example, payment terms might be: "2/10; net 30." That means the buyer will receive a 2% discount if the total invoice is paid within 10 days; otherwise, the total invoice amount is due within 30 days of the invoice date.

Today's POs are often computer generated; needed quantities may also be entered into an online PO format provided on the restaurant supplier's website or submitted to vendors via e-mail or

Purchase order (PO)

A document that communicates to suppliers the quantities to be delivered and the prices to be paid by a restaurant for needed inventory items.

FIGURE 7.5

Sample Purchase Order

Vernon's Restaurant Purchase Order				

From/Ship to:

Vernon's Restaurant
1710 W. Summer Street
Hospitality Island, 00000
Telephone: 000-000-0000

Purchase from:

Rockville Grocers
2451 Elm Rd.
Center Place, NV.
00000

PO No: 34X135
PO Date: 7/16/20xx
Delivery Date: 7/20/20xx
Contact: Eric Davis
Terms: Net 30

Item Purchased	Spec #	Quantity Ordered	Quoted Price	Extended Price
Green beans	1715	4 cases(#10 cans)	34.50	138.00
Flour, all purpose	18100	3 bags (50#)	22.17	66.51
			Total	**783.17**

Terms and Conditions:

This purchase order expressly limits acceptance to the terms and conditions stated above and included on the following page. Any additional terms and conditions are rejected.

Buyer: Eric Davis   Date: 7/16/20xx

Received by: _____ Date: _____
Delivery Instructions: _____
_____
_____

fax. It's always the role of the restaurant manager to ensure that needed ingredients are ordered, received and available for their issue to production staff at the proper time and in the proper quantity.

Receiving

After purchase orders have been prepared and placed, the items will be delivered by a restaurant's chosen suppliers. When they arrive at the restaurant, proper receiving procedures must be in place. Effective product receiving requires attention to personnel, the receiving area, and the tools and equipment needed for receiving activities.

RECEIVING PERSONNEL Only well-trained and qualified staff members should perform receiving tasks. Some receiving procedures are clerical (signing documents) or physical (moving boxes and cases); however, the ability to recognize the quality of incoming products and to confirm that they meet the property's standards is the most important part of a receiving clerk's job, and mastering it requires training and experience. This is especially important for products such as fresh produce, meats, and seafood that aren't typically purchased by a brand name that appears on the item's packaging or label.

Careful observation and inspection of incoming items are essential to ensure that purchase specification requirements are met. Large-volume food service operations may have full-time receiving clerks responsible for all receiving tasks, but most restaurants don't. In either case, restaurant managers must ensure that receiving tasks are consistently performed by staff members who:

- *Maintain food safety standards*: Food safety and sanitation concerns are important aspects of quality. Foods must be carefully inspected upon arrival to ensure that pre-delivery safe food handling procedures have been used by the vendor supplying the product.

GREEN AT WORK!

Restaurant managers know that the cost of removing solid wastes, such as cardboard, cans, and plastic containers from their operations can be expensive. Therefore, many buyers have encouraged suppliers who ship products to them to practice **source reduction** and have aggressively implemented creative programs to reduce the generation of their solid wastes from various forms of food packaging, wrappings, and containers.

Source reduction also decreases the amount of materials or energy used during the manufacturing and distribution of products and packages. Because it stops waste before it starts, source reduction is the top solid waste priority of the U.S. Environmental Protection Agency (EPA).

Source reduction is not the same as recycling. Recycling is collecting already used materials and making them into another product. Recycling begins at the end of a product's life, whereas source reduction takes place when the product and its packaging are being designed. Perhaps the best way to think about source reduction and recycling is as complementary activities: Combined, source reduction and recycling have a significant influence on preventing solid waste, saving resources, and preserving the planet.

Source reduction conserves raw material and energy resources because less packaging material and concentrated products typically use fewer materials and less energy to manufacture and ship. The result is lower purchase prices for products. Source reduction also cuts back on what has to be thrown away, which helps keep solid waste disposal costs down.

Specific source reduction strategies that can be implemented by hospitality buyers include:

Purchasing concentrated products: For example, the cost of packaging and shipping water in products such as broths and stocks can be eliminated by the use of concentrated food bases. Juices may be purchased in concentrated form and reconstituted on-site.

Buying the largest size container that can be used efficiently: In general, per-unit prices for items purchased in large packages are lower than the same items purchased in smaller sizes. The result is lower food costs, less packaging material to throw away, and lower costs of packaging disposal.

Buying refill systems whenever possible: For example, ketchup dispensers that can be refilled generate less waste than individually wrapped single portion packages and reduce product costs as well.

Source reduction

The effort by product manufacturers to design and ship products to minimize waste resulting from a product's shipping and delivery.

- *Maintain quality standards*: The restaurant employee accepting delivery of incoming foods must be able to immediately recognize quality and to determine if the products delivered meet the product specifications the restaurant has established for them. The items delivered by a supplier must be identical in quality to those ordered by the buyer. It's the receiving clerk's job to ensure that this is always true.
- *Are qualified to resolve product delivery issues*: What should be done on those occasions when incoming products don't meet quality requirements? What if incorrect quantities are delivered or products don't arrive when they should? Effective receiving personnel must be trained to address these and related questions in a way that best serve the long-term purchasing objectives of the restaurant.

RECEIVING AREAS The best location for a restaurant's receiving area is often close to the kitchen's back door; however, in very large food service operations—such as those found in hospitals, colleges, and hotels—they may be close to a loading dock that is far from food storage and food production areas. There must always be adequate space to inspect, count, and weigh incoming products. The receiving area may also require space for a desk, file cabinet, or other equipment; computer access is often needed because of the increasing use of technology during receiving tasks.

Useful receiving tools include pocket thermometers, to determine the temperatures of perishable products, and plastic tote boxes or other containers to transport ice for products such as fresh poultry and seafood. Increasingly, smart devices, notebook or laptop computers, and/or other wireless devices are used to access purchasing and inventory records required while receiving.

Restaurant managers must ensure that personnel follow the four steps shown in Figure 7.6 when receiving food and beverage products.

FIGURE 7.6

Four Steps for Effective Receiving

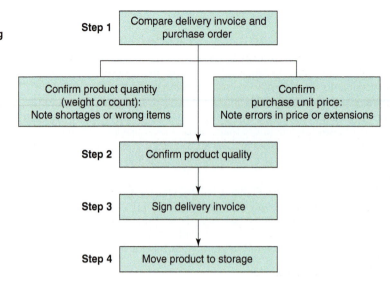

As you review Figure 7.6, note that the first step taken in the receiving process is to compare the delivery invoice to a copy of the PO to help ensure that the quantity and price of products agreed upon when purchased are correct when they're delivered.

Some items, such as cases of canned goods or bags of flour, can be counted, but others, such as fresh meats or seafood ordered by the pound, must be weighed. If prices listed on the delivery invoice don't match those on the PO, management should be alerted to investigate the reason for the difference.

The second step shown in Figure 7.6 involves confirming that the quality of the incoming products meets those contained in the restaurant's purchase specifications. This step is very important and often the most challenging. Standards incorporated into purchase specifications must be easily observable so incoming products can be visually compared with the specifications. If receiving personnel have concerns about product quality they cannot address, they should be instructed to seek guidance from a manager or other qualified restaurant staff member.

If no variations from product standards or other quality-related problems are observed, the delivery invoice can be signed (Step 3). However, if there are product shortages or quality-related problems, adjustments to the delivery invoice must be made and verified by both receiving personnel and the supplier. This is important because the signed delivery invoice is usually the basis for payments that will be made to the supplier. As a result, accurately confirming what was actually delivered, rather than merely what was ordered, is a critical step in the receiving process.

After the delivery invoice has been signed, Step 4 in Figure 7.6 indicates that receiving personnel must quickly move products to their proper storage areas. This helps prevent the loss of quality in refrigerated or frozen products and to reduce the possibility of product theft.

ALL IN A DAY'S WORK: 7.2

"This lettuce doesn't look good at all," said Joan, the receiving clerk at Vernon's Restaurant.

"I know, but it's all like that," replied Dave, the driver for Brother's Produce.

Joan and Dave were talking about a shipment of 10 cases of iceberg lettuce that had been ordered by Vernon's and that Dave was now delivering.

"Well, we're going to lose a lot more product than normal in trimming and cleaning these cases," said Joan. "That may leave us short for the weekend."

"There's nothing wrong with the lettuce," replied Dave. "Look, be a pal. I'm trying to get done early today to get home and see my son's baseball game. Can you just sign the invoice? I gotta get going."

1. If you were Joan, would you sign for the lettuce?
2. If the lettuce were accepted, what steps should Joan take to deal with potential guest feedback related to the quality of the lettuce?

Storage

Experienced kitchen managers know that the quality of most food products will never be better than when they're received; that is, they won't improve while they're in storage. However, product quality can suffer if proper storage practices aren't used. Furthermore, a restaurant's financial goals are directly affected by storage practices. For example, purchased products that are stored effectively will be used to generate revenue. However, if they're not, spoilage will occur, food costs will increase (some products that have been purchased and paid for must be discarded) and more food will need to be purchased at additional cost to replace the discarded food.

Three basic types of storage areas can minimize food loss due to improper storage, including:

- *Dry storage (50°F–70°F; 10°C–21.1°C)*: grocery items, including canned goods, condiments, bakery products such as flour and sugar, and herbs and spices.
- *Refrigerated storage (less than 41°F; 5°C)*: fresh meat, produce, seafood, and dairy products.
- *Frozen storage (less than 0°F; –17.8°C)*: frozen meats, seafood, ice cream, French fries, and other vegetables purchased in this market form.

The location of storage areas is also important. The ideal space is close to the receiving area and between the receiving and food production areas. Storage areas are frequently affected by facility remodeling, however, which can occur several times during the life of the building that houses the food service operation.

Experienced restaurant managers know they have four important concerns directly related to the storage process:

- Quality concerns
- Physical locations
- Record keeping
- Security concerns

QUALITY CONCERNS Products can decline in quality even under the best environmental conditions if, for example, suggested storage times are exceeded or if proper storage temperatures aren't maintained. The recommended temperatures for different storage areas noted earlier in this chapter should be maintained, and they should be monitored on a regular basis.

Storage areas should be cleaned on a regularly scheduled basis. Shelving units should keep products off the floor and away from the walls and ceilings to ease the cleaning process and to

It's essential to keep food storage areas clean and free of clutter.

improve air circulation. Managers who maintain proper storage environments minimize the time that products are in storage. By regularly monitoring the temperatures of storage areas, they're taking significant steps to manage product quality.

PHYSICAL LOCATIONS   Locations for product storage vary in restaurants of different sizes, but typically consist of two main types:

General Storage Areas: These dry, refrigerated, and frozen food storage areas hold the majority of a restaurant's product inventory. In high-volume restaurants, these storage areas will hold a significant proportion of the restaurant's total product inventory.

Production Storage Areas: These dry, refrigerated, and frozen food storage areas hold product inventory that is cooked, ready to be cooked, or served. For example, in a high-volume steakhouse, some meat and seafood products are held in general refrigerated or frozen storage areas, while the steaks and seafood items to be cooked immediately are placed in production storage areas near the restaurant's cooks' line, grill, broiler, or fryer areas. In some restaurants, these storage areas may hold 50% or more of the restaurant's total product inventory.

RECORD KEEPING   Restaurant mangers seeking to accurately record the amount and the value of their product inventories choose from two basic inventory record keeping systems:

Physical inventory
Perpetual inventory

Physical inventory system

A process used to determine the quantity and value of product inventory on hand at a specific point in time.

Physical Inventory   In a **physical inventory system**, managers do a regularly scheduled physical count of the items in storage and then assign a monetary value to those items.

Figure 7.7 shows a sample inventory form used in physical inventory systems; the form may be a hard copy or generated by a computer.

When reviewing Figure 7.7, note that there are three cases of green beans in the general storage area and one case in the production storage area. The case counts in both areas are added together to arrive at the total number of units in storage. Each case has a purchase price of $31.50, for a total inventory value of $126.00 (4 cases (×) $31.50 per case = $126.00 total inventory value).

Physical inventories can be taken daily, weekly, or monthly. While often time-consuming to complete, physical inventories generate the information needed for cost of goods sold calculations (see Chapter 11) and to help ensure that neither too much nor too little inventory is on hand.

Perpetual inventory system

A process that records all products entering and being issued from storage so managers know, on an ongoing basis, the amount of product that should be in inventory.

Perpetual Inventory   In a **perpetual inventory system**, managers don't conduct a physical count of the items in storage prior to assigning a monetary value to their inventories.

The advantage of a perpetual inventory system is that, when used properly, restaurant managers know, at *any* point in time, the quantity of products that should be available in inventory.

A perpetual inventory system works in a way very similar to an individual's personal checkbook. As money (food and beverage products) is deposited in the bank (brought into the storeroom), the balance on the checking account (food products in the storeroom) is increased.

As money is withdrawn from the bank (food products are issued to production areas), the balance of money (food products) in the bank (storeroom) decreases. Therefore, at any point in

FIGURE 7.7

Physical Inventory Form

Item	Purchase Unit	No. of Inventory Units		Total Units	Purchase Price	Total Cost
		In Storage	In Production			
Green Beans	Case	3	1	4	$31.50	$126.00
					Total	$126.00

WEB AT WORK!

Computerized systems are available to help managers with inventory counts and to calculate the value of their inventories. Today, optical scanners can be used to read bar codes on containers of products in storage. This method provides a fast and accurate way to take a physical inventory. To view a bar code scanning system designed specifically for restaurateurs, go to:

www.restaurantinventory.com

time, a person knows the amount of money (quantity of products) that should be in the account (in inventory). Because a perpetual inventory only indicates what "should" be in inventory, experienced managers know that periodic checks to ensure that perpetual inventory and actual inventory amounts are the same are essential.

While it may not be practical or even useful for food service operations to maintain all products under a perpetual inventory system, many restaurant managers use a perpetual inventory system for their most expensive inventory items.

Figure 7.8 shows the format for a perpetual inventory form. The information collected is the same regardless of whether a computerized or manual record keeping system is in use.

When reviewing Figure 7.8, note that strip steaks are considered to be an especially important item because they're expensive and potentially prone to theft. Since they're valuable, they're included in the restaurant's perpetual inventory system.

In this example, there were 37 individual (6 oz.) servings of this item on hand when the new form was begun. On the first date (9/10), 25 steaks were issued, leaving a balance of only 12 steaks in inventory (37 steaks − 25 steaks = 12 steaks). On the next date (9/11), 35 steaks were purchased, and 20 steaks were issued. This left a net balance of 15 steaks, which increased the inventory balance to 27 servings (12 steaks + 35 steaks − 20 steaks = 27 steaks).

On a routine but random basis, the kitchen manager can spot-check the number of strip steaks in the assigned storage area to ensure that the number of servings available in inventory equals the balance recorded on the perpetual inventory form. POS sales records are useful to ensure that the number of steaks indicated as taken from inventory match the number of steaks sold.

SECURITY CONCERNS The products held in a restaurant's various storage locations have been purchased with the intent that they'll be used to generate revenues. If, instead, they're stolen, money will have been spent and food expenses will be increased, but there will be no resulting revenue. Therefore, food and beverage expenses costs will be greater than necessary, and profit levels will be lower than they should be.

Experienced managers should consider their storage areas to be similar to bank vaults. Their storage procedures should address the question, "How should money be managed in a bank vault?" Simple procedures such as storing products in lockable areas with walls that extend to the ceiling and limiting access to storage areas can help reduce employee theft and pilferage. Differences between perpetual inventory quantities as recorded on perpetual inventory forms (if used) and the quantities actually available in storage should be investigated.

FIGURE 7.8
Perpetual Inventory Form

Item: Strip steaks (6 oz.)			
Date	No. of Purchase Units		Balance
	In	Out	
			37
9/10/xx	-----	25	12
9/11/xx	35	20	27

WEB AT WORK!

A perpetual inventory system is a method of immediately accounting for inventory sales in the inventory account, when there is no theft or spoilage. It's an inventory system in which an operation's POS system can easily record product usage after every sale.

Modern POS systems include perpetual inventory modules as well as product usage-costing modules and even programs that create recommended lists of items that must be purchased to replenish inventories to predetermined levels.

To review these types of advanced POS systems, go to your favorite search engine.

Type "perpetual inventory module for POS" in the search field.

Experienced restaurant managers know that problems can arise when employees have unlimited access to storage areas. They also understand that these problems are likely made worse when nonemployees are allowed to enter storage areas. This can happen, for example, in food service operations that allow or even encourage delivery personnel to transport incoming items to storage areas. Ideally, arriving products are formally received in a non storage area and transported to the storage area by a designated receiving clerk (in a large operation) or by a designated food service employee (in smaller operations).

Issuing

Issuing is the process of moving products from storage to production areas. Some operations use an "open-door" approach to issuing. This means that whenever a production worker needs a product, he or she simply goes to the proper storage area and removes it. Employees are "in charge" of their own issuing. For example, production personnel retrieve food products, bartenders re-stock bar areas, dining room servers may pick up bus tubs of pre-prepared salad greens from the refrigerator and bus persons have unlimited access to storage areas for the condiments needed to re-stock server areas. In other operations, the issuing process is formalized. In such cases, employees may be required to obtain management approval prior to removing costly items from inventory.

Restaurant managers must ensure the security of products held in inventory if they're to maintain control over their food and beverage costs.

© Thoma/Shutterstock

While receiving results in added inventory levels, issuing reduces inventory levels. So restaurant managers responsible for preparing their operations' purchase orders must be well aware of:

- The actual amount of product in inventory
- The amount of product the operation wishes to keep on hand (often referred to as "**par stock**")
- The amount of time between the placement of an order for a product and its delivery

Par stock

The predetermined amount of an inventory item that should be kept on hand at all times.

When inventories are managed properly, restaurant operators have the information they need to minimize storage-related product losses and make sound purchasing decisions.

Restaurant Terms and Concepts

Work in Progress

1. Assume you were the area restaurant manager in charge of four separate restaurants. What would be some advantages of utilizing a centralized purchasing system? What would be some advantages of utilizing a decentralized purchasing system?

2. Worker skill affects the product yield percentage of many fresh products. How will you determine if your workers are trained well enough to maximize the product yields they achieve or if they require additional training?

3. Why do you think some food service operations don't permit product deliveries during busy food serving times?

4. Assume that you had been ordering meat products from a specific supplier for a long period of time. Would you still require receiving personnel to weigh every incoming container of meat products? Why or why not?

5. Some food distributors indicate that their delivery personnel will, at no extra cost, help to move in-coming products from receiving to storage areas. If you were a restaurant manager, would you accept this assistance? What security concerns would you have in such an arrangement?

6. Why is accuracy in the preparation of purchase orders (POs) so important in the product cost control process?

7. What are some practical ways to monitor the temperature in refrigerated, frozen, and dry storage areas to best ensure that maximum food quality will be retained while products are stored in these areas?

8. Whom do you believe should be responsible for training a restaurant's receiving personnel?

9. Assume you were experiencing repeated instances of what you believe to be employee initiated inventory theft. What steps could you take to stop or minimize these occurrences?

10. What are two advantages of using a physical inventory system in a restaurant? What are two advantages of using a perpetual inventory system?

Quality Foods

Learning Objectives

After carefully reading and studying the information in this chapter, you will:

1. Know the factors that must be managed to ensure quality food production.
2. Understand the reasons for the increasing importance of a "farm-to-fork" orientation as it relates to quality food services.
3. Recognize the ingredient characteristics, storage, and preparation methods used to produce a variety of high-quality menu items.

IN THIS CHAPTER

Restaurant customers seek value for the dollars they spend dining out. Restaurant managers can help ensure that their customers receive good value when all of the menu items sold are produced and served in ways that consistently achieve pre-established quality standards.

    This chapter begins with an examination of the importance of quality and describes what restaurant managers must do to maximize the quality and value they deliver to their customers.

Increasingly, customer perceptions of the value they receive when dining out are associated with a restaurant's commitment to serving the most healthful and flavorful food possible. Increased consumer awareness and heightened interest on the part of food service professionals has resulted in a careful examination of the way foods are handled from "farm-to-fork."

Maximizing product freshness and minimizing unnecessary processing are key aspects of the farm-to-fork movement. In this chapter, you'll learn about some of the reasons restaurant managers apply farm-to-fork techniques that benefit guests, local economies, and their own restaurants. You'll also learn how decisions related to product sustainability affect the way increasing numbers of guests view a restaurant's commitment to green practices: an increasingly important factor in how these diners assess restaurant quality.

To meet pre-established food quality standards, restaurant managers must know a great deal about the menu ingredients they purchase. When these ingredients are purchased and delivered to the operation, managers must also know how they should be handled and stored until they're prepared and served to guests.

For many restaurant managers, meats, poultry, and seafood represent a large percentage of the total amount their restaurants will spend for food. For that reason, understanding quality standards and proper storage procedures for these popular menu items is of great importance.

Fruits and vegetables are also used to produce a variety of menu items, so an understanding of these items and their quality characteristics is equally important for many restaurant managers.

Finally, dairy products, including milks, creams, butters, and ice cream as well as fresh eggs and egg products, are key ingredients in many popular menu items. For that reason, understanding quality characteristics for all of these highly perishable items is essential to a manager's success. This will be addressed in this chapter.

EMPHASIS ON FOOD QUALITY

For some restaurant managers, the concept of "quality" is hard to define or even conceptualize. Instead, they simply perceive that a product or service is—or is not—of the right quality. They make this determination after they see the finished product or observe service results.

Unfortunately, this subjective assessment cannot be made until a product is received, prepared and served to guests. Although an assessment at each of these points is important to ensure that quality standards *have been* met, the best restaurant managers plan ahead to ensure that quality standards *will be* met. This requires a commitment to quality during the purchasing, storage, and preparation of menu ingredients.

Restaurant customers of all types increasingly demand greater value as they purchase products and services. These guests carefully consider the selling price of menu items and service levels when they consider, "Is the item I'm ordering worth what it costs?" Restaurants that consistently deliver products that guests believe represent real value for their money attract a strong customer base. Those restaurants that consistently *exceed* their guests' value expectations, and thus give them even more than they expect in return for their dining dollars are highly successful. The consistent delivery of quality products is the key to ensuring that guests receive good value for their money.

Quality is simply the consistent delivery of a hospitality organization's products and services according to a restaurant manager's predetermined standards. Achieving consistent quality is a goal that can be difficult to attain. However, it's impossible to attain if the ingredients and products that enable a restaurant's staff to deliver quality menu items are not available, or if the menu items are not properly prepared and served to guests.

Quality assurance refers to all of the activities restaurant managers and their employees undertake to deliver quality products. These include:

- Making good decisions about the specific food and beverage products that must be purchased to provide the best value to customers
- Developing written purchase specifications (see Chapter 7) that reflect quality standards
- Carefully assessing suppliers to identify those that can consistently deliver quality products at a fair price
- Inspecting products when they're received to ensure that quality standards have been met
- Consistently using professional preproduction storage and inventory management procedures
- Using professional preparation methods
- Employing product service (delivery-to-guests) methods that meet or exceed guests' expectations

Quality assurance

Those activities related to ensuring the attainment of high-quality restaurant products and services.

Some restaurant managers think customers only equate value with low menu prices. While it's likely true that a dinner with a selling price of $35.99 would be perceived by guests to be a great value if it were sold for $9.99, the fact is that no restaurant can stay in business selling products at prices far below their costs.

Concerns about customer value perceptions must be addressed in the context of competitive alternatives. Guests paying $35.99 for a meal will think it's a good value if it's "worth" more than any other meal that they can purchase at that price, or at a lower price. Because that is true, restaurant managers are consistently challenged to provide better value for their customers and better value than their competitors. To do this well, incoming menu ingredients must be of high quality.

FARM-TO-FORK SUSTAINABILITY

When restaurant managers demonstrate a real commitment to going "green at work," they often find the number of customers they serve goes up. In increasing numbers, customers care about the quality of their environment. These customers also prefer to patronize food service operations that share their concerns. As a result, guest counts can be increased by marketing restaurant products and services to the growing market segment of informed customers who care about the food they eat and its impact on the world around them. Restaurant managers can make a difference in the eyes of these customers, and the world, when they implement sustainable operating practices and consider rapidly expanding **farm-to-fork** initiatives.

Also referred to as "Farm to Table."

Farm-to-Fork

The farm-to-fork movement arose from an increasing awareness on the part of food service professionals that buying locally produced food and delivering it to their customers is good for business, good for customers, and good for their local economies.

Farm-to-fork

A term used to describe the handling of food through the stages of growing, harvesting, processing, packaging, delivery, storage, and preparation.

Juriah Mosin/Shutterstock

One of a restaurant manager's most important jobs is to make sure that guests receive exceptional product quality and value.

"Farm-to-fork" refers to the path food follows from those who grow or raise it to those who will prepare and serve it. Ideally, this path is short to maximize freshness, minimize health risks, and be environmentally friendly.

Many managers find guest counts increase when they recognize farm-to-fork benefits and openly share their innovative efforts with guests. In addition to its marketing benefits, the advantages of promoting farm-to-fork initiatives are many. They include:

- Improved food quality (freshness and taste) due to a shortened trip from the farm to the dining table
- Lower prices paid for products due to reduced packaging and shipping costs
- Lessened impact on the environment due to reduced amounts of product packaging materials that must be discarded
- Support of local farmers and the local economy by doing business with area growers and producers
- Potential for good press and publicity due to widespread public interest in the farm-to-fork movement
- Enhanced guest appreciation of a business's efforts to operate in an Earth-friendly and responsible manner

Managers who focus part of their procurement efforts on local suppliers committed to conservation and who utilize organic, seasonal, and locally grown products can help build customer and employee loyalty as well as boost their image and their profits.

Restaurant guests are increasingly knowledgeable and concerned about the source of the food and beverage products they buy when dining out. Consumer-related issues of food safety, sustainability, freshness, and quality are all powerful drivers of the farm-to-fork movement. Restaurant managers and chefs who embrace the farm-to-fork philosophy recognize the impact on product freshness, minimal processing, and flavor when buying from local farmers and growers. There's no doubt that fresher ingredients, when properly prepared, produce superior menu items.

Sustainability

Increasingly, restaurant managers understand that nearly all human activity, including their own food service operations, leaves an impact on the planet. Sustainable practices, such as conserving energy where possible, recycling and implementing purchasing practices designed to protect long-term sources of foods, are good for business and for the planet.

One area of sustainability of special interest to those in the hospitality industry relates to the sustainability of endangered fish species. Information from groups such as those operating the Monterey Bay Aquarium Seafood Watch program (www.montereybayaquarium.org) helps consumers and businesses to make choices that support healthy oceans. Their recommendations indicate which seafood items are "best choices," "good alternatives," and which managers should "avoid."

- **Best Choices:** Seafood in this category is abundant, well managed, and caught or farmed in environmentally friendly ways.
- **Good Alternatives:** These items are an option; however, there are concerns about how they're caught or farmed or with the health of their habitat due to other human impacts.
- **Avoid:** These items are caught or farmed in ways that harm other marine life or the environment.

Some restaurant operators feel that an emphasis on sustainable practices might mean putting "planet" before "profit." They may feel businesses can survive only if profits are a manager's primary concern. It's true that an unprofitable business isn't sustainable. It's also true that "planet-friendly" practices yield many positive financial outcomes for businesses as well as for the health of their communities.

For example, as more restaurant managers buy locally grown fresh fruits and vegetables, transportation costs, pollution, and excess packaging costs are all reduced and the money spent on these items stays in the local economy. In addition, consumers are increasingly aware that, when they support businesses committed to sustainability, their purchases make an impact socially and environmentally. Many now actively seek out those restaurants perceived to be operated in an environmentally friendly manner.

In a similar manner, environmentally conscious workers are increasingly realizing that a company's care for the environment is often also reflected in similar care for its employees. Thus, those companies demonstrating a commitment to the environment tend to attract a more committed and higher-quality staff.

MEATS, POULTRY, AND SEAFOOD

Meat, poultry, and seafood are generally a restaurant's highest priced menu items and typically the most highly prized by guests. Paradoxically, meat is also one of the most frequently avoided foods; this is due to concerns about the methods used to raise some animals, to religious restrictions and, in the case of red meat, to health concerns. Despite those reservations, most people do eat meat. As a result, high-quality meat, poultry and seafood items are among the most popular on many restaurant menus.

Quality

The word "meat" generally refers to beef, veal, pork, and lamb products consumed as food. Poultry products are also sometimes called meat. In the United States, the most popular poultry products are chicken, turkey (a bird native to North America) and duck. Other animals eaten for meat include game animals of various types (e.g., deer, boar, bison, and rabbit). Like poultry, seafood is also sometimes referred to as meat. Although there are a variety of ways to classify the many animals taken from the ocean, lakes, and rivers for food, many restaurant managers categorize seafood as either fish or shellfish.

In the past few decades, in response to increased concerns about health, the composition of the animals eaten for food has changed dramatically. Today's meats are younger, leaner, and therefore more prone to be dry and less flavorful if not properly cooked. As a result, today's restaurant managers must have a better understanding of how to buy and prepare high-quality meat products than they had in the past.

Meat can be a very complex item to buy: Each animal raised for food varies somewhat from other animals, and even from other animals in the same species. In addition, meat muscle can be cut in hundreds of ways, and processed and sold in even hundreds of more ways. Although it can be complex, restaurant managers can better understand the meat-buying process by remembering a few key principles. The first of these is that all meat sold in the United States must be federally inspected for wholesomeness. Although it is not mandatory in all cases, the U.S. government also assigns **quality grades** to some types of meat.

Quality grade

Designation of an item's quality rank relative to established standards of excellence. For example, Grade A, Grade B, and so on.

The second major principle that restaurant managers must know is that there are highly established standards for meat products. When these standards are known, buyers can more easily develop detailed product specifications for the meat items they wish to buy. To eliminate the confusing names given to meat cuts in different regions and by different product sellers, a uniform system of designating cuts has been developed. Each beef, pork, and lamb cut is identifiable by a number assigned by the IMPS/NAMP numbering system.

IMPS refers to the U.S. Department of Agriculture (USDA)-approved Institutional Meat Purchase Specifications for fresh beef, veal, pork, and lamb. Under IMPS, meats are indexed by a numerical system (e.g., specific beef cuts are numbered in the 100 series, lamb in the 200 series, veal in the 300 series, and pork in the 400 series). NAMP refers to the North American Meat Processors Association, an organization best known for producing the publication *The Meat Buyer's Guide*.

The Meat Buyer's Guide is intended for meat cutters and commercial meat purchasers and is the recognized reference for meat cuts. It's published annually to enable NAMP to maintain and illustrate the standard numbering system for NAMP-recognized cuts of meat. NAMP has issued its meat buyer's guide since 1963 and now also issues a *Poultry Buyer's Guide*.

Wet aged

The process of storing vacuum-packed meats under refrigeration for up to six weeks.

Dry aged

The storing of fresh meats in an environment of controlled temperature, humidity and airflow for up to six weeks.

A third important principle to know regarding meat buying relates to the age of meat. When an animal is slaughtered, its muscle composition will continue to change as time passes. Some meats (such as beef, veal, and lamb) improve in flavor as they continue to age for longer periods; others, such as pork, poultry, and most seafood do not. Those meats that are aged on purpose may be either **wet aged** or **dry aged**.

Wet and dry aging allows time for natural enzymes and microorganisms to break down connective tissue in meat, which tenderizes and flavors it. An understanding of quality, yield, standards, and aging principles helps managers understand many of the factors needed to ensure quality meat, poultry, and seafood items. Restaurant managers must also understand how these items are best handled, prepared, and cooked.

Preparation

Restaurant managers who wish to ensure that they're serving quality meat, poultry, and seafood items must understand basic cooking principles related to these popular menu items.

BEEF AND PORK   Restaurant managers need not be expert chefs to do their jobs well; however, when it comes to meat, and especially beef and pork, professional buyers need to fully understand the intended use for a meat item before they can effectively create a purchase specification for it. A basic understanding of the two most common meat-cooking procedures is helpful to doing so. This is because a quality piece of meat, when cooked improperly, will be of poor quality. It's best to match the cut of meat purchased with the cooking method that will be used to prepare it.

Dry Heat Cooking Methods: Tender cuts of beef and pork are best cooked with dry cooking methods, such as grilling, broiling, roasting, and sautéing. Grilling is characterized by cooking the meat over a high heat source, generally in excess of 650°F. This leads to searing of the surface of the meat, which creates a flavorful crust.

Broiling is similar to grilling, except that grilling is usually performed with the heat source *under* the meat, and broiling is usually performed with the heat source *above* the meat. Roasting is a method of cooking that uses hot air to cook the meat all the way around the product at the same time. Pan frying and deep-frying are also considered dry heat cooking methods.

Moist Heat Cooking Methods: Tougher cuts of beef and pork are generally best cooked by a moist heat cooking method, such as simmering, or a combination of dry and moist cooking, such as braising, pot-roasting, or stewing. Stewing involves immersing the entire cut of meat in a liquid. Braising involves cooking seared meats in a covered pan containing small amounts of liquids that have been seasoned or flavored.

POULTRY   Poultry is the collective term used to describe domesticated birds bred for eating. The USDA recognizes six categories of poultry: chicken, turkey, duck, goose, guinea, and pigeon. Each poultry type is divided into classes based upon the bird's age, tenderness, and, in some cases, sex. Chickens and turkey make up the overwhelming majority of poultry sold in the United States. The low cost and mild flavor of poultry products mean they will make up a significant portion of many restaurants' overall entrée items. In addition, because of the many processed forms of poultry available to food service operators, poultry consumption continues to rise.

Poultry can be purchased in a wide variety of preprocessed forms. Today, food service buyers selecting poultry products choose from processed alternatives that range from items such as poultry-based "hot dogs," "hams," and "bacon" to breaded, battered, and preseasoned poultry parts and shaped meats. Adding to the complexity of buying and cooking poultry, many poultry products of all forms may be injected with seasoning solutions that significantly increase product weight and thus affect the taste and cost per pound. As a result, buyers of processed poultry products must be especially knowledgeable.

Chicken is the single most widely eaten form of poultry in the United States as well as the rest of the world. Chickens contain white meat (breasts and wings) and dark meat (legs and

---

WEB AT WORK!

USDA's Institutional Meat Purchasing Specifications (IMPS) are widely used as a standard for quality descriptions of products as government agencies, schools, restaurants, hotel, and other food service users specify quality requirements to suppliers. To review these specifications, go to:

www.ams.usda.gov

Enter "IMPS" in the search field to review general requirements and quality assurance provisions of grading systems and to review details for beef, lamb and mutton, veal and calf, pork, and a variety of processed meat items.

thighs). Most chickens have a relatively low fat content and are quite tender. They're served roasted, fried, and stewed as well as in an increasing number of processed forms.

The turkey is a member of the pheasant family and is native to North America. Turkey is the second most popular poultry meat sold in the United States, where it's served roasted whole and in an ever increasing variety of processed products. A longtime food favorite in the southern United States, deep-fried turkey has also grown in popularity, due in large part to its promotion by food celebrities such as Martha Stewart and Emeril Lagasse.

Duck consists of dark meat only and has an extremely high fat content. Duck also has a high bone and fat-to-meat ratio. As a result, those who buy duck must recognize that the edible portion yields are approximately half that of commercial chicken. Thus, for example, whereas a four-pound roasting chicken could serve four people, the same size duck would serve only two people. In the United States, roasting and pan-frying (the breasts) are the most commonly used cooking method for ducks.

SEAFOOD Today, more seafood of outstanding quality is more widely available than ever before. Restaurant managers may choose seafood that comes from all over the world, thus giving them the opportunity to offer new ingredients and creative menu items. At the same time, the variety and variability of seafood make it challenging to purchase and prepare these items: they're more fragile and delicate than many other available meats.

Both fish and shellfish have become increasingly popular on food service menus in recent years. This is in part because seafood is a good source of protein, B vitamins, various minerals and, in the case of cold-water ocean fish, desirable omega-3 fatty acids. These nutrients can't be made very efficiently by the human body yet are essential to the development and function of the brain (explaining why fish is sometimes referred to as "brain food") and to the health of the body's central nervous system. Other documented benefits of omega-3 fatty acids include lowering the incident of heart disease, stroke, and the artery-damaging form of blood cholesterol.

In addition to consumer perceptions of health benefits, fish is increasingly available on food service menus because of the ways it's packaged and stored. Fish is more perishable than other meats; in the past, that limited its use on commercial food service menus. Today, however, improved packaging and processing techniques have resulted in ample availability of most high-quality seafood (both fish and shellfish) at all times of the year.

Commonly served types of fish can be divided into two major classifications, based primarily upon their shape and skeletal structure. "Round" fish swim in a vertical position and have eyes on both sides of their head. These are typically purchased either as filets (horizontal cuts) or steaks (vertical cuts). Salmon and tuna are examples of popular round fish. "Flat fish" have asymmetrical compressed bodies, have both eyes on the top of their heads and are sold as filets only. Sole and turbo are examples of popular flat fish.

Like fish, shellfish can be more easily studied if it's first divided into two major classifications: **mollusks** and **crustaceans**.

Mollusks and crustaceans can be purchased in a variety of market forms and in various sizes or **counts**.

Fish may be broiled, fried, baked or sautéed. Like other meats and poultry, seafood is exceedingly perishable. Great care must be taken ensure that products are at their peak quality at the time of arrival and that they can be maintained as such when they're stored.

Receiving and Storage

In their fresh forms, meat, poultry, and seafood should be delivered to a food service operation at a proper temperature and in proper packaging. For most fresh items, a delivery temperature between 30°F and 34°F (−1°C to 1°C) is best. Frozen foods should arrive at temperatures at or below 0°F. It's essential to use thermometers to check the arriving temperatures of these foods.

Upon their delivery, meat, poultry, and seafood should be immediately placed in their proper storage areas. For meats, poultry, and seafood, refrigerator temperatures between 30°F and 35°F are best, as are freezer temperatures of 0°F or lower. Refrigerated and frozen seafood products may be held at these same refrigerator and freezer temperatures or, in the case of some crustaceans, in a regularly cleaned saltwater tank.

Raw poultry may be kept safely in a refrigerator (40°F) for one to two days. Frozen poultry held in a freezer (0°F) can be thawed and then cooked promptly. Thaw frozen poultry or parts in

Mollusks

Shellfish with soft, unsegmented bodies and no internal skeleton. Examples include conch, clams, and oysters.

Crustaceans

Shellfish with hard outer skeletons or shells and joints that separate the "head" from the "tail" (as in shrimp and lobster), or "leg" from the "body" (as with crabs).

Count

When used to identify crustaceans, this term refers to "the number in a pound." For example, 40–50 "count" shrimp means that, on average, 40–50 individual shrimp of that size will weigh 16 ounces.

Crustaceans are among the most popular types of shellfish sold on restaurant menus.

the refrigerator, or in cold water, changing the water every 30 minutes. Cooked poultry may be kept in the refrigerator, but should be used within two to three days or discarded.

Seafood products that have been received on ice (or refrigerated) can be safely stored before cooking, using the following guidelines:

- If the seafood will be used within one to two days after purchase, store it in the refrigerator.
- If the seafood won't be used within two days after purchase, wrap it tightly in moisture-proof freezer paper or foil to protect it from air and store it in the freezer.
- Always thaw fish and seafood in the refrigerator. Thawing at temperatures higher than 40°F causes excessive drip loss and can negatively affect taste, texture, aroma, and appearance.

FRUITS AND VEGETABLES

Produce is the broad term generally used to describe fruits and vegetables used in restaurants. While most often reserved for foods that are fresh (i.e., those that have not been canned, frozen, or dried), the term is commonly used to describe fruits and vegetables in all of their many market forms.

In the food service industry, buyers most often use the term **fruit** to refer to produce that comes from a flowering plant—apples, berries, oranges, and grapes easily come to mind. From a plant biology standpoint, however, tomatoes, beans, eggplant, and some other items are classified as fruits. However, common practice is to consider these items to be **vegetables**. For restaurant managers, the classification of fruits and vegetables is less important than ensuring that these items are served at their highest levels of quality. Figure 8.1 lists some of the most popular fruits you are most likely to buy for food service use.

Examined strictly from a culinary (rather than botanical) perspective, the items listed in Figure 8.2 are generally considered vegetables and are the ones you are most likely to buy for use in food service.

Cooks and professional buyers know that vegetables typically contain less sugar, and more starch, than fruits. In general, this means that vegetables taste best when carefully cooked and served at their peak quality. Other vegetables (e.g., leafy greens, carrots, and celery) are very popular when eaten raw. Served cooked or raw, fruits and vegetables will likely make up a significant portion of the menu items you sell, so learning to choose and handle these items properly

Produce

Agricultural products, especially fresh fruits and vegetables, grown for human consumption.

Fruit

The reproductive organ of a flowering plant. All species of flowering plants produce seeds (fruits) for reproduction.

Vegetable

Any herbaceous (nonwoody) plant whose leaves, stems, roots, tubers, seeds, or flowers are eaten for food.

FIGURE 8.1

Popular Fruits for Food Service Use

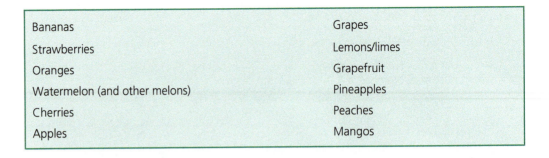

Bananas	Grapes
Strawberries	Lemons/limes
Oranges	Grapefruit
Watermelon (and other melons)	Pineapples
Cherries	Peaches
Apples	Mangos

FIGURE 8.2

A Food Service Buyer's List of Most Popular "Vegetables"

Artichoke	Cucumbers	Radicchio
Asparagus	Eggplant	Radish
Beans	Gourds	Rhubarb
Beet	Kale	Rutabaga
Broccoli	Kohlrabi	Shallots
Brussels sprouts	Leek	Spinach
Cabbage	Lettuce	Squash
Carrot	Mushrooms	Sweet corn
Cauliflower	Okra	Sweet potato
Celery	Onions	Tomatoes
Chard	Parsnips	Turnips
Chicory	Peas	Watercress
Collards	Peppers	Yams
Corn	Potatoes	
Cress	Pumpkins	

can make a big impact on your operation's profitability as well as on your reputation with your customers.

Quality

For most produce buyers, the first step in becoming knowledgeable about produce standards and quality is obtaining *The Fresh Produce Manual* published by the Produce Marketing Association (PMA). Founded in 1949, PMA (www.pma.com) is a not-for-profit global trade association serving more than 2,100 members who market fresh fruits, vegetables, and related products worldwide. Its members are involved in the production, distribution, retail, and food service sectors of the industry. PMA offers its members a wide variety of services, including the publication of many materials related to fresh produce quality and standards.

FRUITS Sweet to the taste when at its peak of flavor, fruit is popular, in large part, because of its naturally occurring sugar (fructose). Purchasing fruit can be especially challenging because different types of fruit have different names in various regions of the world. Suppliers also face their own challenges when selling fruit because no other food group offers a greater variety of colors, flavors, and texture. For convenience in learning about types of fruit, it can be helpful to classify them as either "fresh" or "processed" ingredients.

FRESH FRUITS Top-quality fresh fruits are tasty and nutritious. The quality of fresh fruit is initially judged by its outside appearance. Furthermore, the USDA has established grade standards for most fresh fruit. Fruit grades are used as a basis for trading among growers, shippers, wholesalers, and retailers; however, they're used to only a limited extent in sales between wholesalers

U.S. Fancy: Premium quality. Only the very best (a small percentage) of fruits achieve this grade.

U.S. No. 1: Good quality. The most commonly used grade for most fruits.

U.S. No. 2 and **U.S. No. 3**: U.S. No. 2 is noticeably superior to U.S. No. 3, which is the lowest grade practical to pack under normal commercial conditions.

FIGURE 8.3
USDA Fruit Grades
Source: U.S. Department of Agriculture.

and restaurateurs because the use of USDA grade standards is generally voluntary. If, however, a container of fruit is actually marked with a grade, the packer must ensure that the contents conform to the official requirements of that grade.

As a restaurant manager, you'll most likely encounter USDA fresh fruit grades when you purchase apples or pears. Some other fruits occasionally carry grade designations. Figure 8.3 details the primary fresh fruit grades used by the USDA (grades for some specific fruits may vary slightly).

Fresh fruit has not been subjected to any processing such as canning, freezing, or drying. Increasingly, some consumers prefer organic fruit, which is frequently available for purchase by food service operators.

Fresh fruit can usually be purchased ripe or pre-ripened (also known as "unripened"). Specific fresh fruit groups and their important characteristics can be examined in a variety of ways. One good way is to divide them into the following broad subcategories:

Berries: In a culinary sense, a berry is any small, edible fruit with multiple seeds. Berries don't ripen after they're picked, so they must be purchased fully ripened. These items will deteriorate rather quickly, even when stored properly, so it's essential that they be purchased ripe and used immediately.

Citrus: Citrus fruits grow primarily in warm climates and are characterized by their thick rind coverings. Citrus fruits are acidic and they're a good source of vitamin C. Citrus fruit flavors range from bitter to tart to very sweet. Popular varieties include oranges, grapefruits, lemons, limes, kumquats, and tangerines.

Exotics: Exotic fruits come from a variety of locales. Many are available year-round and include gooseberries, guava, lychees, persimmons, pomegranates, prickly pears, rhubarb, and star fruits. With their unique flavors, these less common fruits most often find their way onto a menu as a garnish.

Grapes: Technically a berry, grapes are the single largest fruit crop in the world, due in great part to their popularity in wine making. Table grapes (those grown for eating) include the Concord—a Native American variety used primarily for cooking—and the Thompson. Today, the Thompson seedless grape is the most popular table grape sold for use in food service. The Thompson is also used for juice as well as wine making and accounts for 95% of the raisins produced in California.

Melons: Melons, squashes, and cucumbers are types of gourds. Many melons originated in the Middle East and gradually spread in popularity across Europe. Melon seeds were transported to the United States by Columbus and eventually cultivated by Spanish explorers in California. Common types include cantaloupes, Casaba, Crenshaw, honeydew, and watermelons.

Pomes: A pome, named after the French word for apple (*pomme*) is a type of fruit that comes from a flowering tree. Pomes have a thin skin and firm flesh. Within this family of fruits are apples of all types, pears, and quince. The food service use of apples is extremely widespread. The flesh of most pomes is eaten raw. Apples and pears are popular when cooked and are offered on menus in a variety of baked items, desserts and sauces.

Pit Fruits: These fruits are characterized by a thin skin, soft flesh and a woody pit (or stone) in the center of the fruit. Apricots, cherries, peaches, nectarines, and plums are popular varieties eaten raw or used for cooking. Storage lives of fresh pit fruits are relatively short, so they must be purchased and used within a few days of their delivery.

Tropicals: Tropical fruit is native to the world's hot tropical and subtropical regions. All can be eaten fresh, without cooking. Popular tropicals, most of which are now available year-round, include bananas, dates, kiwis (also known as the Chinese gooseberry), mangoes, papayas, passion fruits, and pineapples.

PROCESSED FRUITS   Because the storage life of fresh fruit is often short, market forms often involve processing. Fruit suppliers process fruit for a variety of reasons, including reduced shipping costs, increased shelf life, improved utility, and product enhancement. Fruit may be processed in many ways. Sometimes the fruit is simply cleaned, trimmed, and packaged in bags, jars, or other containers. In other cases, it's highly processed to enhance its form or useful life.

The most popular means of preserving fruit include:

Irradiation: Some fruit (as well as many vegetables and meats) can be subject to ionizing radiation to destroy parasites, insects, and bacteria. This treatment is classified as **irradiation** and is considered by the U.S. Food and Drug Administration (FDA) as a food additive. Irradiation may also slow the ripening of the fruit treated. Irradiated fruit is generally purchased, stored and used like any other fresh fruit.

Canning: Many types of fruit are canned (or jarred). Pineapple and peaches are among the most popular. In "solid pack" canning, little or no water is added to the fruit before it's sealed in the cans and heated. "Water pack" canning is accomplished by first adding water or fruit juice to the canned product. In "syrup packing," various amounts of sugar and water are added to the food. Lighter syrups are most often used for sweeter fruits and heavy syrups are used for tart fruits, such as apples, gooseberries, and sour cherries.

Freezing: Freezing is a highly effective method for preserving fruit, even though the process may negatively affect the texture of the fruit because it often damages the product's cell walls. The process does not, however, have a negative effect on the nutritive value of fruit. Many types of fruits are sold individually quick frozen (**IQF**) for ease in use.

Drying: Drying is one of the oldest known methods of preserving fruit. As fruit loses its moisture content, the flavor intensifies, the sugar content increases, and its storage life is extended. Unlike dried beans and legumes, dried fruit is processed in a manner that results in a 16-26% moisture content, leaving the fruit nice and soft. Raisins, prunes, apricots, and figs are among the most popular dried fruit.

VEGETABLES   The term, "vegetable," as commonly used, can be applied to almost any non-woody plant with edible parts used for food. A definition this broad, however, also includes fruits, nuts, and cereals—products that aren't usually considered vegetables by food service buyers or by restaurant guests. As a culinary term, "vegetable" has come to mean those plants and plant parts eaten raw or cooked and served with a main meal. Using this definition, rice and sweet corn are examples of cereals that, while not vegetables in a botanical sense, are considered vegetables by most diners.

Originating from almost any part of a plant, a vegetable can be a leaf (e.g., cabbage, lettuce, spinach), a seed (bean, lentil, pea), a root (beet, carrot, potato), a bulb (garlic, leek, onion), a flower (cauliflower, broccoli, artichoke), a fruit (cucumber, pepper, squash) or a stem (asparagus, celery, kohlrabi).

Vegetables are an important component of most menus. They add color, texture, flavor, and variety to appetizers, salads, and entrées and are often used as side dishes to accompany main courses.

The USDA has established grade standards for most fresh vegetables. Use of the grading standards is generally voluntary, but some state laws and federal marketing programs require certain vegetables to be graded. If a package of vegetables does list a grade, the packer is legally obligated to ensure that the contents meet the grade standards at the time of packing. Grade designations are most often seen on packages of potatoes and onions, but other vegetables occasionally carry a grade name. Figure 8.4 lists the USDA grades that have been established for fresh vegetables.

FRESH VEGETABLES   There are few hard and fast rules for selecting fresh vegetables because each type has its own quality characteristics. The following are broad guidelines for evaluating the quality of many of the most popular vegetables.

Irradiation

The use of x-rays for the purpose of preserving foods.

IQF

An acronym that stands for "individually quick frozen."

FIGURE 8.4
USDA Fresh Vegetable Grades

U.S. Fancy: These vegetables have a more uniform shape and fewer defects than U.S. No. 1.

U.S. No. 1. These vegetables should be tender and fresh appearing, have good color and be relatively free from bruises and decay.

U.S. No. 2 and **No. 3**: While U.S. No. 2 and No. 3 have lower quality requirements than Fancy or No. 1, all grades are nutritious. The differences are mainly in appearance, amount of waste and buyer preference.

Artichokes: Size is not important with respect to quality. Poor-quality artichokes have large areas of brown on the petals and/or spreading petals. This is a sign of age that indicates drying and toughening of the edible portions.

Asparagus: Asparagus is a member of the lily family, which also includes onions, leeks, and garlic. The edible portion of this plant is called a spear. Round spears with closed, compact tips, and a fresh appearance are best. When green, a rich, dark color should cover most of the spear. The tips of poor-quality spears are open and spread out, moldy or decayed.

Beans: Like the word "vegetable," the word "bean" has an imprecise meaning. It's used to refer to the seeds of many different kinds of plants. Varieties include French beans, snap beans (string, stringless, and wax), and kidney beans—to name just a few. Beans can be purchased in their fresh state or dried. Common dry types include black, pinto, navy, great northern, and red kidney. Beans with a fresh, bright appearance, and good color are best. Buyers should reject wilted or flabby bean pods as well as those with serious blemishes or decay.

Beets: Fresh beets are available year-round. Their color and flavor are unique, and they're popular in salads, as a base for soups and as a side vegetable. High-quality beets are firm, round, have a deep red color, and are smooth over most of their surface.

Broccoli: Broccoli is a popular member of the cabbage family and a close relative of cauliflower. High-quality fresh broccoli is firm with a compact cluster of small flower buds, none of which should be opened or showing a yellow color that indicates excessive age.

Cabbage: Cabbage is one of the most popular vegetables in the world. Essentially, there are three types: smooth-leaved green cabbage, crinkly-leaved green (savoy) cabbage, and red cabbage. The savoy and red varieties are more often used in slaw and salads than in cooked dishes. Cabbage with firm, hard heads that are heavy for their size are best. Buyers should avoid cabbage with badly discolored, dried, or decayed outer leaves.

Carrots: Carrots are grown in a variety of colors and sizes. The type of carrot most often purchased in the United States is the Mediterranean. High-quality carrots are well formed, smooth and firm. If the tops are attached, they should be fresh and green. Poor-quality carrots have large green "sunburned" areas at the top (which must be trimmed and discarded) or roots that are flabby from wilting.

Cauliflower: White, green, and purple types of cauliflower are readily available. The white edible portion is called the "curd"; the heavy outer leaf covering is called the "jacket leaves." High-quality cauliflower has a creamy-white color and compact, solid, and clean curds. Poor-quality cauliflower has a spreading curd or dark spots on the curd that indicate excessive age.

Celery: Celery is popular for a variety of uses and is available throughout the year. Most celery is of the "Pascal" type, which includes thick-branched, green varieties. Fresh celery should have a solid, rigid feel, and the leaf tips (if any) should be fresh or only slightly wilted. Poor-quality celery is wilted with flabby upper branches or leaf stems.

Chicory, Endive, Escarole (and other greens): Used mainly in salads, these vegetables are available nearly year-round. The shape, texture, color, and flavor of each make them interesting for mixing with more traditional lettuce in salads. The better-known kinds are spinach, kale, collard, turnip, beet, chard, mustard, broccoli leaves, chicory, endive, escarole, dandelion, cress, and sorrel. The best greens are crisp, tender, and have a good green color. Buyers should reject wilted and yellowing plants or those with insect damage.

Corn: Worldwide, only wheat and rice are cultivated in greater quantities than corn. Much is used for cattle feed, but "sweet" corn is grown for human consumption. Fresh sweet corn is available in frozen form every month of the year, but in the United States, fresh sweet corn is most plentiful from early May until mid-September.

Cucumbers: Cucumbers can be purchased with or without seeds. High-quality cucumbers have a good green color and are firm over their entire length, but not too large in diameter. Poor quality cucumbers are flabby and/or have evidence of spotty soft parts.

Lettuce: Lettuce is popular in salads. Four types of lettuce are generally available year-round: Iceberg (the most common), butter-head, romaine, and leaf. The best-tasting salads are made with a combination of iceberg and other lettuce types. When buying fresh lettuce, buyers should look for good, bright color (in most varieties this means a medium-to-light green). Slight discoloration of the outer or wrapper leaves will usually not hurt the quality of the lettuce, but serious discoloration or decay should be avoided.

Mushrooms: Mushrooms are naturally fat-free and are popular by themselves and when prepared in a variety of ways. There are over 40,000 known varieties. In the United States, the most common is the moonlight (button) mushroom. Other popular mushrooms include portobello, porcini, and shiitake.

Onions (Dry): The many varieties of onions grown commercially fall into three general classes, distinguished by color: yellow, white, and red. Yellow onions make up 88% of those grown. Onions range in size from less than 1 inch to more than 4.5 inches in diameter. The most common sizes of onions sold in the United States are the medium (2 to 3¼ inches in diameter) and the jumbo (3 to 3¾ inches in diameter). Onions should be hard, dry, and have small necks. Poor quality onions are wet, soft, or affected by decay.

Onions (Green), Shallots, and Leeks: Green onions, shallots, and leaks are similar in appearance but differ somewhat in size and flavor. Scallions are a type of onion, and the term is often used when referring to either green onions or shallots. Shallots are onion-like plants that produce small bulbs and edible shoots. Leeks are larger than green onions but share the characteristic of large, green, edible shoots. Green onions are simply ordinary onions harvested very young. They should be fresh looking and free of decay.

Peppers (Green): Most of the green peppers used in the food service industry are considered "sweet" or "bell" peppers. While the taste of these vegetables is not actually sweet, the term is used to distinguish them from "hot" peppers. The best green peppers (and those of other colors, such as red or yellow) have a deep, characteristic color, glossy sheen, relatively heavy weight, and firm walls or sides.

Potatoes: In the restaurant industry, there are three main types of potatoes: russet, round white, and round red. The russet (sometimes called "baker" or "Idaho") is the most popular. The round white potato is used most often in the eastern United States. The round red (redskin) potato is sometimes called a "new" potato; however, technically, "new" refers to any variety of potato that is harvested before reaching maturity.

Squash: The squashes most often used in restaurants are generally either a "summer" or a "winter" variety. Available varieties of summer squash include crookneck, straightneck, and zucchini. Winter squash includes the small-sized acorn (available year-round) and the butternut, buttercup, and Hubbard varieties. Poor quality squash have cuts, punctures, sunken spots, or moldy spots on the rind.

Sweet Potatoes: The sweet potato is not actually a potato (tuber) at all. It's a root, which is a member of the morning glory family. The sweet potato is a Native American plant. Sweet potatoes are often confused with yams; the term "yam" is often used to describe a sweet potato. However, true yams are large, starchy roots grown primarily in Africa and Asia and are rarely available in the United States.

Tomatoes: The tomato, although technically a fruit, is one of the most popular and frequently consumed vegetables. The flavor varies greatly; most restaurant managers agree that the best flavor usually comes from locally grown tomatoes. High-quality tomatoes are smooth, well-ripened, and reasonably free from blemishes. Poor quality tomatoes are too soft, overripe or bruised, with severe growth cracks (deep brown cracks around the stem) that can significantly reduce their Edible Portion (EP) yield percentage.

PROCESSED VEGETABLES   Few menu ingredients have undergone more change in the past decade than processed vegetables. Today, an increased number of vegetables, processed in an evergrowing number of market forms, are readily available. This is so because, vegetables purchased raw must often be cleaned, trimmed, chopped or diced, to make them recipe-ready. These labor-intensive activities can often be performed by processors at a low cost.

A central processing facility usually processes fresh vegetable products in a much more cost-effective way than individual food service units can. Centralized processing can also result in better consistency of product size, shape, and mixture. The quality of vegetable processing has been helped by major advancements in packaging technology used to slow the growth of micro-organisms and the effects of **oxidation**, both of which damage fresh produce.

Oxidation

The chemical reaction (and deterioration) that can occur when a substance is exposed to oxygen.

Storage and Preparation

Proper storage of produce is essential if it's to be served at peak quality levels. It's important to remember that produce items will arrive at the restaurant in their best condition. From the time most of these items are delivered to the time they're served, quality levels will decline: Fruits and vegetables lose moisture after they're harvested, which causes them to decline in quality as they age. To best preserve most vegetables, store them in their original or airtight containers at normal refrigeration temperatures and buy only enough to last for a few days.

Some vegetables, such as tomatoes, do best if held at room temperature until they're fully ripe before being placed in the refrigerator. Others, such as sweet potatoes, should not be refrigerated at all. Avocados and bananas should not be refrigerated until they're completely ripe. Melons can also be held at room temperature until fully ripe before refrigeration. Most fruit should be stored in its original containers, unwashed until ready to use and held at standard refrigerator temperatures. When in doubt, experienced restaurant managers always discuss specific vegetable and fruit storage requirements with their produce suppliers.

Whether served fresh, baked, broiled, sautéed, or fried, fresh fruits and vegetables must be carefully stored, cooked, and served if they're to provide restaurant guests maximum flavor and health benefits.

ALL IN A DAY'S WORK: 8.1

"It does look good," said Amanda, the restaurant manager at Emil's Italian Kitchen. "Very fresh."

"And it's consistent," replied Todd, the sales manager for Brother's Ready Produce.

Todd and Amana were discussing a new processed lettuce blend that Brother's Ready Produce was offering for sale. The blend of arugula, red cabbage, romaine, and iceberg lettuce came packaged in two-pound bags and was ready to serve.

"It's formulated to complement Italian foods," continued Todd. "And with as much salad as you serve at Emil's, you'll save a ton of labor."

"I agree that we would save significantly in labor," replied Amanda, "but what does it cost per serving"?

1. Labor-saving preprocessed foods such as fruits, vegetables, and meats do typically reduce labor costs. In what other areas will cost reductions occur when a restaurant manager buys preprocessed foods?

2. What procedure should Amanda use to determine if the increased as-purchased (AP) cost per serving of salad is more than the labor and any other savings she will incur by purchasing Todd's preprocessed salad blend?

WEB AT WORK!

The Produce Marketing Association (PMA) is the industry association for suppliers of fresh fruits and vegetables.

To view its website, go to:

www.pma.com

Choose "About PMA" to learn more about the goals and mission of this important restaurant industry partner.

DAIRY AND EGG PRODUCTS

The term, "dairy," generally refers to cow's milk and the basic foods that are produced from it, including cheeses, butter, yogurt, cultured dairy products and ice cream. In some cases, food service buyers purchase dairy products produced by mammals other than cows. Products made from goat and sheep's milk are current menu favorites. Dairy products are often consumed alone (beverage milks), but are just as frequently used as ingredients in appetizers, baked goods, entrees, side dishes, and desserts.

Restaurant managers who want to serve high-quality dairy products must know about the three major dairy product categories:

- Milks and creams
- Cheeses
- Other milk-based foods

Milks and Creams

Milk and cream contribute texture, flavor, and nutrients to a wide variety of foods. While milk's vitamin and mineral (especially calcium) content are significant, from a manager's perspective, it's the milk's *fat* content that most influences what you purchase and how much you pay for it. In fact, the milk fat content of beverage milk actually defines the products purchased and how they're used in the kitchen.

In its natural form, cow's milk contains approximately 88% water, 3.5% fat (milk fat), and 8.5% other solids that include proteins, milk sugar, and minerals. Restaurant managers buying milk for drinking or cooking generally select from the following widely available forms:

Whole milk: Must contain a minimum of 3.25% milk fat

Low-fat milk: Has between 0.5 and 2% milk fat

© Palle Christensen/Shutterstock

Because it can be served plain, flavored, hot, or cold, milk is one of the most versatile of all the popular beverages.

Skim milk: Must have less than 0.5% milk fat; also called "nonfat" milk

Flavored milks: Made by adding fruit, fruit juice, or other natural or artificial food flavorings, such as strawberry, chocolate syrup, or cocoa, to pasteurized milk

Dry whole milk: Pasteurized whole milk with the water removed. Dry milk with reduced fat levels or no fat are also readily available. "Instant" nonfat dry milk is made of larger milk particles that dissolve easily in water. The best instant nonfat dry milk will have a sweet, pleasing flavor, and a natural color and will dissolve immediately when mixed with water. Dry milk products are used mainly in baking.

Evaporated milk: Prepared by heating homogenized whole milk under a vacuum to remove 50% of its water and then sealing it in cans or other containers

Condensed (canned) milk: Prepared by removing approximately 50% of the water from whole milk and then adding sugar. Sweetened condensed milk must have at least 40% sugar by weight and is used primarily in baking.

In addition to milks, managers can usually select from the following widely available forms of **cream**:

> **Cream**
>
> A dairy product that must contain a minimum of 18% milk fat.

Half-and-half: Must contain between 10.5% and 18% milk fat.

Light cream: Must contain between 18 and 30% milk fat; also known as coffee cream

Light whipping cream: Must contain between 30 and 36% milk fat; also known as whipping cream

Heavy cream: Must contain at least 36% milk fat

All milk and cream products are highly perishable and must be carefully stored at or below 41°F (5°C) to maintain their best quality.

Cheeses

Milk and products made from milk are popular but also highly perishable. This has always been true, especially in warm climates where, in times before refrigeration was available, milk would spoil easily. Cheese products are the direct result of human efforts to prolong the life of milk products. In European and European-influenced countries, "cheese" is one of the oldest and most widely produced foods. Today's restaurant managers can choose from hundreds of cheeses made in a variety of styles and packaging forms to use in literally thousands of recipes or to serve alone.

Cheeses may be broadly classified as either natural or processed. Essentially, all natural cheeses begin with a mammal's milk (cows, goats, or sheep are the most popular). To make cheese, an enzyme is added to milk to make it coagulate. As it does, it naturally separates into curds, which are solid, and whey, which is the remaining liquid. The whey is removed and the solids are either consumed immediately or specially treated in a variety of ways that may include cutting, kneading, seasoning, or cooking.

Processed cheese is made by combining natural cheese with emulsifiers and flavorings. The resulting mixture is then pasteurized and poured into molds. Processed cheese is generally less expensive to buy than natural cheese. Processed cheese must contain at least 51% cheese, but may also include vegetable oils or milk solids designed to produce a cheese that spreads easily. Processed cheese is often flavored with pimentos, fruits, vegetables, or meats.

In the restaurant industry, natural cheeses are most often purchased. One good way to classify different natural cheese types is by their texture, including:

- Fresh (or unripened)
- Soft
- Semi-soft
- Firm
- Hard

FRESH (UNRIPENED)   Fresh, or unripened, cheese is not cooked and has a moisture content between 40 and 80%. It's highly perishable and extremely popular. The most commonly purchased types of fresh cheese include:

- Cottage cheese
- Cream cheese

- Mozzarella
- Mascarpone
- Queso Oaxaca
- Ricotta

SOFT   Soft cheese is best known for its thin skin and creamy middle. The moisture content of this type of cheese ranges from 50 to 75%. The most commonly purchased types of soft cheese include:

- Brie
- Boursin
- Camembert
- Feta

SEMI-SOFT   Semi-soft cheeses are smooth and sliceable. The moisture content of semi-soft cheese ranges from 40 to 50%. This type of cheese includes what is commonly known as the "blue" or "veined" varieties, which refers to blue-colored molds that produce cheeses with a distinctive look and taste. The most commonly purchased types of semi-soft cheese include:

- Gouda
- Havarti
- Fontina
- Blue
- Roquefort
- Stilton
- Gorgonzola

FIRM   Some firm cheese is solid and often flaky, like Cheddar; others are full of holes like Emmenthaler (better known in the United States as "Swiss"). Most firm cheese has a moisture content in the range of 30 to 50%. The most commonly purchased types of firm cheese includes:

- Cheddar
- Colby
- Emmenthaler
- Gruyere
- Jarlsberg
- Monterey Jack
- Provolone

HARD   Hard cheese is carefully aged for extended periods of time and dried until its moisture content is approximately 30%. Hard cheese is often grated before using. The most commonly purchased types of hard cheese include:

- Asiago
- Parmigiano-Reggiano
- Parmesan
- Romano

Other Milk-Based Foods

In addition to its use as a beverage and in cheese production, milk plays a role in a variety of important foods in the food service industry, including butter, yogurt, sour cream, and ice cream. Restaurant managers often find these items to be challenging to purchase because of their high level of perishability and, with regard to ice cream, the vast array of quality levels generally available to them.

BUTTER   The word "butter" is used in the names of many products, including those made from pureed nuts (such as peanut butter), fruit (apple butter), and fats that are solid at room temperature (cocoa butter). In culinary terms, however, unless it's qualified by another term, the word "butter," almost always refers to the dairy product. The color of butter is mostly

> **ALL IN A DAY'S WORK: 8.2**
>
> "Well, what *do* we have in the box?" asked Raj, the restaurant manager at Sofia's Tuscan Bistro.
>
> "An American blue cheese that I use for making salad dressing," replied Jeanette, the restaurant's kitchen manager.
>
> "But we don't have any Italian gorgonzola for the Tuscan gorgonzola steak?" asked Raj.
>
> "No." said Jeanette. "The distributor shorted us on your order this week. But you know most people can't tell the difference between blue cheese and gorgonzola," said Jeanette. "So why don't we just use the blue cheese?"
>
> Assume you were Raj and that you've included the phrase, "melted gorgonzola" on the menu to describe your popular "Tuscan Gorgonzola Steak" entrée.
>
> 1. Would you use the American blue cheese as a substitute in the Tuscan gorgonzola steak?
> 2. If so, would you inform your guests of the substitution? If not, what would you do?

determined by the feed of the animal from which it's made; however, today's butter colors are most often manipulated in manufacturing to produce the uniform "yellow" common to food service customers.

Butter is typically sold in both salted and unsalted forms. Salted butter has either fine, granular salt or brine added to it during production. In addition to flavoring the butter, salt acts as a preservative.

Butter has a very high milk-fat content. In the United States, all products sold as "butter" must contain a minimum of 80% milk fat (butterfat) by weight, not more than 16% water and 2 to 4% other milk solids.

The USDA has established three butter grades. In general, butter buyers may select from:

U.S. Grade AA: This butter has a smooth, creamy texture and is easy to spread. It contains a light, fresh flavor and may contain a small amount of salt. Grade AA butter is made from cream and is available from most distributors.

U.S. Grade A: This butter is made from cream, has a slightly stronger flavor and possesses a fairly smooth texture. Grade A butter is also widely available.

U.S. Grade B: This butter is less commonly available to food service operators. It's usually made from sour cream and its texture is coarser than that of regular butter. Its major application is in food manufacturing and processing.

Butter may be purchased in a variety of packaging types. These include blocks of varying weights, ¼-pound sticks, individually wrapped patties of various sizes, and pre-formed shapes (such as roses, balls, and chips).

YOGURT Yogurt is a thick, tart, custard consistency dairy product. Commercially sold yogurt can be made from whole, low-fat or non-fat milk, as well as soymilk. Therefore, yogurt contains the same amount of milk fat as the product from which it's made. Yogurt is produced by bacterial fermentation of milk sugar (lactose) which produces lactic acid. The resulting effect on the milk's proteins gives yogurt its characteristic consistency and tart, tangy flavor. In the United States, yogurt may be purchased plain or with a variety of fruit or spice flavorings. The USDA recognizes three yogurt forms commonly available for food service buyers:

Yogurt: Contains at least 3.25% fat and at least 8.25 % milk solids (not fat)

Low-fat yogurt: Contains at least 0.5%, not more than 2.0% fat, and at least 8.25 % milk solids (not fat)

Non-fat yogurt: Contains not more than 0.5% fat and at least 8.25 % milk solids (not fat)

Yogurt for use in restaurants is typically purchased in bulk containers of one to five pounds as well as in single-service-sized containers.

FIGURE 8.5

Minimum Fat Content of Sour Cream
Source: USDA.

Product	Minimum Milk Fat Content
Sour cream	Contains not less than 18% milk fat
Reduced-fat sour cream	Contains 13.5% or less milk fat, but not less than 6% total
Low-fat sour cream	Contains 6.0% or less milk fat, but not less than 1.0% total fat
Nonfat sour cream	Contains less than 1.0% total milk fat

Cultured dairy product

The processed food created when specific bacteria are added to liquid dairy products.

BUTTERMILK AND SOUR CREAM   "Buttermilk" originally described the liquid that was left over after producing butter from milk. Today, the buttermilk available to most food service buyers is actually an artificially **cultured dairy product** (in this case, milk), to which lactic-acid-producing bacteria has been added.

Sour cream, like yogurt, is a cultured dairy product. Both buttermilk and sour cream are produced by adding a specific bacterial culture (*Streptococcus lactis*) to milk. The bacteria convert the milk sugar (lactose) to lactic acid. The acidity of buttermilk and sour cream explain their relatively long refrigerator shelf life, because acid is a natural preservative that inhibits bacterial growth.

Buttermilk is produced when the bacterial culture is added to fresh, pasteurized skim, or low-fat milk to yield a thick milk product with a tart flavor. Sour cream is made by combining the same bacterial culture to cream with a higher fat content, which produces an even thicker product.

The USDA has well-defined fat content minimums for regular sour cream (18%). Figure 8.5 lists the minimum fat contents of the most popular styles of sour cream.

ICE CREAM   Ice cream is a frozen mixture of milk, sugar or other sweeteners, cream, and flavorings such as fruits, nuts, or vanilla. The final, and perhaps most essential ingredient in ice cream is air, without which ice cream would not have the texture that makes it such a popular menu item.

In the United States, ice cream must contain at least 10% milk fat and, at most, 50% air. It must also weigh at least 4.5 pounds per gallon. "Premium" and "super premium" ice cream has higher fat content (13 to 17%) and lower air content.

Despite the fact that the USDA has established rigid standards for various ice-cream quality levels, in common terms, frozen custard, yogurt, and sherbet are also commonly referred to as "ice cream." The following is a partial list of some of the most popular ice-cream-like desserts as well as their identifying characteristics:

Low-fat ice cream: This product contains less than 10% milk fat and lower sweetening content. It's made from milk, stabilizers, sweeteners, and flavorings and contains not more than 3 grams of fat per each 4-ounce serving. Ice cream advertised as "reduced fat" or "light" must have a lower fat content than "regular" ice cream, but may not meet the standard for "low fat."

Frozen custard: Also known as French ice cream or New York ice cream, this product has must contain at least 1.4% egg yolks.

Frozen yogurt: A low-fat or fat-free ice cream alternative made with yogurt.

Gelato: The Italian word for "ice cream," gelato is an Italian-style frozen dessert that must have a 4 to 9% milk-fat content.

Sherbet: This product is made from milk, fruit or fruit juice, and stabilizers and has a level of sweetening much higher than ice cream. It must contain 1 to 2% milk fat.

Sorbet: Technically, sorbet is not a dairy product at all; rather, it's an ice-cream-like product made with fruit puree and without milk.

Ice cream products are highly perishable: they must be stored carefully and used quickly to maintain their high quality. Increasingly, consumer demand in the hospitality industry is for higher quality, more expensive ice cream products, than it's for lower quality, less expensive products.

Ice cream is highly perishable. Outstanding products like this one must be stored properly and for no more than one week.

© DUSAN ZIDAR/Shutterstock

WEB AT WORK!

The International Dairy Foods Association (IDFA) is a professional trade association committed to facilitating the growth of the dairy industry. Its members are involved in the manufacturing and sale of dairy, cheese and ice cream products.

To view its website, go to:

www.idfa.org

Choose "About IDFA" to learn more about the goals and mission of this important restaurant industry partner.

Eggs and Egg Products

Many animals reproduce by laying eggs. Eggs are laid by a female bird, reptile, or fish; the egg's contents, if fertilized, can develop into a new organism, with each egg holding one new animal. Food service buyers generally purchase unfertilized eggs laid by chickens (although duck, pheasant, and quail eggs, among others, are also widely available).

Restaurant managers can choose from chicken eggs available in a variety of market forms. These include fresh eggs (also known as "shell" eggs), processed egg products of various forms and egg substitutes, which are egg-alternative products that can be made entirely or in part from fresh eggs.

FRESH EGGS   From a culinary perspective, the three primary parts of a fresh egg are the shell, yolk and white (**albumen**).

A chicken's breed dictates the color of the eggshell, which can range from white to brown. The color of the shell has no effect on the quality, flavor, or nutritive content of the egg. However, some food distributors consistently charge a premium for brown-colored shell eggs; some restaurant guests prefer their hard-cooked (boiled) eggs to have brown shells. The feed eaten by chickens directly affects the color of the egg yolks. As is true with shell color, however, the color of an egg's yolk is not an indicator of egg quality.

Albumen

Another term for the "white" of a fresh egg.

FIGURE 8.6

Egg Size and Weights
Source: U.S. Department of Agriculture (ounce weights only).

Egg Size	Minimum Weight per Dozen	
	Ounces	Grams
Jumbo	30	850.5
Extra large	27	765.5
Large	24	680.4
Medium	21	595.3
Small	18	510.3
Peewee	15	425.2

Fresh shell eggs are sized by their minimum weight per dozen. Figure 8.6 lists the weight of a dozen eggs of various sizes.

The USDA has established three consumer grades for eggs: U.S. Grade AA, A, and B. The grade is determined by the interior quality of the egg and the appearance and condition of the egg shell. Eggs of any quality grade may differ in weight (size).

U.S. Grade AA: These eggs have whites that are thick and firm; yolks that are high, round, and practically free from defects; and clean, unbroken shells.

U.S. Grade A: These eggs have whites that are reasonably firm; yolks that are high, round, and practically free from defects; and clean, unbroken shells. This is the quality most often sold in stores.

U.S. Grade B: These eggs have whites that may be thinner and yolks that may be wider and flatter than eggs of the higher grades; the shells must be unbroken, but may show slight stains.

Fresh shell eggs can typically be stored in their cartons in the refrigerator for four to five weeks with very little quality loss.

PROCESSED EGGS Most food service distributors sell a variety of processed egg products. These include whole eggs that have been shelled and whites-only or yolks-only products. Processed egg products may be sold fresh (refrigerated), frozen, or dried. Processed eggs are shell

---

GREEN AT WORK!

More and more consumers want to buy products labeled "free range" for use at home and also when they eat out.

The label "free range" on meat, chicken, or fresh eggs implies that animal was given the freedom to roam around a large land area (the range). While the theory behind such an approach to raising animals may be comforting, in practice, there are few regulations imposed on what can be called "free range"; the term may be used misleadingly by producers to suggest that the animal product for sale has been produced more humanely than it actually has been.

In the United States, USDA regulations for the use of the words "free range" apply only to poultry and indicate simply that the animal has been allowed access to the outside. The USDA regulations don't specify the quality or size of the outside range nor the duration of time an animal must have access to the outside. Free-range chicken eggs, however, have no legal definition in the United States. As a result, the term may be used by a producer whose chicken cages are only 2 to 3 feet larger than those producers not using the term.

Free-range egg producers have no common standard for the definition of the term. Other terms such as *cage-free, free-running, free-roaming, naturally nested,* and the like also have no legal definitions that food buyers can count on. Until such time as a legal definition is imposed by the USDA, if it's important to you to offer your guests "free-range" items such as eggs, your guests will count on you to do the supplier research required to know exactly what you are buying and serving.

WEB AT WORK!

The American Egg Board is a professional trade association committed to communicating information about the nutritional and economic values of eggs. To view its website, go to:

www.aeb.org

Choose "Egg Industry" and then "Egg Facts 101" to learn more about eggs and egg products.

eggs broken by special machines at the grading station and then pasteurized before being packaged in cartons. Processed egg products may contain preservatives and flavor or color additives. Because of their built-in labor savings, these products generally cost more per ounce to buy than do in-the-shell eggs.

Another special and popular form of egg processing exists when processors remove yolks from eggs and then further process the whites only. "Whites-only" egg products such as ConAgra Foods' popular "Egg Beaters" is such a product. The processed egg products typically contain 99% egg whites. The other 1% consists of coloring, salt, and other ingredients. In addition, nutrients may be added to make up for those lost from the yolk.

EGG SUBSTITUTES   Eggs contain **cholesterol**, and a significant numbers of people are allergic to eggs. These two facts explain why the use of total egg substitutes has increased greatly in recent years.

Egg substitutes are generally of two types, and restaurant managers must understand the difference between the two. The first type is a complete substitution made from soy or milk proteins. This substitute cannot typically be used for baking or other uses where egg is intended to provide thickening or leavening in the item to be produced.

The second type contains real albumen (egg white), but the yolk is removed and replaced with dairy or vegetable products. While these products have a different taste than whole eggs, the whites they contain do make them suitable for many cooking purposes.

Cholesterol

A soft, waxy substance found in animal tissues and other foods of animal origin. Its level in the bloodstream can influence certain unwanted health conditions, such as plaque buildup in the arteries and heart disease.

© Simone Voigt/Shutterstock

Proper Storage and Rotation of Fresh Eggs are Critical to Their Serving Quality.

Dairy and Egg Storage

Fluid milks, butter, cream, yogurt, most cheeses, and egg products should be refrigerated at 41°F (5°C). Dairy products easily absorb off-odors and should be stored in airtight containers. Butter should be stored in its original container to avoid absorbing flavors from other foods.

Frozen desserts stored at temperatures below 0°F (−18°C) keep for about a month but have the best quality when stored for shorter periods of time. To maintain their quality, frozen desserts should be stored in tightly closed cartons.

Restaurant Terms and Concepts

Work in Progress

1. Private-label meats that use their own quality standards (rather than those developed by the USDA) are increasingly available from food service distributors. Examples include "Black Angus" and "Angus Beef." What are the advantages of selecting such products for a food service buyer? What are the potential disadvantages?

2. Many varieties of fish and shellfish have been overfished to the point that they're in danger of being completely exhausted for commercial use (e.g., see the list found at: www.fishonline.org/advice/avoid/). Assume that consumer demand for such products remains strong and that they're available for purchase from your distributor. What specific responsibility, if any, do you believe you and other buyers in food service have toward such overfished species?

3. What cost factors should restaurant managers consider before deciding to process their own fresh fruits and vegetables rather than buying them in a preprocessed market form?

4. Increasing labor costs and a lack of skilled kitchen personnel have resulted in many restaurants choosing to purchase pre-cut beef steaks and other meats (such as poultry breasts and other chicken parts) to ensure quality and consistency. What unique quality assurance challenges do you think managers who choose to purchase such products face?

5. Some animal rights advocates oppose on moral or ethical grounds the serving of certain types of meat dishes, such as veal or goose livers. How should restaurant managers respond to those guests who may question an operation's use of these (or other) sometimes controversial menu items?

6. When used to describe fruits and vegetables, "fresh" can mean anything from "never frozen" to "never processed." Choose one fruit and one vegetable (e.g., peaches and broccoli) and write a complete menu description of "fresh" for them. Do you think the customers for whom you buy would agree with your definition of fresh? Why or why not?

7. U.S. consumers increasingly purchase organic fruits and vegetables for their use at home because they perceive these products to be healthier (though more expensive) alternatives to highly processed fruits, vegetables, dairy products and eggs. Do you think this consumer trend will ultimately affect the products these consumers want to purchase when dining out? Explain your answer.

8. Assume that you are the food service manager at a large college. Would you offer all possible versions of beverage milks (e.g., nonfat, 1%, 2%, and whole) to your residence hall students? As a manager, what factors should you consider as you seek to balance your guests' preferences with your operation's storage and other production limitations?

9. Like many other food products, some fruits, vegetables and dairy products are packaged under nationally labeled brands (e.g., Dole® brand pineapples, Green Giant® brand vegetables, and Ben and Jerry's® brand ice cream). How important do you feel name-brand products in these categories would be to your restaurant guests? How would you best communicate the use of these name-brand products to your guests?

10. Americans are increasingly discussing steps that can be taken to address the country's rising obesity rates. What, if any, role do you feel is best for managers in the restaurant industry to play in this dialogue?

9

Serving Guests

Chapter Outline

Learning Objectives

After carefully reading and studying the information in this chapter, you will:

1. Understand the increasing importance of social media sites to the contemporary marketing of restaurant services.
2. Know the principles and practices used by restaurant professionals for the effective management of dining areas.

IN THIS CHAPTER

The long-term success of a restaurant requires that it first attract and then maintain and expand a strong customer base. Marketing is the management activity used to attract customers, and quality service is the tool used to ensure that those restaurant guests return again and again.

In this chapter, you'll learn how managers plan, and then implement, marketing activities that are most effective for attracting guests. Increasingly, those marketing activities include the use of advanced technology and social networking sites as well as more traditional marketing methods. The best managers understand both traditional and recently emerging marketing activities; in this chapter, you'll learn about both types.

When guests arrive at a restaurant, managers must turn their attention to ensuring that these guests receive the best customer service possible. A quality dining experience actually begins as soon as a guest arrives on the restaurant's property. As a result, managers must take care to maintain parking, arrival, and waiting areas at the same high standards as they do their actual production and dining areas.

Upon arrival, guests must be greeted, seated, and then served in a manner that optimizes each diner's service experience. Upon completion of their meals, guest must be presented with an accurate summary of their charges. The best restaurant managers are concerned about their ability to efficiently service guests; revenue per available seat hour (RevPASH) is one good way to measure the effectiveness of a restaurant's marketing and service efforts. Thus, the calculation of RevPASH and an assessment of RevPASH results are reviewed in this chapter.

Finally, a restaurant's ability to properly service its guests can and should be objectively measured with guest feedback systems. Restaurant managers can do that by addressing those service errors and shortcomings that have been brought to their attention. They also must monitor those social media sites on which guests post personal reviews of the restaurants they have visited and respond as needed to the postings. In this chapter, you'll learn how managers can best respond to fair and even unfair customer feedback.

ATTRACTING GUESTS

It has been said that management's primary function in the restaurant business is simply to obtain and retain customers. Without a sufficient number of customers, a restaurant cannot generate the revenue it needs to stay in business. Marketing is the means by which management attracts those customers it seeks to serve.

Target Markets

Features

Specific menu items and services that a restaurant offers for sale.

Benefits

An advantage or desirable consequence that results from the purchase of a product or service feature.

To determine which marketing activities should be undertaken, restaurant managers must understand well the products and services they offer and the target markets (see Chapter 1) they can serve best. To effectively market a restaurant, managers must understand that the products they sell will have **features** and will provide **benefits**.

Consider, for example, a hardware store salesperson who sells power drills. To be effective, he or she must understand that potential customers don't really want to buy a drill as much as they want to buy holes! Features are what businesses offer for sale (the drill); benefits are what the customers gain (the holes).

Similarly, the mother with young children who purchases lunch at a quick-service drive-through restaurant is buying food (the feature). Just as importantly, however, she is purchasing convenience, speed, value and, because she does not have to cook, she buys quality time with her family (benefits). When considering how to best identify a target market, managers must consider both the features and the benefits they can offer to their potential guests.

It might appear that all restaurants are similar because they serve food to a hungry public. However, the couple seeking an intimate restaurant to celebrate their wedding anniversary is looking for a different experience than is a grandmother hosting her six-year-old granddaughter and friends for a birthday/pizza party.

Guest profile

The personal characteristics of the guests who would be attracted to a restaurant.

Demographic

A distinctive characteristic of a group used to identify a target market. Examples are age, gender, and income level.

Psychographic

Any distinctive attribute of guests relating to personality, values, attitudes, interests, or lifestyles.

Examples are hobbies, ethical values, political affiliations, and social class.

Similarly, the health-conscious person desiring a "lunch on the run" during a lunch break is seeking a different type of restaurant than are teenagers wanting to eat pizza and "hang out" with their friends on a Friday night. Specific restaurants appeal to specific target markets. An important role of management, then, is to identify their restaurants' target market(s) and to effectively communicate their restaurants' features and benefits to those target markets.

Identifying current and potential guests as well as those features and benefits that appeal to them is a first step in developing a successful marketing plan. One of the best methods for determining the target market is to develop a **guest profile**. This marketing tool helps managers focus on specific characteristics of those guests who would be attracted to the restaurant. Guest profiles may be determined by age, gender, geographic location, or any other **demographic** characteristics that make sense for a particular restaurant. Guest profiles may also include one or more **psychographic** characteristics of guests.

THE MARKETING PLAN

After the restaurant's manager has identified the product/service features and benefits to be sold and has precisely defined the target market(s), it's time to plan a unified strategy for marketing the property. Effective restaurant marketing begins by developing a **marketing plan**.

A marketing plan is like a road map for the restaurant's selling efforts. It tells what and when activities will be undertaken to achieve sales goals. Developing a marketing plan is a process that involves answering the following questions:

- What is to be done?
- Who will do it?
- When should it be done?
- What funding will be required?
- How will results be monitored?
- How will results be measured?
- How will results be evaluated?

Assessing alternative marketing activities generally involves evaluating the potential of each activity to effectively deliver a restaurant's product and service message to its targeted audience. In some cases, the timing of a marketing activity is just as important as the activity itself. For example, assume that a restaurant has a large private banquet room in addition to its regular dining area. The restaurant is located in a city with many large businesses that sponsor social events in December. The restaurant manager wants to maximize banquet room revenue during this time by offering a special "Holiday Party" menu targeting areas companies and including drinks, appetizers, dinner, and dessert. Clearly, early December is too late to market these holiday parties. By that time, corporate planners will have already made party arrangements. In this example, mid-summer or early fall will likely be the best time to contact potential customers about booking the banquet room for holiday events. Because of the importance of timing market activities, many managers use a marketing calendar. Figure 9.1 is an example of a calendar that managers can use to plan their marketing activities.

Note the marketing calendar identifies:

- What is to be done
- Who will do it
- When it's to be completed

There's no easy answer to the question, "How much should be spent on restaurant marketing?" Funds must, however, be allocated for the restaurant's marketing budget. Generally, the

Marketing plan

A calendar of specific activities designed to the meet the restaurant's revenue goals.

Monthly Marketing Activities Checklist		
Restaurant: VERNON'S	Month/Year November, 20xx	
Activity	**Assigned To**	**Completion Date**
1. Attend chamber of commerce monthly social	Kitchen manager	_____
2. Place holiday ad in local newspapers	Restaurant manager	_____
3. Train new service staff on selling three recently introduced menu items	Executive chef	_____
4. Attend meeting of local restaurant association	Kitchen manager	_____
5. Revise/update employee dress code	Dining room manager	_____
6. Attend citywide chili cook-off	Executive chef	_____
7. Conduct "Guest of the Month" business card drawing/draft letter to winner	Dining room manager	_____
8. Insert new website photos/content	Restaurant manager	_____
9. Update Facebook wall	Restaurant manager	_____

FIGURE 9.1

Marketing Activities Calendar and Checklist

more marketing activities undertaken, the larger the marketing budget needed. A restaurant's total marketing budget can only be finalized after restaurant managers have carefully assessed the marketing methods included in their marketing plans.

MARKETING METHODS

Restaurant managers who develop a marketing plan carefully choose from a variety of marketing-related activities. Marketing methods available to restaurateurs may be viewed as either traditional or contemporary marketing approaches.

Traditional Marketing

Historically, marketing activities have been considered to be one of four distinct types:

- Advertising
- Promotions
- Publicity
- Public Relations

ADVERTISING   While a thorough discussion of advertising principles and philosophies is beyond the scope of this book, the primary goal of advertising is always to bring the restaurant's products and services to the attention of its current and potential target markets. Traditional restaurant advertising is typically done using one or more of the following:

- Exterior signage
- On-premise interior signage
- Brochures/flyers
- Coupons
- Radio or television commercials
- Direct mailings
- Property websites
- E-mailings
- Yellow Pages

© Simon Gurney/Shutterstock

Exterior signage can be one of a restaurant's most effective advertising tools.

- Billboards
- Personal contact

Good advertising can be costly, and thus its effectiveness must be constantly evaluated. While there's a great deal of variability in successful advertising pieces and campaigns, the best of these:

- Are eye or ear catching
- Are memorable
- Sell the restaurant's features and benefits
- Are cost-effective
- Don't become quickly outdated
- Reflect positively on the restaurant's image
- Can be easily directed to the restaurant's target market

An effective restaurant marketing plan will include the advertising activities (and their costs) that will be carried out in the period covered by the plan as well as a method for measuring the advertising's value.

PROMOTIONS In addition to advertising, an effective marketing plan includes promotion, publicity, and public relations activities. These three terms are closely related, sometimes overlap, and are often confused; however, each plays a part in the successful marketing of a restaurant.

In the restaurant industry, the term "promotion" most often refers to a "special" packaging of products or services. For example, a restaurant may create a "Summer Menu" promotion to be marketed in the late spring and early summer and which announces new menu items that feature seasonally available foods. Information about this promotion would be disseminated through internal and external advertising and, possibly, through publicity.

PUBLICITY Publicity refers to information about the restaurant that is distributed, free of charge, by the media. The good news is that publicity costs the restaurant nothing. The less good news is that the publicity may be either good or bad. The news media is, of necessity, an independent force in the shaping of public opinion. Cultivating good relationships with the media is an important job of a restaurant manager. When such a relationship exists, it may be easier for the restaurant to achieve positive publicity. If, for example, a major newspaper prints an article about the use of locally grown foods on restaurant menus, the fact that your restaurant is mentioned in the newspaper means the publicity would likely be very good.

However, even with good media relationships, a highly publicized foodborne illness outbreak in a nearby restaurant carrying the same brand affiliation as your restaurant will likely reflect poorly on your own business. In situations such as this, it's important that the restaurant have an active public relations program in place.

PUBLIC RELATIONS **Public relations**, or PR, include all activities designed to ensure that a restaurant has a positive public image. PR activities help the restaurant let its target market know that it's a good community citizen. PR efforts can include, among many other activities, hosting charity events, contributing cash or in-kind services to worthy causes or the donation of the restaurant staff's time for a worthy cause.

The restaurant's community can, depending on the property, be viewed as including local, state, national, and even international residents. In all cases, it's should be the intent of the operation's PR activities to positively reflect the values of the restaurant and its owners.

Contemporary Marketing

Increasingly, effective contemporary marketing is characterized by a restaurant's successful use of **social media**.

To best understand the incredible impact of social media on restaurant marketing, it's important to understand that, historically, customers gained information about a restaurant from print and electronic media such as newspapers, magazines, TV, and radio. Today's social media are different from these traditional marketing forms in a variety of ways:

Public relations
The active process of managing communications between an organization and those interested in the organization's activities. Also known as "PR."

Social media
The use of web-based and mobile technologies to turn communication into interactive dialogue between a restaurant and its customers.
Examples include Facebook and Twitter.

Cost of communication: Reaching large numbers of people using TV or radio, for example, is expensive, and the additional airing of a TV or radio ad usually means increased marketing costs. Social media technologies such as Facebook can reach a global audience of hundreds or even thousands of recipients for the same small fixed cost incurred to reach only a small number. The result is that social media sites can provide low-cost advertising, promotion, publicity, and public relations vehicles to even the smallest of restaurants.

Cost of acquisition: Creating memorable TV, radio, and print ads can be costly because they require the use of skilled professionals to produce the advertisement or other communication vehicle. Generally, the use of social media sites such as Facebook or Twitter requires little more than the sincere efforts of restaurateurs to communicate personally and directly with their guests.

Immediacy: Traditional media messages such as radio commercials or printed flyers can take days or even weeks to create. Social media messages can be delivered to audiences instantly. For example, if a restaurant manager decided to offer a chef-created special menu item at 4:00 P.M. on a Friday night, that message could, theoretically, be delivered to the restaurant's Facebook followers at 4:01 P.M.!

Alterability: Once a magazine or newsprint ad has been developed and printed, it cannot be changed until its next printing. Communication delivered on social media sites can be instantly altered, revised, or expanded.

One factor driving the expansion of social media as a form of marketing is the tendency for people to place more trust in those they feel are unbiased than in messages delivered by traditional advertising. Thus, a strong recommendation to visit a particular restaurant posted on a restaurant review site may have more appeal than the same restaurant's ad placed in a more traditional media outlet.

The popularity of social media networks is based on the fact that many individuals want to stay electronically connected for reasons that include friendship, hobbies and other common interests, romantic relationships, or shared knowledge such as that about foods and wines. While some of these individuals may spend significant amounts of time maintaining the connection, others spend much less time. From a restaurant manager's point of view, however, the most important aspect of social media is that it's heavily based on customer-to-customer communication. That means managers cannot directly control this nontraditional communication channel. However, they shouldn't underestimate how much they can influence it.

Increasing numbers of guests consult social network sites prior to making dinner reservations, locating a restaurant, ordering takeout food, or choosing a pizza for delivery. As a result, those managers who use social media sites most effectively can position their operations for success. Those who don't, however, seriously risk being left out of vital customer-initiated conversations.

That is true because communication is the primary reason for the existence of social networking sites. Users of social media sites register to use the sites, create content, connect with like-minded users, and share information. Managers can employ a variety of strategies to leverage the rapidly changing landscape of social media sites and applications. Those that are successful recognize that when it comes to having meaningful social media conversations, there must be two-way communication.

Some managers mistakenly feel that a social media page is essentially an extension of their websites. But they aren't the same. Website site visitors typically seek information. Social media users, however, seek two-way communication. A potential guest may go to an operation's website to find driving directions; the same guest will turn to a social media site to find out if others felt the drive would be worth making in the first place!

A second mistake some restaurant managers make is that of using their social media presence only to advertise their promotions or specials. When they do, their social media presence exists only to increase short-term sales. While this approach may increase revenue in the short run, it fails to take advantage of the more dynamic features of social media networks by ignoring the interest of social media users to share their insights and post impressions of their dining experiences. Few social media site users want to visit a site only to receive advertisements. Rather, social media users seek information they find of interest to them.

To meet this need, managers can supply their network contacts with information about new and exciting things happening in their operations. This can include providing detailed

> **WEB AT WORK!**
>
> Restaurant managers who wish to better understand the role they should play in marketing their properties can find ample resources to help them. One of the best is the book *Marketing for Hospitality and Tourism* by Philip Kotler. To learn more about it go to:
>
> www.amazon.com
>
> Enter the book's title, the author's name or the book's ISBN number (ISBN: 978-0135045596) to review its table of contents.

descriptions of new menu items, identifying links to positive reviews posted on other social media sites, providing discount coupons, or sending holiday greetings. Some restaurants also provide their customers with the opportunity to make reservations directly from social media sites.

Social media sites will continue to expand and change. They will likely play an ever larger role in the marketing programs of successful restaurants. For that reason, their use and evolution must be continually monitored by managers.

THE IMPORTANCE OF QUALITY SERVICE

Guests receive three distinct things when they visit a restaurant, including:

- Menu items
- Service
- Dining experience

Of course, restaurant guests purchase menu items; these items must be of high quality and represent value for the dining dollars expended. In Chapter 8, you learned that properly choosing, storing, and preparing quality foods are important management tasks. Just as restaurant managers must set quality standards for the menu items they sell, they must also establish standards for the service they will deliver and the overall dining experience they will offer their guests.

Most managers would agree that the number one complaint in restaurants is not bad food; it's poor service. Guest can encounter poor service even before they're seated. For example, a guest may receive poor service when he or she calls a restaurant to make a reservation, parks a car in lots that are littered or are poorly lighted, enters through doors with glass that is spotted or dirty, and arrives in a cluttered entrance way that needs sweeping or vacuuming. The best managers know that they must control their guests' service experiences through pre-arrival, arrival, and seating.

PRE-ARRIVAL   Pre-arrival service includes providing guests with information they need to make reservations and arrive at the restaurant. Because guests increasingly go online to find information about the restaurants they want to visit, providing good pre-arrival service means making it easy for guest to find key information about a restaurant, including:

Address

Hours of operation

Location

Driving directions

An operation's internet presence can be professionally designed and managed to provide this (and other) critical information in a way that is easy to navigate and read. In those operations where reservations are taken, pre-arrival service also includes professionalism when taking the guest reservations.

ARRIVAL   Guests often arrive at a restaurant by automobile or bus. Guests form initial quality and service perceptions by observing an operation's landscaping, grounds, and parking areas. Landscaping should be kept well trimmed and attractive. Grassy and other landscaped areas should look appealing. Parking areas should be kept well lighted and litter-free. Parking lot surfaces should be kept in good repair. Exterior spaces are very important, so these critical areas should be inspected on a daily basis.

When entering a restaurant, customers immediately assess the cleanliness and attractiveness of its doors, windows, entrance areas, and waiting areas. Restrooms are also critical in affecting guest perceptions about the service, cleanliness, and quality of an entire operation. In fact, restroom areas are so important that many managers require those areas to be inspected on an hourly or even half-hourly basis.

SEATING   Regardless of how they reach the operation, guests should be made to feel welcome when they arrive. A well-trained staff should be available to greet the guests enthusiastically and sincerely. When guests cannot be served or seated immediately upon arrival, they should be kept well informed about the how long it will be until they're served. While waiting for seating, guests should be made as comfortable as possible in waiting areas that are clean and inviting.

When guests are seated, their assigned tables and chairs should be clean, attractive, and in good repair. Assistance for special-needs guests such as the elderly or children should be readily available to ensure that quality service is also provided to these guests. Managers who spend large amounts of their time in dining areas observing guests are in an excellent position to determine the quality of service being provided.

Service Standards

The level of service provided by a restaurant will vary based on the restaurant's industry segment. Thus the *level* of service provided by a quick service restaurant will be different from that of a fine dining restaurant, but the *quality* of service should be the same.

© Dmitry Kalinovsky/Shutterstock

Service staff should be neat, well-groomed, in proper uniform and smiling when they greet guests.

Providing high-quality customer service is critical to the long-term success of any restaurant. High-quality service is the result of careful planning, extensive employee training, and continual assessment of the service levels actually experienced by guests. The consistent delivery of high-quality restaurant service requires the collective efforts of professional managers and servers.

Increasingly, guests are willing to pay more for dining experiences that meet or exceed their service quality expectations. The role of restaurant managers and servers is, then, much more than to simply "deliver" food and beverages ordered by guests. In fact, the goal of service staff should be to help ensure that each guest is satisfied with the service each has received. This requires that servers create experiences "one at a time" for their guests. Certain service basics, including cleanliness, courtesy, and product knowledge, are of obvious importance. However, the ability to satisfy guests goes far beyond the delivery of these "basics." Service staff must have a genuine interest in helping their guests and must be empowered by their manager to provide the "little extras" that make a difference from the guests' perspective between an acceptable and a high-quality dining experience.

The consistent delivery of service that meets the standards established by a restaurant requires the combined efforts of management and servers.

THE MANAGER'S ROLE   In addition to being responsible for food and beverage product quality, restaurant managers are responsible for maintaining targeted service quality levels and ensuring that each guest receives a memorable dining experience.

It may be easy to describe the quality service that management strives for. Friendly greetings offered to arriving guests, prompt and courteous order taking, accurate delivery of ordered items, and well-designed billing and payment collection procedures are characteristics all professional managers seek to offer their guests.

In some restaurants, however, service delivery falls short of the standards established by management. This happens because it's usually the restaurant's employees, not its managers, who actually deliver guest service. Managers understand that it's in their own best interests and the interests of their customers to do all they can to create a positive guest dining experience and ensure that their staff has the needed training to deliver it. The benefits of providing quality service to guests are many and include these facts:

1. Guest loyalty increases when excellent service is consistently delivered.
2. Minor mistakes in service delivery are more often forgiven when it's clear the restaurant is striving to do its best for customers and apologizes for the errors.
3. Guests who have a positive experience will tell others about it (just as they will share their negative experiences!).
4. Customer feedback systems work better because guests know management truly cares about service improvements.

THE SERVER'S ROLE   It would be difficult to overemphasize the importance of restaurant employees in the delivery of quality service. Professional restaurant servers share many similar characteristics regardless of the restaurant segment in which they work:

- They think and act as if they're the "host" of the guests being served.
- They remember and use the names of guest "regulars" whom they serve.
- They make a genuine effort to ensure that each guest has a memorable dining experience.
- They anticipate and respond to the needs of their guests.
- They're proud of their appearance and personal grooming practices.
- They help other members of the restaurant service team whenever they can.
- They sincerely thank guests for their business and invite them to return.

Dining Experience Standards

Certainly, a positive dining experience is greatly influenced by the quality of food and beverage served to guests, the service standards established by the management, and the guests' interactions with service personnel. In addition, however, ambiance plays a central role in a restaurant's ability to deliver a high-quality experience.

In Chapter 1, you learned that ambiance is the feeling or mood created by an environment, such as the inside of a restaurant. Ambience is an important aspect of the overall dining experience that customers receive when they visit your restaurant. To better understand the importance of ambiance, consider how you would view your overall dining experience in these scenarios:

- You visited a restaurant that served excellent food, but the tables were sticky from spilled food, the chairs were poorly cleaned, the floor was littered with crumbs and food scraps, and the restrooms were extremely dirty.
- You visited a restaurant that served excellent food, but the lighting level was so low you could not read the menu.
- You visited a restaurant that provided excellent service, but the dining room was so cold you couldn't enjoy your food.
- You visited a restaurant that provided excellent service, but the seats were so hard and uncomfortable they distracted you from enjoying your meal.
- You visited a restaurant that provided excellent food and service, but the guests seated next to you were loud and used foul language that quickly made you and your dining companion feel very uncomfortable.
- You visited a restaurant that provided excellent food and service, but the tabletop was so small and littered with promotional materials and condiments, that you found it difficult to arrange the plates you were served in a way that would allow you to thoroughly enjoy your meal.

ALL IN A DAY'S WORK: 9.1

"So how does everything taste tonight?" Jana, the manager of the Seafood Shack Restaurant said with a big smile as she approached a four-top table on the west side of her restaurant's dining room on a busy Thursday night.

"Not so great," began the man, wearing a suit and tie, and sitting at the table with his wife and two teenage daughters. "This is our first time here," he continued.

"It's not so bad," interrupted his wife "Really, the food is fine."

Jana was concerned. Having new customers state that the food at the Seafood Shack was "not so bad" or only "fine" wasn't a good sign. She knew the food quality at her restaurant was excellent.

"Is there a problem with your order?" asked Jana. "We want to correct that if there is."

"Well, for one thing," continued the man, "it's really hot in here. We asked the server to lower the shade on the window over there because the sun is making our table so warm I'm actually sweating. She said she would, but she hasn't. That was 10 minutes ago."

Jana looked up and saw that the setting sun was in fact streaming through the window directly onto these guests' table.

"I think our server just got busy and forgot," said the woman at the table, apologetically. "It's fine, really it is. We're almost done now anyway. It's fine. We're fine."

1. Do you think the man at this table will remember the food quality at the Seafood Shack when he recalls his meal experience? Do you think he or his wife felt everything was "fine"? Do you think he and his family are likely to return?
2. What action should Jana have taken prior to opening that day to prevent this type of incident? What should she do now?

WEB AT WORK!

Guests don't always share their feelings with management during a negative dining experience. They may, however, post comments online. User-supplied restaurant reviews are increasingly popular; many guests refer to them when they choose a restaurant. To see restaurant reviews in your own town, go to:

www.dine.com

Enter the name of your town. Read several reviews. Do you think the managers of the reviewed restaurants would consider the posted reviews to be fair and objective? Do you think it matters if they do or if they don't?

Item	Okay As Is	Needs Immediate Attention
Exterior signage properly lit		
Parking lot areas litter-free and well lighted		
Entrance areas free of ice and snow		
Entrance doors clean and functioning properly		
Entrance foyers clean and litter-free		
Windows clean/interior sills insect-free		
All interior light bulbs/lamps working		
All lighting at appropriate levels		
Dining-room floors clean		
Child/booster chairs cleaned and sanitized		
All tables clean and level (not wobbly)		
Chairs/booths clean and in good repair		
Temperature at appropriate levels		
Interior walls clean/free of food debris		
Restrooms clean and well stocked		
Reception waiting area clean/litter-free		
Other		
Other		
Other		
Other		

FIGURE 9.2

Pre-Opening Ambiance Checklist for Restaurants

In each of these scenarios, you would likely feel that you had a poor dining experience regardless of the food and service quality delivered by the restaurant. For that reason, managers must be concerned with establishing and maintaining an ambiance that ensures that their guests will receive a positive dining experience.

Figure 9.2 is a checklist of some of the many features that restaurant managers must consider in maintaining an ambiance designed to help their guests receive a positive overall dining experience. It can be modified as managers see fit to better address the ambiance-related issues present in their own restaurants.

SERVING GUESTS

Because of the wide range of restaurant types, it can be challenging to identify the specific methods managers must employ to deliver quality guest service. Those features important in a fine-dining restaurant (e.g., proper table setting and napkin folding) are not tasks undertaken in a takeout only restaurant. Despite the variation in restaurant operations and guest expectations, however, there are common features in nearly all restaurant guest service interactions. These include:

- Managing guest arrivals
- Greeting guests
- Taking and delivering guest orders
- Guest payment
- Table clearing and resetting

Managing Guest Arrivals

It's important to realize that guests' opinions of their dining experiences begin to form long before they enter a restaurant and receive their food. Their initial reactions to a restaurant take shape as they call ahead to make a reservation or as arrive at the restaurant and see the parking lot or restaurant's exterior. For that reason, restaurateurs must carefully consider how best to manage these experiences.

FACILITY APPEARANCE   Clean, well-lighted parking and walk-up areas are a critical part of forming positive guest perceptions about a restaurant's quality and management's attention to detail. The exterior of a restaurant must be kept completely free of litter and debris. Any landscaping around the property should be kept weed-free and well trimmed. Trash and ashtray receptacles should be clean, checked daily and emptied frequently.

The best restaurant managers recognize that a restaurant's exterior gives arriving guests important visual clues about what they can expect inside. Clean and well-maintained entrance areas, foyers, restrooms, and waiting areas help to make a first impression positive. Poorly maintained arrival areas can cause guests to become wary of their restaurant choice even before they enter the dining room.

STAFF   Restaurants in all segments work hard to ensure that their guests receive excellent service. The appearance, attitude, and skill level of a restaurant's staff work together to shape guests' perceptions of service quality and will directly impact guests' views of their overall dining experiences. For this reason, managers must pay close attention to these important staff-related issues.

APPEARANCE   The visual impressions given to guests by restaurant staff directly relate to the appearance of the staff's uniforms and their personal grooming habits.

In most restaurants, policies regulate the work uniforms worn by **front-of-house staff** and **back-of-house staff**.

The uniforms worn by restaurant employees can range from casual to formal. When arriving guests first encounter uniformed staff members, the uniforms worn by staff members should:

- Fit properly
- Be clean
- Be pressed (or wrinkle free)
- Be in good taste and allow for an appropriate level of modesty
- Include proper hair restraint (if nets, hats, or caps are worn)
- Include appropriate close-toed shoes
- Include a clean and easy-to-read name tag

Front-of-house staff

Employees whose jobs put them in direct contact with guests. Examples include hosts and hostesses, bartenders, servers, bussers, and cashiers.

Back-of-house staff

Employees whose jobs don't typically put them in direct contact with guests. Examples include cooks, bakers, and dish washers.

© Yuri Arcurs/Shutterstock

In well-managed restaurants, uniform and grooming standards for the back-of-house employees are just as high as those for the front-of-house staff.

Do	Do Not
Shower or bath daily	Wear excessive amounts of fragrance
Use deodorant	Wear excessive amounts of makeup or lipstick
Brush teeth and tongue frequently	Chew gum while on duty
Keep fingernails trimmed and clean	Smoke while on duty
Wash hands frequently	Wear jewelry or nail polish that can interfere with work or create a safety hazard.
Keep facial hair (beards and mustaches) trimmed	Allow hair to cover the face while working (keep it tied back)
Keep hair clean	Wear excessive amounts of body jewelry or piercing jewelry

FIGURE 9.3

Restaurant Server Personal Grooming Dos and Don'ts

A restaurant's uniform policy should be legally defensible and carefully explained to employees during the selection and orientation process. Specifically, employees should be asked if there are any parts of the dress code with which they're uncomfortable. If they express concerns, their issues should be fully addressed and, if reasonable, accommodations may be made. After dress code requirements have been fully explained to employees, however, these standards should be strictly enforced by management.

Poorly fitting or dirty, wrinkled uniforms speak to guests long before the employees wearing them have said a word. They convey that management cares little about cleanliness or quality, and that standards for the operation are lax. A clean, properly fitting uniform relays the opposite impression: that management insists on a neat and orderly business while delivering service defined by its attention to detail. In the eyes of customers, clean uniforms mean a clean restaurant.

In addition to the uniforms, the personal grooming habits of restaurant employees silently express information guests use to assess their overall dining experiences. Figure 9.3 lists some important server "Dos and Don'ts" that can form the basis of a server's personal grooming policy.

Policies on potentially controversial issues as unusual hair coloring and styles, visible tattoos and body piercings vary widely in the hospitality industry, but policies about these issues should be carefully explained to all affected employees.

ATTITUDE   It has often been said that a "smile" is the most important thing for a restaurant server to wear at work. When servers genuinely smile at arriving guests, they convey a positive attitude and welcoming feeling that create memorable experiences. Restaurant managers can train staff to portray a positive attitude when they emphasize the fact that when it comes to guests, all restaurant employees need to be SERVE oriented.

- Smiling
- Energetic
- Respectful
- Visible
- Engaged

Arriving guests know when they're being genuinely welcomed or when their arrival is seen by staff to be unimportant, or even a bother! For that reason, many restaurant managers prefer to hire untrained service workers who consistently exhibit a positive attitude and then train them as servers, rather than hire more experienced, but less welcoming servers who must then be taught to convey a positive attitude.

Greeting Guests

Whether they "arrive" at a drive-up window or the most upscale of dining rooms, the formal greeting of guests is a **moment of truth** for all restaurants.

Sometimes, arriving guests can be seated or served immediately. In other cases, the guests name will be placed on a **wait list**.

Moment of truth

An instance of interaction between a customer and a business that gives the customer an opportunity to form or change his or her impression about the business.

Wait list

A document or software program that contains the names of guests who have arrived at a restaurant but haven't yet been escorted to their tables.

MANAGING WAIT LISTS   When a restaurant is busy, arriving guests who don't have reservations may not be seated immediately. It's in the best interest of both the guests and the restaurant to manage the wait list in a manner that minimizes wait times for guests and maximizes the number of seated guests.

The process of managing wait lists can be manual or automated. The goal of the restaurant should be to:

1. Manage the wait list in a manner guests consider to be fair
2. Provide waiting guests with realistic estimates of the amount of time they will wait for their tables

Few guests want to wait to be seated and served. Restaurant managers can make their guests' wait times as pleasant as possible by:

- Providing a clean and pleasant foyer, lobby, or bar area for waiting guests
- Allowing guests easy access to continually updated information about the estimated length of their wait times
- Managing the wait list on a strict first-come, first-served basis
- Providing guests the option of alternative seating arrangements where practical (e.g., offering immediate bar area seating if no dining areas seating is immediately available)
- Providing music, videos, or television programming to make wait times pass more pleasantly
- Ensuring all bussing and service staff are aware that there are guests in the restaurant's waiting area
- Implementing an *effective* communication method to ensure that waiting guests know when their tables are ready

Sometimes guests who have reserved tables in advance will arrive on time but can't be immediately seated. While this can happen for a variety of legitimate reasons, it's important to recognize that such a situation, if not handled properly, can lead to extreme customer dissatisfaction. When guests who have confirmed reservations are required to wait more than a few minutes beyond their reserved table times, it's imperative that a sincere apology for the delay is given, the reason for the delay is made clear, and that these guests are seated at the earliest available opportunity.

The proper management of wait lists is important to quality guest service; restaurant managers must ensure that the process is fully integrated into the restaurant's table management system.

TABLE MANAGEMENT   Consider a busy restaurant whose dining room contains "two-top" tables (those that seat two guests), three-person tables, and four-person tables. Assume also that 20 two-person parties are currently on a wait list. If these guests are seated at available three- and four-top tables, their waits will be reduced, but the restaurant won't operate at full capacity. Table management is the process used to carefully balance guests' wait times with dining room capacity.

In restaurants where tables can be easily moved to create larger or smaller seating arrangements, table management is an easier process than in restaurants where tables are stationary and cannot be rearranged to optimize dining room capacity.

At times, waiting guests can become disturbed if they observe empty tables in the dining room while they're waiting to be seated. This can happen, for example, when a customer without a reservation sees empty tables reserved for dining parties that haven't yet arrived at the restaurant or that haven't yet been seated. In such cases, clear and polite communication with waiting customers is essential.

> ### WEB AT WORK!
>
> Increasingly, modern restaurant POS systems include an automated "Wait-list management" application. To view a popular system, go to:
>
> http://www.rmpos.com/reservations_table.html
>
> Read the information provided about wait list and table management software programs.

SEATING GUESTS   When an appropriate-sized table is available, waiting guests should immediately be escorted to their seats. Hosts or hostesses escorting guests to their tables should walk slightly ahead of the guests and slowly enough so the guests can follow easily. When a dining area isn't crowded, asking guests to indicate their own seating preferences (e.g., near the window, near the fireplace, at a booth rather than at a table) is a good way to make a positive impact on the guests' overall dining experience. Special attention should be paid to seating disabled guests and those guests dining with small children.

Upon arriving at the table, the employee seating the guests should check to make sure that the table is clean and that there are complete place settings for each guest seated. Menus should be distributed to each guest (not merely tossed on the table), and seated guests should be told when their server will arrive. In many restaurants, the name of the server who will handle the table is stated by the hostess, for example, "Laura will be serving you tonight. . . ."

TAKING AND DELIVERING GUEST ORDERS   The actual taking of guest orders can varies greatly in the Quick Service Restaurant (QSR), fast casual, casual, and fine dining restaurant segments. The traditional method of talking orders (i.e., a server takes the order from the guest seated in the dining area) is an exceptionally critical part of a guest's overall dining experience in many restaurants. Order taking and food delivery is a skillful art that reflects on the quality of the server and the restaurant. Guest orders that are recorded accurately better ensure that guests receive exactly what they want. Orders that aren't taken precisely will result in guest dissatisfaction, excessive costs (from returned foods), and wasted effort on the part of servers and back-of-house production personnel.

Well-trained servers can significantly impact the profitability of a restaurant by suggestively selling selected menu items. Building **check averages** with **suggestive selling** increases a restaurant's revenue and, because tips are most often calculated as a percentage of a guest's total bill, it increases server tips as well.

Well-trained servers not only get guest orders "right," they also use a system to ensure that food is *delivered* to the guest who ordered it, avoiding the *"Who's the ham sandwich!"* questions associated with poor order taking and delivery.

To make sure that food is delivered to the proper guest, trained servers use a system to associate each order with a specific guest. Ordering guests may be numbered in a clockwise direction starting from one designated guest or some designated point in the dining area (e.g., the person sitting closest to the entrance, or to the kitchen). Many different order-taking systems are in use in the restaurant industry, but all are designed to ensure that guests receive exactly what they have ordered, and that orders are delivered in a professional manner.

Check average

The average amount of money spent per guest served in restaurant. Also known as "average sale per guest." Check average is calculated as:
Total food and beverage revenue ÷ Total number of guests served = Check average

Suggestive selling

Encouraging diners to buy more, or to buy selected menu items, by emphasizing their availability to a restaurant's customers.

Guest Payment

Guest payment processes are another area in which the overall dining experience can be affected in either a positive or a negative way. Certainly, guests' bills should accurately reflect the amounts they owe. The processes put in place for handling payments should be especially **customer-centric**.

Guests seek accuracy and speed in processing their bills. Experienced restaurant managers know that an otherwise excellent dining experience can be ruined when:

Customer-centric

A decision-making approach that emphasizes a course of action's impact on customers prior to its implementation.

- A bill is too slowly delivered to the guest's table by the server
- A bill is processed too slowly after it has been returned to the server for payment
- A bill is delivered too quickly to the guest's table, resulting in the guest's feeling rushed to leave
- The guest check contains errors (e.g., charges are made for items that weren't delivered, or incorrect prices were charged for ordered items)
- Credit or debit card charges don't match the original guest check amounts
- Improper change (cash and/or coin) is returned to the guest after the bill has been paid

Table Clearing and Resetting

When guests have paid their bills and departed, dining area tables should be immediately cleared and reset. Having a well-established plan to do so efficiently leads to improved dining room capacity management and improves the look of the dining room to seated guests and those being escorted to their tables.

© Tatiana Popova/Shutterstock

The restaurant staff's ability to quickly clear and reset tables for use by new guests is an important measure of their skill.

Busser and other service staff who will clear and reset tables should be trained to work quickly and carefully. After uneaten food, used dishware, glassware, and eating utensils have been removed, large crumbs or other food debris should be placed in the hand or onto a plate or napkin (not brushed to the floor) and then removed.

If soiled, tablecloths may need to be carefully examined for possible replacement and hard surface tabletops should be cleaned and sanitized (see Chapter 5) before the table is reset for use by the next guests. Chairs, booths, and child seats should be cleaned between uses so diners don't have to brush crumbs off their seats before sitting down. Table-top items such as menus, condiments, and condiment holders should be checked between each seated party to ensure that they're clean and free of food spills.

From the time guests arrive at a restaurant's entrance until the time they leave, the opportunities to capitalize on moments of truth are great; however, that can only happen when restaurant managers train their service staff well.

RevPASH

Stands for "revenue per available seat hour," a measurement designed to assess efficiency in using the seating capacity of a restaurant.

EVALUATION OF GUEST SERVICE

Restaurant managers can assess the quality of their guest service efforts in two important ways. The first is by objectively measuring the efficiency with which guests are served. This can be done by performing a **RevPASH** analysis.

WEB AT WORK!

Restaurant managers can choose from a wide variety of server training materials. One of the most popular is *Service That Sells*. To view the website for this concept, go to:

www.servicethatsells.com

Read the information about various wait staff training programs.

The second way to assess a restaurant's guest service quality is to monitor both on-premise and off-premise guest feedback.

Revenue Per Available Seat Hour (RevPASH)

To best understand the importance of RevPASH as a measure of serving efficiency, it's important for restaurant managers to recognize that they're in the business of renting space as well as selling food and beverages. Restaurants typically have a fixed number of seats. Their total revenue generation depends on how many customers are seated during the period the restaurant is open, the amount of time each customer remains seated and how much money each customer spends during the time he or she is seated. An increase in the number of guests seated typically results in higher sales levels. In a well-managed restaurant, higher sales levels should produce higher levels of profit.

An assessment of RevPASH helps managers better understand the length of their customers' dining experiences and the amount they spend. Of course, restaurant managers cannot typically control the menu items selected by guests or the speed with which they eat. However, monitoring RevPASH can give managers a good idea of the speed at which a kitchen produces menu items and the speed at which guests are served.

The formula used to calculate RevPASH is:

$$\frac{\text{Total revenue}}{\text{Seat hours available}} = \text{Revenue per available seat hour (RevPASH)}$$

To calculate RevPASH, managers identify the sales level and number of customers served for each hour their restaurants are open. This information is easily retrievable from a typical restaurant POS system. To illustrate the calculation of RevPASH, assume that a restaurant has 125 seats and is open from 4:00 P.M. to 11:00 P.M. Figure 9.4 details the revenue achieved during a single night of operation.

In this example, the dining room holds 125 seats, thus, from 4–5 P.M., there are 125 seat hours available for guests. Because the restaurant is open for 7 hours, the total number of seat hours available is 875 (125 seats available per hour ($\times$) 7 hours = 875 seat hours available). Total RevPASH for the day is $20.06 ($17,550 ÷ 875 = $20.06).

Note that RevPASH is calculated on an hourly basis as well as a daily (total) basis. On this day, the restaurant was most efficient in using its seats to generate sales during the 6:00 P.M. to 10:00 P.M. time periods. During each of these time periods, the individual (hourly) RevPASH values achieved exceeded the operation's overall RevPASH average of $20.06.

Managers reviewing the data in Figure 9.4 could come to several sales and service-related conclusions. The most obvious is the fact that the restaurant's available seating was significantly underused during the following time periods:

- 4–5 P.M.
- 5–6 P.M.
- 10–11 P.M.

Hour	Seat hours Available	Customers Served	Revenue	Check Average	RevPASH
4–5 P.M.	125	30	750.00	$ 25.00	$ 6.00
5–6 P.M.	125	50	1,275.00	25.50	10.20
6–7 P.M.	125	75	2,800.00	37.33	22.40
7–8 P.M.	125	100	3,625.00	36.25	29.00
8–9 P.M.	125	125	4,100.00	32.80	32.80
9–10 P.M.	125	100	3,350.00	33.50	26.80
10–11 P.M.	125	60	1,650.00	27.50	13.20
Total	875	540	$ 17,550.00	**$ 32.50**	**$ 20.06**

FIGURE 9.4

RevPASH Calculation Per Available Seat Hour (RevPASH) For: Saturday Night

If the restaurant's manager could offer special programs or promotions that attracted more customers to earlier periods (4:00 P.M. to 6:00 P.M.), or later periods (10:00 P.M. to 11:00 P.M.), an increase in revenue and profit would likely result. Secondly, while check average is an important measure of sales, the highest RevPASH period, 8:00 P.M. to 9:00 P.M., was *not* the period generating the highest check average. That is because increases in RevPASH are determined in large part by optimizing the *number* of guests served, rather than the amount purchased by each guest. Finally, a variety of strategies might be evaluated to determine if they could help increase this restaurant's RevPASH, including:

- Promoting off-hour (slow period) food and drink specials
- Adding staff during high RevPASH periods to ensure quality service
- Eliminating or not promoting any menu or drink specials that take extra kitchen time to *prepare* (e.g., complex entrees or soufflé desserts) during high RevPASH periods
- Eliminating or not promoting any menu or drink specials that take extra time to *serve* (e.g., tableside-served salads or desserts) during high RevPASH periods
- Offering special "add-on" menu items with higher-than-normal selling prices and profitability during times of high seat utilization to maximize the potential sale of these items
- Ensuring that reservation programs optimally match diner arrival times with potentially available seating
- Reviewing table and wait-list management programs and procedures to ensure that optimal seat usage decisions are made during busy serving periods (*Manager's tip: a larger number of smaller tables generally leads to higher RevPASH levels than can be achieved in restaurants with a smaller number of large tables. Smaller tables can be moved together to accommodate larger parties, but larger tables can't be reduced in size to serve smaller parties.*)

Responding to Guest Feedback

Despite their best efforts, most restaurants will encounter some guests who are unhappy with the quality of service they've received. Sometimes the guests will indeed have received sub-standard service. At other times, service was probably provided just as the restaurant intended, but the guest's service expectations were not reasonable.

Complicating matters further is the fact that some guests will provide service-quality-related feedback while they're in the restaurant, while others will make their displeasure know only after they've departed. From the perspective of the restaurant manager, however, it's important that feedback from both types of customers be addressed promptly and professionally.

ALL IN A DAY'S WORK: 9.2

"What I don't understand," said the woman at the hostess stand, "is why you took my reservation for 7 o'clock but then make us wait for 45 minutes. I can clearly see empty tables in the dining room."

Emily, the hostess at the Fleur-de-Lis French restaurant, looked toward the 125-seat main dining room. She too could see a large number of tables that were indeed empty. But the tables hadn't yet been cleared and reset. There was no way she could immediately seat the increasingly agitated customer and her four dining companions. She could also see the one busser on duty, working as quickly as possible to clear one of the cluttered tables.

It was Friday night. The restaurant was very busy, and the wait times for guests were getting longer by the hour. Emily looked at the reservation list and saw that a number of large groups were scheduled to arrive at 8:00 P.M. With only one busser on the schedule, Emily knew it was going to be a long night.

"I'm sorry ma'am," said Emily apologetically, "we'll get you seated in just a few minutes."

"Well, this is just unacceptable," replied the woman. "I want to see your manager!"

1. Assume you were the manager at the Fleur-de-Lis. What is the likely cause of empty unreset tables while guests are waiting to be seated? What would you say to this customer?
2. Assume you were Emily. What would be your view of management's commitment to providing quality guest service during periods of high volume?

ON-PREMISE FEEDBACK   Responding to positive guest feedback is typically one of a restaurant manager's most rewarding experiences. Having a guest take the time to tell a restaurant's manager that the guest especially enjoyed a specific menu item or the actions of a particular employee almost always makes managers feel that they're doing a good job.

Unfortunately, guest feedback is not always positive. Mistakes made cooking food, preparing drinks, or serving menu items can happen even in the best-managed restaurants. Sometimes guests' expectations aren't reasonable, or guests may be upset about other areas of their own lives and be critical or unfair in their criticism of a restaurant.

Regardless of the type or source of the negative guest feedback, as a restaurant manager, you'll likely be the person called upon to address it. When you do so, follow these five recommended steps:

Five Steps for Addressing Negative Guest Feedback

Step 1   **Introduce yourself by name and position.**   Make it clear to the guest that you're there to help resolve their issues and that you're committed to doing so.

Step 2   **Seek information.**   Asking guests to relay the cause of their issue or complaint is a helpful way to calm guests and show that you care. It's essential that you avoid interruptions and let the guest talk. Even if the guest is wrong (or unreasonable) about some aspects of the situation, it's important to hear his or her perspective on the issue.

Step 3   **Empathize with the guest.**   Stating that you can understand how the guest feels because you would likely feel the same way (e.g., if your food were served cold, the wrong drink was delivered, or service was slow) shows you take the guest's complaint seriously.

Step 4   **Fix the problem and apologize on behalf of the restaurant.**   In most cases, service errors can be corrected by replacing a menu item, removing its charge from the guest's bill, or simply apologizing for an unintentional service error. A sincere apology should always conclude the actions taken by the manager.

Step 5   **Thank the guest for bring the issue to your attention.**   While dealing with an upset guest can be challenging, experienced restaurant managers know it's better to be made aware of problems than not. The final step in the guest complaint resolution process is to sincerely thank the guest for bringing the problem to your attention.

Some unhappy guests may not be reasonable in their complaints or in their reactions to the service-related errors that can be made by a restaurant. There's an old saying in the hospitality industry: "The customer is always right." In fact, however, the customer is *not* always right. When customers are verbally abusive to staff, engage in unwelcomed behavior such as touching or making suggestive and/or threatening comments to workers or other guests, managers have an ethical and legal responsibility to do what they must to ensure the safety of all of those in their restaurants (see Chapter 3). In most cases, this can be achieved simply by talking reasonably to the guest and asking him or her to stop the offensive behavior.

While managers should never physically confront an unruly guest, they should make it known that if the guest's inappropriate behavior doesn't stop, the manager will be forced to ask the guest to leave or to seek the assistance of the proper authorities to remove that guest from the premises.

SOCIAL MEDIA SITE FEEDBACK   Increasingly, restaurant guests go online to seek information about the restaurants they're thinking about visiting. So restaurant managers must understand

---

WEB AT WORK!

Restaurant managers should make it a point to regularly monitor social media sites that provide restaurant reviews. To view one such site, go to:

www.urbanspoon.com

Carefully read the information on the site about your favorite local restaurant and consider how you would respond to any negative reviews.

10

Beverage Products and Service

Chapter Outline

Alcoholic Beverages
Types of Beverage Operations
Physiological Effects of Alcohol
Regulation of Alcohol Sales

Wine and Foods
Wine
Wine and Food Pairings
Wine Lists

Other Alcoholic Beverages
Beer
Spirits

Bar Operations
Quality Beverage Service
Responsible Beverage Service

Learning Objectives

After carefully reading and studying the information in this chapter, you will:

1. Recognize the importance of restaurant wine lists to the effective marketing of wine.
2. Understand the manager's role in ensuring both high-quality and responsible service of alcoholic beverages.

IN THIS CHAPTER

For restaurant guests, the choices of alcoholic beverages that can be enjoyed while dining out are greater than ever before. However, the responsibilities of those who serve alcoholic beverages to these guests are also greater. Diners have long enjoyed alcoholic beverages with their meals and will no doubt continue to do so. For that reason, it's important that restaurant managers know the fundamental characteristics of the different alcoholic beverages they sell. They must also know how these products are best served. Finally, they must understand the legal liability that's assumed by a restaurant when it decides to offer alcoholic beverages on its menu.

Good food and good wine make meals memorable. The choice of which wine goes best with which food is a personal one. Historically, however, many wine drinkers have found that specific types of wine complement certain groups of foods. In this chapter, you'll learn about some of those traditional wine and food pairings and how to make lists of the kinds of wine you offer for sale to guests.

Wine isn't the only alcoholic beverage enjoyed by diners and sold by restaurant managers. Beer, ales and spirits are also popular with guests. As a manager you must know about these well-liked products and how you can ensure that what you offer guests is of high quality.

Experienced restaurant managers know that it's profitable to sell alcoholic beverages. In today's marketplace, however, the emphasis on beverage profitability must come from serving more customers responsibly, not by serving more beverages to just a few individuals. From a legal perspective, those who are allowed to sell alcoholic beverages must do so in socially acceptable ways or face significant penalties. This chapter concludes with an examination of how to serve alcoholic beverages in a highly responsible manner.

ALCOHOLIC BEVERAGES

Alcohol is a colorless liquid created by fermenting a liquid containing sugar.

Fermentation is a chemical reaction that splits a molecule of sugar into equal parts of ethyl alcohol and carbon dioxide. The carbon dioxide escapes into the air, and the drinkable ethyl alcohol remains.

Government regulations set minimum and maximum amounts of alcohol content for various types of alcoholic beverages. Generally speaking, alcoholic beverages can contain as little as 2% alcohol (certain types of beers) or as much as 75.5% alcohol (151 rum).

An alcoholic beverage is broadly classified as either a wine, beer, or spirit. Each is unique.

Wine is the term used for an alcoholic beverage produced from fermented grapes or other fruits.

Beer is fermented from cereals and malts and generally flavored with hops.

Spirits utilize the **distillation** process to remove water from a liquid that contains alcohol. Spirits are sometimes referred to as "hard liquor" (liquor) because of the large quantity of alcohol they contain.

Types of Beverage Operations

Businesses that sell alcoholic beverages include restaurants, neighborhood bars, hotels, night-clubs, breweries, sports complexes and specialty clubs. These can be grouped as:

- Beverage and food operations
- Beverage-only operations

BEVERAGE AND FOOD OPERATIONS Facilities that sell both alcoholic beverages and food are the predominant type of beverage operations in the United States and a major industry in the world today. Examples include restaurants that serve wine, beer, and liquor and bars that serve limited food items or light meals.

The profit margins for alcoholic beverages are generally much higher than that for food; thus, it makes good business sense for many restaurants to serve alcoholic beverages along with food.

While it's impossible to state the "appropriate" profit levels for alcoholic beverages, they're generally two to five times greater for beverage products than for food products. So it's most likely that the profit made from a pitcher of beer sold with a pizza would exceed the profit made if the pizza were sold by itself.

Many alcoholic beverages were created specifically to be enjoyed with food, so it's only natural that restaurant managers in a variety of restaurant segments should know how these beverages can be legally, responsibly, and profitably sold to guests.

BEVERAGE-ONLY OPERATIONS Beverage-only operations have been in existence in the United States for many years and include taverns, bars, lounges, and clubs. The décor in beverage-only operations can range from comfortably casual to upscale. Entertainment, when provided, may consist of television, live or recorded music, a pool table, or video games. This can make beverage-only operations very popular because many customers want to "do" something while they consume their favorite alcoholic beverage. Dance and music clubs, comedy clubs, and piano bars are popular in many cities; at times, an outdoor setting may be used to attract customers.

Many beverage-only businesses provide their customers with such snacks as pretzels, chips, and nuts, but the sale of beverages is their primary purpose. At the very least, however, these

Alcohol

A colorless beverage created by fermenting a liquid containing sugar.

Fermentation

The conversion of carbohydrates to alcohol and carbon dioxide using yeast or bacteria to initiate the conversion process.

Distillation

A process in the production of alcoholic beverages that's used to increase the amount of alcohol contained in the beverage.

operations should offer some level of food service to help counter the physiological effects of drinking alcohol. For that reason, restaurant managers are often called upon to manage a beverage and food business as well as a beverage-only business. As a result, knowledge of wine, beer, spirits, and their proper service is important for most professional restaurant managers.

Physiological Effects of Alcohol

Alcohol has a direct physiological effect on those who drink it. So managers, bartenders, servers, and other key restaurant personnel must understand its effect on customers. The three basic processes that take place when alcohol enters the body are absorption, distribution, and oxidation.

Alcohol that's consumed is absorbed into the bloodstream. A small percentage is absorbed through blood veins in the mouth and stomach, but most of the alcohol is absorbed by veins in the small intestine. If the stomach is full of food, the absorption process is slowed down: the food must be digested before it goes to the small intestine, and the alcohol does not act on the system as quickly. The type of food consumed also affects the absorption rate. Fatty foods, such as cheese, nuts, and fried foods, take longer to digest than high-carbohydrate foods, such as pasta, breads, and fruits.

Once the alcohol is absorbed into the bloodstream, it's distributed to the different organs in the body in a ratio based on the amount of water each organ contains. The brain, which has a high water content, receives a high percentage of the alcohol. For legal purposes, once alcohol is absorbed into the bloodstream, the amount contained in a person's body is measured as a percentage of **blood alcohol content (BAC).**

Blood alcohol content (BAC)

The amount of alcohol contained in a liter of an alcohol drinker's blood. BAC is also known as blood alcohol concentration and is expressed as a percentage.

For example, a BAC of 0.0008 is expressed as the percentage: 0.08%.

As a person's BAC increases, it affects his or her inhibitions, motor control, and thinking. Clearly, it's not in the best interests of restaurant management to allow the BAC of customers to get so high that it could result in harmful behavior.

Many factors alter the way BAC levels affect different people. Some of these include:

- Body weight: The larger the body, the more the alcohol is diluted. Because of this, given the same amount of alcohol, a large person will be less affected by alcohol than a smaller person.
- Amount of sleep: Tired people feel the effects of alcohol more than those who are well rested.
- Age: Younger people feel the effects of alcohol more quickly than older people. However, the eyesight of older customers is more affected by drinking.
- Health: The liver plays an important part in removing alcohol from the system. Customers with liver problems are more apt to become intoxicated.
- Speed of consumption: BAC increases when the same number of drinks are consumed over a shorter period of time.
- Medication: Many medications don't mix well with alcohol; these mixtures can be very dangerous.
- General metabolism: Some people simply eliminate alcohol from their bloodstream faster than others.

In the final step, oxidation—the process by which the liver breaks alcohol down into water and carbon monoxide—takes place and as a result, BAC is reduced.

Contrary to popular opinion, fresh air, black coffee, and concoctions featuring raw eggs don't affect the oxidation process. The only thing that will reduce a drinker's BAC is time. State laws set very specific maximum levels of BAC that people may have, for example, before they're allowed to operate a motor vehicle.

Unfortunately, a person's BAC level and ability to function at various BAC levels vary from individual to individual; this makes it a challenge to know when a customer has had too much alcohol.

A typical serving of these drinks have the same amount of alcohol:

Proof

A measure of a beverage's alcohol content. The proof of an alcoholic beverage is equal to two times the amount of alcohol it contains.

For example, an alcoholic beverage that contains 40% alcohol would be labeled as 80 proof (40% alcohol content (×) 2 = 80 proof).

- A 12-ounce serving of beer
- A 5-ounce serving of wine
- A drink prepared with $1\frac{1}{4}$ ounces of 80 **proof** spirits

Managers, bartenders, and servers must understand alcohol equivalents because some customers erroneously think that wine and beer contain less alcohol per drink than spirits.

Regulation of Alcohol Sales

Since alcohol can affect behavior, states in the United States are granted a great deal of leeway in regulating the sale and consumption of alcoholic beverages. Each state has a Department of Alcohol Beverage Control (ABC). The ABC sets the legal requirements that must be met in order to sell alcoholic beverages and monitors the actions of those who do.

Because alcoholic beverage laws vary so greatly between states (and even city to city), professional restaurant managers must have a thorough understanding of local beverage service rules and regulations. These rules can cover many topics, such as:

- Permitted hours of operation
- Approved purchasing sources
- Restrictions on admittance of customers
- Employee-related regulations
- Prohibitions on certain types of promotions
- Regulations regarding certain types of pricing decisions
- Required record keeping

It isn't possible to know all of the local rules for selling alcohol throughout the country or state. Therefore, managers should contact the local regulatory agency in their area for detailed information on what is and isn't allowed under the liquor licenses granted to their individual operations.

WINE AND FOODS

The history of man is intertwined with the history of wine. While no one knows when wine was first made, even the earliest known literature makes reference to its production. While wine has probably been made since the beginning of time, it was not until the mid-1800s that scientists discovered exactly how it came to be. Louis Pasteur, the famous scientist, was the first to discover and in fact prove that fermentation was caused by yeasts in the air. The knowledge of "why" fermentation started helped wine producers improve their products greatly.

Today, as in the past, wine and food are often consumed at the same time. So restaurant managers should know basic information about wine, be familiar with traditional wine and food pairings, and know how to produce wine lists that help their customers make informed choices about which wine to buy.

www.thinkstock.com/comstock

The purchase and sale of alcoholic beverages to restaurants is highly regulated by state and federal law.

Wine

Due to soil conditions, weather, and other geographic characteristics, some areas of the world produce spectacular wine, while other areas produce either no wine or very poor wine. Many countries, however, produce a good, solid wine. Wine is particularly fascinating to people because no two types of wine are identical. There are significant differences in wines, even those made from the same grapes. Location, climate, soil, the winemaker's skill, and the age of a wine are but a few of the characteristics that influence a wine's taste.

Good wine appeals to the eye, the nose, and the mouth. To the eye, the wine should appear clear and brilliant. Red wine should appear rich, and whites should sparkle. To the nose, the wine should be pleasant, with a hint of flowers, spices, or other characteristics common to the wine type. The aroma, or **bouquet**, should linger and, above all, be an indicator of the taste to come.

Finally, the flavor of the wine should appeal to the drinker. From inexpensive to the very highest price, there is a type of wine for every taste and preference.

Some restaurant managers can be intimidated by the great variety and voluminous amount of information associated with wine. They need not be. While some beverage-management positions require tremendous wine knowledge, most restaurant managers can do quite well if they know a few wine basics and truly seek to understand the likes and dislikes of their own customer base.

Wines can be grouped in a variety of ways. The country in which the wine was made, its age, and the grapes used to make it are examples of ways wine can be classified. Wine can also be grouped on the basis of its sugar content. Thus, wine is often classified as dry, semi-dry, and sweet. These terms are used to describe the sweetness of a wine and refer to the residual sugar content, or the amount of grape sugar remaining in the wine after fermentation has occurred.

Dry wine is the least sweet and has a sugar content below 0.8%, semi-dry wine has a sugar content that's between 0.8–2.2%, and sweet wine has more than 2.2% sugar content. While sugar content is an important characteristic, there are a variety of other ways to group types of wine. In the United States, color is probably the most common method of classification.

Wine color does not depend on the type of grapes from which it's made. A wine's color depends on how long the grape skins stayed in the beverage during fermentation. Since all grape juice is clear in color, any juice can be used to make white wine. If grape skins are allowed to stay in contact with the juice during production, the juice will take on the color of the grape skins.

If the red grape skins stay in contact for a long time, red wine is the result. If they're allowed to stay in contact for only a short time a light red, or rosé, wine is the result.

RED WINE   Red wine has traditionally been associated with hearty, full-bodied flavor. The classic red wines are made from the Cabernet Sauvignon (cab-er-nay so-veen-yohn) grape and were made famous by wine producers in the Bordeaux region of France. This wine is a complex, outstanding product that goes very well with food and is also fine for drinking by itself. Red wine often accompanies such menu items as beef, wild game, and other dark meat entrées that require a bold, hearty flavor.

A second outstanding grape used for making red wine is the Pinot Noir (pee-no nwar). The famous French Burgundies are made from this grape. This is the same grape used to make champagne.

Other notable grapes used in making red wine include the Merlot (mer-low), the Gamay, or Napa Gamay, grown in France and California, the Shiraz (or Syrah), and the Zinfandel (zin-fan-del) grape grown in California and popular for making a very light red, or blush, wine. These light red wines can range from just barely pink to nearly red. They're called white Zinfandels (if they're made from that type of grape), blush or Rosé. They're popular for sipping in the summertime and as an accompaniment to light foods, such as fish and poultry. Generally, they resemble white wines. Red wine that's made from a blend of different grapes may be labeled as simply "red" or "table red": it's less expensive, yet may prove to be exactly what your customers want.

Restaurant managers must remember that wine is an integral part of a beverage menu. It's critical that the red wine selected for sale match the tastes and price range of the intended consumer.

Red wine is best served at a temperature of 55–65°F (12.8–18.3°C). Red wine is stronger in flavor and heavier in body than white wine. It can range in taste from "sweet" to "dry," and its alcoholic content ranges from 10 to 14%.

Bouquet

The aroma of wine.

WHITE WINE   While red wine has traditionally been associated with robust food, white wine, with its more delicate taste, has become far and away the most popular wine for drinking by the glass in bars, at receptions, and with lighter foods. White wine complements delicate foods such as fish, poultry, and pork.

White wine is typically served chilled. It ranges in flavor from dry and tart to sweet and mellow and its colors range from pale yellow to very deep gold. White wine has a more delicate flavor than red wine. Its alcohol content ranges from a low of 10% to as much as 14%. Most of the white wine served in the United States is produced in Italy, Germany, France, South America, South Africa, or California.

The grapes used to produce fine white wine vary according to the country that makes the wine. In the Rhine and Moselle valleys of Europe, the Riesling grape is most often used to produce the sweet, flavorful wines associated with German whites. Pinot Bianco, Pinot Grigio, and Traminer are other popular grapes used for making white wine.

By far the most popular white wine in the United States is Chardonnay. This complex wine is aged in oak. While many white wines are fermented in stainless steel tanks, fermenting and aging in oak and other woods give wine unique and quite complex flavor, color, and aroma characteristics. Like many red wines, Chardonnay wine will improve with age prior to its bottling. Chardonnay is made from the same grape used in the Burgundy and Champagne regions of France. Excellent Chardonnay wine is produced in France, the United States, Argentina, and Australia.

SPARKLING WINE   Sparkling wine is characterized by the presence of carbonic acid in solution in the wine. Sparkling wine is generally white, but can vary from light red (Rosé) to dark red. Champagne, a type of sparkling white wine, is actually made from grapes that are bluish-black on the outside and red on the inside. Their juice, however, is clear and will produce white sparkling wine provided it's not allowed to be colored by the dark skins of the grapes.

Sparkling wine is available in many flavors and can range from dry to sweet. Its alcohol content ranges from 10–14% by volume.

Champagne is the most popular sparkling wine and the standard drink of celebrations. Only sparkling wine from the Champagne region in France and domestic sparkling wine that is fermented in thick glass bottles (referred to as the champagne method) may be called champagne. Champagne and sparkling wine should be served well chilled.

OTHER WINE   Wine that isn't considered red, white, or sparkling can also be an important part of a restaurant's wine menu. A list of some of the more notable types of wine follows.

Vermouth
Vermouth can be either sweet (Italian) or dry (French). Vermouth is a **fortified wine**: Its alcohol level has been increased after fermentation is complete. The alcohol level of vermouth is increased to about 18% (36 proof). Vermouth is also an **aromatized wine**: It has been flavored with a product other than the grapes used for its production.

Sake
Sake is often called rice wine; the word means "essence of rice spirit." In fact, sake is a product made from rice, but its production method is closer to a beer than a wine. At 14–16% alcohol content, however, its alcohol content is closer to wine than beer. Sake is served warm to release its entire aroma.

Sherry
Sherry is a blended wine and was originally produced in Spain. The name is said to be derived from the Spanish word *Jerez* (the grapes in sherry were grown near the city of Jerez de la Frontera in southern Spain). There are many types of sherry, from the very dry Manzanilla to the sweet, deep golden cream varieties. Sherry contains anywhere between 13 and 20% alcohol and is popular both before and after dinner.

Port
Port is a variety of wine produced in Portugal. It became widely distributed and popular in English-speaking countries during the early 1700s. All port bottled in Portugal is certified as "Porto" by the Portuguese government. Port made outside Portugal is called port or port wine. Port is a rich, popular after-dinner drink.

Wine is purchased by restaurant managers in a variety of container sizes and then sold to guests in a number of ways, including by the glass, in a **carafe** of various sizes, and by the bottle.

Fortified wine

A wine that has had a spirit added to it to increase its alcohol content.

Aromatized wine

A fortified wine to which a flavoring ingredient has been added.

Carafe

A glass container used to serve wine or water.

FIGURE 10.1
Wine Bottle Sizes and Capacities

Bottle Size (Capacity)	Common Name	Description
0.100 liters	Miniature (mini)	A single serving bottle
0.187 liters	Split	$1/4$ standard bottle
0.375 liters	Half bottle	$1/2$ standard bottle
0.750 liters	Bottle	Standard wine bottle
1.5 liters	Magnum	Two bottles in one
3.0 liters	Double magnum	Four bottles in one

Note:
1 U.S. quart = 0.946 liters
1 U.S. gallon = 3.785 liters

The sizes of wine bottles legally sold in the United States are listed in Figure 10.1. Note: The common names for these bottles date to before the U.S. beverage industry's conversion to metric measurements in the 1980s.

Wine and Food Pairings

A basic knowledge of wine is very useful for every restaurant manager whose operation sells wine. Wine should complement the food on the menu and sell at a price level consistent with the selling prices of the food.

Wise restaurant managers know that when wine is served with a meal, it can elevate the dining experience to become a special occasion. This in turn will result in increased guest satisfaction and greater restaurant profits.

Wine and food pairings

The concept that certain types of wine go better with specific foods and that a wine should be selected *after* the food item to be served with it has been chosen.

There is a long tradition of suggested **wine and food pairings**.

Since wine should complement the food with which it's served, many diners wish to match (pair) a specific wine to a specific menu item. While this is of interest to some wine drinkers and, probably, to almost everyone who enjoy fine dining, the individual preferences of guests is always most important. Experienced restaurant managers know that regardless of any tradition, the best wine to accompany a menu item is always the one the guest likes and wants to buy.

Some menus offer wine suggestions with entrées as a suggestive selling tactic. However, managers must carefully weigh this idea. Consider, for example, a couple dining out; one has ordered a beef dish and the other a pork item. If the menu suggests only one wine for each dish, it will likely be a red wine for the beef and a white or rosé (blush) wine for the pork. If the suggested wine is only available for purchase by the bottle, it's possible that neither person will order it because it's not available by the glass. Despite that possibility, it's usually a good idea for restaurant managers and servers to have a basic understanding of the characteristics of all the wine included on the restaurant's **wine list**, as well as those specific menu items these wines best complement.

Wine list

The total number and kinds of wine sold in a restaurant as well as its price per bottle, carafe, or glass.

Also known as a "wine menu."

Figure 10.2 lists information of help in developing a restaurant's recommended wine and food pairings.

Wine Lists

A well-developed wine list is a vital tool for selling wine in many restaurants. Many of the principles used to design food menus also apply to the planning and design of wine lists. In addition, restaurant managers should:

- Remember food and wine pairings.
  The pairings suggested should complement the food being served. For example, a restaurant offering a wide variety of menu items will likely offer a number of different types of wine from many areas. By contrast, Italian restaurants may emphasize Italian wine and offer a wider selection of wine from Italy rather than from other wine-producing regions.

Wine Type	Serve With
Robust Red Wines	
Cabernet Sauvignon and red Bordeaux	Lamb roasts and lamb chops, all cuts of beef steak, roast duck, goose
Merlot	Beef and lamb roasts, venison, sirloin steaks, grilled or roast chicken
Pinot Noir	Roast chicken, rabbit, duck, grilled salmon, grilled tuna
Shiraz	Grilled or roast beef, game meats, BBQ, pizza
Sangiovese (Chianti)	Roast pork, roast chicken, pasta, grilled vegetables, Italian sausages, pizza
Rosé/Blush Wines	
White Zinfandel/white Merlot	Seafood salads, pastas, grilled chicken, grilled pork loin, Mexican food
White Wines	
Chardonnay	Sole, halibut, cod, scallops, lobster, roast chicken, pasta with seafood or chicken
White Riesling	Roasted pork, chicken, veal, smoked salmon, sushi
Sauvignon Blanc	Fish, shrimp, calamari, fresh oysters, sashimi
Pinot Grigio	Pastas, grilled chicken and shrimp, veal
Sparkling (champagne)	Caviar, fresh oysters, sushi, sashimi, lobster

FIGURE 10.2
Sample Food and Wine Pairings

- Make sure wine prices complement food prices.
  Those restaurant managers with experience in developing wine lists know that it's normally unwise to offer exceptionally high-priced wine when the food items offered are relatively inexpensive; the reverse is also true.
- Ensure that wine lists make it easy for guests to order wine.
  Guests visiting some restaurants may not be very knowledgeable about wine and might be embarrassed to mispronounce the name of the wine they wish to order. One common tactic used to make wine ordering easier to assign a **bin number** to each wine so, for example, a guest can merely order "wine (in bin) number 21."
- Offer some types of wine "by the glass."
  Offering wine by the glass allows guests ordering two different entrées to each enjoy a wine that matches their food choice. Additionally, many customers limit their alcohol consumption during meals and might purchase one glass, but not an entire bottle, of wine. An alternative to wine "by the glass" is the offering of wine in splits (1/4 bottles) or halves (1/2 bottles).
- Include wine descriptions.
  When possible, write some information about each wine. Examples include its origin, flavor, and special characteristics.
- Avoid repetition.
  It's not usually necessary to offer several merlot (for example) wines on a relatively short wine list. Most wine buyers prefer expanded numbers of choices to many wines of the exact same type.
- Be sure information on the wine list is accurate and correctly spelled.
  Some guests are very well informed about wine and will spot errors in information and spelling. It's always best to obtain the spelling of a wine directly from the bottle label and information about **vintage**, region, and vineyard from wine distributors.
- Make sure the wines listed on the menu are consistently available.
- To the degree possible, store wine at cellar temperature (55° F (12.8° C)).
- To the degree possible, serve wine at the proper temperature (see Figure 10.3).

Wines that aren't always available from suppliers and not always in the operation's inventory should not be placed on the wine list to avoid disappointing guests who want to order them.

- Carefully consider the appearance of the wine list.
  Wine lists should be attractive. The wine list, like the food menu, should represent the quality standards of the restaurant. A wine list that's torn, dirty, and with price changes

Bin number

A number that indicates the location in a wine cellar where a specific wine is being held for service. Bin numbers are often provided to guests so they can order a wine by a number, rather than by its name.

Vintage

Wine grown from grapes in one vineyard during one growing season.

FIGURE 10.3
Recommended Wine Service
Temperatures

Wine Type	Recommended Service
Champagne and sparkling wines	Serve well chilled. Place in refrigerator 1 to 2 hours before serving or in an ice bucket with an ice-water mixture for at least 20 minutes before serving.
Sauvignon Blanc, Pinot Grigio, white Zinfandel, and other light white wines, as well as dry sherry	Serve between 35° and 40°F (1.7° and 2.5°C). If stored in the refrigerator, allow it to warm slightly (10 to 20 minutes) before service.
White burgundy, chardonnay, and other barrel-aged white wines as well as dessert wines (e.g. Port, sweet sherry)	Serve at 55°F (12.8°C). If stored in the refrigerator, allow it to warm approximately 20 minutes before service.
Nearly all red wines of good quality	Serve at 65°F (18.3°C). Store at cellar temperature (55°F (12.8°C) if possible; if stored at room temperature, allow to chill in refrigerator approximately 20 minutes before service.

scribbled on top of old prices, for example, would not meet the quality standards established by a professional manager.

- Ensure that staff are trained in the proper service of wine (see Figure 10.4).

Restaurant managers creating wine lists can choose from several alternative formats. They may:

1. List wines in the order they would be consumed: (e.g., appetizer wines, followed by entrée wines and dessert wines).
2. List wines by their color (e.g., white wines followed by blush wines, followed by red wines).
3. List wines by their selling prices (e.g., lowest price to highest price).
4. List wines by their origin (e.g., country or state, such as Italian, French, German, or Californian).
5. List wines using a combination of two or more of the above formats (e.g., by color and price).

The pricing of wine is heavily influenced by the type of restaurants where it's sold. As a general rule, every wine list should include some lower-priced wines so that even cost-conscious

FIGURE 10.4
Proper Wine Service

Proper wine service in any operation requires the completion of 12 key steps:

1. Upon presentation of the wine at the table, clearly pronounce the name and vintage of the wine to ensure that it's what the guest ordered.
2. Present the bottle with the label facing the guest who ordered it for ease of bottle identification.
3. Ensure that each person who will drink wine has the appropriate glassware.
4. Remove the foil cork cover with a foil knife and place it in an apron or pocket.
5. Wipe the bottle opening with a clean napkin or cloth.
6. Open the wine at the table, removing the cork and placing it to the right of the person who ordered the wine.
7. If the wine is chilled, wrap it in a napkin or hold it at the base while pouring to minimize warming due to contact with the server's hand.
8. Pour a small amount (approximately 1/2 ounce) to be tasted by the guest who ordered the wine, or the person designated as the taster.
9. Allow time for the taster to visually inspect and taste the wine, then confirm that the wine meets the guest's expectation.
10. Pour wine for all other guests in the order established by the restaurant (some managers prefer a clockwise or counterclockwise rotation; while other managers prefer that females seated at the table are served first) finishing with the taster's glass. Fill glasses no more than half full.
11. After pouring, place the bottle on the table (if red) or in ice on, or near, the table (if white).
12. Monitor the table's wine consumption and refill glasses as needed.

High-quality wine complements quality food and helps build repeat business.

guests can enjoy wine with their meals. Of course, every wine list should include high-quality wines for customers who enjoy drinking a finer wine with their meals.

OTHER ALCOHOLIC BEVERAGES

While wine is the alcoholic beverage most often served with food, beer and some spirits are also popular when consumed with food or alone. Alcoholic beverages of all types are produced in nearly every country. Increasingly, wine as well as beer and some sprits are made and distributed on a regional basis. Restaurants that include popular regional beverage products on their menus can leverage local favorites and set themselves apart from their competitors.

While a complete description of all the popular alcoholic beverage products on the market today is beyond the scope of this book, restaurant managers should have a basic understanding of beer and spirits as well as their production, storage, and proper service.

WEB AT WORK!

There's a wide variety of information available for restaurant managers who want to stay up-to-date on wine trends. To view one of the best online sources designed for those who buy, sell, and serve wine in the restaurant industry, go to:

www.restaurantwine.com

Select "About Restaurant Wine" to review the types of wine-related information available to restaurant managers.

ALL IN A DAY'S WORK 10.1

"Normally I agree with you, Connie, but this time I really don't!" Clare, the kitchen manager at Duke's Restaurant, was meeting with the property's dining room manager.

"Well," said Connie, "I really think we should recommend a specific wine for each entrée on our menu. You could train the service staff to suggest them. But the guests don't have to take our suggestion. We would make sure the staff knows that whatever wine the guest wants, is the wine the guest should have. What's wrong with that approach, Clare?"

"For one thing, I think there are lots of good wines to go with every one of our entrées," replied Clare. "So how do we select one to recommend? Plus, I get kind of turned off by all the fancy adjectives like "oaky," "a hint of fruit nectar," and "earthy." Maybe a wine expert can understand or explain these things, but most people can't. I think we should just list our wines and then indicate the types of foods that most people enjoy with them. For example, we could suggest dry reds with our steaks, rather than try to recommend a specific wine for a specific item."

1. What is your opinion about the two approaches to selling wine at Duke's Restaurant?
2. Assume you were the restaurant manager and it was your job to make a decision about which approach to use. Which would you choose? Why?

Beer

Beer is an extremely popular beverage, and the United States brews more beer than any other country in the world. National, regional, and local breweries provide many restaurant operators with hundreds of beer choices to offer guests.

Beer is any fermented alcoholic beverage made from malted grain and flavored with hops. There are two general classes of beer: lagers and ales. Lagers include bock, dark lager, light lager, light beer, dry beer, ice beer, malt liquor, and the very popular pilsner. Ales include light ale, brown ale, porter, and stout.

Lagers and ales are brewed basically the same way, but various types of yeasts and methods of fermentation give them different bodies and tastes. When restaurant customers order a "beer" in the United States, they're usually ordering a *lager* product made in the *pilsner* style (referring to the lager beer first made in the city of Pilsen in the Czech Republic).

In the United States, ales are typically ordered by their brand names. Most ales have a higher alcohol content, more body and a stronger taste than lager beer. Light beer is also popular in the United States. Light beer is essentially pilsner-style beer brewed with extra enzymes to give it a lower calorie, carbohydrate, and alcohol content. While regular beer contains approximately 150 to 200 calories per a 12-ounce serving, light beer generally ranges from 75 to 150 calories. The milder-tasting lager beer is most popular in the United States.

Less popular in the United States but more popular worldwide are the darker brews such as porter and stout. Dark brown, heavy bodied, and malty flavored, porters have a slightly less sweet taste and less pronounced hop flavor than light ales. Porter has an alcohol content of approximately 5%.

Stout is a heavy beer made with roasted malted barley. The traditional English stouts are "sweet" because they use lactose (milk sugar) in their production. This explains why they're sometimes called "cream" stouts. Porter, stouts, and ales are gaining in popularity in the United States as microbreweries broaden the taste preferences of American beer drinkers. **Microbreweries** are small breweries that produce limited quantities of unique beer. While the amount of beer produced in a microbrewery is small, the variety of beer produced in microbreweries is quite large.

The unique beer created in microbreweries is most often purchased locally or may even be produced inside the restaurants or pubs where it's served. Sometimes called "varietal" beer (in the same way wine produced from a specific grape type is called varietal wine), this beer is usually brewed in a distinctive manner and with specific flavors:

Fruit beer: Flavored with raspberry, strawberry, peach, apple, blackberry, cherry, lemon, or limes.

Spice beer: Flavored with spices such as ginger, coriander, clove, allspice, cinnamon, vanilla bean, or ginger.

Wood-aged beer: Aged in wooden casks previously used to age (for example) wine, bourbon, scotch, or sherry.

Microbrewery

A brewery that produces limited amounts of specialized beer. Sometimes referred to as a brewpub if the beer is produced in the same facility in which it's served.

Regardless of the size of brewery in which it's produced, beer is sold in the United States in bottles, cans, and in kegs with varying capacities. (Note: The standard keg size used in most restaurant operations ranges in volume from 14 to 16 gallons). In most cases, bottled and canned beer can be stored at room temperature until it's ready to be chilled in a refrigerator.

Beer sold in kegs is referred to as "**draft beer**" or "tap" beer and is an unpasteurized product. It requires special handling and should be kept refrigerated at all times.

The ideal temperature for a keg of draft beer is 36 to 40°F (2.2 to 4.4°C). Even if a keg is kept well cooled, its shelf life is approximately 30 to 45 days, so it should be used as quickly as possible. It's important to keep the lines used to run keg beer to the **tap** very clean.

Restaurant managers should ensure that the lines running from beer kegs to taps are cleaned at least once every 30 days. If this cleaning isn't done, the result will be microorganism growth in the beer lines, an inferior beer product, and lowered customer satisfaction.

How a beer is served has a great deal to do with the way it will taste. To be served properly, beer should be at the right temperature (40°F [4.4°C] for a lager and approximately 45°F [7.2°C] for ale). Beer glasses and pitchers must be clean, or the **head** of foam will lose its firmness and break up. Tap beer must be poured as soon as it's to be served. The glass or pitcher should be held at a 45-degree angle for half the pour, and then straightened for the last half of the pour. The head on beer normally measures from one-half to one inch.

Not every person can or wants to drink wine, beer, or spirits, because these products all contain alcohol. Agreeing to serve as a designated driver for friends, health concerns related to medications, and religious beliefs are a few of the reasons some restaurant customers prefer not to order alcoholic beverages. To address the preferences of these customers, **nonalcoholic beer (NA beer)** and to a lesser degree, nonalcoholic wine, is increasingly popular.

NA beer is fermented in the same way as regular beer, but the brewers then use a process that removes the majority of the beer's alcoholic content. The resulting product is not classified by the government as an alcoholic beverage because it contains less than 0.5% alcohol. In fact, the alcohol level in NA beer is so low that the alcohol in eight cans of NA beer equals the amount in one 12-ounce can of regular beer. The number of calories in a serving of NA beer is also lower. A standard glass of beer contains 150 to 180 calories. A glass of NA beer contains approximately 60 calories. Today, most major breweries produce an NA beer, and it's increasingly common for restaurant managers to offer it to guests.

Draft beer

An unpasteurized beer product sold in kegs. Also known as "tap beer."

Tap

The mechanism used to dispense draft (tap) beer.

Head

The foam that accumulates on the top of a properly poured beer or ale.

Nonalcoholic beer (NA beer)

Beer with an alcohol content less than 0.5%.

The proper-sized head on a draft beer affects the beer's appearance, flavor, and profitability.

© Valentyn Volkov/Shutterstock

Spirits

Spirits are the most potent of alcoholic beverages because they contain the highest concentration of alcohol. Water and alcohol boil at different temperatures. Because of this difference, spirit makers can use the distillation process to increase the alcohol content of any fermented beverage.

While beer is the result of the fermentation of grain, and wine is the result of the fermentation of grape juice, spirits are the distillation of these and other fermented sugar products. For example, vodka is a spirit made from grain, rum is made from sugar cane, and brandy is the result of distilling grape juice. Other spirits include whisky, gin, tequila, and liqueurs. Most spirits consist of approximately one-half water and one-half alcohol (80–100 proof), with the exception of some liqueurs. Generally, spirits are served before or after lunch or dinner.

Spirits are differentiated by their flavors and body. Flavor and body are determined by the food product used to make the beverage; the amount of alcohol in the beverage; and special product treatments during processing, such as aging, flavoring, blending, and bottling.

Taste differences occur among types of spirits (for example, gin versus vodka), within product categories (Irish whiskey versus Scotch whisky) and among different brands of the same product (one brand of vodka versus another).

Restaurant managers whose operations serve spirits should know basic information about the most popular of these widely sold alcoholic beverage products.

VODKA   Vodka is the largest selling spirit in the U.S. market today, accounting for over 25% of all the spirit beverages sold. It's distinguished by its aroma, texture, weight, and smooth, silky character. It's also noted for its refreshing bite, which makes it a good accompaniment to oily and smoked foods such as caviar and salmon. It's also famous for the warming sensation it provides the body as it is drunk, perhaps a reason for its popularity in colder climates.

The best vodka is most often made from fermented grain mash. Vodka is bottled for sale in proofs ranging from 80–100. Vodka is normally produced with the objective of creating a tasteless, colorless, odorless product. In order to achieve this result, the vodka is filtered through charcoal. It requires no aging and mixes easily with other beverages because of its neutral qualities. Most recently, a variety of flavored vodkas have appeared on the market. These products are flavored with a variety of ingredients including oak, honey, pepper, currants, pineapple, and citron.

GIN   In the 1950s, gin outsold vodka in the United States by nearly a three-to-one margin. It's still the key ingredient in the gin martini, a consistently popular before- and after-dinner drink. The flavor of gin comes from juniper berries and spices.

Today, gin is available in two basic types: Dutch and English. Dutch gin is meant to be drunk straight and cold and is rarely diluted or mixed with other beverages. English (dry) gin is made in England and the United States and is used most often in **mixed drinks**.

Mixed drink

A drink made by combining a spirit with water, fruit juice or another alcoholic or nonalcoholic beverage. Also known as a cocktail.

The martini was originally a drink made with equal parts of gin and dry (French) vermouth. Over the years, the amount of vermouth was reduced until an eight-to-one (eight parts gin to one part vermouth) ratio became the more accepted standard. The lesser amount of vermouth in a martini, the "drier" the martini is said to be.

RUM   Rum is perhaps the oldest distilled beverage known to man. It's a spirit with a significant history in the development of the New World. It's said that Columbus brought sugar cane cuttings to the West Indies from the Caribbean Islands in the early 15th century. Molasses, which is produced when sugar crystallizes, became to Caribbean countries what malted barley (the basis for Scotch whisky) was for the Scots and grape juice was for the French and Italians—the essence of a unique and flavorful distilled spirit.

Rums of many flavors and color are produced throughout the Caribbean as well as in Central and South America. They can be either light or full-bodied. The great majority of rum sold in the United States is of the light variety. Darker rums tend to be fuller flavored than the lighter varieties.

In addition to light and dark rums, customers often request spiced and fruit-flavored rums. These flavored rums can be spiced with a variety of ingredients. Popular spiced rums include Captain Morgan's (flavored with apricot, fig, vanilla, and other ingredients) as well as Malibu rum (flavored with coconut).

Rum mixes well with fruit and fruit juices. It sells particularly well in the summer, but is popular all year long, including the year-end holidays, where it's a favorite when mixed with eggnog.

TEQUILA   Tequila is a product of Mexico and is **aged** in oak. It can only be produced in a very tightly controlled area of the country, Tequilas, which is the official district surrounding the town of Tequila, Mexico. Tequila is made from the blue agave plant; in order to earn its name, it must be distilled from at least 51% fermented agave juice.

Tequila is often drunk straight (as a **shot**), with salt and lime. In the United States, the most popular tequila-based drink is the margarita. A margarita is a mixture of fruit juice and tequila that can be served frozen or over ice.

In the late 1990s, some traditional tequila distillers launched premium tequila products. These upscale products contain as much as 100% agave juice. Like lower-cost tequilas, they can be sipped or used to make premium margaritas.

Aging

The process of holding a beverage for a period of time before releasing it for sale. Aging may be done in bottles (e.g., wine) or wooden kegs (e.g., whiskey and some wines), but the intent is always to improve the beverage product.

Shot

A small (1- to 2-ounce) drink consisting only of a single spirit.

WHISKEY   Whiskey is a "brown" (colored) spirit, rather than a "white" (clear) spirit. A basic understanding of whiskey is essential for every professional restaurant manager serving spirits.

One aspect of whiskey that can be confusing is the spelling of the word. Scottish and many Canadian distillers spell "whisky" without an *e*; while Irish and American distillers most often include the *e* when labeling their whiskey products.

Aging is what gives whiskey its color. The type of wooden barrel in which the whiskey is aged adds flavor and aroma. After whiskey is bottled, the aging process stops. There are two general types of whiskey: straight and blended.

Straight whiskies are unmixed or are mixed with whiskey from the same distiller or distillation period. Blended whiskies are a mixture of similar straight whiskies from different distillers or distillation periods. By government standards, an American whiskey can be labeled as straight if the **mash** used to make it contains at least 51% of a certain grain (for example, corn or rye).

Whisky is categorized according to country of origin and includes:

Mash

A mixture of grain, malt, and water used to produce beverage whiskey.

- Scotch whisky. This is the whisky of Scotland and is light-bodied and smoky-flavored. Barley, and sometimes corn, is used to create the mash. Most Scotch whisky is blended rather than straight and is bottled at 80–86 proof. The grain used is dried over open, peat fires that give the product its smoky taste. The grain is then combined with water, fermented, distilled, and aged at least four years.
- Canadian whisky. This blended product is light in body. It may contain corn, rye, wheat, and barley as base grains. It's aged six years or more and bottled at 80–90 proof.
- Irish whiskey. This product is made using the same ingredients and procedures as Scotch whisky. The main difference is that the malted barley isn't exposed to peat smoke when it's dried, so there's no smoky taste. The product also goes through a triple distillation process and uses several grains in addition to malted barley. The result is a very smooth, high-quality whiskey. Irish whiskey must be aged a minimum of seven years before it can be sold.
- U.S. whiskey. This product includes bourbon, rye, corn, bottled-in-bond, blended, and light whiskey.

Bourbon is the most popular whiskey in the United States. It's a straight whiskey distilled from a fermented mash containing a minimum of 51% corn. It's aged in charred oak barrels from 2 to 12 years, reaching peak mellowness in about 6 years. Bourbon has a strong flavor and a full body. It's generally bottled at 80–90 proof.

Rye is produced in much the same way as bourbon, except it's distilled from a fermented mash containing at least 51% rye. True rye is an unblended whiskey.

Corn whiskey is produced from a fermented mash containing no less than 80% corn grain. It's aged in un-charred oak containers for at least two years.

Bottled-in-bond is a straight whiskey bottled at 100 proof and aged for at least four years.

Blended whiskey is a combination of straight whiskies (whiskies with neutral spirits) that must contain at least 20% straight whiskey. Close to one half of the whiskies consumed in the United States are blends. These are designated by the words "American whiskey" on their labels. If a blended whiskey contains 50% or more of one type of straight whiskey, it must use the name of that specific whiskey. One example is blended rye whiskey. There are no aging requirements for blended whiskies.

BRANDY   Brandy is a distilled spirit made from a fermented mash of fruit. The fruit is usually grapes, but apples, cherries, apricots, and plums may also be used. The word itself has its origins in Holland; it's derived from the Dutch word *brandewijn*, or "burned wine," a reference to the fact that the product was heated when distilled.

If brandy is made from grape juice, the term "brandy" stands alone on the label. If it's made from other fruits, the name of the fruit appears with the term "brandy" (for example, apricot brandy). Brandy must be bottled at 80 proof or more. Different types of brandies include:

- Cognac—considered the finest of brandies and produced in the Cognac region of France. Cognac is the distillation of grape juice only.
- Apple Brandy—an American favorite in early New England days.
- Calvados—the French equivalent to apple brandy.
- Kirsch or Kirschwasser—German brandy made from wild black cherries.
- Ouzo—Greek brandy that's colorless and has a licorice-like taste.
- Per William—made from Swiss or French pears.
- Elderberry—made from the elderberry.
- Fraise—made from strawberries.
- Framboise—made from raspberries.
- Slivovitz—plum brandy from central Europe.

LIQUEURS   Liqueurs or cordials are spirits that have been redistilled or steeped with fruits, plants, flowers, or other natural flavorings and then sweetened with sugar. When the sugar content is high, liqueur has a creamy quality and is designated "crème de" (as in crème de cacao). Some popular liqueurs include:

- Anisette—red or clear color with an anise or licorice flavor.
- Amaretto—almond flavor, but made from apricot pits.
- Coffee liqueur—made from coffee beans.
- Crème de bananas—yellow color, banana flavored.
- Crème de cacao—brown or clear color with a chocolate-vanilla flavor.
- Crème de menthe—green or clear color with a mint flavor.
- Crème de cassis—deep red color with a red currant flavor.
- Curaçao—orange, blue, or clear color with an orange peel flavor.
- Triple sec—a white Curaçao (orange flavor).
- Kummel—clear color with a caraway seed flavor.
- Maraschino—clear color with a nutty, cherry flavor.
- Rock and rye—whiskey and rock candy syrup.
- Sambuca—licorice flavored, usually clear in color.
- Sloe gin—red color with a plum flavor, made from the sloe berry.

FLAVORED SCHNAPPS   In the United States, the word "schnapps" is usually associated with peppermint schnapps. In Germany, the word "schnapps" is a generic term for distilled spirits.

Peppermint schnapps, which people drank as a cold-weather "warmer" or as a "shooter" with beer, increased in popularity during the 1970s as it found its way into ski resorts and college bars. Until very recently, the primary flavors were peppermint, spearmint, and cinnamon. As consumers searched for lighter drinks, the industry began to introduce a wide range of flavors in lower proofs.

The new, flavored schnapps are sweet, light, and combine well with mixers and fruit juices. As a result, drinks such as the fuzzy navel (a cocktail made with equal parts orange juice and peach schnapps) continue to be popular. Best-selling schnapps flavors include banana, amaretto, mint, pear, orange, peach, strawberry, apple, raspberry, root beer, licorice, and cola.

BAR OPERATIONS

Because alcoholic beverages play such a significant part in the overall dining experience of a restaurant guest, care must be taken to ensure that beverages are prepared and served in a professional manner. Thus, restaurant managers must address two important and related beverage management issues:

Quality beverage service

Responsible beverage service

Quality Beverage Service

The layout and design of the facilities used as bartending areas can vary greatly from one operation to the next. Carefully controlling the way high-quality alcoholic beverages are prepared and

© svry/Shutterstock

Restaurant managers and bartenders know creative drink presentation is an important part of any successful beverage program.

served is important for three reasons: 1) managers must control their beverage product costs; 2) improperly prepared drinks can result in guests who are dissatisfied with what they have been served; and 3) the restaurant must know the quantity of alcohol served to each guest in order to demonstrate that it exercised reasonable care in its service.

To control costs and ensure quality, beverage managers must standardize drink production. This requires careful monitoring of bar recipes and drink sizes. Some bartenders feel that "the more alcohol the better" is the way to go when producing drinks for guests. These bartenders simply don't understand **mixology**.

These bartenders are similar to the chef who refuses to use standardized recipes "because they're not necessary." In fact, standardized recipes are required for both high-quality food and beverage production. While experienced bartenders don't need to consult a standardized recipe file every time they produce a common mixed drink such as a "gin and tonic," they do need to use the ingredients, quantities, glass type, and garnish procedures specified by the standardized drink recipe.

Alternatively, bartenders may need to consult a recipe file to prepare a less common drink, such as a "horse's neck," "queen bee," or "Smith and Kerns." Today, drink recipes are as likely to be available on a computer as in a book or recipe file. The use of standardized recipes for drinks and food ensures that the guests receive exactly what was requested, and that the restaurant provides exactly what it intended to give.

Standardized drink recipes, like those for food, should include the information needed to properly prepare and serve a drink. Special attention must be given to the issue of drink size, especially as it relates to the amount of alcohol in the drink. For example, a standardized recipe for a gin and tonic may suggest two parts tonic water to one part gin (for example, 1 ounce of gin and 2 ounce of tonic water). In this example, the manager calculates the cost of the beverage with this assumption about ingredient use. As long as that proportion is maintained, the guest will find the drink acceptable, and product costs will be in line with expectations. If, however, managers allow bartenders to **free pour**, controlling beverage production costs become more difficult to control.

A properly prepared drink with the correct amount of alcohol served in a properly sized glass ensures that both you and your guests will be pleased with the final result.

Mixology

The practice and study of alcoholic beverage drink production.

Free pour

A manual system of making mixed drinks that relies upon the bartender to control the quantity of alcohol in the drink without the use of a portioning device.

WEB AT WORK!
There are many good books with drink recipes. However, online recipe referencing, especially through a high-speed Internet connection, is an efficient way to provide bartenders with quick access to recipes for nearly every imaginable drink. To view one such site, go to:
<div align="center">www.webtender.com</div>
Select "Browse Drink Recipes" to search thousands of recipes. See how long it would take one of your bartenders to look up the recipe for a horse's neck or a queen bee!

Restaurant managers who wish to offer high-quality beverage service must, of course, begin with quality beverage products. In addition, they must be concerned with both the glassware and the ice they use when serving alcoholic beverages.

GLASSWARE There are as many different types of glasses available to restaurant managers as there are imaginative glassware designers. In fact, uniquely shaped and/or logo glassware can add to the festive atmosphere of an environment in a bar. In addition, sophisticated drinkers want their drinks served in the type of glass that has been specially designed for the beverage they've ordered.

Managers must carefully select the glassware needed to properly serve those beverages that are most frequently ordered. The following glassware types are common and are usually included in the glassware stock of restaurants and bars serving significant amounts of alcoholic beverages.

Champagne flute: Typically holding 6 to 8 ounces, this glass is tall, elegant, thin, and often made of crystal. It's widely used at formal functions and celebrations. Its long stem is designed to be grasped by the fingers. This keeps the drinker's hand from transferring the higher body temperature to the cold contents of the glass. In addition, the small amount of beverage surface area permitted by the design of the glass helps preserve the carbonation of the champagne.

Martini: Typically holding 4 to 6 ounces, the martini glass is proper for a variety of drinks, but is used most commonly for a martini or a cosmopolitan. The classic martini glass is defined by the straight edges of the glass expanding outward from the stem at approximately a 60-degree angle. A clear glass is typically used for serving traditional recipes; however, glass color and stem shape may vary to add interest to the glassware.

Wine glass: Typically holding 4 to 12 ounces, wine glasses come in a variety of shapes and sizes. Red wine is typically served in larger glasses to allow the wine's bouquet to be maximized and enjoyed by the drinker.

White wine is generally served in smaller wine glasses to allow them to more easily retain their cooler serving temperatures. Dessert wine glasses may be even smaller. Some managers use a single all-purpose wine glass for both red and white wine; however, more elegant beverage facilities generally use at least two sizes/shapes of wine glasses.

Rocks glass: Typically holding 8 to 10 ounces, a rocks glass is a short, heavy-for-its-size, wide-rimmed glass, which is essential for any bar. It's typically used for straight "on the rocks" (on ice) drinks, some alcohol and fruit juice drinks and for some specialty drinks such as white Russians and whisky sours.

Highball Glass: Also holding 8 to 10 ounces, the highball glass is tall, slender, and used for drinks such as Tom Collins, Bloody Mary, or fruit juice and ice drinks. It's a versatile glass that shows off colorful drinks very well.

Shot glass: Shot glasses typically range in size from 2 to 3 ounces and are used for many types of liquor that are served "straight up" (without ice). Drinks served in a shot glass range from the very potent (tequila) to the very sweet (fruit schnapps).

Beer glass(es): Typically 12 to 16 ounces (or more), beer can be served in a variety of beer glass styles. Many managers view the pilsner-style glass as the best for beer. It has a narrow, footed base that expands outward toward the top. The Pilsner Urquell brewery originally

WEB AT WORK!
Buyers of bar glassware can choose from an extremely large selection of shapes and styles. One of the largest manufacturers of commercial glassware is Libbey Glass Inc. See its online selection of over 900 glass styles at: www.libbey.com

developed the pilsner glass in 1842. It's popular for its ability to clearly display the varying colors of the beer it contains. In addition, its narrow base helps prevent temperature transfer from the drinker's hand. Other popular beer glass styles include mugs and steins of various sizes as well as pitchers (made of plastic or glass) and all-purpose glasses.

All-purpose glasses: These are typically sold in sizes ranging from 6 to 16 ounces. Some restaurant guests request water, soft drinks, juice, or other nonalcoholic beverages that may be served from the bar. For these requests, a general, all-purpose glass of a size in keeping with the bar's pricing structure is required.

Specialty glasses: A variety of glassware shapes and sizes designed for specialty cocktails are also widely available. Popular cocktails in these types of glasses include a hurricane, piña colada, mai tai and frozen, and on-the-rocks daiquiris.

ICE   What does ice have to do with standardized beverage production? A lot! Large ice cubes leave space between them when scooped into a glass. This permits a larger amount of mixers to be added, which may dilute the drink more than was intended. By contrast, smaller cubes or shaved ice (in particular) pack a glass and permit less mixer to be added. This may, in turn, give the impression of a "stronger" drink.

Large ice cubes have less exposed surface area relative to their smaller counterparts and melt (and dilute the drink) at a slower pace than smaller cubes.

Experienced restaurant managers know that quality beverage products, standardized recipes, the right glassware, and the right type of ice are essential to quality beverage service. These managers know that the service of quality beverages is essential to success. They also recognize that while *quality* beverage service is important, *responsible* beverage service must always be their number one priority.

Responsible Beverage Service

While the choices of alcoholic beverages that can be served are greater than ever before, the legal responsibilities of those who serve alcohol are also greater. The requirements for obtaining a **liquor license** vary from state to state; however, in all cases, the granting of the license requires every restaurant holding the license to be aware of their responsibilities related to the following factors:

What is sold. Holders of liquor licenses aren't free to sell any alcoholic beverages they choose. In fact, the type of license granted indicates whether the license holder is permitted to sell beer only; beer and wine only; or beer, wine, and spirits. In addition, the selling of these products, regardless of their type, will only be allowed if the products have been purchased from a state-approved alcoholic beverage supplier. This ensures product wholesomeness, allows the state to carefully monitor alcoholic beverage sales, and assists in the collection of alcohol sales-related taxes.

Where it's sold. A liquor license generally designates a very specific geographic location in which alcohol may be served. This may be identified as an individual building address or even a particular section(s) of a building. Restaurant managers must know exactly where their license allows them to serve alcohol and where the boundaries of that permitted area are located. Generally, the license will require that guests drink only in those designated areas and that they not be allowed to remove alcohol from the premises (although some states do allow the removal of small amounts of unfinished wine served with guest meals). For example, a New York State law allows unfinished wine to be taken out of a restaurant

Liquor license

A state-authorized permit that allows the holder of the license (the licensee) to sell alcoholic beverages in accordance with state, local, and federal law. Some times called a liquor permit.

The use of the right glassware for the right drink shows guests that management understands the importance of presentation when serving quality beverages.

provided the wine was ordered with a meal, part of the wine was consumed with the meal, and the bottle is sealed in a transparent bag with the receipt for the meal and wine.

Some licenses may allow the restaurant manager to serve alcohol in alternative locations. For example, a restaurant manager may hold a license authorizing beverage service at catered events in off-site locations. The terms of the license will clearly spell out the circumstances in which off-site alcoholic beverage service is allowed.

When it's sold. Operating hours for restaurants that serve alcohol are strictly controlled. While few localities place restrictions on when food may be sold, all states regulate the time of day alcohol may be sold, at what time service must stop and on what days of the week, holidays or special occasions (such as election days) if any, that service is prohibited or is restricted.

How it's sold. The responsible service of alcohol requires that managers carefully institute procedures to control sales. Holders of liquor licenses may be instructed by their state about how alcohol can or cannot be sold. For example, in many locales, guests may not be served more than one alcoholic drink at a time or, perhaps, only guests seated at a table or bar may be served. In other locales, these practices may be permitted. Restaurant managers holding liquor licenses of any type must be aware of all restrictions on how these products can be sold.

In what quantity it's sold. In most jurisdictions, beer may be sold by the glass or the pitcher, wine can be sold by the glass or bottle, and spirits are typically sold by the drink. This isn't however, always true. Depending upon local regulations, restrictions on the quantity of alcohol that can be sold at one time and to a specific individual may be quite extensive. Restaurant managers should know about any restrictions placed on the quantity of alcohol they can sell to any buyer of alcohol.

To whom it's sold. In all 50 states and the District of Columbia, those who purchase alcoholic beverages must be 21 years old. Restaurants and bars are responsible for taking reasonable steps to ensure that they only serve alcohol to those who are legally entitled to consume it. However, restaurant managers are likely to encounter guests who are over 21 but are still prohibited from purchasing alcohol (e.g., those who appear to be obviously and visibly intoxicated or those who pose a threat to others).

Ensuring the responsible service of alcohol in their operations is among a restaurant manager's most critical responsibilities.

It's a well-established fact of case law that restaurant managers who exercise reasonable care don't serve alcohol to those who are intoxicated. Knowingly serving an intoxicated person is a sign that the restaurant has *not* exercised reasonable care and may be held responsible under third-party liability (dram shop) laws for damages resulting from the actions of the intoxicated person.

A restaurant manager has a responsibility to serve alcoholic beverages responsibly. Increasingly restaurants are held accountable when safe products are sold in unsafe ways. This changing view by society is especially important for restaurateurs who sell alcoholic beverages.

Alcoholic beverages are absolutely safe and healthful when consumed properly, but they can be extremely dangerous if served or consumed unsafely. The law considers the responsibility of serving alcohol seriously. In fact, those who serve it improperly are committing a crime or may otherwise be held responsible for what may happen as a result of an improper sale.

To illustrate the impact of dram-shop laws, consider the fact that when too much alcohol is served to a guest and an accident or injury results, there are actually three (not two) distinct parties to the accident:

- First party: The individual consuming the alcohol
- Second party: The restaurant serving the alcohol
- Third party: An injured individual not involved in the specific instance of consuming or selling the alcohol

To better understand the legal impact of improper alcohol service, assume that Terri, a guest (the first party) is served an excessive amount of alcohol by Erick, the bartender at your restaurant (the second party). As a result, Terri drives her car and causes an accident that severely injures Crystal (the third party).

WEB AT WORK!

The Education Foundation of the National Restaurant Association produces "ServSafe Alcohol," an excellent program consisting of training materials for those who sell and serve alcohol. You can find more information about the program at:

www.servesafe.com

Click on "Responsible Alcohol."

In such a situation, the restaurant (and perhaps the bartender) may be held liable for Crystal's injuries. This legal concept, known as third-party liability, forms the basis for dram-shop laws enacted to penalize those who serve alcohol improperly and to compensate the innocent victims of the improper service.

Restaurant managers must recognize that society views the proper serving of alcohol to be of critical importance. Prior to the 1980s, most states did not hold servers of alcohol responsible for the damages caused to third parties. Today, 43 states and the District of Columbia have some variation of dram shop law (see Chapter 3) in effect.

Managers must recognize that dram-shop legislation means that criminal charges may be involved, as well as civil liability, when alcohol is sold irresponsibly. Civil liability means that a manager's operation could be held responsible for an injured person's expenses. That may include paying for medical bills, lost wages, damages to property, or making cash awards to the estates of deceased persons. Criminal liability can subject a hospitality manager to loss of liquor license, fines, and even imprisonment. As a result, businesses should secure third-party liability (dram shop) insurance and train staff properly in the responsible service of alcohol. Even if your restaurant is located in a community that doesn't specifically require alcohol server education or certification, it's still a good idea to mandate responsible alcohol service training programs for every bartender and alcohol server.

Restaurant Terms and Concepts

Alcohol *201*	Fortified wine *205*	Vintage *207*	Mixed drink *212*
Fermentation *201*	Aromatized wine *205*	Microbrewery *210*	Aging *213*
Distillation *201*	Carafe *205*	Draft beer *211*	Shot *213*
Blood alcohol content (BAC) *202*	Wine and food pairings *206*	Tap *211*	Mash *213*
Proof *202*	Wine list *206*	Head *211*	Mixology *215*
Bouquet *204*	Bin number *207*	Nonalcoholic beer (NA beer) *211*	Free pour *215*
			Liquor license *217*

Work in Progress

1. What are the principal differences between the way fermented beverages and distilled beverages are produced? Why are these differences important to restaurant managers?

2. To be safe, some restaurant managers require all their guests (regardless of age) to show proof of age prior to serving them alcohol. Assume you've implemented such a policy. How would you respond to a 65-year-old guest who complains about the policy and refuses to comply?

3. Society carefully regulates the sale of alcoholic beverages. What alcohol service-related restrictions are in place in your state? Do you feel they're appropriate?

4. Some popular types of beer are sold in bottles, cans, and kegs. Which serving form do you think most beer drinkers prefer? Why?

5. Some managers feel that their wine lists must be extensive to optimize guest choice; other managers feel wine lists should be designed to minimize inventory costs. What factors would you consider when deciding how extensive the wine list should be in a restaurant you manage?

6. In addition to California, many states now produce wine. How should restaurant managers determine the number, if any, of locally produced wines that they include in their wine lists?

7. The popularity of different spirit products can fluctuate according to the time of year and geographic region in which a restaurant operates. How can restaurant managers stay abreast of changes in spirits consumption that could affect their businesses?

8. Managers must keep up with changing consumer preferences related to alcoholic beverage products. What methods and information sources can be used to help managers do so?

9. Both bartenders and customers tend to like "free pour" beverage operations. Why do you think that's very often the case?

10. You discover that a trusted bartender in your restaurant routinely serves one of your regular customers too much alcohol. What would you say to the bartender? What would you say to the customer?

11

Cost Control

Chapter Outline

Managing Food and Beverage Costs
    Calculation of Cost of Goods Sold
    Food and Beverage Cost Percentages
    Concerns About Cost of Goods Sold

Managing Labor Costs
    Factors Affecting Labor Costs
    Five-Step Labor Control System
    Management of Salaried Labor

Managing Other Costs
    Variable Costs and Fixed Costs
    Common Restaurant Costs

Learning Objectives

After carefully reading and studying the information in this chapter, you will be able to:

1. Calculate the cost of goods sold for food and beverage.

2. Explain basic procedures to plan for and control labor costs.

3. Describe other costs incurred in restaurant operations.

IN THIS CHAPTER

Restaurant managers must control costs as they plan and implement procedures to reach their financial goals. Many tactics to control food and beverage costs have already been explained in Chapter 5 during our discussion of standardized recipes and in Chapter 7 when we reviewed the basic purchasing, receiving, storing, and issuing procedures. However, wise restaurant managers understand that their costs must be known before they can be controlled.

    The amount spent to purchase foods and beverages is referred to as "cost of goods sold," and calculations to determine these costs are routinely made. Restaurant managers must understand all of the components that contribute to actual food and beverage costs. These components will be carefully examined in this chapter.

    Labor cost control is also a significant concern to every restaurant manager. What major factors impact the number of employees and labor hours that are needed? This chapter will answer this question and present a five-step system to plan and manage the labor hours that are required.

Two other important labor cost concerns—the management of salaried labor and the role of technology in labor cost control—will also be addressed.

While paying attention to controlling product (food and beverage) and labor costs is a priority, numerous other costs that must also be managed. Many of these will be noted in a concluding section of this chapter.

MANAGING FOOD AND BEVERAGE COSTS

What is food cost? What is beverage cost? Your first responses to these questions are probably, "What the restaurant spent for food and beverage during a specific time period." However, as you'll soon learn, the answers are more complicated. Restaurant managers use an **accrual accounting system** to match the revenue generated during a specific accounting period with the costs incurred to generate that revenue. This allows them to compare their actual product costs with what they had budgeted as a basic step in the control process.

An accrual accounting system is more useful than a **cash accounting system**, which considers revenues to be earned when they're received and expenses to be incurred when payments are made. Consider, for example, products that are purchased on the last day of the month that generate revenue on that day. If the food isn't paid for until a week later (during the next month), the revenue won't be matched with the cost of food that generated it. Therefore, the food cost percentage would be understated in the first month and overstated in the second month.

Calculation of Cost of Goods Sold

The cost of goods sold information for food and beverages is used by restaurant managers for two purposes:

1. To compare with **operating budget** estimates of these costs to determine whether corrective actions are needed to bring future actual costs more in line with budget plans.
2. To include as a cost on the property's **income statement** (see Chapter 13) that summarizes the restaurant's profitability for the accounting period.

Figure 11.1 shows the calculations necessary to compute the **cost of goods sold: food** for Vernon's Restaurant during January, 20xx.

Sidebar definitions

Accrual accounting system

An accounting system that matches costs incurred with revenues generated.

Cash accounting system

An accounting system that considers revenues to be earned when they're received and expenses to be incurred when payments are made.

Operating budget

A financial plan that estimates revenues and expenses for a specific time period.

Income statement

A summary of the restaurant's profitability that details revenues generated, costs incurred, and profits or losses realized during a specific accounting period; also called a profit and loss (P & L) statement or an income and expense statement.

Cost of goods sold: food

The actual cost of the food used to generate food revenue for a specific time period; also called adjusted food cost or net food cost.

FIGURE 11.1

Calculation of the Cost of Goods Sold: Food (January 20xx)

Line		Vernon's Restaurant	
(1)	Value of Food Inventory (Beginning of Period, Jan. 1)	$83,575	
(2)	Value of Food Purchases (During January)	187,615	
(3)	Total Value of Food Available (During January)		271,190
(4)	Value of Food Inventory (End of Period: January)		(89,540)
(5)	Unadjusted Cost of Goods Sold: Food (January)		181,650
(6)	Add Adjustments to Cost of Goods Sold: Food		
(7)	Transfers from Beverage		6,550
(8)	Deduct Adjustments to Cost of Goods Sold: Food		
(9)	Transfers to Beverage	(4,175)	
(10)	Transfers to Labor Cost (Employee Meals)	(8,900)	
(11)	Transfers to Marketing	(3,750)	(16,825)
(12)	Cost of Goods Sold: Food (January)		$171,375

Adapted from Ninemeier, J., and Hayes, D. (2006). *Restaurant Operations Management.* Pearson Education, Inc.

Let's look at Figure 11.1 carefully, remembering that its purpose is to allow the restaurant manager to determine the cost of goods sold: food for January. The calculation requires knowledge about:

- Changes in inventory values (lines 1–5)
- An adjustment that increases cost of goods sold (line 7)
- Three adjustments that decrease the cost of goods sold (lines 9–11)

CHANGES IN INVENTORY VALUES   Note that the value of food inventory (line 1) at the beginning of the accounting period (January 1) is added to the value of purchases during January (line 2). This yields the total value of food available for sale during January ($271,190 in line 3). Then the value of inventory at the end of January ($89,540 in line 4) is *deducted* to determine the unadjusted cost of food ($181,650 in line 5) used during January.

Some restaurant managers conclude their calculations at this point and consider the unadjusted cost of goods sold to represent their food costs for the period. Other managers, however, want to more closely match product revenue with product costs and make additional calculations.

ADJUSTMENTS THAT INCREASE COST OF GOODS SOLD   Note in Figure 11.1 that the unadjusted cost of goods sold (line 5) is increased by the value of **transfers** from beverage ($6,550 in line 7).

Beverage transfers increase food costs because they generate food revenues. Examples of transfers from beverage include wine used in cooking and liqueurs used to flambé desserts. The value of the transfers represents costs initially charged to beverage ("cost of food: beverage") that actually generated revenue for food ("cost of goods sold: food"). This transfer is in line with the intent of accrual accounting, which is to match revenues generated with expenses incurred to generate the revenue.

ADJUSTMENTS THAT DECREASE COST OF GOODS SOLD   Figure 11.1 also shows that some adjustments can be made that reduce the cost of goods sold: food. Note the value of transfers

Transfer

An adjustment to the "cost of goods sold" that increases or decreases food or beverage costs to better match product costs with the revenue generated by the product's sale.

Restaurant accounting systems will capture the cost of this coffee. Will the revenue for it be collected?

©kameleonmedia/Fotolia

to beverage ($4,175 in line 9), to labor costs ($8,900 in line 10), and to marketing ($3,750 in line 11).

Transfers from food *to* beverage costs may include the cost of produce (examples: lemons and celery sticks) used to make drink garnishes and ice cream used for specialty drinks. Transfers of food costs to labor costs represent, for example, the cost of employee meals, which is a labor cost, not a food cost).

Transfers from food cost to marketing cost might include the cost of complimentary meals provided to potential guests looking for a site for a future banquet and to dissatisfied guests who receive a "comp" meal.

After the above adjustments are made, the cost of goods sold: food ($171,375 in line 12) can be determined.

The calculations to determine the **cost of goods sold: beverage** are very similar to the process you have just learned and are shown in Figure 11.2.

As with the calculations for cost of goods sold: food, restaurant managers must add the value of beginning beverage inventory ($19,550 in line 1) to the value of beverage purchases ($38,950 in line 2) to determine the total value of beverages available ($58,500 in line 3). Then the value of ending beverage inventory ($15,715 in line 4) is *deducted* to determine the unadjusted cost of beverages ($42,785 in line 5).

The adjustment process involves increasing the unadjusted cost of beverages by the cost of transfers from food ($4,175 in line 7). Examples of these transfers include the cost of produce and ice cream noted during the discussion of Figure 11.1 that generated beverage revenue.

Figure 11.2 indicates that the adjustments for transfers to food ($6,550 in line 9) and to marketing ($1,275 in line 10) reduce the cost of goods sold: beverage. As indicated in the discussion of Figure 11.1, the transfers to food were for wine and liquors that were originally charged to beverage costs but, instead, generated food revenue. The transfer to marketing is for the cost of beverages that were really marketing-related expenses, such as for "comp" beverages.

Do the calculations involving adjustments to reflect accurate cost of goods sold data make any "real" difference? We'll answer this question next.

Cost of goods sold: beverage

The actual cost of the beverages used to generate beverage revenue for a specific time period; also called adjusted beverage cost or net beverage cost.

FIGURE 11.2

Calculation of Cost of Goods Sold: Beverage (January 20xx)

Line		Vernon's Restaurant	
(1)	Value of Beverage Inventory (Beginning of Period, Jan. 1)	$19,550	
(2)	Value of Beverage Purchases (During January)	38, 950	
(3)	Total Value of Beverage Available (During January)		58,500
(4)	Value of Beverage Inventory (End of Period: January)		(15,715)
(5)	Unadjusted Cost of Goods Sold: Beverage (January)		42,785
(6)	Add Adjustments to Cost of Goods Sold: Beverage		
(7)	Transfers from Food		4,175
(8)	Deduct Adjustments to Cost of Goods Sold: Beverage		
(9)	Transfers to Food	(6,550)	
(10)	Transfers to Marketing	(1,275)	(7,825)
(11)	Cost of Goods Sold: Beverage (January)		$39,135

Adapted from Ninemeier, J., and Hayes, D. (2006). *Restaurant Operations Management.* Pearson Education, Inc.

Food and Beverage Cost Percentages

Restaurant managers are very concerned about their **food cost percentage** and their **beverage cost percentage**. The reason is that food and beverage purchases are considered **prime costs** and, because they're so large, they must be carefully controlled.

Managers' concerns begin when budgets are planned and continue when they review the cost of goods sold calculations for each product. Budgeted (estimated) food and beverage cost calculations are compared to the cost of goods sold for food and beverages (actual costs), and corrective actions are undertaken when there are excessive variances between the planned and actual costs. Note: The corrective action process used to identify variances and to properly address them is discussed in depth in Chapter 13.

The calculation of food and beverage cost percentages is straightforward. We will use the data in Figures 11.1 and 11.2 to illustrate the process. First, let's assume that the January food revenue was $508,620. We'll calculate the unadjusted and adjusted food cost percentages in Figure 11.1:

$$\text{Food cost \% (unadjusted)} = \frac{\text{Unadjusted cost of goods sold: food}}{\text{Food revenue}} = \frac{\$181,650}{\$508,620} = 35.7\%$$

$$\text{Food cost \% (adjusted)} = \frac{\text{Adjusted cost of goods sold: food}}{\text{Food revenue}} = \frac{\$171,375}{\$508,620} = 33.7\%$$

Note that there is a 2.0 percentage point difference (35.7% − 33.7% = 2.0%) between the unadjusted and adjusted food cost percentages when adjustments such as transfers, labor costs, and marketing-related expenses are considered. It's important that managers use the same factors to consider food costs when they plan budgets and evaluate actual costs, because doing so can help to explain when and where costs are out of line.

Now let's assume that the January beverage revenue was $168,750. We calculate the beverage cost percentages in Figure 11.2 as the following:

$$\text{Beverage cost \% (Unadjusted)} = \frac{\text{Unadjusted cost of goods sold: beverage}}{\text{Beverage revenue}}$$
$$= \frac{\$42,785}{\$168,750} = 25.4\%$$

$$\text{Beverage cost \% (Adjusted)} = \frac{\text{Adjusted cost of goods sold: beverage}}{\text{Beverage revenue}}$$
$$= \frac{\$39,135}{\$168,750} = 23.2\%$$

Note that there is a 2.2 percentage point difference (25.4% − 23.2% = 2.2%) between the unadjusted and adjusted beverage cost percentages.

The differences between the unadjusted and adjusted food and beverage cost percentages seem small; however, in operations of any size, every dollar counts. For example, the restaurant's food revenue in January was $508,620. The property's food costs would have been overstated by $10,172 ($508,620 × 2.0) if its food costs had not been adjusted. In addition, since its beverage revenue was $168,750, the month's beverage cost would have been overstated by $3,713 ($168,750 × 2.20) without adjustments. The restaurant manager could not have obtained a clear picture of the property's financial results. This could result in valuable time being spent to address the question, "Why are our food and beverage costs so high?" This time could be better spent on other management issues.

Restaurant managers must be consistent and always use the same (or no) adjustment factors when estimating food and beverage costs for the budget and when preparing financial information for the income statement. In small restaurants without accounting specialist positions, managers and those who direct the food and beverage departments must "speak the same language" about the components of product costs. Their peers in large operations with accountants or bookkeepers and in multiunit organizations where some accounting and control functions may be managed off-site should also define product costs in exactly the same way.

Food cost percentage

The percentage of food revenue used to purchase the food that generated the revenue.

Beverage cost percentage

The percentage of beverage revenue used to purchase the beverage that generated the revenue.

Prime costs

The term used to categorize product (food and beverage) costs and labor costs; these are the largest expenses in most restaurants.

┃ **WEB AT WORK!**

To learn more about procedures to manage and calculate food costs, go to the website for the Restaurant Report:

www.restaurantreport.com

Click on "Restaurant Accounting & Finance" to select articles and reports of interest.

Cost of Goods Sold Concerns

Profit center

A revenue-producing department within the restaurant.

Inventory turnover rate

The speed with which food or beverage inventory is turned into revenue within a specific time period, determined as follows:

$$\frac{\text{Cost of goods sold (food or beverage)}}{\text{Average inventory (food or beverage)*}} = \text{Inventory turnover rate}$$

*Average inventory = (Beginning inventory + ending inventory) ÷ 2.

You've just learned about the importance of considering food and beverage inventory values and the value of transfers between food and beverage **profit centers** when making cost of goods sold calculations. This section discusses these concepts in more detail.

Wise restaurant managers recognize the significant amount of money that's tied up in food and beverage inventories even if there's a fast **inventory turnover rate**. There's more to managing inventory than just keeping expensive items under lock and key (although this would be a good start in many less-professionally managed operations!).

Procedures for taking inventory counts must incorporate basic control principles. First, inventory values shouldn't be assessed by the person responsible for maintaining inventory, since a priority objective of the process is to confirm that the amount of product that *should* be available *is* in storage. Perhaps, for example, the restaurant manager and the accountant/bookkeeper can determine food inventory quantities. The head bartender, if not involved in storage or issuing, can also work with the accountant/bookkeeper to assume responsibility for inventory of beverage products. In small operations, the manager and owner can take inventory counts.

There are four basic methods used to determine the value of products in inventory.

FIRST-IN-FIRST-OUT (FIFO) METHOD The first-in-first-out (FIFO) method assumes that products are removed from inventory in the order they were received. In other words, the products in storage are the most recently purchased items. Thus, inventory value can be assigned on the basis of the prices paid for the most recently purchased products.

Assume that, on January 31, there are 35 cases of canned peaches with a value of $31.00 per case in inventory. On February 1, the date of the beginning inventory for February, there will also be 35 cases valued at $31.00 each. Let's also assume that 18 cases costing $33.00 per case were purchased during February and, on February 28 (the last day of the month), there are 22 cases of peaches in inventory.

The FIFO method of inventory valuation yields the following value of peaches in inventory on February 28:

$$\text{Most recent costs 18 cases @ \$33.00 per case} = \$594.00$$

$$\text{February 1 inventory} \frac{4 \text{ @ \$31.00 per case}}{22 \text{ cases}} = \underline{124.00}$$

$$\text{Inventory cost (peaches)} \quad \underline{\$718.00}$$

As you'll notice, the manager assumes that 18 of the 22 cases in inventory at the end of February are the most recent purchases ($33.00 per case); therefore, the remaining four cases remain from February 1 and are valued at $31.00 per case. The number of cases available at each cost are multiplied and added together to arrive at an inventory value for peaches of $718.00.

LAST-IN-FIRST-OUT (LIFO) METHOD This method assumes the reverse of the FIFO method: the most recently purchased products are used first. Inventory value is represented by the cost of items that have been in inventory the longest.

Let's use the same information about peaches presented above to calculate inventory cost using the LIFO method.

Since there are fewer end-of-inventory cases (22) than beginning-inventory cases (35), it's assumed that all cases in inventory remain from the beginning of the month.

Earliest cost = 22 cases @ $31.00 per case = $682.00 (inventory value of peaches)

ACTUAL COST METHOD   This inventory valuation method assumes that the value at the end of the month is based on the actual cost paid for each case available and that inventory value is the sum of the actual case costs.

To use this method, each case of peaches is marked with the case cost taken from delivery invoice.

Let's assume the following about the cost of the 22 cases in inventory on February 28:

$$6 \text{ cases @ } \$31.00 \text{ per case} = \$186.00$$

$$\frac{16 \text{ cases @ } 33.00 \text{ per case}}{22 \text{ cases}} = \underline{528.00}$$

$$\text{Inventory value (peaches)} \quad \underline{\$714.00}$$

As noted above, 6 cases of peaches remained from the earliest purchase date (at $31.00 per case), and 16 cases were purchased during the month (at $33.00 per case) so the value of the 22 cases of peaches in inventory on February 28 is $714.00.

WEIGHTED AVERAGE METHOD   The weighted average method of inventory evaluation considers the quantity of each product purchased at different prices. The inventory value is then determined by the average price for each product.

Let's continue with our example:

$$\text{February 1 inventory} = 35 \text{ cases @ } \$31.00 \text{ per case} = \$1,085.00$$

$$\text{February purchases} = \frac{18 \text{ cases @ } \$33.00 \text{ per case}}{53 \text{ cases}} = \frac{\$ 594.00}{\$1,679.00}$$

$$\text{Average case cost} = \$1679.00 \div 53 \text{ cases} = \$31.67$$

$$\underset{\text{Inventory cost}}{\frac{\$696.74}{}} = \text{No. of cases in inventory} \overset{22}{\times} \underset{\text{Average case cost}}{\overset{\$31.67}{}}$$
$$\text{(February 28)}$$

INVENTORY COST SUMMARY   You've noted that each inventory valuation method yields a different inventory value. This can create a total inventory cost difference for all products of several thousand dollars (or more) depending upon the inventory valuation method selected. Restaurant managers should consult a tax expert to determine the inventory valuation method to use. They should also ensure that the agreed-upon method is used consistently, because there are tax implications and possible restrictions on changing inventory valuation methods.

FOOD AND BEVERAGE TRANSFERS   The role of food and beverage transfers to adjust cost of goods sold calculations was explained above. An electronic or printed copy of a food/beverage transfer memo serves as a **source document** for each occasion when a product transfer is made between the food and beverage departments. After transfers are made, they can be held (hard-copy system) or electronically summarized until the end of the accounting period, after which transfer cost information can be used to make applicable cost of goods sold adjustments.

Source document

A document that provides an entry point for financial information into the restaurant's accounting system.

WEB AT WORK!

To learn about inventory management restaurant software, go to the CostGuard website:

www.costguard.com

Click on "Tutorial" and then "Inventory."

FIGURE 11.3

Food/Beverage Transfer Memo

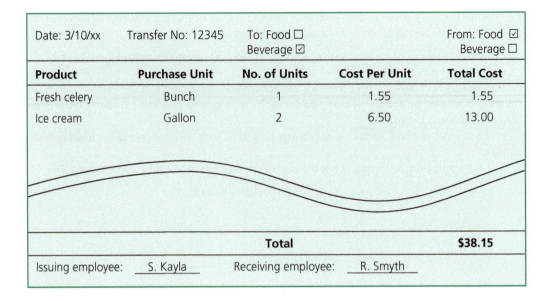

Date: 3/10/xx	Transfer No: 12345	To: Food ☐ Beverage ☑		From: Food ☑ Beverage ☐
Product	**Purchase Unit**	**No. of Units**	**Cost Per Unit**	**Total Cost**
Fresh celery	Bunch	1	1.55	1.55
Ice cream	Gallon	2	6.50	13.00
			Total	**$38.15**

Issuing employee:	S. Kayla	Receiving employee:	R. Smyth

Figure 11.3 shows a sample of a food/beverage transfer memo. When you review Figure 11.3, note that fresh celery and ice cream were transferred to the beverage department from the food operation. Information about purchase unit and number of units transferred along with unit cost and total cost for each product are summarized on the form. You'll see that products totaling $38.15 were involved in this transfer memo. Finally, note that the document includes the names of the employees issuing and receiving the products.

Recall that transfers *from* the food department *to* the beverage department *decrease* the cost of goods sold: food and *increase* the cost of goods sold: beverage.

Conversely, transfers *to* food *from* beverage *increase* cost of goods sold: food and *decrease* cost of goods sold: beverage.

©mcphotos/Shutterstock

A food and beverage cost transfer system should be in place to accurately determine the real costs of producing these specialty drinks.

> ### ALL IN A DAY'S WORK 11.1
>
> "I thought we were supposed to work as a team," said Jerome, the bar manager at Vernon's Restaurant. He was speaking to Colleen, the restaurant manager. "I've always given the kitchen wines for cooking, liqueurs for tableside flambéing and even the maraschino cherries used in some desserts. Food production personnel have always provided me with the garnishes and ingredients I need for our specialty drinks, and the appetizers they provide for our cocktail hour specials are great!" he continued.
>
> "We will always work as a team," said Colleen, "although we do need to start keeping track of the food and beverage products being transferred between departments. This is a new policy. All of the properties in the chain have to start doing this next month."
>
> 1. What do you think prompted "headquarters" to require this new policy and procedures?
> 2. What can Colleen do to ease the transition into these new accounting procedures at her property?

MANAGING LABOR COSTS

For many restaurants, labor costs are the largest category of expenses and the one most difficult to control. The right number of employees must be available at the right times to meet guests' needs. With too few employees, labor costs may be low, but service levels will suffer. With too many employees, labor costs will be excessive, and this may mean the difference between a profitable restaurant and one that loses money. Therefore, the control of labor costs is an important part of every restaurant manager's job.

Factors Affecting Labor Costs

The best labor cost control systems ensure that guests are well served while financial goals are attained. The quality and number of staff required to effectively operate a restaurant vary based on factors that we will discuss below.

THE MENU   The menu may be the most important factor impacting the restaurant manager's ability to control labor costs. Menus with many and/or complex items typically require more production time and skills, unless **convenience foods** are used. Managers must provide guests with sufficient menu variety while ensuring that employees can adequately prepare and serve the items at a reasonable cost.

Convenience food

Food that has some labor built-in that otherwise would need to be added on-site. Examples include pre-sliced meats, processed vegetables, and baked desserts.

FOOD PREPARATION METHODS   It's rare for a restaurant to prepare all its menu items from "scratch." Convenience foods are commonly purchased; their use results in increased food costs that are, hopefully, offset (or more than offset!) by reduced labor costs. Restaurant managers and their food production team should select convenience foods on the basis of required (acceptable) quality and their ability to reduce labor costs. For example, a restaurant manager may decide to buy a premade cheesecake rather than prepare the product in-house with the belief that lower labor costs will offset the higher purchase price.

The decision to "buy convenience" or "make from scratch" involves the consideration of two major factors: product quality and labor savings. A manager who buys inferior products to save labor costs will quickly learn that guests won't accept poor quality foods. Spending less for products that aren't acceptable to guests doesn't make business sense or save money.

DESIRED SERVICE LEVELS   Increased levels of guest service typically result in increased labor costs. For example, the costs of providing an attentive, well-trained, and professional service staff in a restaurant with **tableside food preparation** can be high. If, alternatively, guests receive only limited service (for example, when food is purchased at a drive-up window or walk-up counter), service-related costs will be reduced. Managers must ensure that they know the service level desired by their guests (and what they'll pay for).

Tableside food preparation

Food preparation in the dining room or at or near the guest's table. Popular tableside-prepared items include Caesar salad, flambé desserts and specialty drinks.

QUALITY OF EMPLOYEE TRAINING   You learned in Chapter 4 that effective training helps to improve the knowledge and skills of restaurant staff and that its benefits include increased productivity and lowered labor costs. Training is good for the restaurant, its guests and its

FIGURE 11.4

Five-Step Labor Cost Control System

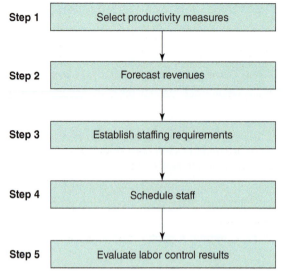

Adapted from Ninemeier, J., and Hayes, D. (2006). *Restaurant Operations Management.* Pearson Education, Inc.

employees. Restaurants with high-quality employee training programs generally spend fewer labor dollars than do their competitors that don't take advantage of these programs.

Five-Step Labor Control System

Restaurant managers can use a five-step sequential process to determine how many staff members must be available at specific times to ensure that production and service standards are met. These steps are previewed in Figure 11.4 and discussed below.

Let's discuss these steps to learn why they're important.

STEP 1: SELECT PRODUCTIVITY MEASURES   Restaurant managers measure productivity because they want to compare labor goals with actual results. To do so, the goals must be measurable and appropriate for the operation.

For example, assume that LaToya, a restaurant manager, wishes to evaluate the productivity of a cook. She knows from experience that a well-trained and motivated cook can produce 75 quality meals per hour. Lewis is a cook who prepares only 35 meals per hour; he doesn't meet her expectations. Since she knows about Lewis's low productivity, corrective action can be undertaken. This could just involve making sure that Lewis has the necessary tools and supplies needed to do his job, or it may mean he needs extensive re-training. Unless LaToya identifies an expected performance level and then compares her workers' actual performance to those expectations, productivity levels will remain unknown and unimproved.

The first step in establishing productivity standards is to select which measure(s) to use. Several are popular and can be computed for various accounting periods such as day, week, or month.

Labor Cost Percentage

Labor cost percentage

The ratio of labor costs incurred in a specific accounting period relative to the revenue dollars generated in that same accounting period, as computed as:

Cost of labor (÷) Revenue = Labor cost percentage

Restaurant managers who use **labor cost percentages** compare their revenue to the labor-related dollars spent to generate that revenue. The ratio between these two numbers is called the labor cost percentage and is expressed as:

$$\frac{\text{Cost of labor}}{\text{Revenue}} = \text{Labor cost \%}$$

Assume that LaToya's restaurant generates $1,000,000 per year in revenue and incurs $350,000 in labor costs the same year. The labor cost percentage is:

$$\frac{\$350,000}{\$1,000,000} = 35\%$$

In other words, of all the revenue generated ($1,000,000), 35% of it ($350,000) is used for labor.

The labor cost percentage is relatively easy to compute and is one of the most popular labor productivity measures used in the restaurant industry.

Meal Period	Cost of Labor	Revenue	Labor Cost %
Lunch	$2,500.00	$5,000.00	50.0
Dinner	$4,000.00	$12,000.00	33.3
Total	$6,500.00	$17,000.00	38.2

Adapted from Ninemeier, J., and Hayes, D. (2006). *Restaurant Operations Management.* Pearson Education, Inc.

FIGURE 11.5

LaToya's Lunch and Dinner Labor Cost Percentages

Some managers only consider "**payroll**" dollars when calculating a labor cost percentage.

"Payroll" generally means the total salaries and wages paid to employees. Labor costs, however, consist of more than just payroll and include all other labor-related costs, including:

Payroll

The total wages and salaries paid to employees.

- FICA (Social Security taxes)
- Unemployment and workers' compensation taxes
- Employee health, dental, and vision insurance premiums paid by the employer
- Vacation/sick leave/personal days
- Employee meals
- Employee training expenses

Restaurant managers should include all related costs when calculating their **cost of labor**.

There's no universally accepted "best" or "target" labor cost percentage. Depending upon the type of restaurant, an ideal labor cost percentage (one used for budget development) can range from 20 to 30% (or even more) of a restaurant's revenue.

Cost of labor

Salaries, wages, fringe benefits, and all other employee-related expenses required for restaurant personnel.

Managers often calculate labor productivity ratios separately for different meal periods. LaToya's property serves lunch and dinner, and she computes separate labor cost percentages for them, as shown in Figure 11.5.

Note the different productivity ratios for both meal shifts and that the total labor cost percent (38.2%) could be misleading. Therefore, it's better to schedule employees and evaluate lunch and dinner staffing patterns separately to control labor costs.

While low labor cost percentages are generally desirable, three things should always be remembered:

- Always use the same types of labor cost information when computing and comparing labor cost percentages. For example, always include or exclude nonpayroll costs or management costs when you compare your labor cost percentage from one period to another.
- Realize that labor cost percentages are affected by changes in wage rates. When the price paid for labor increases and there is no change in revenue, the labor cost percentage increases. For example, if LaToya granted all employees a 3% pay increase, the new cost of labor would be computed as:

$350,000 × .03 = $10,500 (labor cost increase resulting from changed labor)

$350,000 + $10,500 = $360,500 (total (new) labor cost)

$360,500/$1,000,000 = 36% (labor cost percentage)

In this case, LaToya's labor cost percentage increased from 35 to 36%, and productivity defined by the labor cost percentage decreased because labor costs increased without an increase in revenue.

- Recognize that labor cost percentages are affected by changes in menu selling prices and in total revenues generated. When selling prices and revenues increase without a change in labor costs, the labor cost percentage decreases. Note: The reverse is also true. If menu prices and revenues decrease without a change in labor costs, the labor cost percentage will increase.

If LaToya raised all menu prices by 5 percent on the first day of a new accounting period and guest counts were not affected, the labor cost percent would be computed as:

$1,000,000 × .05 = $50,000 revenue increase

$1,000,000 + $50,000 = $1,050,000 total revenue

$350,000/$1,050,000 = 33.3% (labor cost percentage)

Here, the labor cost percentage decreased from 35 to 33.3%. Note that this does not suggest a productivity increase because it was created by an increase in menu selling prices.

Historical data should be considered in conjunction with the most recent data available. Assume that revenues increased 5% each month from the same period last year for several months but that, in the last two months, the increase has been closer to zero. This may mean that the increase trend has slowed or stopped, and good managers modify historical trends as they examine current conditions.

It's also necessary to estimate the effect of future events on revenue. As you learned in Chapter 7, the opening of new competitive restaurants; scheduled occurrences, including sporting events and concerts; or significant changes in your own operating hours may increase or decrease future revenues.

When all available information has been considered, future revenues can be forecasted and, with knowledge of the productivity measurements already established, an employee schedule can be developed.

STEP 3: ESTABLISH STAFFING REQUIREMENTS Assume that LaToya has estimated next week's revenue as shown in Figure 11.6.

Figure 11.6 indicates that LaToya anticipates generating $50,000 in revenue for the coming week. Assume that she has evaluated past productivity ratios and is satisfied with the service levels they provide. Therefore, she knows she can allocate 30% of estimated food revenue for food-related labor costs and 25% of anticipated beverage revenues for beverage-related labor costs.

Since LaToya has forecasted $36,850 in food revenue, she can spend $11,055 in weekly food-related labor costs ($36,850 × .30 = $11,055) and $3,287.50 ($13,150 × .25 = $3,287.50) in labor to generate beverage revenues.

If revenue levels exceed LaToya's estimates, she may not need more employees, since some positions aren't directly affected by the level of revenue or number of guests served. For example, one salaried manager can be responsible for LaToya's dining area when $3,000 in revenue is generated; that same manager can probably also manage her dining room when $4,000 in revenue is generated. Of course, when significant increases in revenues are planned, LaToya will need to increase the hours in some positions, including service staff, bus persons, dishwashers, and cooks.

Employee schedules should be developed by considering labor dollars, which can then be converted to a labor cost percentage. The labor dollars committed when an employee schedule is built must be sufficient to adequately serve the anticipated number of guests. To create the appropriate percentage amounts, the payroll forecast should be separated, at minimum, into **required shift labor** and **additional shift labor**, and each should be forecast independently.

Required shift labor

The amount of labor and associated costs required to operate the restaurant for a specific shift regardless of revenue volume.

The number of additional shift labor hours and costs to be scheduled is determined by considering productivity requirements, and these figures change as revenue levels change. Costs for required shift labor, however, remain constant regardless of the revenue level and/or the number of hours of fixed labor used.

Additional shift labor

The amount of labor and related costs required to serve guests above the maximum number that can be served by required shift labor. As revenue increases, additional shift labor costs also increase.

STEP 4: SCHEDULE STAFF Restaurant managers can develop their employee schedules after revenue forecasts have been made. Proper scheduling impacts the quality of products and services provided to guests, their employees' levels of job satisfaction and the restaurant's profitability.

Developing the Schedule

Managers can choose from numerous software programs to create employee schedules. These tools allow managers to preload employee data, including requested days off, vacations,

FIGURE 11.6

LaToya's Restaurant: Weekly Revenue Forecast

Day	Food Revenues	Beverage Revenues	Total Revenues
Monday	$ 3,000	$ 1,000	$ 4,000
Tuesday	$ 2,500	$ 800	$ 3,300
Wednesday	$ 3,500	$ 1,100	$ 4,600
Thursday	$ 5,500	$ 700	$ 6,200
Friday	$ 8,500	$ 4,000	$12,500
Saturday	$ 9,000	$ 4,800	$13,800
Sunday	$ 4,850	$ 750	$ 5,600
Total	**$36,850**	**$ 13,150**	**$50,000**

Adapted from Ninemeier, J., and Hayes, D. (2006). *Restaurant Operations Management*. Pearson Education, Inc.

maximum allowable work hours, restrictions about work hours for minors, and employee time preferences. Effective employee schedules should indicate, at minimum:

- Days and dates covered by the schedule
- Employees' first and last names
- Days to work and scheduled days off
- Scheduled start and stop times (A.M./P.M.)
- Total hours to work, excluding meal periods
- Requested vacation time or personal days off
- On/off days for salaried personnel
- Date of schedule preparation
- Name of manager preparing/approving the schedule

Figure 11.7 shows an Excel spreadsheet work schedule created for a week with busy Friday and Saturday nights. A one-half hour break is included in scheduled hours. Note that this schedule includes the information listed above.

Regardless of whether schedules are developed manually or with software, several guiding principles should be used:

- Develop a productivity target and a schedule to meet it. If, for example, your productivity measurement is a labor cost percentage, compute the anticipated percentage you would achieve with your schedule.
- Determine the forecasted revenue and consider the employee hours required to generate that revenue.
- Schedule for the needs of guests first and employees second. A manager's job is to ensure that employees are available when they're needed, not just when they prefer to work.
- Avoid scheduling **overtime** when possible. Overtime pay is expensive, and these labor hours increase total payroll costs but don't increase productivity. Some overtime may be unavoidable, as scheduled employees are absent from work and on-duty employees work additional hours, revenue unexpectedly increases and/or as extra work must be completed. However, employee schedules should not normally be developed with "built-in" overtime.

  Overtime

  The number of hours of work after which an employee must receive a premium pay rate, usually one and one-half times the hourly rate.

- Use part-time employees for peak-volume periods. Increased guest counts typically occur during traditional meal periods. For example, the hours between 6:00 A.M. and 9:00 A.M. may be very busy for a restaurant serving breakfast and additional staff, particularly in guest service positions, may be needed. This time period may be one in which part-time employees may be helpful. Note: Good managers remember that the total number of hours worked is important for many employees, and managers attempt to make part-time jobs desirable.
- Minimize **split shifts**. Some managers address meal period fluctuations by scheduling employees for "split shifts." Most employees don't like this arrangement. While it may sometimes be necessary to schedule employees for these shifts, the negative long-term impact on employee morale will likely more than offset any cost savings.

  Split shift

  A work schedule in which an employee works a specified number of hours, leaves the restaurant and returns later the same day to work a second shift.

- Grant employee schedule requests when possible. Restaurant managers must balance employees' personal needs with the property's scheduling requirements. Employees typically request earned vacation, preferred days and special days off, and wise managers consider these requests with a system by which each employee has a reasonable chance for requests to be granted.
- Be fair when scheduling preferred work periods. The workweek at many restaurants often includes some shifts that are busier than others. Tipped employees working busier shifts receive greater tip income than those working at other times. Managers should ensure that, given the employees' skill levels and scheduling policies in effect, the most desirable work shifts are assigned fairly and equitably.
- Comply with all applicable laws and company policies. This includes scheduling minors under 18 years of age according to restrictions imposed by the Fair Labor Standards Act. Note: Those under 18 must obtain a work permit unless they've graduated from high school or have obtained a General Education Development (GED) diploma. Only one work permit may be issued at a time, and it can be denied or revoked if the minor does not remain in good standing with the school. Generally, minors are restricted in the number

FIGURE 11.7

Sample Employee Schedule

ANYTOWN STEAK HOUSE

From	1-Oct	thru	7-Oct				
Area/Employee	**Monday** 10/1	**Tuesday** 10/2	**Wednesday** 10/3	**Thursday** 10/4	**Friday** 10/5	**Saturday** 10/6	**Sunday** 10/7	**Total Hours**
Dining Room								
Janet F.	7:00a–1:00p	OFF	7:00a–1:00p	OFF	7:00a–1:00p	1:00p–8:30p	7:00a–1:00p	29.0
Anthony H.	OFF	7:00a–1:00p	1:00p–8:30p	7:00a–1:00p	1:00p–8:30p	7:00a–1:00p	OFF	30.5
Bill C.	7:00a–1:00p	OFF	7:00a–1:00p	OFF	7:00a–1:00p	1:00p–8:30p	7:00a–1:00p	29.0
Mike C.	1:00p–8:30p	7:00a–1:00p	OFF	7:00a–1:00p	1:00p–8:30p	7:00a–1:00p	OFF	30.5
Talisha C.	1:00p–8:30p	1:00p–8:30p	1:00p–8:30p	1:00p–8:30p	OFF	OFF	OFF	28.0
Ray S.	OFF	OFF	OFF	OFF	1:00p–8:30p	1:00p–8:30p	Vacation	14.0
Dan M.	OFF	1:00p–8:30p	OFF	1:00p–8:30p	1:00p–8:30p	1:00p–8:30p	1:00p–8:30p	35.0
Kitchen								
Lorenzo T.	OFF	6:00a–2:30p	6:00a–2:30p	6:00a–2:30p	1:00p–9:00p	1:00p–9:00p	OFF	39.0
Ron C.	6:00a–2:30p	OFF	OFF	OFF	6:00a–2:30p	6:00a–2:30p	6:00a–2:30p	32.0
Arthur A.	1:00p–9:00p	1:00p–9:00p	OFF	OFF	11:30a–8:00p	11:30a–8:00p	1:00p–9:30p	39.0
Shanna A.	OFF	OFF	1:00p–9:00p	1:00p–9:00p	OFF	OFF	OFF	15.0
Dishroom								
George G.	11:00a–4:00p	OFF	OFF	11:00a–4:00p	11:00a–4:00p	11:00a–4:00p	11:00a–4:00p	22.5
Janna A.	OFF	11:00a–4:00p	11:00a–4:00p	OFF	5:00p–10:30p	5:00p–10:30p	OFF	19.0
Bob D.	5:00p–10:30p	5:30p–10:30p	5:00p–10:30p	OFF	OFF	5:00p–10:30p	5:00p–10:30p	25.0
Cindy T.	OFF	OFF	OFF	5:00p–10:30p	5:00p–10:30p	OFF	OFF	10.0
Manager								
Shingi R.	On	On	On	On	On	On	OFF	6 Days
Sam V.	On	On	OFF	OFF	On	On	On	5 Days
Herman Z.	OFF	OFF	On	On	On	On	On	5 Days
Prepared 9/26		**Approved By**		J Davids				

Adapted from Ninemeier, J., and Hayes, D. (2006). *Restaurant Operations Management*. Pearson Education, Inc.

WEB AT WORK!

Creating an employee schedule shouldn't require a significant amount of time. To learn about electronic scheduling systems, check out:

www.schedulesource.com

or

www.asgardsystems.com

of hours they can work as well as when they can work. (Additional information about the legal aspects of human resources management was presented in Chapter 3.)

- Communicate scheduling decisions in a timely manner. The employees' work schedules dictate a significant portion of their personal lives, so schedules should be made available at a reasonable time.

DISTRIBUTING THE SCHEDULE   Employee schedules should be distributed quickly and accurately. In many restaurants, schedules are posted in one or more central areas. In others, managers include the schedule with paychecks. Increasingly, managers e-mail schedules, make them available on the restaurant's intranet system, or post them on the web.

When work schedules must be modified, changes should be communicated to affected employees as quickly as possible. In some restaurants, employees who get to work at the scheduled time but aren't needed or are sent home early receive a minimum pay regardless of the time they actually worked. You must know your restaurant's policies before making schedule adjustments and communicate schedule adjustments and modifications appropriately.

Managers should monitor employee schedules carefully and adjust them for:

- Significant changes in forecasted business volumes
- Unanticipated employee separations
- Employee **call-ins** or **no-shows**
- Unanticipated changes in operating hours or work assignments

Call-in

Employees who are scheduled to work but notify their managers that they are not coming to work.

No-show

Employees who are scheduled to work but don't report for their assigned shift or notify their managers that they are not coming to work.

©nyul/Fotolia

Technology provides new ways for restaurant employees to learn their work schedules.

> ### WEB AT WORK!
>
> Some restaurant managers develop employee schedules and place them on the Internet so their employees can see them on a 24/7 basis. To learn about this type of program, go to:
>
> http://www.workschedule.net

STEP 5: EVALUATE LABOR CONTROL RESULTS   The final step in the labor cost control system involves the evaluation of its financial and guest service results.

Meeting Financial Goals

Restaurant managers who have developed one or more specific labor productivity measurements can evaluate actual operating results against schedule plans to determine if their goals were met. The amount by which actual performance differs from the goal or plan is called a **variance**.

Variance

The difference between planned and actual operating results.

For example, assume that LaToya anticipates $50,000 in revenue with a 30% labor cost: $15,000 ($50,000 × .30 = $15,000) for a specific accounting period. She discovers that she did generate $50,000 in revenue, but she spent $ 20,000 on labor, resulting in a 40% labor cost: ($20,000/$50,000 = 40%). LaToya can compute the labor cost variance in dollars and/or a percentage:

Dollar Variance:

$20,000 actual cost (−) $15,000 targeted costs = $5,000 negative variance

Percent Variance:

40% actual labor cost percentage (−) 30% targeted labor cost percentage = 10% negative variance

It's also possible to have a positive variance. Consider another manager who anticipates the same $50,000 in revenue and a $15,000 labor cost. While the revenue goal was attained, actual labor costs were only $13,000. Let's look at the variance in dollars and percentage:

Dollar Variance:

$15,000 targeted cost − $13,000 actual cost = $2,000 positive variance

Percent Variance:

Planned cost: $\frac{\$15,000 \text{ labor cost}}{\$50,000 \text{ revenue}}$ = 30% targeted labor cost percentage

Actual cost: $\frac{\$13,000 \text{ labor cost}}{\$50,000 \text{ revenue}}$ = 26% actual labor cost

30% − 26% = 4% positive variance

There's generally some variance between forecasted and actual operating results because it's very difficult to estimate the exact amount of revenue to be achieved and labor to be utilized. A small variance may be considered insignificant. For example, a variance of $5.00 in payroll costs that's part of an estimated payroll of $10,000 is irrelevant. By contrast, if variances in business volume and/or labor costs are very significant, managers must investigate that variance and take corrective action.

Figure 11.8 shows how restaurant managers can compute the estimated labor cost for the schedule they create. The actual labor cost to which the estimated (scheduled) labor cost is compared is available from the restaurant's payroll records generated by accounting personnel or the payroll processing company it uses. Data used is for the employee schedule shown in Figure 11.7. Note: Times for management staff aren't included because they're salaried (fixed cost) personnel.

Variances can be computed by comparing the actual payroll cost or labor hours used to the estimated costs/hours scheduled (see Figure 11.7). As noted earlier, estimated and actual results can be assessed by position (for example, servers and cooks), for meal periods (breakfast and lunch) and/or for days of the week. Variations between scheduled

FIGURE 11.8

Estimated Total Payroll Cost per Shift (Meal Period)

ANYTOWN STEAK HOUSE

Date: _____ October 1 _____

Employee	Schedule (AM 12–11, PM 12–12)	Total Hours	Hourly Rate	Total Pay
Dining Room				
Janet F.	(7 AM – 2 PM)	7	$ 6.25	$ 43.75
Sarah H.		---		
Bill C.	(7 AM – 2 PM)	7	6.75	47.25
Mike C.	(2 PM – 9 PM)	7	7.00	49.00
Talisha C.	(2 PM – 9 PM)	7	7.00	49.00
Ray S.		---		
Kylie M.				
Kitchen				
Lorenzo T.		---		
Ron C.	(6 AM – 2 PM)	8	10.50	84.00
Arthur A.	(1 PM – 8.5 PM)	7.5	12.50	93.75
Shanna A.		---		
Dishroom				
George G.	(1 PM – 5.5 PM)	4.5	7.00	31.50
Janna A.		----		
Bob D.	(6 PM – 11 PM)	5	7.25	36.25
Cindy T.		---		
		Total Labor Cost/Shift		**$ 434.50**

NOTE: "Total Pay" is payroll costs; it is not total labor costs because, for example, fringe benefit costs are not included.

Adapted from Ninemeier, J., and Hayes, D. (2006). *Restaurant Operations Management.* Pearson Education, Inc.

(expected) results and actual results will likely occur. It's the manager's responsibility to evaluate these differences to determine their cause and to take corrective action as needed. Note: Details about variance analysis and the corrective action process will be presented in Chapter 13.

Meeting Service Goals

Restaurant managers should have service goals as well as financial goals. For example, a quick-service restaurant with a targeted labor cost percentage will also likely have goals relating to the number of drive-through, take-out, and counter orders to be processed in a specified period (for example, 10 minutes or one hour).

If too few employees are available to meet the needs of drive-through guests, the restaurant won't meet its service goals even if its labor cost percent is *below* the target set by the manager. The reason: The lower-than-targeted labor cost percentage came at the expense of guest service levels.

While some restaurants may not find it as easy to measure service levels, the number of guest complaints, the average time required for preparing and serving items listed on a single guest check and the number of guests assigned to each server are some ways to determine if measurable service goals have been met.

The Operating Results Summary Chart (Figure 11.9) shows the possible combinations that managers face as they evaluate effectiveness in meeting realistic financial and service goals.

Management of Salaried Labor

Many restaurant managers faced with rising labor costs and other operating challenges consider whether some employees should be paid a salary rather than a wage. Their reasoning: Employees can then work more than 40 hours a week without being paid overtime. However, there are strictly-enforced laws governing precisely who can be legally considered salaried employees. Regardless of legal definitions, managers should also recall that staff members quickly learn if they're being manipulated.

FIGURE 11.9

**Operating Results Summary
Chart**

Review each of the four types of operating results below. Consider the future strategies that apply to the outcome that best represents your operation.

Outcome 1   **Goals Met?**
Financial Goals Met   ☐ Yes
Service Goals Met   ☐ Yes

Future Strategy: Congratulations! Continue to monitor your results. Celebrate your success with staff members to let them know how well they are doing.

Outcome 2   **Goals Met?**
Financial Goals Met   ☐ Yes
Service Goals Met   ☐ No

Future Strategy: Don't allow service levels to suffer even though you are meeting your financial goals. Review your staffing patterns to identify "under-staffed" time periods that caused poor service levels. Review your service-related training procedures for weaknesses.

Outcome 3   **Goals Met?**
Financial Goals Met   ☐ No
Service Goals Met   ☐ Yes

Future Strategy: Overstaffing may ensure that you meet your service goals, but the financial success of the operation is also critical. Study your schedule for possible overstaffing. Ask your employees for ideas about how to better serve guests. Start now!

Outcome 4   **Goals Met?**
Financial Goals Met   ☐ No
Service Goals Met   ☐ No

Future Strategy: You are not alone. Many managers find themselves in this position when they take over a new or existing operation and/or when financial and/or service goals are increased. Don't panic. Build employee schedules that meet your targeted financial goals and then observe staff carefully to identify service bottlenecks. Intensify your training efforts to help employees meet their service-related goals. Monitor your improvements!

Adapted from Ninemeier, J., and Hayes, D. (2006). *Restaurant Operations Management.* Pearson Education, Inc.

Legal Distinctions

Compensation for salaried employees cannot fluctuate based on the quality or quantity of work. If a salaried employee works only a part of the day, compensation cannot be reduced for missing part of that day. However, in keeping with appropriate company policies, salaried employees may receive reduced pay for missing an entire day for personal reasons. In addition, if the employee is paid a salary, he or she must meet certain defined requirements. For restaurants, these are:

- At least 60% of an employee's primary duties must involve managing the business or a department within it
- The employee must regularly direct the work of two or more other employees
- The employee must have the authority to hire, fire, or recommend these courses of action

ALL IN A DAY'S WORK (11.2)

"It was just awful," said Mrs. Kline, to Carlos, the owner and manager of the Mexican Cantina restaurant.

"I made dinner reservations for myself and four of my friends for tonight, and everything went wrong! It took us 40 minutes to get a table, and when we finally got seated, it took 15 minutes to place our drink order!"

"I'm sorry," said Carlos.

"That's not all," replied Mrs. Kline. "It took a long time to get our food and longer to get our dinner check after we'd finished!"

1. What can happen in a restaurant if too few staff members are available and what are the hidden costs of having too few servers?
2. If you were Carlos, what would you do about Mrs. Kline?

> ## GREEN AT WORK
>
> Restaurant managers must address numerous concerns and priorities at the same time. For example, in this chapter, you're learning about the importance of controlling food and labor costs. We have already reviewed the priorities for food safety concerns and for emphasizing food quality, and the need to consistently attain guest service standards is a theme of almost every chapter.
>
> Each chapter also addresses the issue of restaurant managers and their team implementing environmentally friendly and sustainable work practices. You've learned that many guests are concerned about the environment, and that this trend will very likely continue. You've learned that many "green" practices can be very cost-effective and an emphasis on sustainability is the "right thing to do" because successful restaurants are contributing members of their communities.
>
> An organized discussion of restaurant management requires that topics be presented one at a time. Restaurant managers must think about how to overcome challenges and achieve a wide variety—all at once. What goals take priority in the day-to-day decision making: financial, guest-service, quality, "green" or others?
>
> As a practical example, one of this book's authors worked in a food service operation in which management consistently emphasized cost control and quality. He remembers retrieving the leftover greens from the previous day's salad bar and seeing that some of the lettuce and spinach pieces were starting to turn brown. What did the restaurant manager want him to do at that moment? Use the salad greens to save money or discard them because of quality concerns?
>
> What should be the most important priorities of the restaurant manager? The practical answer really violates the definition of "priority" (that which is most important) because the correct answer is "many things—and all at the same time"!

Violations of these regulations can subject a restaurant to significant penalties and fines so requirements must be carefully followed.

Scheduling Salaried Employees

Salaried employees, like their hourly paid counterparts, may be assigned a work schedule that can be enforced in the same manner as it is for hourly workers. If the salary for an employee is computed at less than a 40-hour week, that employee will be eligible for time and one-half for any

This beverage manager also works some bartender shifts. Whether he should be paid a salary or an hourly rate may depend upon a variety of labor law-related factors.

©yamix/Shutterstock

| | **WEB AT WORK!** |

To read a detailed description of requirements placed upon employers of salaried workers and to learn the definition of a salaried employee, go to the Federal Government's Department of Labor (DOL) website at:

http://www.dol.gov/dol/siteindex.htm

Enter "salary" in the site's search box.

hours worked beyond 40 hours per week. For example, if an employee is hired at a weekly salary of $350.00 and, if it's understood that this is compensation for a regular workweek of 35 hours, the employee's regular rate of pay is $10.00 ($350.00 (÷) 35 hours = $10.00). If the employee works overtime (more than 35 hours weekly), he or she should receive $10.00 for each of the first 40 hours and $15.00 ($10.00 × 1.5= $15.00) for each additional hour worked over 40 hours.

Many salaried employees are hired to work 40 or more hours weekly. Restaurant managers should not schedule salaried employees beyond a reasonable number of hours weekly even if they can do so because the inevitable result will be employee dissatisfaction, lessened productivity, burnout, and turnover.

MANAGING OTHER COSTS

This chapter has presented detailed information about food and labor costs because they're the largest category of expenses in most restaurants.

There are, however, numerous other types of costs that must be managed, and the process to do so involves the same basic strategies used to manage food and labor costs. It involves a budgeting process to estimate what these costs should be, an accounting process to determine the actual costs incurred, and a corrective action process to address variances. Note: Details about corrective action process will be presented in Chapter 13.

Restaurant owners, managers, and those with accounting knowledge must determine how costs will be categorized. Once identified, formats for budgeting, operating reports, and income statements can be developed.[*]

Variable Costs and Fixed Costs

Variable cost

A cost that changes in direct proportion to revenue.

Fixed cost

A cost that does not vary as revenue changes

One way to classify all costs is to consider whether they're variable or fixed. **Variable costs** are those that change in direct proportion to revenue, and **fixed costs** are those that don't vary as revenue changes. Note: Some fixed costs, such as insurance, taxes and salaries remain constant for an annual accounting period but may change from year-to-year when a new fixed cost amount is created. Other fixed costs, such as a mortgage, may remain constant for many years.

Cost of goods sold: food is an excellent example of a variable cost because this cost increases in direct proportion to revenue. Here's an example:

Assume that 25 steak sandwiches are sold with a food cost of $4.50 and a selling price of $14.25. The food cost percentage is:

$$\frac{\text{Food cost}}{\text{Food revenue}} = \frac{\$4.50 \times 25}{\$14.25 \times 25} = \frac{\$112.50}{\$356.25} = 31.6\% \text{ (rounded)}$$

Now let's assume that only 15 sandwiches are sold on the following day. The food cost percentage is:

$$\frac{\text{Food cost}}{\text{Food revenue}} = \frac{\$4.50 \times 15}{\$14.25 \times 15} = \frac{\$67.50}{\$213.75} = 31.6\% \text{ (rounded)}$$

---

[*]Note: one excellent source of information is the "Uniform System of Accounts for Restaurants" published by the National Restaurant Association.

As you see above, the food cost percentage for steak sandwiches will be 31.6% regardless of the number sold assuming that the standard recipe is followed and ingredient costs don't increase.

There are few restaurant costs that are truly variable; however, other examples typically include cost of goods sold: beverage and supplies such as disposable plates, napkins, or cups used in carry-out operations.

Labor, the other prime cost, is not a variable cost because it doesn't maintain a fixed relationship to revenue levels. For example, assume that a 30% labor cost is ideal for a restaurant when $10,000 in revenue is forecasted. If actual revenue is $10,500, the actual labor cost percentage will be lower than 30% because the fixed labor component (that paid for salaried staff) will be spread over a larger revenue base. Note: The reverse is also true: the actual labor cost percentage will be higher than planned when revenue is less than expected because the fixed labor will be spread over a smaller revenue base.

Common examples of fixed costs include salaries, expenses for rent and insurance, property taxes, interest expense, and depreciation expense.

Common Restaurant Costs

What kind of costs do most restaurants incur? Figure 11.10 summarizes common examples of restaurant costs.

While the cost categories listed in Figure 11.10 are common, the specific types of costs within each category depend more specifically on each property. For this reason **supporting schedules** are typically used to identify specific costs in each category. Consider, for example, "direct operating expenses" in Figure 11.10. Examples of costs that may be carried in this category are those for uniforms, laundry and dry-cleaning, linen rental, tableware and linen, kitchen utensils and production, and service supplies.

Busy restaurant managers cannot spend significant time addressing variances between budgeted and actual costs for each of these expense categories. Instead, they focus their attention on those expenses that create the most significant opportunities for financial savings. The process by which they do this will be addressed in Chapter 13.

FIGURE 11.10

Common Restaurant Costs

Cost of Sales (Food and Beverage Costs)
- Cost of goods sold: food
- Cost of goods sold: beverage

Operating Expenses (Nonproduct costs most impacted by management decisions)
- Salaries and wages
- Employee benefits
- Direct operating expenses
- Music and entertainment
- Marketing
- Utilities
- General and administrative expenses
- Repairs and maintenance
- Other income expenses

Other Costs (Costs not generally within managers' control)
- Occupancy costs
- Deprecation
- Interest
- Income tax

Restaurant Terms and Concepts

Work in Progress

1. What are practical ways to determine food and beverage transfer costs for cost of goods sold calculations?
2. How would you select the method of inventory valuation used in a restaurant?
3. Some properties share cost of goods sold information with their employees. What are the advantages and disadvantages of doing this?
4. This chapter's "Green At Work" discussion introduced the idea that a restaurant manager has many "priorities," basically all at the same time. Do you agree? Why or why not?
5. What do you think is the best productivity measure for evaluating a labor control system?
6. How can a restaurant manager use technology to control labor costs?
7. Labor has replaced food as the most costly expense of many restaurants. What can restaurant managers do to control labor costs without sacrificing quality standards?
8. Some restaurant managers feel that full-time employees should receive preferential treatment over part-time employees when weekly schedules are developed. What are the advantages and disadvantages to doing this?
9. Some managers think that long hours are a "given" in the restaurant business. How many hours would you expect salaried members of your management staff to work?
10. Suppose your restaurant used one propane gas tank each month for three months during the summer to fuel a barbeque grill on the outside terrace. Also assume that the cost was $15.00 per tank ($45.00 total cost for the year). Should a separate cost in the property's supporting schedule for utilities be established? Why or why not?

12
Managing Revenue

Chapter Outline

Revenue Analysis
    Total Revenue Indicators
    Guest Check Average Indicators
    Revenue Variance Indicators

Menu Analysis
    Menu Pricing Basics
    Menu Engineering

Revenue Control
    Importance of Revenue Control
    Technology and Revenue Control
    Revenue Control Systems
    Minimizing Guest Theft
    Minimizing Employee Theft

Learning Objectives

After carefully studying and reading the information in this chapter, you will be able to:

1. Review procedures to conduct a source of revenue analysis.

2. Explain how to use menu engineering to analyze menu profitability and popularity.

3. Discuss tactics to record and protect revenues.

IN THIS CHAPTER

Restaurants are in business to make money. To do so, restaurant managers must control costs and revenue. While you have learned much about cost control in this text, this chapter is the first that explores procedures to manage revenue.

Fortunately, point-of-sale (POS) systems provide a significant amount of revenue information. Effective restaurant managers analyze revenue to learn about past performance and to plan changes to improve future operating results. This chapter discusses common revenue analysis procedures.

The menu is integral to revenue control. It informs guests about menu items' selling prices, and these prices impact the profitability of each item. Effectively designed menus also influence the popularity (sales) of profitable items. Details about menu analysis will be explored here so that you can learn how to use these procedures.

Restaurant managers must plan, implement, and monitor systems to control revenue collected from guests until it is deposited in the property's bank account. This goal is best attained if you implement the three major components of a revenue control system: 1) determine the amount of money owed, 2) collect the money owed, and 3) secure these funds until they're deposited. A discussion of this three-part revenue control system concludes the chapter.

REVENUE ANALYSIS

This chapter details procedures to manage revenue. The term "revenue," relates to the money that a restaurant receives from the sale of its products and services. However, other terms are also commonly used and can cause confusion. For example, some managers use "sales" interchangeably with revenue, while others consider sales to mean the number of units sold ("We had sales of 35 sandwiches today."). Some managers think income and revenue have the same definition, while others think of income as profit. In this chapter, the term "revenue" will represent money received from guests for the products and services they purchase.

While technology makes revenue data available on a real-time basis, many restaurant managers analyze revenue at month's end. The POS system data helps to develop income statements; that information can also be compared with budget estimates (a topic that will be addressed in Chapter 13).

Revenue information can be compared more frequently than monthly. For example, key indicators such as guest check average might be reviewed daily and weekly if more timely corrective actions are of interest. Special situations such as the use of a new menu or advertising campaign highlighting specific menu items may also create the need for more frequent revenue analysis.

Let's explore three general types of key revenue indicators that can be generated by the revenue analysis process.

Total Revenue Indicators

Day-part

A segment of the day that represents a change in menu and customer response patterns; for example, the time during which breakfast or lunch menus are offered.

Every restaurant manager wants to know the total revenue generated during the month, week, and day. Some may also want that information for the **day-part** or even by the hour.

Figure 12.1 reviews examples of total revenue indicators that can help managers with decision making. Note: Each calculation can be made for a month, week, day, or other time period.

Total revenue calculations may be easier to understand when the percentage of revenue of each type is determined. Then the calculation is simple:

$$\text{Revenue from source} \div \text{Total revenue} = \text{Revenue source contribution percentage}$$

For example, to determine the percentage of total revenue generated from dine-in operations in Figure 12.1 C, the calculation would be:

$$\frac{\text{Revenue \%}}{\text{Dine-In Operations}} = \frac{\text{Revenue from Dine-In Operations}}{\text{Total Revenue}} = \frac{\$47,500}{\$96,000} = 49.5\% \text{ (rounded)}$$

In the above example, almost 50% of the restaurant's total revenue is generated from dine-in operations.

Guest Check Average Indicators

A guest check average is the amount of money spent by an average guest during one visit. The calculation is easy:

$$\text{Total food \& beverage revenue} \div \text{Number of guests served} = \text{Guest check average}$$

Assume that Figure 12.1 B represents the total à la carte dining room revenue for the month, and that 6,065 guests were served. The monthly guest check average is:

$$\frac{\text{Total Food \& Beverage Revenue}}{\text{Number of Guests Served}} = \frac{\$96,000}{6,065 \text{ Guests}} = \$15.85 \text{ (rounded) guest check average}$$

Figure 12.2 shows common variations of the guest check average indicator.

FIGURE 12.1
Common Total Revenue
Indicators

A. Total Revenue from Restaurant Operations

Purpose: To separate revenue by products/services sold:

	Example
Food revenue	$780,000
Beverage revenue	$210,000
Other revenue*	$35,000
Total revenue	$1,025,000

*May include souvenirs, banquet room rental, or audio/visual charges for meetings conducted at the property.

B. Total Revenue by Location

Purpose: To separate revenue generated in separate areas within the restaurant:

	Example
À la carte dining room	$97,000
Banquet room	$40,000
Lounge/bar	$19,000
Total revenue	$156,000

C. Total Revenue by Type of Guest

Purpose: To separate revenue by the type of services purchased by guests:

	Example
Dine-in	$47,500
Carryout	$8,200
Drive-through	$16,800
Banquet	$14,000
Bar/lounge	$9,500
Total revenue	$96,000

Revenue Variance Indicators

Variances between budgeted (expected) and actual revenues typically occur; these are key revenue indicators for many restaurant managers. Figure 12.3 presents three examples. In each case, forecasted revenue from the budget (Column 2) is compared to the revenue actually received (Column 3); the differences are expressed in dollars (Column 4) and as a percentage difference from the forecasted amount (Column 5).

Revenue variances can be caused by fewer guests and/or lower guest check averages. Restaurant managers can easily determine this; the knowledge will be helpful as they plan corrective actions.

Let's review situation B in Figure 12.3. Note that the actual revenue for lunch was $3,600 less than forecasted. What's the reason?

If the lunch check average is $12.75, this suggests that 2,235 guests were expected to be served during March:

$$\underset{\text{Forecasted revenue}}{\$28,500} \div \underset{\text{Check average}}{\$12.75} = 2,235 \text{ Guests}$$

Analysis of POS data indicates that 1,995 persons were actually served. The check average for these guests is easy to determine.

$$\underset{\text{Actual revenue}}{\$24,900} \div \underset{\text{Guests}}{1,995} = \$12.48$$

FIGURE 12.2

Common Guest Check Average Indicators

A. Guest Check Average (Meal)

Purpose: To determine the guest check average for each meal period.

Assume the following information for one week and use the guest check average equation:

Meal Period	Total Revenue	Number of Guests	Guest Check Average
Breakfast	$9,500	985	$9.64*
Lunch	$18,400	1,225	$15.02
Dinner	$27,095	1,231	$22.01

*Total breakfast revenue ($9,500)/number of guests (985) = $9.64 guest check average

B. Guest Check Average (Location)

Purpose: To determine the guest check average in each location.

$$\text{Guest check average (location)} = \frac{Revenue \text{ Per Location}}{\text{Number of Guests Served}}$$

Assume the following for one day:

Location	Total Revenue	Number of Guests	Guest Check Average
À la carte dining room	$1,710	120	$14.25*
Banquet room	$1,112	65	$17.11 (actual is $17.108)

*Total à la carte revenue ($1,710)/no. of guests (120) = $14.25 guest check average

Note: Restaurant managers typically compare guest check averages by location to similar calculations for different time periods rather than comparing them between locations. This is important because the menus and item selling prices are likely different.

C. Guest Check Average (Guest Type)

Purpose: To learn the guest check average based upon the type of food services purchased.

$$\text{Guest check average} = \frac{Revenue \text{ by Type of Guest}}{\text{Number of Guests}}$$

Assume the following for one month:

Type of Guest	Total Revenue	Number of Guests	Check Average
Dine-in	$30,375	2,250	$13.50*
Carryout	$11,288	1,050	$10.75
Banquet	$17,100	1,200	$14.25

*Example: Total revenue for dine-in guests ($30,375)/number of guests (2,250) = $13.50

In this example, the check average was approximately the same as in previous periods, but the number of guests visiting for lunch was lower. What marketing tactics might be useful to increase guest counts?

Now let's assume that POS data indicates that 2,210 luncheon guests were actually served in March. The guest check average is calculated as follows:

$$\underset{\text{Actual revenue}}{\$24,900} \div \underset{\text{Guests}}{2,210} = \$11.25$$

The manager now knows that the number of guests served was about as expected, but the guest check average was lower. What can be done to increase the check average?

FIGURE 12.3
Common Revenue Variance Indicators

A. Revenue Variance (Location)

Purpose: To indicate the variance between budgeted (expected) and actual revenues by location.

Assume the following for February, 20xx:

Location (1)	Forecasted Revenue (2)	Actual Revenue (3)	Variance (4)	Variance (5)
À la carte dining room	$90,000	$94,000	$4,000*	4.4%
Banquet room	$54,000	$48,000	−$6,000	−11.1%**

$$\$94,000 - \$90,000 = \$4,000$$

*Example: Actual revenue − Forecasted revenue = Revenue variance

**Revenue percentage differences are calculated as follows:

$$\frac{Actual\ \text{Revenue} - Forecasted\ \text{Revenue}}{Forecasted\ \text{Revenue}}$$

Example for banquet room: $\dfrac{\$48,000 - \$54,000}{\$54,000} = -11.1\%$ (column 5)

B. Revenue Variance (Meal)

Assume the following for March, 20xx:

Meal Period (1)	Revenue Forecasted (2)	Revenue Actual (3)	Variance (4)	Variance (5)
Lunch	$28,500	$24,900	−$3,600*	−12.6%
Dinner	$42,500	$44,500	$2,000	4.7%

$$\$24,900 - \$28,500 = -\$3,600$$

*Actual Revenue − Forecasted Revenue = Revenue Difference

Revenue percentage differences are calculated as follows:

$$\frac{Actual\ \text{Revenue} - Forecasted\ \text{Revenue}}{Forecasted\ \text{Revenue}}$$

**Example for dinner: $\dfrac{\$44,500 - \$42,500}{\$42,500} = 4.7\%$

C. Revenue Variance (Guest Type)

Assume the following for the week of July 16, 20xx:

Guest Type (1)	Revenue Forecasted (2)	Revenue Actual (3)	Variance (4)	Variance (5)
Dine-in	$8,400	$8,150	−$250*	−3.0%
Carryout	$2,700	$2,400	−$300	−11.1%**

*$8,150 − $8,400 = −$250

Actual revenue − Forecasted revenue = Revenue difference

**Example for carryout guests:

$$\frac{Actual\ \text{Revenue} - Forecasted\ \text{Revenue}}{Forecasted\ \text{Revenue}} = \frac{\$2,400 - \$2,700}{\$2,700} = -11.1\%\ (\text{column 5})$$

The best restaurant managers monitor their guest check averages and know how to influence them.

MENU ANALYSIS

Restaurant revenue is directly affected by the sale price of menu items. The prices charged must help the property meet its financial goals and provide value for their guests.

Menu Pricing Basics

Restaurant managers should incorporate the restaurant's financial plans into selling price decisions. Methods emphasizing mark-up pricing and contribution margin pricing are objective and address financial concerns.

Mark-up factor

An objective menu pricing method that considers an item's fair "share" of all costs and desired profit.

MARK-UP PRICING METHOD A **mark-up factor** can be applied to the food costs of a menu item to recover the item's fair "share" of all costs and desired profit.

One common approach involves three steps:

1. Determine food costs for the item(s) being priced.
2. Determine the mark-up.
3. Establish a **base selling price** by multiplying the food cost by the mark-up.

Base selling price

The benchmark selling price of a menu item calculated by use of an objective pricing method.

Note: A base selling price is not necessarily the final selling price. Rather, it is a starting point from which other factors must be assessed, including guest value, supply and demand, production volume concerns, and competitors' prices.

Here's how the food cost mark-up pricing method can be used:

Step 1 **Determine food costs.** Assume that a chicken dinner has a food cost of $3.32. This cost represents the total food costs for all items making up the "chicken dinner" (chicken entrée, salad, potato, and vegetable, for example) when prepared according to applicable standard recipes that have been costed (see Chapter 5) using current ingredient costs.

Step 2 **Determine the mark-up.** One approach uses the planned food cost percentage from the operating budget. Menu items priced, on average, to yield the budgeted food cost percentage create a foundation to generate revenue sufficient to cover food and all other costs and budgeted profit requirements. For example, assume:

- Budgeted food revenues: $875,000
- Budgeted food costs: $325,000
- Budgeted food cost percentage: 37.1% (food costs ÷ food revenues)

A mark-up can now be calculated:

$$\frac{1}{Budgeted \text{ Food Cost Percentage}} = \frac{1}{37.1} = 2.7\% \text{ (rounded)}$$

Step 3 **Establish a base selling price.** Multiply the food cost to make the chicken dinner by the mark-up:

$$\underset{\text{(Ingredient cost)}}{\$3.32} \times \underset{\text{(Multiplier)}}{2.7} = \underset{\text{(Base selling price)}}{\$8.96}$$

If this base selling price appears reasonable, the chicken dinner is sold for about $9.00.

CONTRIBUTION MARGIN METHOD   In Chapter 5, you learned that an item's contribution margin is found by subtracting the item's total food costs from its selling price. This becomes the amount the item "contributes" to nonfood costs and profit.

Two steps are used in contribution margin pricing:

1. Determine the average contribution margin per guest.
2. Determine the base selling price for the menu item and then add the average contribution margin per guest to the item's standard food cost.

For example, assume that the approved operating budget indicates that all non-food costs in a budget period will be $395,000. The operation's profit goal for the period is $50,000, and 85,000 guests are expected to be served during the budget period:

Step 1 **Determine the average contribution margin per guest:** Divide all nonfood costs plus profit by the number of expected guests.

$$\frac{\text{(Nonfood costs)} + \text{profit}}{\text{Number of expected guests}} = \text{Average contribution margin per guest}$$

$$\frac{\$395,000 + \$50,000}{85,000} = \$5.24 \text{ (Rounded)}$$

Step 2 **Determine the base selling price for the menu item:** Add the average contribution margin per guest to the item's food cost. The base selling price for menu item with a $3.60 food cost would be $8.85:

$$\underset{\text{Food cost}}{\$3.60} + \underset{\text{Contribution margin}}{\$5.24} = \underset{\text{Base selling price}}{\$8.85 \text{ (rounded)}}$$

The contribution margin method is easy to use with information from the operating budget. It's practical when costs associated with serving each guest are basically the same, with the exception of variations in food costs. This method tends to reduce the range of selling prices on the menu since the only difference in selling price is reflected by differences in actual menu item food costs.

Managers should use the contribution margin method carefully. For example, one would probably not add $5.24 to the cost of an inexpensive hamburger sandwich as well as to an expensive steak. Remember that the required contribution margin is an average. The add-on will likely be less for inexpensive items and more for the most expensive items so the mark-up on food costs will average the required amount ($5.24).

The two objective pricing methods just discussed are easy to use because they incorporate financial information from the operating budget that must be developed for other purposes. Perhaps the most "challenging" calculation in all the above methods involves food cost. Standardized recipes must be pre-costed with current financial information. The need for standard recipes extends throughout all aspects of operating control, and costing them accurately and quickly has become easier with the use of recipe management software.

These menus have been carefully designed to sell items with the highest contribution margins, and the server has been trained in suggestive selling tactics.

Menu Engineering

Menu engineering

An evaluation method that attempts to maximize the sale of a menu's most popular and profitable items.

Competing menu items

Menu items that normally compete with each other as guests make their selection decisions.

Menu engineering helps restaurant managers to increase the popularity and profitability of their menu items.

Assume a menu has 10 **competing menu items**. If all items were equally popular, each would generate 10% of total sales (100% divided by 10 items = 10% per item).

Traditionally, menu item profitability focused on the food cost percentage of an item, with the belief that a lower food cost percentage yields a more profitable operation. However, the menu engineering model focuses attention on an item's contribution margin. Figure 12.4 illustrates the difference between the two concepts.

Let's look at Figure 12.4 more closely:

- Item A has a food cost of $3.50 and a selling price of $10.95. Its food cost percentage is 32.0% ($3.50 ÷ $10.95 = 32.0%) and its contribution margin is $7.45 ($10.95 [−] $3.50 = $7.45).
- Item B has a food cost of $8.00 and a selling price of $18.25. Its food cost percentage is 43.8% ($8.00 ÷ $18.25 = 43.8%), and its contribution margin is $10.25 ($18.25 [−] $8.00 = $10.25).
- Item C has a food cost of $12.50 and a selling price of $26.50. Its food cost percentage is 47.2% ($12.50 ÷ $26.50 = 47.2%), and its contribution margin is $14.00 ($26.50 [−] $12.50 = $14.00).

Item A has a lower food cost percentage (32.0%) than either Item B (43.8%) or Item C (47.2%). If the goal is to minimize food cost percentage, Item A is the best.

FIGURE 12.4

Maximize the Contribution Margin

Menu Item	Item Food Cost	Item Selling Price	Food Cost Percentage	Contribution Margin
Item A	$3.50	$10.95	32.0%	$7.45
Item B	$8.00	$18.25	43.8%	$10.25
Item C	$12.50	$26.50	47.2%	$14.00

Adapted from Ninemeier, J., and Hayes, D. (2006). *Restaurant Operations Management.* Pearson Education, Inc.

However, look at the contribution margins of the three items: Item A, with the lowest food cost percentage (32%), also has the lowest contribution margin ($7.45). By contrast, Item C, with the highest food cost percentage (47.2%), has the highest contribution margin ($14.00). Remember that the contribution margin is the amount that remains from an item's selling price after deducting its food cost. Therefore, Item C is the best item to sell because there is $6.55 more remaining from the revenue generated from the sale of Item C than from the sale of Item A after product costs are deducted from selling price. This additional $6.55 can be used to pay for all costs and to make a larger "contribution" to the property's profit goals.

It should be clear that the goal of restaurant managers should be to maximize the contribution margins of their menus, rather than minimize a menu's food cost percentage.

Figure 12.5 shows a worksheet that can be used to manually evaluate restaurant menus. While software programs are now available to assist them in the process, restaurant managers should understand the basic concepts used to evaluate their menus even when they use automated systems.

Let's see how the menu engineering worksheet in Figure 12.5 is produced.

- *Column A (Menu Item)* lists competing menu items. The menu in this example has four competing items. While few restaurants offer only four competing items, this simplified example illustrates major menu engineering concepts. Since menu engineering analyzes competing items, restaurants with different breakfast, lunch, and dinner menus require a separate analysis for each.
- *Column B (Number Sold)* reports the number sold of each item in Column A. Data is from sales history information, which compiles sales over a previous fiscal period and can be easily retrieved from an operation's POS system.
- *Box M* adds together all menu items sold during the analysis period. Note that 1,890 portions of the four menu items in Column A were sold.
- *Column C (Sales %)* indicates the percentage of total sales (Box N) represented by each menu item (in Column A). Note that 270 portions of tuna salad plate were sold

FIGURE 12.5

Menu Engineering Worksheet

(A) Menu Item	(B) Number Sold	(C) Sales %	(D) Food Cost	(E) Sales Price	(F) Item CM	(G) Total Food Cost	(H) Total Revenues	(I) Item CM	(J) CM Type	(K) Sales % Type	(L) Menu Item Classification
Tuna salad plate	270	14.3	$3.25	$7.25	$4.00	$877.50	$1957.50	$1080.00	Low	Low	Dog
Beef stew	490	25.9	$4.25	$8.50	$4.25	$2082.50	$4165.00	$2082.50	Low	High	Plow horse
Fried chicken	810	42.9	$5.15	$9.75	$4.60	$4171.50	$7897.50	$3726.00	High	High	Star
Sirloin steak	320	16.9	$8.25	$13.50	$5.25	$2640.00	$4320.00	$1680.00	High	Low	Puzzle
	(M)					(N)	(O)	(P)			
Column Total	1890					$9771.50	$18,340.00	$8568.50			

Restaurant: _____   Date of Analysis: _____

Meal Period: ❏ Breakfast   ❏ Lunch   ❏ Dinner

Additional Computations: $Q = M/N$ — $4.53; R (Popularity) = 100% ÷ No. items × 70% — 17.5%

Adapted from Ninemeier, J., and Hayes, D. (2006). *Restaurant Operations Management.* Pearson Education, Inc.

(see Column B). This represents (in Column C) 14.3% of the total items (Box M): 270 portions (÷) 1,890 portions sold equals 14.3% of all items sold.

- *Column D (Food Cost)* is the per-portion cost for each menu item in Column A when (a) items are prepared according to standard recipes and (b) when the recipes have been pre-costed with current ingredient costs. One portion of tuna salad plate (Column A) has a food cost of $3.25 (Column D) when it's prepared with accurately costed standardized recipes.

- *Column E (Sales Price)* is the selling price listed on the menu. The selling price of tuna salad plate (Column A) is $7.25 (Column E).

- *Column F (Item CM)* reports the contribution margin (item selling price [−] food cost) for each item in Column A. Tuna salad plate has a contribution margin (Column F) of $4.00 (selling price [$7.25] minus its food cost [$3.25] = $4.00 contribution margin).

- *Column G (Total Food Cost)* indicates the total food cost required to produce all portions of each menu item. For example, 270 servings of tuna salad plate were sold (see Column B). Each portion has a $3.25 food cost (see Column D). The total food cost for all portions of tuna salad plate was $877.50 (in Column G: 270 portions [×] $3.25).

- *Box N* indicates the total food cost incurred to produce all portions of all menu items. The total food cost to produce all 1,890 items (Box M) is $9,771.50 (the sum of Column G).

- *Column H (Total Revenues)* tells the total revenue from the sale of all menu items. Since 270 servings of tuna salad plate were sold (Column B) at a per-portion sales price of $7.25 (Column E), the total revenue generated is $1,957.50 (270 portions [×] $7.25 = $1,957.50).

- *Box O* indicates the sum of all revenue generated from all menu items. In this example, $18,340.00 was generated from the sale of all 1,890 menu items (in Box M).

- *Column I (Item CM)* indicates the total contribution margin from the sale of the menu items. Tuna salad plate generated a total contribution margin of $1,080.00: menu revenue ($1,957.50 in Column H) less total food cost ($877.50 in Column G).

- *Box P* indicates the total contribution margin from all menu items. In this example, the 1,890 menu items sold (Box M) generated a total contribution margin of $8,568.50.

- *Box Q* indicates the average contribution margin generated from all menu items. To calculate this number, the total menu contribution margin ($8,568.50 in Box P) is divided by the total number of meals (1,890 in Box M) and equals $4.53. Menu planners now have a "definition" of profitability for this menu: they would most like to sell those items with a contribution margin of $4.53 or more. Note: This is often referred to as the "**seat tax**."

- *Box R (Popularity)* is used to calculate the "popularity" factor for the menu. Note: The menu engineering model defines "popularity" to be 70% of expected sales. In our example, there are four menu items. If each were equally popular, it would represent 25% of all sales (100% ÷ 4 = 25%). However, menu engineering defines a popular item as one that sells at least 70% of its expected sales percentage (25% [×] 70% = 17.5%). Restaurant managers analyzing this menu would now know the most popular items. Popular items are those that have a sales percentage (Column C) of 17.5% or higher.

- *Column J (CM Type)* indicates whether the contribution margin of each item in Column A is lower or higher than the average contribution margin in Box Q. Tuna salad plate has an item contribution margin (Column F) of $4.00, which is lower than the average contribution margin ($4.53 in Box Q); it's listed as a low contribution margin item in Column J. By contrast, fried chicken has an item contribution margin of $4.60 (Column F), which is higher than the average contribution margin ($4.53 in Box Q). It's listed as a high contribution margin in Column J.

- *Column K (Sales % Type)* indicates whether the popularity of each menu item is higher or lower than the menu's average popularity. For example, tuna salad plate has a sales percentage of 14.3% (see Column C). This is lower than the menu's popularity index (17.5% in Box R). It's reported to have a low sales percentage in Column K. By contrast, fried chicken has a sales percentage of 42.9% (see Column C), which is higher than the menu's popularity requirement (17.5% in Box R). As a result, it's reported to have a high sales percentage in Column K.

Seat tax

The contribution margin of a menu item or (in menu engineering) the weighted average contribution margin for all items sold during the period under study.

- *Column L (Menu Item Classification)* names each menu item in Column A. The traditional names assigned by menu engineering for each classification are:
  - *Plow horse.* Unprofitable (low contribution margin) but popular (high sales percentage) items; beef stew is a plow horse.
  - *Puzzle.* Profitable (high contribution margin) but unpopular (low sales percentage) items; sirloin steak is a puzzle.
  - *Dog.* Unprofitable (low contribution margin) and unpopular (low sales percentage) items; tuna salad plate is a dog.
  - *Star.* Profitable (high contribution margin) and popular (high sales percentage) items; fried chicken is a star.

Restaurant managers can use information about each menu item's profitability and popularity to make decisions about menu planning and design. Here are some tactics to manage each type of menu item.

PLOW HORSES   A plow horse has a low contribution margin (profitability) but high popularity. Action plans include increasing pricing for these items gradually and carefully. If demand is not affected, the contribution margin will increase, and the item will become more profitable.

Managers can also shift demand by relocating plow horses to lower-profile "real estate" sections on the menu. The vacated menu space can be used to promote more profitable and popular items. Point-of-sale advertising and suggestive selling by service staff can also emphasize other, more profitable, items.

Demand can also be shifted by providing alternatives with better value. Puzzles (items with high contribution margin and low popularity) may be offered with a free or reduced price dessert. This may increase sales of the puzzle and, even though a dessert is provided, the puzzle may have a higher total contribution margin than plow horses.

Plow horses can also be combined with items with a lower food cost to increase contribution margins. For example, a high-cost, twice-baked potato might be eliminated as a potato choice and be re-listed as an à la carte item.

PUZZLES   A puzzle has a high contribution margin but low popularity. Restaurant managers like these items but guests don't. What can be done to effectively manage puzzles?

First, they can be repositioned to "prime real estate" areas on the menu. Menus can feature these items by highlighting them with boxes, colors, shades, photos, or drawings. In addition, more extensive menu descriptions can be provided.

© auremar/Fotolia

This server is using suggestive selling to emphasize puzzles and stars.

WEB AT WORK!

Want to learn more about menu engineering? There are numerous web sites to review. Just type "menu engineering" in your favorite search engine.

Renaming the item may also be useful. Restaurant managers can consider decreasing the price of puzzles. If the selling price is decreased to where it will generate an average or higher contribution margin, the item will still be "profitable," and its sales may increase.

Increased sales of puzzles might also be generated by point-of-sale advertising and suggestive selling. Increasing an item's presentation, such as serving a steak on a sizzling platter or using creative garnishes, may also help to increase sales.

STARS   A star is a profitable and popular item. The best tactic to manage them is often to do nothing! Purchase specifications for ingredients should remain the same. Stars should be located in highly visible menu locations. Merchandising including point-of-sale advertising and suggestive selling should continue. In some cases, the selling prices of these items may be carefully increased to make them even more profitable.

DOGS   A dog is an unprofitable and unpopular item that should probably be eliminated. If a dog is kept on the menu, its price should at least be raised to equal the price of puzzles.

REVENUE CONTROL

Liquid asset

Assets (something of value) that are cash or that can easily be converted into cash.

Revenue collection

The process of properly identifying and recording guest charges and collecting their payments.

In balance

The concept that the amount of money owed by guests is received from guests.

Restaurant managers and their teams work hard to generate revenue. Procedures, policies, and systems are required to ensure that the money earned by the restaurant will ultimately be deposited in its bank account. The restaurant's owners depend on management to safeguard cash, which is the restaurant's most **liquid asset**. Guests expect that they will be billed properly and fairly for their purchases.

Importance of Revenue Control

Revenue collection involves identifying and recording guest charges and collecting payments. Doing this properly is critical, but not always easy. When a restaurant manager adds up all the guest purchases for a specific period and collects that exact amount of money from guests, the revenue is said to be "**in balance**."

GREEN AT WORK!

How does the concept of environmental sustainability pertain to menu engineering? The answer relates to the emphasis on "green" in the previous chapter: Restaurant managers are confronted with numerous priorities that must be addressed at the same time.

Menu engineering analysis has historically addressed two priorities when menu items were analyzed: contribution margin (profitability) and popularity. Some industry observers point out that labor costs should also be considered. For example, a low contribution margin menu item with little production labor may actually be more profitable than a high contribution margin item with extensive labor costs.

Will restaurant managers in the future also consider sustainability when undertaking menu item analysis? For example, what if a fresh seafood item is profitable and popular but also endangered? What if some items could be better marketed if they were made with organic ingredients even though they're more costly and reduce the contribution margin?

Which is more important: labor cost control, menu analysis, or marketing efforts? In Chapter 11, you learned that they're all priorities and must be considered as a routine part of the restaurant manager's job. This current discussion emphasizes that, within a priority such as menu analysis, there are numerous factors to be considered that may perhaps be of equal priority.

You'll find that the job of a restaurant manager is unique, challenging and different every day. This is why the position is of so much interest to many people.

WEB AT WORK!

Some restaurant managers select their property's credit card processing company. To learn about the services offered by alternative companies, enter "credit card processing companies" in your favorite search engine.

Short indicates that the amount of money collected is less than the sum of guest charges that should have been generated. **Over** indicates that the amount of money collected is more than the guest charges that were expected.

When revenue collection systems are inadequate, shortages will continue:

- If the time and specific cause(s) of the shortage cannot be identified
- If the cause of a cash shortage cannot be traced to a single individual
- When "small" shortages are ignored

Revenue control also relates to securely retaining revenue on-site until it is deposited. Assume that a restaurant accepts credit cards. In this case, the restaurant won't receive cash from credit card sales but, rather, an electronic funds transfer will be generated by a **credit card processing** company.

Even though revenue from credit card sales are never physically on-site, managers must still have procedures and systems in place to ensure that the operation is not defrauded. Therefore, whether the revenue consists of **currency**, credit or debit cards, and/or personal checks, these revenues must be effectively safeguarded. For example, personal checks that are accepted should be endorsed "For Deposit Only" and included with the bank deposit for that shift's sales.

When managers don't implement proper revenue controls, they leave their operations subject to **embezzlement**.

Embezzlement may go undetected for a long time because many embezzlers are actually trusted employees. Embezzlement may take a variety of forms. Simply stealing money intended for deposit in the restaurant's bank accounts is one common method. More sophisticated methods involve elaborate record falsification schemes intended to divert money to the employee who is embezzling the money.

Technology and Revenue Control

Much of the technology used in revenue control involves the restaurant's POS system, and few areas within restaurants have undergone more technological change in recent years than those related to revenue control. Enhancements to already advanced hardware and software technology make the gathering of important management information easier-to-use than ever before.

TECHNOLOGY HARDWARE The technology available in modern point-of-sale (POS) systems continues to expand, and hardware advances in POS systems come rapidly.

Common hardware items include:

- *Monitors.* Monitors can serve as input and/or display devices. In dining areas, monitors often feature touch screen entry and maximize server effectiveness by thoughtful placement of data entry functions, easy-to-view content displays, and efficient print function.
- *Input Devices.* Input devices allow servers to place orders. Traditionally this has been done with a keypad or touch screen. New handheld devices allow wireless connection to the main POS terminal. Servers can enter guest orders without returning to a central POS station or waiting in line while other servers manually enter orders into a POS terminal. New models can be programmed to recognize an individual server's handwriting.
- *Receipt Printers.* Receipt printers allow servers to quickly and quietly print guest receipts with speed, accuracy, and reliability.
- *Charge Card Readers.* Card readers that authorize payment cards have advanced in speed and ease-of-use. Increasingly, these devices are wirelessly connected to an operation's POS to allow for easy at-the-table guest payment.

Short
When the amount of money collected is less than the sum of guest charges that are owed.

Over
When the revenue collected is more than the sum of guest charges that are owed.

Credit card processing
Procedures used to transfer funds from a credit card holder's account to the bank account of the business charging the guest's card.

Currency
Bills and coins (money) used to make purchases.

Embezzlement
The crime of fraudulently taking the money or property of an employer.

> ▍**WEB AT WORK!**
>
> Some new input devices have been designed to read a server's handwriting and send requested orders directly to the kitchen or bar. To see one such handwriting recognition program, go to:
>
> www.actionsystems.com
>
> When you arrive, click on "The Write on Handheld."

TECHNOLOGY SOFTWARE Today's sophisticated software programs are designed either as stand-alone personal computer programs or are included as part of a larger POS system. Helpful software packages related to revenue collection and control include those that:

- Maintain revenue totals from different POS locations within one restaurant or within a group of restaurants.
- Compare products produced per POS sales to actual inventory reductions.
- Reconcile guest check totals with total revenue collected.
- Identify the revenue generated by the restaurant, day, menu item, shift, and/or server.
- Separate revenue generated by type of guest (dine-in, carryout, drive-through, delivery, banquets, off-site catering, and bar/lounge).
- Reconcile payment card deposits with payment card sales.
- Maintain **accounts receivable** records.
- Create the revenue portion of the income statement after reconciling bank deposits, charge card sales deposits, returned checks, and bank deposits.

Accounts receivable

Money owed to a restaurant that hasn't been received.

Those who select software programs understand that interfacing (electronically connecting the various programs) is essential. For example, a software program that computes total server gratuities (tips) for a specific payroll period is good. One that interfaces those server gratuity totals with the payroll-generating software is better!

POS REVENUE DATA Today, even the most basic POS systems can generate a wide variety of revenue-related data. In fact, restaurant managers must ensure that they capture and use only the data that's relevant to their operation.

Revenue data generated by POS systems is typically used for several purposes:
- To control revenue—Managers can compare POS revenue totals to budgets and to actual revenues collected. This is critical to any control procedure. Operating statements typically allow readers to compare present levels of revenue to those of previous periods.
- To develop income statements—A restaurant's profitability is impacted by revenue levels, and income statements report POS revenue data when this important financial management tool is developed.
- To facilitate revenue analysis—This topic was discussed earlier in this chapter. You now recognize that data generated by the POS system is used for many of these calculations.

What types of revenue data can be generated by POS systems? A short answer is "almost anything the restaurant manager wants." Examples include total revenues sorted by:

- Profit center (food, beverage, other)
- À la carte by meal period, hour or other period
- Type (examples: à la carte and banquet)

> ▍**WEB AT WORK!**
>
> Point of sale (POS) systems are becoming increasingly sophisticated. To view a website developed exclusively to selling advanced technology POS products go to:
>
> www.posworld.com

- Hours or part-hours of operation
- Servers and bartenders
- Food types (examples: appetizers and entrees) and specific menu items within each type
- Months and/or days of operation

Restaurant managers can program their POS systems to supply a variety of information. Examples include reports on revenue per server by hour or by shift, breakfast revenue by day and revenue by menu item for a week or other time period.

While this discussion addresses POS technology that's useful for revenue control, POS systems can be used for numerous other purposes, including:

- As a source of employee hours worked for compensation purposes and as input to scheduling labor hours.
- To track the sale of menu items for menu engineering, promotion results, employee contests, and other purposes.
- To facilitate purchasing and inventory management. The POS systems can determine the quantities of ingredients that should have been used to prepare the number of each menu item sold. This information can be used to reconcile changes in inventory levels and to determine when additional quantities of products should be ordered. Now that you have learned some background information about the role of technology in revenue control, let us review procedures that can help ensure that the correct amount of revenue collected from guests is available for bank deposit.

Revenue Control Systems

An effective revenue control system must address three components:

- Charging the guest
- Collecting revenue
- Protecting revenue

Let's review each of these components.

CHARGING THE GUEST   Guests must be fairly charged for their purchases, and the restaurant manager must ensure that this occurs. **Undercharging** occurs when guests receive products and services but don't pay for them. This can happen, for example, when employees "give" free products to their friends, neglect to charge other guests for legitimate purchases or fail to collect money rightfully owed to the restaurant.

Overcharging guests for their purchases can be just as bad for a restaurant's financial success. This can occur as a result of inadvertent errors when servers ring (add) up sales, when employees purposely overcharge guests to defraud them and when guests are charged for items they did not order.

To avoid undercharging and overcharging, the guests and the restaurant must have a clearly written record of charges. This may consist of a server physically writing the guest's order on a **guest check** and, at the appropriate time, presenting it to the guest. Note: A basic food and beverage production control procedure requires that products should be prepared and issued from the kitchen only when a record has been made of the guest's order. This safeguards against servers securing prepared items, serving them to guests and keeping the money collected from the guests.

Many restaurants use computer-based systems in which servers enter guest orders directly into a POS terminal or a hand-held transmitting device. The order appears on a screen in the restaurant's production area at the same time it is recorded in the POS. At the proper time, information is transmitted to a printer to create the written record (guest check) presented to the guest.

Regardless of the restaurant's size or its level of automation, basic revenue control principles require that:

- The name of items purchased must be accurately recorded.
- The quantity of items purchased must be accurately recorded.
- The prices of items purchased are correct (the same as that printed on the menu or recited by the server).

Undercharging

The incidence of charging a guest a lower amount for a food or beverage product than its actual selling price.

Overcharging

The incidence of charging a guest more for a food or beverage product than its actual selling price.

Guest check

A written record of what a guest has ordered and the price the guest will be charged for the item(s). Guest checks may be prepared manually or generated electronically by a POS system.

FIGURE 12.6
Principles to Determine Guest Charges

1. Guests know about menu item prices before they place their orders.
2. Individually numbered guest checks are printed by machine (POS systems identify each guest's bill with a unique transaction number) or by hand. One copy of the guest check is given to guests; at least one copy is retained by the restaurant.
3. Menu item prices and the number of items purchased are identified on the guest check.
4. **Extensions** (if any) are clearly indicated on the guest check.
5. Where possible, guest checks are totaled by machine to reduce error. Total charges are plainly indicated on the guest check when they're presented to guests.
6. Guest check totals clearly indicate whether **tips** or **service charges** are included in the totals. If so, they're listed as a separate item.
7. The guest check is presented to the guest before accepting payment.
8. Guests can review their bills before payment.
9. All unresolved disputes are promptly addressed by management.

Adapted from Ninemeier, J., and Hayes, D. (2006). *Restaurant Operations Management.* Pearson Education, Inc.

Extensions

The price of an item multiplied by the number of items purchased.
For example, if one guest orders three beverages for $4.00 each, the extension is: 3 beverages @ $4.00 = $12.00.

Tips

Money voluntarily given to a server by a guest for appreciation of good service.

Service charges

A guest charge added by management that's typically computed as a percentage of a guest's food and beverage expenditures. Service charges are legally the property of the restaurant.

- The sum of the costs of all items purchased (the guest check total) is accurate.
- Applicable taxes are correctly charged to the guest's purchase total.

When these principles are practiced, guest charges will be correct. Figure 12.6 is a checklist of specific features to help ensure that guests are charged precisely what management has predetermined they *should* be charged.

COLLECTING REVENUE The second step in a revenue control system is to collect the revenue. The collection process may be as simple as a guest paying cash at a drive-up window in a quick-service restaurant or as complex as processing a payment card transaction. However, the goals of revenue collection are the same:

- Identify the employee collecting the money.
- Collect the correct amount of revenue.
- Properly record the transaction.

Today's POS systems allow these goals to be completed electronically, minimizing the need for employees to exchange cash and for service personnel (in some traditional systems) to keep cash banks of revenue received until the end of a shift.

PROTECTING REVENUE In many cases, it's most difficult to keep revenue safe right after it's been collected because the risk of theft or **fraud** is greatest from the restaurant's employees.

The safeguarding of revenue begins with matching the funds received with the funds to be deposited. These funds must be held in a secure location until they're transported to the appropriate site for deposit. Most restaurants use a safe with a combination lock that can only be accessed by designated personnel.

Fraud

The intentional use of a trick, deceit, or other dishonest means to unlawfully take the property of another.

ALL IN A DAY'S WORK 12.1

"Kim," said Peggy, "This doesn't make sense." "This" was a significant shortage in Kim's cash drawer at the end of her bartender's shift at the restaurant Peggy managed.

"Were you at the register the entire shift? Did anyone else use the drawer?" asked Peggy.

"Well, Pat took over the register during my break, and the assistant manager got some change for the cashiers once," replied Kim.

1. Do you think Peggy will find the missing money? Why or why not?
2. What should Peggy do to prevent these kinds of revenue collection problems?

FIGURE 12.7
Revenue Recap Sheet

Name of Restaurant _____ Date _____

Revenue Generated:

        Breakfast _____

        Lunch _____

        Dinner _____

Total Revenue Generated _____ (1)

Revenue Collection:

        Credit card charges _____

        Debit card charges _____

        Checks received _____

        Direct bill (customer accounts) _____

    Currency on Hand (Excluding Cashier Banks)

        Bills _____

        Coins _____

        Total Revenue Collected _____ (2)

Net revenue collected _____ (3)

Net Over (or Short) _____ (4)

Deposit Amount _____ (5)

Prepared By _____

Adapted from Ninemeier, J., and Hayes, D. (2006). *Restaurant Operations Management.* Pearson Education, Inc.

The funds to be placed in the safe must be verified by completing a **revenue recap sheet**. Figure 12.7 identifies the information needed. This sheet should be created daily and retained for at least three years.

The revenue recap sheet documents important information critical for revenue control:

- Line (1) Total revenue generated: This data is taken from the restaurant's POS system or can be computed manually. Managers must identify the total revenue charged/collected from guests.
- Line (2) Total revenue collected: This is the revenue that's accounted for and does not include the value of any in-house **cashier bank**. It does include all payment card charges, checks received and currency on hand.
- Line (3) Net revenue collected: This is the sum of the total revenue on hand.
- Line (4) Net Over (or Short): This reflects the difference between the revenue that should have been collected and the revenue that's accounted for. When significant shortages (or overages) occur, managers must investigate thoroughly and take necessary corrective action.

Remember that the goal of a revenue recap sheet is to identify the total amount of revenue received from the employees who collected it and to determine the amount to be deposited.

It is generally recommended that a bank deposit of sales receipts be made daily to avoid keeping too much cash in the restaurant. The confirmation slips or monthly statements verifying the total amount of the daily deposits must be matched against the original deposit documentation prepared by the restaurant.

Falsification of bank deposit totals is a common embezzlement method. To prevent this, you can take the following steps:

- Make daily bank deposits.
- Ensure that the individual(s) making the daily revenue deposit is **bonded**.

Revenue recap sheet

A document prepared daily that details the total revenue generated, type of payment received, cash on hand, and appropriate deposit amounts for one day's sales.

Cashier bank

Currency used to provide guests with change.

Bonding

The purchase of an insurance policy to reimburse a restaurant when there is proven employee fraud.

- Establish and enforce written policies for completing bank reconciliations by the monthly (or more frequent) comparison of bank statements and daily deposit records.
- Use online banking features to reduce the time between performance and verification of banking activities.
- Review and reconcile all bank deposit and checking statements received from the bank with operating account balances.
- Use an annual external audit to examine the accuracy of deposits and account activities.

Minimizing Guest Theft

Unfortunately, dishonest guests may want to steal from your business, so it's important to examine potential threats related to the forms of payment your restaurant accepts. Some guests make purchases from restaurants with no intention of paying for them, and they **walk** their bill.

Walk

The act of a purchasing products in a restaurant and then leaving without paying for them.

Walks are a potential problem in the many restaurants where guests pay for their food and drinks after they have consumed them. It can be easy for a dishonest guest to leave when the server or cashier responsible for revenue collection is busy with other activities and doesn't notice that the guest who owes money has departed. Experienced restaurant managers implement steps to reduce opportunities for guests to leave without paying, and some of these are detailed in Figure 12.8.

In some restaurants, the majority of guests use credit and debit cards to pay their bills. Despite significant fines and even prison terms for misuse, some guests will still use them to fraudulently obtain products and services.

Card issuers are creating payment cards that help limit the chance of guest fraud. Cards are now issued with three-dimensional designs, magnetic strips, encoded numbers, smart chips, and other features. In addition, today's preauthorization verification systems are fast, accurate, and designed to reduce the chances of loss. Each card-issuing company provides information that can help restaurateurs reduce potential loss.

Your restaurant will be required to follow specific card-processing procedures established by the companies whose payment cards you accept. In most cases, the cards will be electronically authorized, and their use will be denied if the card is not valid. However, the fact that a card is valid does not guarantee that its use is legitimate or that the rightful owner is presenting the card for payment. Restaurant personnel should use the following procedures when accepting payment cards:

- Examine the card for signs of alteration.
- Verify the card's expiration date.

FIGURE 12.8
Steps to Reduce Walks

1. Present guest checks promptly upon serving guests their last ordered item or as directed by management policy.
2. Encourage servers to carefully monitor guest checks delivered to guests who haven't yet paid them.
3. If guests are observed leaving their table prior to paying their bills and are still in the restaurant, approach them politely with the assumption that they have simply forgotten to pay.
4. If guests actually leave before paying their bills, don't attempt to physically restrain them. Note the descriptions of the guests' clothing and automobile (if applicable) used to leave the area.
5. Place cashier stations, if used, in areas that ensure maximum visibility of dining areas.
6. Encourage employees to continually monitor remote exits that could allow guests to leave without paying their bill.
7. If a walk is observed, instruct servers and cashiers to notify management immediately.
8. Report all walks (include amount, date, time, and description of guests) to local law enforcement authorities.

Adapted from Ninemeier, J., and Hayes, D. (2006). *Restaurant Operations Management.* Pearson Education, Inc.

Hopefully, this restaurant has an excellent revenue collection system that makes it difficult for a guest to "walk" without paying for their meal.

- Compare the signature on the charge slip with the one on the card's back.
- Refuse to accept unsigned cards.
- If necessary, ask the guest for a driver's license or other form of picture identification to confirm he/she is the person named on the card.

Threats to Personal Check Collection

Some restaurants still accept personal checks; doing so creates some level of risk. Checks that are accepted may be declared **NSF** by the bank, and checks may be written on closed accounts.

You can reduce your restaurant's risk of loss from NSF or fraudulent personal checks by using the procedures listed in Figure 12.9.

NSF

Short for "non-sufficient funds." NSF checking accounts are those without sufficient funds to pay the full amount of the check.

Minimizing Employee Theft

Restaurant managers must protect their property's assets from employees who would otherwise steal. Control systems must protect the guests and the restaurant from numerous theft possibilities.

When significant losses from employee theft are detected, it's most likely that there are control procedure weaknesses that are related to one or more of the following:

- Ineffective internal controls
- Excessive control limited to one or two individuals
- Inadequate management of controls
- Failure to adequately prescreen employees

WEB AT WORK!

Want to learn how restaurant managers can protect their properties from credit card fraud? If so, go to:

www.merchantaccount.com

Click on "Merchant Accounts."

FIGURE 12.9
Procedures to Reduce Personal Check Fraud

1. Develop written guidelines about the types of checks you accept: personal, two-party, payroll, and/or traveler's checks.
2. Insist on proper picture identification.
3. Verify that the check writer's name and mailing address are printed on the check and secure the check writer's driver's license and telephone numbers.
4. Compare the check signature with the signature on the picture identification.
5. Don't accept checks written for amounts in excess of that required to pay the guest check.
6. Deposit checks into your bank account as rapidly as possible.
7. Consider using a check verification or check guarantee company.
8. Require a manager's initials or signature before accepting checks.
9. If you're the victim of fraud, send a certified letter requesting repayment to the individual writing the check. If there is no response, report the fraud to your bank and local police.
10. Monitor losses incurred from accepting checks and revise check acceptance policies if losses reach unacceptable levels.

Adapted from Ninemeier, J., and Hayes, D. (2006). *Restaurant Operations Management.* Pearson Education, Inc.

Cashiers and servers have opportunities to steal, and specific internal controls are needed to reduce theft by these restaurant employees.

Dishonest cashiers don't typically remove money from their cashier banks before their shifts are over; doing so would produce cash shortages that would be relatively easy to detect. Therefore, they must make it appear that their bank matches expected revenue totals.

Dishonest cashiers have two potential victims: guests and the restaurant. The ways cashiers attempt to defraud guests and the restaurant include:

- Making incorrect (too high) totals of legitimate purchases and keeping the difference between the correct and the artificially high totals.
- Charging guests for items not purchased and keeping the extra money.
- Returning less-than-the-correct amount of change from guest purchases with the hope the guest does not detect it.
- Reducing guest check totals in the POS or manual revenue system after the guest has paid and keeping the difference between the original and modified charge.
- **Voiding** (deleting) sales from the POS after the guest has paid for the full amount of the sale.

Void

The removal of a sale from a revenue total after the sale amount has been added to the revenue total.

In some operations, servers act as their own cashiers and can perform the fraudulent acts described above. In others, the server and cashier functions are performed by different individuals. Regardless of the payment collection method, there must be a system to identify missing guest checks and to match individual guest check totals with those of POS sales totals.

Experienced restaurant managers recognize the need to investigate cash banks that are "short" and "over" the expected balances. If cash "overs" are not analyzed, a dishonest cashier can, for example, remove $8.00 from a cash drawer but falsify sales records by voiding $10.00 in sales. This will result in a $2.00 cash "overage" that the cashier may know from prior experience

WEB AT WORK!

The National Check Fraud Center is a private organization that provides information to support the law enforcement, federal agency, financial, and retail communities in the detection, investigation, and the prosecution of check fraud. To view its website, go to:

www.ckfraud.org

won't be investigated. As a matter of policy, managers should have a system to determine the cause of all:

- Overages
- Shortages
- Cashier-initiated voids

Servers in many restaurants bring menu items to the guests and collect applicable revenue. A dishonest server can:

- Charge too much for items ordered and keep the excess payment.
- Charge the appropriate amount but not record the sale and keep the payment.
- Charge the appropriate amount and record the sale, but later falsify the sales record to keep all or part of the payment.
- Fail to charge for the items ordered and collect a reward (for example, a higher tip) from the guest.

A vigilant manager can often detect the above and related methods, but detection can be difficult if there is **collusion** among employees.

To explain how a manager can develop a system that helps reduce or eliminate server theft, consider the four basic steps required to serve a menu item to a guest:

- Step 1 - place the order
- Step 2 - prepare the order
- Step 3 - serve the order
- Step 4 - collect payment

If a server is normally responsible for steps 1, 3, and 4 and colludes with a cook responsible for step 2, the restaurant can be defrauded in the short run. The theft might be detected, however, when changes in food inventory levels are compared to revenue. Assume that a server colludes with a line cook and places an order for a steak (step 1) with the cook but makes no record of the sale. The steak is prepared (step 2) and served (step 3). The guest consumes and pays the server for the steak (step 4) and leaves. In this example, the restaurant receives no revenue, the cash totals balance, and the server and cook could split the money paid by the guest. The theft would be detected, however, if the inventory system can match the number of steaks removed from inventory to the number of steaks sold. This could be done if managers know how many steaks were on hand when the shift began, how many were sold during the shift, and how many steaks remain at the end of the shift.

Managers can use a **pre-check/post-check** system to help prevent employee theft. The server records (pre-checks) the order taken from the guest on a guest check or in the POS system. Kitchen production personnel cannot produce any products without a pre-checked guest check or POS record. When the guest is served and later pays, the server (or cashier) recalls the pre-check total, and the guest pays that bill.

When the system is used, the products ordered by the guest and issued by the kitchen or bar should match exactly the items and money collected (post-checked) by the cashier. If servers enter all orders into the pre-check/post-check system and, if production personnel cannot issue menu items without a pre-checked order, server theft can be eliminated or greatly reduced.

Dishonest bartenders and beverage servers also use common theft methods to defraud their employers. For example, bartenders can:

- Substitute lower cost products for higher cost products and keep the extra money collected. To illustrate, assume a guest orders a drink made with **call-brand** liquor that sells for $7.00. The bartender substitutes a lower cost **house-brand liquor** that sells for $5.00 and charges the guest $7.00. The bartender then keeps the $2.00. This type of theft happens

Collusion

An agreement between two or more people to commit fraud.

Pre-check/post-check

A system that matches the quantity and value of orders placed by servers to the number of items paid for by guests.

Call-brand liquor

A specific brand of liquor requested by a guest.

House-brand liquor

Alcoholic beverages sold by generic type (e.g., gin, rum, or scotch) rather than by brand (e.g., Tanqueray gin, Bacardi rum, or Glenlivet scotch).

WEB AT WORK!

New computer software related to restaurant revenue control appears on the market frequently. To stay abreast of new products, go to:

www.foodsoftware.com

Bookmark the website and return to it regularly for updates.

WEB AT WORK!

Automated beverage control systems allow managers to be much more vigilant in their overview of beverage revenue. To learn about one system, go to:

www.berg-controls.com

most often when the bar is busy, when guests are distracted, and when managers don't match actual product sales volumes with the specific products used.

- Under pour to create unaccounted-for liquor by removing a small amount from each drink made. For example, assume 1.5 ounces of liquor per drink should be poured but instead, the bartender pours only 1.25 ounces.. In this scenario, for each 6 drinks served, one additional 1.5 ounce drink can be served (.25/drink × 6 drinks = 1.5 ounces) at full price with the bartender keeping the revenue.

In this situation, both the restaurant and the guest are defrauded. Metered pour spouts are one way to prevent this, and mechanical or electronic pouring systems are another. Note: Many bartenders prefer to "free-pour" (prepare drinks without measuring the amount of alcohol that goes into them). This is usually the sign of poor control procedures, and in most cases should not be allowed.

Beverage servers can also defraud the operation and its guests. Common forms of server theft can include:

- *Shortchanging.* When guests aren't paying attention, servers can give incorrect change for drinks sold. The server might "forget" that a guest paid with a $20 bill and return change from a $10 bill. The server may also return no change and, if questioned, explain that he

© CandyBox/Fotolia

This bartender may look friendly and honest, but a good revenue control system is still absolutely necessary to prevent revenue theft.

or she assumed the change due the guest was thought to be a "tip." While shortchanging is fraud committed against a guest, the restaurant's reputation will also suffer if this is allowed to occur.

- Beverage servers can overcharge either by charging for drinks that were never served, or by charging for high-priced drinks but serving guests lower cost drinks. When the bill is presented, it may be nearly impossible for the guest to determine precisely what was ordered, especially if the bill includes charges for drinks consumed by a large group of guests.
- Dishonest beverage servers can deliver undocumented drinks that were ordered by guests but not entered in the property's POS system. This may occur when servers make their own drinks, when bartenders collude with servers, or when records in the POS system can be revised (voided) to remove evidence of sales. In this situation, the server can keep the guests' payments, and the restaurant loses the cost of each drink's ingredients and the profit from the sale.

Reducing bartender and beverage server fraud requires constant management diligence. If revenue collection and control systems are well designed, this type of fraud can be significantly reduced.

In most properties, mid-level managers and supervisors may also have the opportunity to steal money or products. Preventing managerial theft can be more difficult than preventing employee theft because of the greater access these employees have to the restaurant's assets.

Managers and supervisors can pose threats to a restaurant's cash assets before revenue deposits are made. These threats include those related to:

- *Revenue Collection*: In most restaurants, the manager or a supervisor monitors the revenue collection system. If one of them uses knowledge of the revenue collection system to steal, significant losses can occur. No manager should modify revenue reports from the POS system without a double-check by another manager. For example, if a manager or supervisor enters the POS system to void a sale, that activity should be reviewed by a different restaurant manager at the end of the shift or the next day.
- *Revenue Control*: Every manager who has a role in revenue control, including the preparation of revenue deposits, should be bonded. In the event of proven fraud by any restaurant employee, corrective actions that may include reporting the crime to the appropriate law enforcement authorities and/or termination are in order.

WEB AT WORK!

Many restaurants use mystery (anonymous) shopper services to evaluate their service, food, and operational controls. To view the website of one such company, go to:

www.restaurantprofits.com

Click on "Mystery Shopper" to read about the services provided.

ALL IN A DAY'S WORK 12.2

"Are you sure?" asked AJ, as he looked up from the report he was reading.

"Positive," replied Sheila. AJ was the manager of the Cattleman's Club Restaurant, and Sheila was employed by Sullivan's Shopper Services. Her report indicated that Trey, one of the restaurant's bartenders, had given free drinks to three guests during the secret shopping service visit Sheila had recently conducted.

"Well," said AJ, "From your report, it looks like the bartender had served the guests two drinks but only charged them for one, so he didn't actually take money."

"You're correct," replied Sheila, "He isn't taking your money; he's giving away your drinks. The guests loved it, and his tips were great!"

1. What should AJ do about Trey?
2. Do you believe employees who are caught stealing should be allowed a second chance to prove they won't steal again in the future? Why?

Restaurant Terms and Concepts

Work in Progress

1. What are several items of information generated by POS systems that you, as a restaurant manager, would like to know about each day?

2. Some restaurant managers use employee contests and award prizes to employees with, for example, the highest check averages. What do you think of this practice?

3. Much of the information used to objectively price menus is readily available in the restaurant's operating budget. Therefore, could be some reasons why some restaurant managers don't want to use this information?

4. This chapter has listed several tactics that managers can use once knowledge about stars, puzzles, plow horses, and dogs are known. What are additional tactics you could use to manage items in these categories?

5. In some properties, servers must reimburse the restaurant for any money lost because of guests who "walk." In other restaurants, the property absorbs the loss. Who do you think should be held responsible? Why?

6. Some restaurant managers have moved aggressively to automate their beverage dispensing systems to reduce potential bartender and server theft. Other managers feel that this depersonalizes the dining experience, and most guests like to see a bartender actually "pour" drinks. What do you think?

7. What are three actions you can take to remain informed about the most current tools and procedures to help you implement effective revenue collection and control procedures?

8. Some restaurant managers require all cash handling employees to submit to a criminal background check before they're considered for employment. Would you do this? Would the length of time between the crime and the employment decision influence your decision to hire, or not to hire, the potential employee? Why?

9. What would you do if you were a beverage server and you knew a bartender was stealing from the restaurant?

10. Have you ever been cheated by an employee of a restaurant you visited? Who did you blame for the problem? Why?

13

Managing for Profit

Learning Objectives

After carefully reading and studying the information in this chapter, you will be able to:

1. Explain why restaurant managers must know how to prepare and use operating budgets and describe procedures used in analyzing budget variances.

2. Review procedures to correct significant variances between expected results from the budget and actual results from the income statement.

IN THIS CHAPTER

To achieve the financial results they want, restaurant managers prepare budget plans that identify financial goals and then implement their plans. The development of a budget helps predict the amount of sales that will be generated during a specific time period and the amount of expenses required to generate the sales.

    A completed budget provides financial **benchmarks** that allow managers to compare actual sales and expenses to budget forecasts; in the process, they can assess any variances between budget plans and their actual operating results expressed in the income statement. Variances that are considered to be significant can be identified, and reasons for the differences can be assessed. In this chapter, you'll learn how to use the budget by comparing it to actual performance and to implement corrective actions to best manage sales, expenses and profits. You'll also learn about the balance sheet, an important financial management tool that details the results of the manager's activities to operate a financially sustainable restaurant.

THE BUDGET PROCESS

Benchmark

A goal or standard against which actual operating results are compared.

Experienced restaurant managers understand the value of accurately forecasting their operation's future financial standing, and they do so as they develop an operating budget. They know that, by closely monitoring these financial tools and revising them as business conditions change, they can influence their property's financial results.

No one can accurately predict the future all of the time, and sales and expense levels in restaurants are affected by many external and internal variables. Regardless of the difficulty in projecting future events, however, an operating budget is critical because it:

- Requires managers to consider future external events and their financial impacts.
- Challenges managers to recognize the importance of sales when projecting expenses and allows them to carefully prioritize competing sales demands.
- Creates a standard against which to compare actual versus budgeted performance.
- Helps managers establish an appropriate menu pricing structure.
- Communicates a realistic estimate of future financial results to owners so they can evaluate the restaurant as an investment.

Fiscal year

Any 365 day accounting period that does not begin on January 1.

Restaurant managers most typically use an annual operating budget with a 365-day time interval as its accounting period. The 365 days need not be a calendar year beginning on January 1 and ending on December 31. A restaurant could, for example, begin its **fiscal year** October 1 and end it September 30.

The best budgets are prepared with input from managers of each profit center in the restaurant. For example, in addition to the restaurant manager, the kitchen manager, chef, or other food production manager can be very helpful in estimating food-related costs. Similarly, the dining room manager can provide insight about service staffing, and the beverage manager can advise about beverage costs based upon projected sales. While the ultimate responsibility to produce the final budget rests with the restaurant manager or owner, a development team consisting of those who can best develop sales and expense estimates is vital to create a useful budget.

Budgeting Sales

Most restaurant managers begin their budgets by estimating sales because they largely determine the level of expenses and resulting profit that will be incurred. Their calculations involve a simple formula:

$$\text{Budgeted sales} - \text{Budgeted expense} = \text{Budgeted profit}$$

The budgeted profit can be attained when the planned sales levels are achieved and when only the amounts budgeted for the expenses are spent to generate that sales. If sales fall short of forecast and expenses aren't reduced accordingly, profit shortfalls will occur.

Similarly, if actual sales exceed forecasted levels, expenses will also likely increase. If the increases are monitored carefully and aren't excessive, increased profits should result. If, however, managers allow expenses to exceed the levels required to support the sales increase, budgeted profits are less likely to be realized.

Restaurant sales may be estimated on a weekly basis and then combined to create monthly budgets that are further merged to develop the annual sales budget. This is an effective tactic because many restaurants have seasonal sales variations. For example, a restaurant in a shopping mall may generate significantly higher sales during the holiday season than in the summer, when shopping mall sales are generally lower.

Forecasting sales is not an exact science; however, one useful strategy involves the five-step process reviewed in Figure 13.1.

Let's consider each of the steps in Figure 13.1:

Step 1   **Review sales data from previous years**.   When a restaurant has been open for a period of time, its sales history may help predict future sales levels. Modern POS systems provide a wealth of information about historic sales broken down in a variety of ways, which restaurant managers may find helpful.

Step 2   **Evaluate changes in internal environment**.   Noteworthy activities that are within the control of the restaurant manager can dramatically affect sales projections. Consider a significant change in the type, quantity, and/or direction of marketing efforts. In

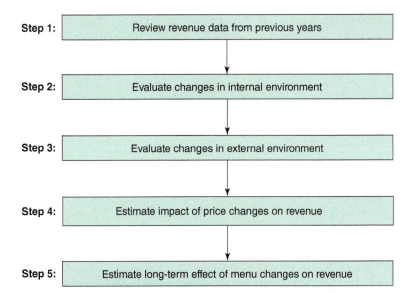

FIGURE 13.1
Five-Step Sales Forecasting Process
Adapted from Ninemeier, J., and Hayes, D. (2006). *Restaurant Operations Management.* Pearson Education, Inc.

addition, server training programs addressing suggestive selling can yield sales increases. Facility renovations may increase seating capacity and sales, although disruption due to the renovation may temporarily decrease sales. A final example: when the restaurant's operating hours are changed, the sales generated will also likely change.

Step 3   **Evaluate changes in external environment**.   External issues that can affect a restaurant's sales forecasts include the opening and closing of competitive restaurants, road construction that disrupts normal traffic patterns and changes in the economy that affect potential guests' discretionary spending on dining out.

Step 4   **Estimate the impact of price changes on sales**.   Some managers think an increase in menu selling prices "automatically" results in sales increases. In fact, if menu prices increase and guest counts significantly decrease, sales will decline. Managers who factor menu price increases into their sales forecasts must do so cautiously and with the understanding that a $1.00 price increase may yield less than $1.00 in increased sales because of the **law of supply and demand**.

Law of supply and demand

Economic beliefs about the supply of an item and its price relative to its demand. Sometimes, as the price of an item increases, demand for that item decreases (and vice-versa).

Food production managers must be good cooks, but they must also be good with the "numbers."

© Tetra Images/Alamy

Roll out

Introducing a new menu item on an existing menu.

Step 5   **Estimate the long-term effect of menu changes on sales.**   Some restaurateurs believe that a key to increasing sales is to expand menu offerings and they "**roll out**" new products to drive up total sales. Sometimes, incremental sales occur. In other cases, however, short-term increases in sales are achieved, but longer-term sales do not increase significantly because the new items are purchased by the same guests who had previously purchased other menu items. Additionally, if some items are dropped to make room for new items, total sales may actually decline if guests visit competitors because their favorite menu selections are no longer available.

It isn't possible to make an exact forecast of a restaurant's sales one week, one month, or one year into the future as operating budgets are developed. However, with practice and good information, many managers can typically attain budget forecasts within 10% (plus or minus) of actual results for the forecast period.

Budgeting Expenses

After budgeted sales are forecasted, the next step is to estimate expenses. This is an important skill for restaurant managers. Sometimes estimating costs is easy. For example, assume you manage a restaurant. You know the monthly rent payments for your operation are $7,000. Creating the annual budget for "rent" expense is simple:

$7,000 a month for 12 months = $84,000.00 rent expense
($7,000 × 12 months = $84,000 rent expense).

Rent is a fixed cost that remains unchanged regardless of the restaurant's sales.

Other expenses increase or decrease as sales change. For example, as more guests are served, more napkins will be used, and more napkin laundry expense will be incurred because it's a variable cost. Most types of expenses incurred by restaurants are variable costs.

Some expenses may be **mixed costs**. Restaurant utilities is one example.

Mixed cost

A cost that contains both fixed and variable components.

Consider a restaurant located in an area with a warm climate. Air-conditioning costs will be incurred. The restaurant must spend some money (fixed expense) to properly cool its dining areas regardless of the number of guests served. As the number of guests served increases, additional costs (variable expense) are incurred to maintain the appropriate temperature when the dining area is filled with guests.

Managers must understand the concepts of fixed, variable, and mixed costs and must also practice principles of **cost allocation** between profit centers.

Cost allocation

The assignment of specific costs to the profit center that generates the cost.

Ensuring proper cost allocation requires managers to consider all costs and to make assignment decisions about them. Consider the cost of making a Bloody Mary cocktail. Because this drink contains alcohol, it generates beverage sales. However, it also contains tomato juice, vegetable garnishes, and spices. In Chapter 11, you learned that the cost of these food items should be deducted from the cost of food (food profit center) and should be allocated (assigned) to the beverage profit center through a food/beverage transfer process.

Restaurant managers recognize the need to budget for departmental food, beverage, and labor expenses. In Chapter 11, you learned about the wide variety of expenses that are incurred. Managers must carefully consider all of these costs as they and their budget teams develop budgets that represent profit plans for their business.

Note: The National Restaurant Association (NRA) has developed and published the *Uniform System of Accounts for Restaurants* that includes, among much other information, a complete list of typical restaurant costs. It's helpful to review all the expenses identified in this

WEB AT WORK!

To learn more about restaurant budgeting basics, go to:

www.foodservicewarehouse.com

Type "Restaurant Operations" in the search box and then click on "Restaurant Accounting."

publication to ensure that you don't miss any when preparing your budget. Two other publications can also be helpful to budget planners: NRA's *Restaurant Industry Forecast* and its *Restaurant Industry Operations Report*.

Monitoring the Budget

An operating budget is a forecast of future financial activity. The budget team's view of the future may or may not be accurate, and wise restaurant managers know that one way to best ensure profitability is to analyze the differences between budgeted (planned for) and actual operating results. To do this effectively, managers must receive timely income statements that accurately detail actual operating results. These actual results can then be compared to the budget for the same accounting period.

In Chapter 11, you learned that the difference between planned and actual results is called a variance, and we explored how to calculate dollar and percentage variances for labor costs. We reviewed these calculations for addressing sales variances in Chapter 12.

A **positive variance** (favorable) is an improvement on the budget (sales are higher; expenses are lower); a **negative variance** (unfavorable) occurs when actual results are less than budget expectations (sales are lower; expenses are higher).

Procedures to calculate variances in all budget sales and expense categories are the same as for determining labor cost and sales variance. For example, assume the budget for landscape services is $1,000 per month, but the actual expense was $1,150 for a specific month. The variance may be expressed as a dollar amount ($1150 − $1000 = $150) or as a percentage of the original budget as follows:

$$\frac{\text{Actual expense } (-) \text{ Budgeted expense}}{\text{Budgeted expense}} = \text{Variance percentage}$$

$$\frac{\$1,150 \, (-) \, \$1,000}{\$1,000} = 15\% \text{ variance}$$

This variance is negative because it's unfavorable to the restaurant.

It's the manager's task to identify **significant variances** between planned and actual operating results. This is an important concept because not all variances should be investigated. Assume a restaurant manager allocates $3,000 for the December utility bill, and the actual amount of one particular bill is $3,025. Given the $25.00 variance ($3,025.00 − $3,000.00 = $25.00) and the difficulty of estimating utility expenses, the $25.00 probably doesn't represent a significant variance from the budget estimate.

Alternatively, if the manager estimated office supplies usage at $100.00 for that same month, but the actual supplies cost was $500.00, the $400.00 difference ($500.00 − $100.00) probably represents a significant (500%) difference between planned and actual results and should be investigated.

Managers must decide what represents a significant variance for their operation based on their knowledge of the specific operation. You should remember that small percentage differences can be important if they represent large dollar amounts. Consider the following:

Expense	Actual	Budgeted	Difference $	Difference %
Food Cost	$805,000	$850,000	($45,000)	(5.3)
Landscaping	$1,150	$1,000	($150)	(15.0)

Note above that there is a 5.3% variance between budgeted and actual food costs and a 15.0% difference between budgeted and actual landscaping service costs. Inexperienced managers might conclude that the landscaping variance represents the biggest problem. However, wise managers realize that the operation's profitability is impacted much more by the $45,000 excessive food costs than it is by the $150 increased landscaping cost. There's an old saying in the restaurant business that "You can't bank a percentage," and this is very clear from our analysis of the above variance information. Restaurant managers would rather save $45,000 in food costs than $150 in landscaping costs, even though the $150 represents a larger percentage difference

Positive variance

A favorable difference between planned and actual operating results.

Negative variance

An unfavorable difference between planned and actual operating results.

Significant variance

A difference in dollars or percentage between planned and actual operating results that warrants further investigation.

FIGURE 13.2

Four-Step Budget Monitoring Process

Adapted from Ninemeier, J., and Hayes, D. (2006). *Restaurant Operations Management.* Pearson Education, Inc.

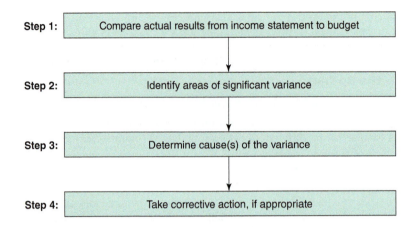

Step 1: Compare actual results from income statement to budget

Step 2: Identify areas of significant variance

Step 3: Determine cause(s) of the variance

Step 4: Take corrective action, if appropriate

between budgeted and actual landscaping costs than does the $45,000 difference between budgeted and actual food costs.

Variations from budgeted results can occur in sales, expenses, or profit, and restaurant managers can monitor each of these important areas using the four-step process illustrated in Figure 13.2.

Let's look at these steps more closely.

In Step 1, the manager studies income statement and budget data in each of the income statement's three major sections (sales, expenses, and income before income taxes—commonly called profit) for the accounting period. In Steps 2 and 3, actual operating results are compared to the budget, and significant variances, if any, are identified and analyzed. Finally (in Step 4), corrective action is taken to reduce significant unfavorable variances. Note: The corrective action process is examined in detail in the next section of this chapter.

Let's see how the budget monitoring process works using the data for Vernon's Restaurant in Figure 13.3. It shows income statement data for January, 20XX, and compares it to the budget for the same month.

You learned in Chapter 11 that an income statement is a summary of a restaurant's profitability that details sales generated, costs incurred, and profits or losses realized during a specific accounting period. In other words, it represents the operation's actual operating results, and it can be compared to the expected financial results expressed in the operating budget. The manager uses the same categories of sales and expenses for the income statement and budget to make the comparison process easy.

SALES ANALYSIS For several reasons, sales are the first area to examine when comparing actual and budgeted results for Vernon's Restaurant. First, if sales fall significantly below projected levels, there is likely to be a significant negative impact on profit goals. Second, when sales vary from projections, costs are also affected:

• Variable cost dollars should be *less-than-budgeted* if sales are short of forecast and *higher-than-budgeted* if sales exceed budgeted levels.
• Fixed and mixed cost percentages should be *higher-than-budgeted* when sales fall short of budgeted levels; these cost percentages will likely be *less-than-budgeted* when sales are greater than budgeted.

Another reason to initially examine how actual sales vary from the budget is to understand what is, and what should be, happening with expenses and profits. For example, if sales exceed forecasts, most operating expenses should increase, at least in part, because they're variable expenses. The impacts on budgeted expenses that result from variations in sales are listed in Figure 13.4.

Note in Figure 13.3 that Vernon's Restaurant has a shortfall in actual food and beverage sale(s) when compared to budgeted results. Food sales were budgeted at $91,000 and beverage sales were expected to be $40,000. In fact, food sales were $85,000, and beverage sales

January 20XX				
	Current Period		**Year-to-Date**	
SALES	**Actual**	**%**	**Budget**	**%**
Food	$ 85,000	70.8	$ 91,000	69.5
Beverage	35,000	29.2	40,000	30.5
Total Sales	120,000	100.0	131,000	100.0
COST OF SALES				
Food	32,600	38.4	31,850	35.0
Beverage	9,660	27.6	10,000	25.0
Total Cost of Sales	**42,260**	**35.2**	**41,850**	**31.9**
LABOR				
Salaries and Wages	28,400	23.7	26,100	20.0
Benefits	8,150	6.8	7,775	5.9
Total Labor	36,550	30.5	33,875	25.9
Prime Cost	**78,810**	**65.6**	**75,725**	**57.8**
Other Controllable Expenses				
Marketing	2,000	1.7	2,850	2.2
Utilities	2,810	2.3	2,750	2.1
General/Administrative	4,410	3.6	4,060	3.1
Repairs/Maintenance	2,100	1.8	2,750	2.1
Insurance	1,700	1.4	1,700	1.3
Direct Operating Expenses	2,000	1.7	1,800	1.4
Total Other Controllable Expenses	15,020	12.5	15,910	12.2
Controllable Income	26,170	21.8	39,356	30.0
Noncontrollable Expenses				
Occupancy Costs	10,440	8.7	10,440	8.0
Equipment Leases	2,880	2.4	2,880	2.2
Depreciation	3,480	2.9	3,480	2.7
Total Non-Controllable Expenses	16,800	14.0	16,800	12.9
Restaurant Operating Income	9,370	7.8	22,556	17.2
Interest Expense	1,560	1.3	1,560	1.2
Other (Income) Expense	1,080	0.9	1,100	0.9
Income Before Income Taxes	**$ 6,730**	**5.6**	**$ 19,896**	**15.1**

FIGURE 13.3

Vernon's Restaurant Income Statement and Budget Forecast*
Adapted from Ninemeier, J., and Hayes, D. (2006). *Restaurant Operations Management.* Pearson Education, Inc.

*Note: This format is adopted from *The Uniform System of Accounts for Restaurants, Eighth Edition* (2010). National Restaurant Association.
All percentages are calculated as a percentage of total sales except cost of sales line items (food and beverage), which are based on their respective sales.

FIGURE 13.4
Impact of Sales Variation on
Fixed and Variable Expenses
Adapted from Ninemeier, J.,
and Hayes, D. (2006). *Restaurant
Operations Management.*
Pearson Education, Inc.

Budget Impact	If Actual Sales Greater than Budgeted	If Actual Sales Lesser than Budgeted
Fixed Expenses		
Dollars	None	None
Percentage of Sales	Decreases	Increases
Variable Expenses		
Dollars	Increases	Decreases
Percentage of Sales	May fluctuate*	May fluctuate*

*100% variable expenses increase or decrease in direct proportion to sales increases or decreases. In actuality, most expenses have a partially fixed component. Therefore, as sales increase, variable expense percentages may actually decline. Similarly, when sales fail to meet budget, some increases in the variable expense percentages will likely result.

were $35,000. When sales consistently fall short of forecast, managers may need to review service levels and use additional marketing tactics, such as coupons, increased advertising, price discounting, and specials, to address sales challenges.

EXPENSE ANALYSIS   Identifying significant expense variances is a critical part of the budget monitoring process. While managers may be limited in their ability to directly influence sales, many expenses are under their direct control. Some variation between budgeted and actual expenses can be expected because, as noted above, some variable operating expenses fluctuate with sales volumes. Variances can, however, indicate something about operational efficiencies, and experienced managers know that properly controlling operating costs is one key to ensuring profitability.

Costs in an income statement and operating budget are typically expressed in dollars and as a percentage of sales. As you learned in Chapter 11, food and beverage cost percentages are calculated as follows:

$$\frac{\text{Cost of goods sold: Food}}{\text{Food sales}} = \text{Food cost percentage}$$

$$\frac{\text{Cost of goods sold: Beverage}}{\text{Beverage sales}} = \text{Beverage cost percentage}$$

Costs for food and beverages use the sales generated from their respective sales in the calculation because these cost ratios are important in order to learn about restaurant profitability. Vernon's food costs (Figure 13.3), were 3.4% percentage points higher than budgeted (38.4% actual food costs − 35.0% budgeted food costs = 3.4 % more). The beverage cost percentage was 2.6% points higher than budgeted (27.6% actual − 25.0% budgeted = 2.6% difference).

You'll note in Figure 13.3 that all nonfood and beverage cost percentages are calculated on the basis of total sales (food sales + beverage sales). For example, the *actual* salaries and wages percentage is calculated as:

$$\frac{\text{Salaries and wage cost}}{\text{Food and beverage sales}} = \text{Salaries and wage cost percentage}$$

In this example:

$$\frac{\$28,400}{(\$85,000 + \$35,000)}$$

$$\frac{\$28,400}{\$120,000} = 23.7\% \text{ Salaries and wage cost percentage}$$

Note in Figure 13.3 that while total prime costs (food, beverage, salaries, and benefits) were budgeted at 57.8% of total sales, the actual results were much higher (65.6%). Reasons for the higher costs must be evaluated, and variances should be analyzed using the four-step budget monitoring process being discussed.

Unfortunately, all of the other controllable costs, except marketing and repairs/maintenance, were higher or the same as planned even though the sales were lower than planned. Reasons for these variances should be closely examined.

It's ironic that marketing costs (dollars) were lower than budgeted because higher marketing expenditures may have improved sales. In addition, the manager may have reduced repairs/maintenance expenses because of the lowered sales. This is usually a poorly-thought-through, short-term tactic to reduce costs that will have long-term negative impacts on the upkeep of the facility and equipment.

Note that the actual and budgeted costs for the three categories of noncontrollable expenses (occupancy costs, equipment leases, and depreciation) are the same because they're fixed costs that don't vary with changing sales levels. Note also, as explained in Figure 13.4 above, that these fixed costs produced a higher cost percentage because of reduced sales.

PROFIT ANALYSIS   When the sales and expense assumptions initially used to develop the budget change, the result is often a change in profit. In Figure 13.3, profit is described as "**income before income taxes**." Because of its placement at the end of the income statement, income before income taxes is often referred to as the "**bottom line**." However, since the term "profit" is the one most commonly used in the hospitality industry, that term will be used throughout this chapter.

Income before income taxes in dollars and as a percentage of sales is an important management concern. As seen in Figure 13.3, the actual income before income taxes for Vernon's Restaurant was $6,730 or 5.6% of total sales. This is far less than the $19,896 (15.1%) of sales that were budgeted.

Income before income taxes

The "bottom line" of an income statement. It's calculated as:

Total sales − (prime costs + other controllable expenses + noncontrollable expenses + interest expense + other expense); most often called "profit"

Bottom line

Industry slang meaning "profit" or "net income."

This guest is not aware of the significant financial calculations that occur when revenues for his purchase are planned and when they are analyzed.

© Konstantin Sutyagin/Shutterstock

This shortfall relates directly to lower sales and, in some categories, higher expenses. The inability to meet budget means either that the budget was ineffectively developed, internal/external conditions changed, and/or managers were not effective. Corrective actions are needed to prevent more serious problems. This topic is addressed later in the chapter.

Profit Percentages and Dollars

Figure 13.3 reveals that Vernon's Restaurant achieved an income before income taxes (profit) that was lower in dollars and in percentages than the forecasted amounts ($6,730; 5.6% actual vs. $19,896; 15.1% budgeted).

However, assume the actual profit was 16.0%, which would be greater than the 15.1% budgeted. The total profit dollars ($120,000 actual sales × 16% = $19,200) would still be less than the budgeted profit of $19,896. This should make you think about a point made earlier in this chapter: "You can't bank a percentage!"

Evaluating profit dollars is important, but managers must be careful when doing so. Let's look at two identical restaurants. The first manager achieves $1,000 in profits on $10,000 of sales ($1,000 ÷ $10,000 = 10% operating profit). The second manager achieves profits of $1,100 on sales of $50,000 ($1,100 ÷ $50,000 = 2.2% operating profit). While the second manager realized a greater dollar level of profits, the first manager likely operates a restaurant with lower food, labor, and other costs—the result of which is a higher operating profit percentage.

Effective managers review operating profit percentages *and* dollars when monitoring budgets. They also want to know how their operating results relate to the money invested in the business.

Return on Investment

A restaurant can achieve a good amount of income before income taxes but not be a good investment for the owner. In other cases, a restaurant with a not-as-good profit can be a better investment. The reason is that the return on investment (ROI) in the two restaurants can be very different.

To illustrate, assume two restaurant owners generate $100,000 in income before income taxes (profit) after a year of operating their restaurants. The first owner invested $1,000,000 in the operation, and the second owner invested $2,000,000. The first owner achieved an ROI of 10% ($100,000 ÷ $1,000,000 = 10% ROI); the second owner achieved an ROI of 5% ($100,000 ÷ $2,000,000 = 5% ROI). Maximizing an owner's return on investment is critical for a restaurant manager. Actual returns on investment can vary greatly, but few people will invest in a restaurant if the return is less than what could be achieved in other investment opportunities with the same or lesser risks.

To maximize profitability, managers must carefully create budgets, aggressively pursue sales targets, actively manage and control expenses, analyze significant variations between budgeted and actual results, and revise their operating budgets when necessary.

Revising the Budget

Budgets should be active documents with great potential for change. They require regular review and modification as new and better information replaces the information that was available when the budget was initially developed.

WEB AT WORK!

The website for Small Business Notes provides basic information about financial management, including budgeting. To view the website, go to:

www.smallbusinessnotes.com

Click on "Business Finances" and then "Financial Management."

The budget should be reviewed anytime it's believed that the assumptions upon which it's based are unfounded. For example, assume that a restaurant owner employs 50 full-time employees, and each is covered under the restaurant's group health insurance policy. Last year, the restaurant owner paid 50% of the $200 per month, per employee, insurance cost:

$$50 \text{ employees } (\times) \ \$200.00 \text{ per employee } = \$10,000 \text{ monthly cost}$$

When the budget was developed, the manager assumed a 10% increase in health insurance premiums. If the premiums actually rose 20%, employee benefit costs will be greater than projections; In this case, the owner has several choices:

- Modify the budget to reflect the increase
- Reduce the amount contributed by the restaurant to stay within the original budget
- Change (reduce) health insurance benefits or coverage to stay within allocated costs

Regardless of the owner's decision, the budget, if affected, should be modified. Figure 13.5 identifies some of many situations that may result in modifications to a budget.

1. The opening or closing of a competitor.
2. Opening, by the same or different ownership, of an identical restaurant in the property's market area.
3. A significant and long-term change in major menu ingredient prices.
4. Significant and unanticipated increases in fixed expenses, such as insurance or taxes.
5. Unplanned road construction that significantly affects consumers' abilities to reach the restaurant.
6. Natural disasters, such as floods and hurricanes, that significantly affect forecasted sales.
7. Significant changes in operating hours.
8. Permanent changes in service style that appreciably affect labor costs.
9. Changes in financial statement formats and/or bases for allocation of financial resources.
10. The loss of especially skilled or talented employees.

FIGURE 13.5

Factors That May Require Budget Revisions

Adapted from Ninemeier, J., and Hayes, D. (2006). *Restaurant Operations Management.* Pearson Education, Inc.

GREEN AT WORK!

You've been learning about budgets in this section of the chapter. Bear in mind that a restaurant manager's decision to "go green" can have numerous budget implications.

Assume, for example, that energy-saving light bulbs or "eco-friendly" cleaning detergents are purchased. These products may have a higher purchase cost than their traditional counterparts, and these extra costs will increase the applicable budget accounts. The light bulbs may also reduce energy consumption; this, in turn, will decrease the restaurant's utility bills. Note: The decision to purchase them may have been based upon recognition that it was "the right thing to do" or because of the belief that energy savings will exceed purchase costs over the specified time period.

Capital budgets can also be affected by decisions to be environmentally correct. The manager may, for example, purchase expensive equipment, system controls, and/or technology to reduce energy consumption. This will likely be considered a **fixed asset** that will be **depreciated** on the property's income statement.

Large-volume restaurants often use **cash budgets** to help manage cash flow; funds to purchase energy-saving equipment might be allocated for it in a property's cash budget.

As you can see in the above examples, financial aspects pertaining to environmentally friendly purchases can have numerous budget implications.

Capital budget

A budget that outlines a property's plans to invest in projects dealing with assets; see fixed assets.

Fixed assets

Assets with a cost greater than an amount specified by the restaurant that will benefit the restaurant for more than one year in the future.

Depreciation

A cost allocation system that charges a portion of the original cost of equipment to specific accounting periods.

Cash budget

A budget that estimates cash receipts and disbursements during a specified time period to determine cash flow: the ability to pay bills when due.

FIGURE 13.7

Prioritizing Problems: Assess the Economic Impact

Adapted from Ninemeier, J., and Hayes, D. (2006). *Restaurant Operations Management.* Pearson Education, Inc.

A. Would you rather increase sales or decrease variable costs? (Answer: Ideally, both!) What about in the example below?

Priority: To increase sales by $2,000 or to decrease variable costs by $2,000.

Assume	Current Data	Increase Sales by $2,000	Decrease Costs by $2,000
Sales	$ 12,000.00	$ 14,000.00	$ 12,000.00
Variable Costs (70%)	(8,400.00)	(9,800.00)	(6,400.00)
Fixed Costs (20%)	(2,400.00)	(2,400.00)	(2,400.00)
"Profit"	$ 1,200.00	$ 1,800.00	$ 3,200.00

Increasing sales by $2,000 only yields a $600 increase in profit ($1,800 increased profit [–] $1,200 current profit). The reason: Variable costs that, by definition, will be 70% of sales at any level, increase from $8,400 to $9,800 and reduce the amount of sales that drops to the "bottom line."

By contrast, if variable costs are reduced by $2,000, profitability is increased by that entire amount: $1,200 (original profit) + $2,000 (decreased variable cost) = $3,200 (new profit level).

B. Which of the following costs would you first "manage?" (Answer: Hopefully, both at the same time!) If not, which is the priority?

	Budget	Actual	Difference
Food Cost	34%	36%	(2%)
Beverage Cost	26%	31%	(5%)

At first examination, it appears "obvious" that beverage costs represent the biggest problem: a 5% variance from expected costs compared to only 2% variance for food costs. However, after we learn more details, our opinion of the largest problem changes:

FOOD			
	Actual	Budget	Difference
Food Sales	$450,000.00	$450,000.00	
Food Cost %	36%	34%	
Food Cost	$162,000.00	$153,000.00	($9,000.00)

BEVERAGE			
	Actual	Budget	Difference
Beverage Sales	$105,000.00	$105,000.00	
Beverage Cost %	31%	26%	
Beverage Cost	$32,550.00	$27,300.00	($5,250.00)

As seen above, a 2 percentage-point variance in food costs (36% – 34% = 2%) represents $9,000 in higher-than-expected costs (and lower profits). By contrast, a 5 percentage point variance in beverage costs (315 – 26% = 5%) results in $5,250 in higher-than-expected costs (and lower profits). Clearly, after any "quick fix" with the beverage operation, the manager's attention must be directed to food cost control activities.

Step 1 Define the Problem. Sometimes (but not always) the problem is obvious. Declining volumes of sales and/or increasing costs may be examples. Sometimes, however, it's much more difficult to identify the problem. Consider, for example, the view of some

| SALES PROBLEMS ||
Potentially Manageable Reasons	Potentially Unmanageable Reasons
• Sales theft by employees • Ineffective marketing/sales tactics • Guest-relations issues • New and significant competition for the same guest market • Operating hours are longer than necessary, and incurred labor costs aren't offset by sufficient sales	• Significant layoffs within the community, reducing the size of the guest market • Economic **recession** • Significant capital improvement/remodeling project leading to restaurant downtime • Street/other community improvement project yielding difficult/no access to property • Shortage (lack) of key menu ingredients, which require popular items to be temporarily removed from the menu
FOOD COST PROBLEMS	
Potentially Manageable Reasons	Potentially Unmanageable Reasons
• Sales theft[1] • Failure to follow procedures for effective purchasing, storing, issuing, or preparation of food products • Improper/inaccurate procedures used to calculate actual food costs[2] • Ineffective selling techniques, resulting in the sale of higher-than-desirable food cost items • Portion control issues	• Significant increases in costs paid for food due to increases in raw ingredient prices • Shift of guests' preferences to higher-food cost menu selections • Storage losses (for example, refrigerator/freezer breakdown due to power outage, requiring stored food to be destroyed) • Corporate-mandated shift to more convenience foods in efforts to reduce labor costs
LABOR COST PROBLEMS	
Potentially Manageable Reasons	Potentially Unmanageable Reasons
• Lack of training yields reduced productivity • Misuse of electronic time clock • Ineffective employee scheduling • Out-of-date productivity standards in use • Failure to enforce employee break times	• Government-mandated minimum wage increases • Increased employee benefits costs • Changes in union-negotiated working conditions • Very low unemployment in community: difficult to fill vacant positions and higher compensation rates result • Must provide employee housing because of property location

[1.] The food cost percentage is a function of food costs divided by sales; therefore, sales theft yields a higher food cost percentage. The real problem could be theft of sales rather than excess funds being spent for food.
[2] Review the discussion of actual food cost calculations in Chapter 11.

FIGURE 13.8

Manageable and Unmanageable Reasons for Sales, Food Cost and Labor Cost Problems
Adapted from Ninemeier, J., and Hayes, D. (2006). *Restaurant Operations Management.* Pearson Education, Inc.

Recession

A downturn in the economy that creates job losses, stock market decreases, and uncertainty about the financial future.

restaurant managers that an increasing number of job applicants enter the workforce with a lower work ethic than did their counterparts in prior generations. While this may be true, there are, probably, numerous societal, cultural, and other components of this issue that make problem identification and correction by a single restaurant manager difficult or even impossible.

Some managers ask themselves, "What would the situation be like in the absence of the problem?" to help define the problem. In other words, if the manager were gone for 10 years and then returned and said, "The situation is perfect," what would the manager have to notice in order for him/her to make this statement?

Unfortunately, in the real world, problems don't occur on a one-at-a-time basis. Instead, managers are typically confronted with numerous (or more!) problems at

FIGURE 13.9

Basics of the Decision-Making (Problem-Solving) Process

Adapted from Ninemeier, J., and Hayes, D. (2006). *Restaurant Operations Management.* Pearson Education, Inc.

Mystery shoppers

Persons retained by the restaurant to pose as guests and to observe and report any service, food quality, cleanliness, sales security, or other problems that are observed.

Step	Example
Step 1: Define the Problem	Sales have been decreasing for each of the last three months. Guest counts have remained about the same, so the guest check average is decreasing.
Step 2: Generate Solution Alternatives	• Need to utilize suggestive selling • Need to evaluate menu components and design to determine if changes can increase sales • Errors in equipment/procedures used to calculate data • Theft of sales by food servers
Step 3: Evaluate Solution Alternatives	• **Mystery shoppers** did not observe suggestive selling; training needed to implement suggestive selling program • Menu recently redesigned; guest counts are up slightly • An auditor has found no bookkeeping problems suggesting employee theft
Step 4: Select the "Best" Solution Alternative	Implement a suggestive selling program for food servers
Step 5: Implement the Solution Alternative	Train service staff; implement a contest (all servers with a specified minimum guest check average win complimentary meals and sweatshirts)
Step 6: Evaluate the Effectiveness of the Solution	Determine the extent to which the guest check average increases after the suggestive selling training program has been implemented

Cross-functional team

A group of employees from different departments within the restaurant that work together to resolve operating problems.

the same time. They must, then, set a priority using procedures such as those noted above.

Step 2 **Generate Solution Alternatives.** What can be done to address the problem? The manager should have some answers, but affected employees may also have suggestions—for example, "what did and didn't work" in their previous places of employment. The use of **cross-functional teams** can help to identify potential solutions. For example, the problem that "some guests complain about slow service" should probably be addressed by the manager, servers, cooks (and, perhaps, others) who can provide solution alternatives.

Step 3 **Evaluate Solution Alternatives.** Factors including perceived ability to resolve the problem, time, cost and ease of implementation, and impact upon other work processes are among the factors that can be used to evaluate the solution alternatives generated in Step 2 above.

Step 4 **Select the "Best" Solution Alternative.** The experience of the manager and the problem-solving team will be very helpful in selecting the alternative that should be implemented. Sometimes, the "best" solution involves utilizing aspects of several possible alternatives generated in Step 2.

Step 5 **Implement the Solution Alternative.** Employee training, purchase of necessary equipment/tools, changes to work methods, and trial study are among the tactics that may be necessary during the implementation phases of decision-making and problem-solving.

Step 6 **Evaluate the Effectiveness of the Solution.** If the manager has considered what the situation would be like if the problem no longer existed (Step 1), this step becomes easier. Often, solutions that are implemented aren't optimal; the problem may still exist but, as a result of the decision-making process, its impact on the organization has been lessened. If the problem is still significant relative to others confronting the restaurant, the manager may choose to repeat the problem-solving process with the hope of identifying and implementing other solution alternatives that can further reduce the impact of the problem.

TACTICS TO IMPLEMENT CHANGE   Sometimes the corrective action process helps managers to realize that existing procedures are good ones, but that they're being used incorrectly or inconsistently. While retraining, closer supervision or coaching may be in order, the employees at least know about the procedure and won't resist it because it's new. Frequently, however, the decision-making team will recognize that new and different procedures will be necessary to keep sales or costs in line with budget estimates or to resolve other operating challenges. It is at this point that the managers must become masters of implementing change.

One of the first obstacles that potentially must be overcome involves affected employees resisting proposed changes. For example, employees who are used to doing something one way may resist changes in standard operating procedures. "We have always done it this way!" or "We have never done it that way!" may be some employees' initial response. These workers may be uncertain about how they'll be affected by the change, they may not want to take the time to learn "new ways of doing things" or they may be concerned about the closer coaching and supervision interactions which will likely be necessary as the change is implemented and evaluated. If this human nature to resist change is understood and addressed, the restaurant manager is much more likely to be successful in managing change.

OVERCOMING RESISTANCE TO CHANGE   Knowledgeable restaurant managers can use several tactics to overcome resistance to change. All will be more effective if the manager has had a history of 1) involving employees and explaining, defending, and justifying why the change is necessary; and 2) if he/she has historically been correct; if the situation was "better" after the change.

Let's look at some tactics to reduce resistance to change:

- Involve employees in the decision-making process. A democratic management style improves the quality of the decision-making process. Implementing corrective actions is easier when the decision is "ours" rather than that of the manager alone.
- Inform employees in advance about changes that will impact them.
- Select an appropriate time to implement the change. "Trying something new" during an extremely busy shift is never a good idea!
- Share past successes Review related changes that have benefited the employees and the organization.
- Reward employees for sharing ideas in the decision-making process that benefit the restaurant and the employees.

CHANGE MUST BE MANAGED   Restaurant managers who truly believe in involving their employees in the decision-making process will lead their staff members through a **continuous quality improvement (CQI)** initiative.

These restaurant managers recognize that, regardless of how small a change may be, the restaurant is "better" because of any change that helps the organization to better meet its mission and goals. Employees working within a CQI environment will be conditioned for change, will look forward to it because they know its benefits and will be active participants in it. Another advantage: CQI typically works "from the bottom up" in the restaurant because employees closest

Continuous quality improvement (CQI)

Ongoing efforts within the restaurant to better meet or exceed guests' expectations and to define ways to perform work with better, less-costly, and faster methods.

WEB AT WORK!

Restaurant managers and owners may want the services of a foodservice consultant to help with problem identification/resolution if the on-site managers cannot sufficiently address the issue. To learn about food service consultants and what they do, go to the website of the Foodservice Consultants Society International. To view the website, go to:

www.fcsi.org

This organization's homepage provides wonderful information about the professionals it represents. You'll learn what a food service consultant does, and you can search a database for members within any specific area.

This restaurant owner is talking about problems and how to reoslve them with her chef.

to the situation are very likely to have ideas to help improve it. Their ideas about increasing sales and controlling costs, for example, can be very creative and of great assistance to the restaurant manager. With CQI efforts, the restaurant manager is really a facilitator who, after defining a problem, utilizes a team approach to analyzing, taking corrective action, and implementing necessary changes.

Corrective Action Tactics: A "Case Study"

This chapter has emphasized the importance of monitoring budget estimates against actual operating results and taking corrective actions to address significant negative variances. It has also noted the benefits of utilizing decision-making assistance from employees, including cross-functional teams.

This section provides a "case study" of how corrective actions might be planned by using the property's most important resource: the employees.

Executive committee

The restaurant's top-level decision makers, including managers with property-wide responsibilities and department heads responsible for specific functions.

THE SITUATION AT VERNON'S RESTAURANT   The executive management team at Vernon's Restaurant was not surprised about how the restaurant's owner opened the weekly meeting of his **executive committee**: "Our comparisons of budgeted and actual sales for the last four months have indicated a serious problem: Our sales are way down, even though our guest counts are right on target."

"Our POS system suggests some clues," he continued. "First, our check averages are lower by about $2.00 per person. Second, and even worse, the items we want to sell the most based on our ongoing menu engineering analysis are losing popularity."

"We're a closely-knit management team, and we've never had the all-too-typical comments from service personnel that if the cooks would prepare better food we could sell it. I have also never heard comments from our food production team that we could increase the check average if only the servers would do a better job of suggestively selling appetizers, desserts, and high-contribution entrees."

"I know we're all very busy, but we must make determining what's wrong and fixing it a priority. Here's what I want you to do:

- Luke (the kitchen manager) should meet with the production team to carefully consider why we're experiencing lower check averages and reduced sales of our most profitable items based on our menu engineering results.
- Jasmine (the dining room manager) should meet with the front-of-house staff to discuss the same two concerns.
- I'm asking both teams to identify potential problems and suggest how they can be resolved.
- Then Luke and Jasmine should meet to discuss each team's recommendations and to develop a proposal for our next executive management meeting. This will take place in about 10 days."

"If you have any questions, or if I can help in any way while your teams address these concerns, let me know. Otherwise, I want to hear your suggestions, and then our executive management team will consider what to do."

RESTAURANT SEGMENTS BY PRICE AND SERVICE LEVEL   The kitchen manager's team met a total of three times. Their ideas for resolving the problems were as follows:

- *Increase the check average*: We can offer a value-priced special dessert and appetizer-of-the-day that will contribute money above the contribution margin to increase our check average. Maybe we can begin a "dessert club" with a free dessert or appetizer after a specified number is purchased.
- *Management of the menu*: Our most profitable items are often, but not always, our highest-priced items. As the sale of our profitable items decrease, the check average also decreases. However, the financial problem is made worse because the contribution margin that's "buried" in the check average also goes down. We could redo our menu engineering analysis to confirm which items are currently the most popular, or get the information from our POS system.
- *Ensure food quality and portion size*: Our food quality has suffered a little in recent months. The reasons, while explainable, aren't defensible. We've had to purchase many of our products from a new supplier since the previous one (who provided many ingredients for our entrées) went out of business. Unfortunately, we've paid a little less attention to food purchase specifications for our most expensive items, and the reduced quality of some ingredients has affected some of our menu items—including our most profitable ones. As a result, many of these items aren't being reordered by our regular guests. Needless to say, an emphasis on suppliers following purchase specifications has already begun.

THE DINING ROOM MANAGER'S REPORT   The dining room team also met several times. It's ideas are summarized here:

- One reason the check average may be low is that we have discontinued our suggestive selling contest (all servers with a check average above a specified amount for five shifts in a row received a gift certificate for use at several local retail stores). Suggestive selling training along with the reimplementation of this program should help increase the check average. The same tactic (suggestive selling) should also help to increase the sale of our profitable items as identified by the menu engineering process.
- Our team doesn't have any comments about food quality or portion sizes. Our servers say they're receiving some negative feedback from the guests compared to the past. However, they don't notice a significant trend.

CASE STUDY WRAP-UP   In just 10 days, selected members of Vernon's Restaurant's executive committee had generated several ideas about the three challenges that confronted them:

- Lower check averages could be caused by the lack of suggestive selling by servers. This might be resolved by suggestive selling training, implementation of a server check average contest, and the offering of daily special value-added appetizers and desserts.
- The lower popularity of profitable menu items could be caused by a lack of suggestive selling and potential guests' concerns about food quality and portion size.

Professional restaurant managers know that highly motivated employees who work together as a team are essential to success.

- Food quality complaints may be due to a failure to follow through on the use of food-purchase specifications because of a supplier change.

After the reports with recommendations about the problems were given, the restaurant's owner met with the executive committee again and summarized the experience:

"I have always felt that a food service operation is comprised of several closely-related subsystems and, when one subsystem is affected, so are all the others."

"I think that this concept was proven in the problem–resolution process we just experienced. Production staff can cause problems for service staff and the restaurant. Service employees may also create issues for production personnel and the restaurant. We really do need to work as a team. We cannot separate sales control and food production by convenient ideas such as "servers are responsible for sales," and "kitchen personnel are responsible for food production."

"In fact, we're all responsible for every activity that impacts our operation because we're all affected by it. Our next step will be to develop an action plan with individual responsibilities and due dates for task completion. This plan should be finished in 30 days so it can be implemented."

The Balance Sheet: Summary of Financial Status

The best managers develop detailed operating budgets and carefully review their income statements. They then control their restaurant by comparing information from both accounting tools and taking the necessary corrective actions to keep on track with their financial goals. Another financial statement, the **balance sheet**, provides a summary of **financial sustainability**: Is the restaurant generating profits that meet the owner's financial risk requirements so the restaurant will continue operating? It also indicates the amount of **retained earnings**: the amount of profits made that have not been withdrawn from the business.

Balance sheets are developed according to a **basic accounting equation**:

Assets = Liabilities + **Shareholders' equity** (also called owner's equity)

Balance sheet

The financial document that details the value of a restaurant's assets, the total debt (liabilities) owed by the restaurant and the amount of equity held by its owners or shareholders at a specific point in time.

Financial sustainability

The situation in which a restaurant continues to operate because the owner's investment is generating an adequate return.

Retained earnings

The amount of profit that has not been withdrawn from the business.

Basic accounting equation

Assets = liabilities + shareholders' equity

Shareholders' equity

What remains after subtracting what the business shareholders (if a corporation) or owners (if not a corporation) owe to others (liabilities) from what the business owns (its assets).

This equation is the fundamental concept used to report the financial condition of a business.

A balance sheet reports information at a specific point in time. For example, many restaurant owners prepare a balance sheet at year's end. It reflects the value of assets, liabilities, and owner's equity as of December 31 of the year reported. Alternatively, some restaurant operators want a balance sheet prepared at the end of each month. In either case, the balance sheet reports its information as of the last day of the accounting period to which it applies. Figure 13.10 is a simplified balance sheet for Vernon's Restaurant.

Note that there are three types of assets. **Current assets** include cash or other assets that can quickly (currently) be converted to cash, such as food, beverage, and supplies (inventories). **Property and equipment** represent the physical portion of the restaurant, including leasehold improvements and furniture, fixtures, and equipment less any accumulated depreciation. **Other assets** include the cost of the liquor license and deposits. **Total assets** are the combined value of all the restaurant's assets.

The liabilities section of the balance sheet in Figure 13.10 shows the claims by others against the restaurant's assets. Vernon's has total liabilities of $305,000. This includes $137,000 in **current liabilities** (those payable within one year) and the currently due portion of long-term debt. The total liabilities also include $168,000 in other long-term debt.

The total liabilities must be paid before the owners can determine their own portion of the restaurant's assets. In this case, the owners have a total claim of $228,000 against the restaurant's assets, represented by **capital stock** and retained earnings.

The fundamental accounting equation discussed earlier in this chapter holds true:

$$\text{Assets} = \text{Liabilities} + \text{Shareholder's equity}$$

or

$$\$533,000 = \$305,400 + \$228,000$$

Understanding the effect of an operation's profitability on the balance sheet is essential for many reasons. Two of the most important reasons are related to **liquidity** and long-term debt.

Since the balance sheet identifies the cash on hand and other assets that can quickly be converted to cash and short-term debt (liabilities), it can be used to evaluate the ability of the restaurant to meet its short-term debt. This is done with the **current ratio**:

$$\text{current ratio} = \frac{\text{Current assets}}{\text{Current liabilities}} = \frac{\$124,200}{\$137,400} = .90$$

Vernon's Restaurant has 90 cents in current assets for each $1.00 in current liabilities. Current ratios less than 1.00 suggest that short-term obligations may be difficult to meet without drawing down on the owners' investments.

The balance sheet also indicates the total amount of long-term debt owed by the business. Vernon's owners have an obligation to repay this debt. It's possible to be profitable and still be unable to make debt payments according to the debt repayment agreements. In many cases, even profitable restaurants default on long-term debt repayments. The reason: The profit was insufficient to meet long-term debt payment obligations for the land, buildings, and furnishing loans used to generate the restaurant's profits. A **solvency ratio** allows the reader of a balance sheet to see how the restaurant's assets relate to its liabilities. This can indicate whether the owners are able to pay off debts with their assets:

$$\text{Solvency ratio} = \frac{\text{Total assets}}{\text{Total liabilities}} = \frac{\$533,400}{\$305,400} = 1.74$$

In this example, the owners have $1.74 of balance sheet assets for every $1.00 in balance sheet liabilities; if necessary, it's likely that they could sell their assets (even at less than book value) to pay all their debts. Thus, in this example, while the ability of the restaurant to pay its short-term debts is limited, it's in a strong position (solvency ratio) to pay its overall debts.

Current assets

Cash or other assets that can quickly (in less than one year) be converted to cash, such as food, beverage, and supplies inventories.

Property and equipment

The physical portion of the restaurant, including leasehold improvements and furniture, fixtures, and equipment, less any accumulated depreciation.

Other assets

Examples include the cost of the liquor license and deposits.

Total assets

The combined value of the restaurant's assets.

Current liabilities

Liabilities that are payable within one year.

Capital stock

The amount of money invested in a restaurant by its corporate owners and the amount, if any, of profit retained by the restaurant that has been reinvested in it.

Liquidity

The ability of a restaurant to pay its short-term (current) bills.

Current ratio

A measure of liquidity computed as:
Current assets ÷ Current liabilities

Solvency ratio

A comparison of a business's total assets to its total liabilities.

FIGURE 13.10

Balance Sheet: Vernon's Restaurant*

Adopted and recommended by the National Restaurant Association.

Assets			
CURRENT ASSETS			
Cash			
House Banks	$ 6,500		
Cash in Banks	35,800		
Accounts Receivable:		$ 42,300	
Credit Cards	13,800		
Customer House Accounts	8,500		
Inventories:		22,300	
Food	18,000		
Beverage	15,600		
Supplies & Other	7,500	41,100	
Prepaid Expenses		18,500	
Total Current Assets			$ 124,200
PROPERTY AND EQUIPMENT			
Leasehold Improvements		321,400	
Furniture, Fixtures, Equipment		133,000	
Less: Accumulated Depreciation and Amortization		(68,500)	
Total Property and Equipment: Net			385,900
OTHER ASSETS			
Cost of Liquor License		15,800	
Lease and Utility Deposits		7,500	
Total Other Assets			23,300
TOTAL ASSETS			**$ 533,400**
Liabilities and Shareholders' Equity			
CURRENT LIABILITIES			
Accounts Payable		$ 38,600	
Payroll Taxes Payable		21,900	
Sales Taxes Payable		27,800	
Accrued Expenses		21,500	
Current Portion, Long-Term Debt		27,600	
Total Current Liabilities			$ 137,400
Long-Term Debt, net of Current Portion			168,000
Total Liabilities			305,400
SHAREHOLDER'S EQUITY			
Capital Stock		35,000	
Retained Earnings		193,000	
Total Equity			228,000
TOTAL LIABILITIES AND SHAREHOLDER'S EQUITY			**$ 533,400**

*Format from *The Uniform System of Accounts for Restaurants, Eighth Edition.* (2010).

ALL IN A DAY'S WORK 13.2

"We've never done it that way," said Mandy, as she walked out of the restaurant with Danny. She was referring to the new procedures outlined at the restaurant's staff meeting for dining room cleanup at the end of each shift.

Penny, the restaurant's manager, was frustrated with ever-increasing labor costs that exceeded budget estimates and was making numerous changes to reduce labor costs without, allegedly, sacrificing quality.

One proposed dining room change involved the early closing of certain sections and associated server stations. As service slowed toward the end of each shift, all servers on duty would help with clean-up.

"Why should I help other people with their clean-up duties so they can go home, when I just have to stick around to do my own clean-up duties later?" Mandy asked Danny, another server.

"You're right, it doesn't sound fair," said Danny. "But Penny did say we would rotate shifts so that we could each leave early sometimes and do more work later at other times."

"Yes, but let's see how long that type of schedule works," replied Mandy. "Servers who have been here a long time will get the 'early-out' shifts!" she continued. "Why do we have to change anything? I think the restaurant is making big money at our expense, so what's the big deal if we save a few hours? How much more money does the manager have to make, especially if it's an inconvenience to us?"

1. What techniques might a restaurant manager using a democratic leadership style have tried to reduce the possibility of this conversation and the server attitudes that it suggests?

2. What, if anything, should Penny do next when she learns about the server's negative reactions to the new dining room scheduling plan?

IN CONCLUSION

You have now reached the end of the last chapter in this book. Along the journey through the book, you've learned about many important principles that restaurant managers use to help ensure that their properties are successful. The profession of hospitality management, including restaurant operations, is exciting, and every day is different. A grounding in basic knowledge about "how a restaurant works" coupled with the experience you'll gain as you advance in your career will prove to be invaluable.

The book's authors congratulate you in the completion of this milestone. We sincerely wish you the very best as you learn and practice the art and science of professional restaurant management.

Restaurant Terms and Concepts Glossary

Work in Progress

1. Severe weather can have a significant short-term effect on a restaurant's sales levels. Assume you own a restaurant chain where business is likely to be affected by severe winter weather. How would this impact the development of your budget?

2. Should restaurant managers share financial results with restaurant employees? What might be two advantages and two disadvantages to doing so?

3. Restaurant managers are busy. Their ongoing work involving scheduling and supervising staff, maintaining quality standards and monitoring the budget to identify the need for corrective actions, among many duties, is a full-time job. How much priority should a manager give to longer-term planning and improvement concerns? Should the manager delegate some/all of this responsibility to others? If so, to whom?

4. Restaurant managers are responsible for the "numbers"; however, in many large-volume operations, accountants develop record-keeping systems, collect the information, summarize it and report it to owners and managers. What type of initial and ongoing communication between the manager and the accountant is necessary to define terms (what elements will be included and excluded from food and beverage costs, for example) and to interpret "what the numbers mean"?

5. The chapter describes a variance analysis process to determine where financial problems are occurring and what corrective actions can be helpful. To what extent should a restaurant manager involve subordinate personnel in the variance analysis process?

6. This chapter reviews examples of reasons that would explain sales levels that fall short of budget expectations. What are some additional potential causes of sales-related challenges that could be within the restaurant manager's control?

7. This chapter reviews examples of reasons that would explain higher-than-expected food costs that don't meet budget expectations. What are some additional causes of food cost-related challenges that could be within the restaurant manager's control?

8. The chapter reviews examples of reasons that would explain higher-than-expected labor costs that don't meet budget expectations. What are some additional causes of labor cost-related challenges that could be within the restaurant manager's control?

9. Assume you are a district manager for a restaurant chain. You directly supervise five unit managers. All the restaurants are in the same metropolitan area and have the same menu. Purchasing is done centrally for all the units. What do these demographics suggest about the budget development process and for the assistance you give the unit managers as they analyze variances between budgeted and actual sales and food and beverage costs?

10. Do you think using mystery shoppers to review restaurant operations is a good idea? Explain your response. What can you do to make sure the mystery shopper reviews your special concerns during the visit?

GLOSSARY

À la carte menu A meal chosen item-by-item; each item is priced separately.

Accompaniment An item such as a salad or potato offered with and included within an entrée's selling price.

Accounts receivable Money owed to a restaurant that hasn't been received.

Accrual accounting system An accounting system that matches costs incurred with revenues generated.

Additional shift labor The amount of labor and related costs required to serve guests above the maximum number that can be served by required shift labor. As revenue increases, additional shift labor costs also increase.

Advertising The distribution of information about a business that is paid for by the business.

Aging The process of holding a beverage for a period of time before releasing it for sale. Aging may be done in bottles (e.g., wines) or wooden kegs (e.g., whiskey and some wines), but the intent is always to improve the beverage product.

Albumen Another term for the "white" of a fresh egg.

Alcohol A colorless beverage created by fermenting a liquid containing sugar.

Ambiance The feeling or mood created by an environment.

Application form A document job applicants fill out with employment-related information about themselves when they're applying for a job.

Aromatized wine A fortified wine to which a flavoring ingredient has been added.

As purchased (AP) The weight of a product before it's prepared or cooked; also called "AP weight."

Asset Property, including cash, that is owned by an individual or a business.

At-will employment An employment contract that can be terminated by either the employer or the employee at any time for any reason.

Attrition A reduction in the workforce caused by voluntary separation.

Authority The power and responsibility to make decisions.

Autocratic A leadership approach in which decisions are typically made and problems are resolved without input from affected staff members.

Background check A review of an applicant's criminal history, credit, driving record or other information relating to employment qualifications.

Back-of-house staff Employees whose jobs don't typically put them in direct contact with guests.

Bain marie A cooking utensil containing hot water into which another container is placed to keep food warm or to cook it gently.

Balance sheet The financial document that details the value of a restaurant's assets, the total debt (liabilities) owed by the restaurant and the amount of equity held by its owners or shareholders at a specific point in time.

Base selling price The benchmark selling price of a menu item calculated by use of an objective pricing method.

Basic accounting equation Assets = liabilities + shareholders' equity

Batch cooking The preparation of food in large quantities in small volumes (batches) rather than at one time; this maximizes food quality by reducing holding times until service.

Benchmark A goal or standard against which actual operating results are compared.

Benefits An advantage or desirable consequence that results from the purchase of a product or service feature.

Beverage cost percentage The percentage of beverage revenue used to purchase the beverage that generated the revenue.

Bin number A number that indicates the location in a wine cellar where a specific wine is being held for service. Bin numbers are often provided to guests so they can order wines by a number, rather than by their names.

Blood alcohol content (BAC) The amount of alcohol contained in a liter of an alcohol drinker's blood. BAC is also known as blood alcohol concentration and is expressed as a percentage.

Body language Nonverbal communication, including gestures and eye movements, that sends information about a person's feelings or intentions to another person.

Bona fide occupational qualifications (BOQ) Employment qualifications that employers are allowed to consider when making decisions about hiring and retaining employees.

Bonding The purchase of an insurance policy to reimburse a restaurant when there is proven employee fraud.

Bottom line Industry slang meaning "profit" or "net income."

Bouquet The aroma of wine.

Bureaucratic A leadership approach that involves "management by the book" and the enforcement of policies, procedures and written rules.

Business model The plan implemented by a company to generate revenue and make a profit from operations.

Business plan A formal, written statement of business goals and strategies for how those goals will be achieved.

Business structure A legally recognized business entity.

C corporation A corporation that may be formed without restriction on the number of foreign or domestic shareholders. Also known as a "C Corp."

Cajun cuisine A style of cooking named for the French-speaking Acadian (Cajun) immigrants deported by the British from the area that is now Nova Scotia (Canada) to the area around New Orleans, Louisiana, in the late 1700s and early 1800s.

Call-brand liquor A specific brand of liquor requested by a guest.

Call-in Employees who are scheduled to work but notify their managers that they are not coming to work.

Capital The investment cash used to start a new restaurant.

Capital budget A budget that outlines a property's plans to invest in projects dealing with assets; see fixed assets.

Capital stock The amount of money invested in a restaurant by its corporate owners and the amount, if any, of profit retained by the restaurant that has been reinvested in it.

Cappuccino A classic recipe uses typically equal portions of espresso, steamed milk and whipped cream foam (often sprinkled with powdered cinnamon).

Carafe A glass container used to serve wine or water.

Career ladder A plan that shows how one can advance to more responsible positions within a restaurant.

Cash accounting system An accounting system that considers revenues to be earned when they're received and expenses to be incurred when payments are made.

Cash budget A budget that estimates cash receipts and disbursements during a specified time period to determine cash flow: the ability to pay bills when due.

Cashier bank Currency used to provide guests with change.

Center of the plate The concept that the entrée should be positioned in the center of the plate with the other items slightly overlapped and moving toward the plate's rim, so that all center-plate areas are covered with food.

Centralized purchasing A system in which purchasing is the responsibility of a specialist in the purchasing department in a large restaurant or is coordinated with purchasing specialists outside the restaurant in a multiunit operation.

Chain restaurant A restaurant that shares the name, menu and operating practices with other restaurants that are part of the same organization. Well-known examples include McDonald's, Wendy's, Subway, Panda Express and Qdoba Mexican Grill.

Change order Revisions to building plans after construction has begun.

Check average The average amount of money spent per guest served in restaurant. Also known as "average sale per guest."

Cholesterol A soft, waxy substance found in animal tissues and other foods of animal origin. Its level in the bloodstream can influence certain unwanted health conditions, such as plaque buildup in the arteries and heart disease.

Cleaning Removal of soil and food from the items being processed.

Clip-on menu A menu insert or attachment that advertises daily specials or emphasizes other menu items.

Coaching Efforts made by restaurant managers to encourage proper job behavior and guidelines.

Code of ethics A formal statement that defines how restaurant employees should relate to each other and the persons and groups with whom they interact.

Collusion An agreement between two or more people to commit fraud.

Commercial food service Food service operations that are typically open to the general public. These operations most often seek to make a profit by providing food and beverages to as wide an audience of customers as possible.

Compensation package The money and other valuable items (fringe benefits) provided in exchange for the work employees do.

Competency A recognized standard level of knowledge, skills and abilities required for successful job performance.

Competing menu items Menu items that normally compete with each other as guests make their selection decisions.

Competitive bidding A tactic used by purchasers who compare suppliers' prices for those products meeting specifications to determine which supplier is offering the best price.

Computer-assisted design (CAD) software Used to draw (develop) sketches of building plans/layouts.

Concept A clearly stated and well-thought-out idea for a restaurant.

Condiment Salt, pepper, mustard, ketchup, or a similar flavoring substance added in small amounts to food (usually at the table) to improve its taste.

Continuous quality improvement (CQI) Ongoing efforts within the restaurant to better meet or exceed guests' expectations and to define ways to perform work with better, less-costly and faster methods.

Controller The person who records and summarizes a restaurant's business transactions, develops financial statements and provides suggestions about what "the numbers say"; another word for accountant.

Convection oven An oven that heats by circulating air (convection currents) rather than using a conventional heating process (conduction currents).

Convenience food Food that has some labor built-in that otherwise would need to be added on-site.

Cooks' line The work station containing the major food production and food holding equipment used to prepare items for plating and pick-up by service personnel.

Corporation A formal business structure recognized as a legal entity, with privileges and liabilities separate from those of its owners.

Cost allocation The assignment of specific costs to the profit center that generates the cost.

Cost of goods sold: beverage The actual cost of the beverages used to generate beverage revenue for a specific time period; also called adjusted beverage cost or net beverage cost.

Cost of goods sold: food The actual cost of the food used to generate food revenue for a specific time period; also called adjusted food cost or net food cost.

Cost of labor Salaries, wages, fringe benefits and all other employee-related expenses required for restaurant personnel.

Cost-effective A situation in which time and money gained is greater than incurred costs.

Cost justification The process of ensuring that what is done attains the highest-possible purpose and costs less than the expenses required for its implementation.

Count When used to label crustaceans, this term refers to "the number in a pound."

Cream A dairy product that must contain a minimum of 18% milk fat.

Credit card processing Procedures used to transfer funds from a credit card holder's account to the bank account of the business charging the guest's card.

Creole cuisine A style of cooking named for the European aristocrats who moved to New Orleans, Louisiana, in the late 1600s. The word Creole comes from the Spanish word criallo; meaning a mixture of cultures or colors. The various cultures that contributed to the creation of Creole cuisine include Native American, Caribbean, African, French, Spanish, English, German and Italian.

Critical control point (CCP) Something done in the management of food from receiving to service to helping prevent, eliminate or reduce hazards.

Critical limit Maximum/minimum limits that define the extent to which a critical control point must be controlled to minimize foodborne illness risks.

Cross-contamination The transfer of harmful germs or bacteria from one surface to another.

Cross-functional team A group of employees from different departments within the restaurant that work together to resolve operating problems.

Cross-selling Tactics to advertise other products or services offered by the restaurant in addition to those on a specific menu.

Crustaceans Shellfish with hard outer skeletons or shells and joints that separate the "head" from the "tail" (as in shrimp and lobster), or "leg" from the "body" (as with crabs).

Cuisine A specific group of cooking traditions and practices associated with a specific culture. Most often named after the cooking style or the region where the culture is found. Examples include French, Italian, Creole, German and Asian cuisines.

Cultured dairy product The processed food created when specific bacteria are added to liquid dairy products.

Currency Bills and coins (money) used to make purchases.

Current assets Cash or other assets that can quickly (in less than one year) be converted to cash, such as food, beverage and supplies inventories.

Current liabilities Liabilities that are payable within one year.

Current ratio A measure of liquidity computed as Current assets ÷ Current liabilities

Custom equipment Equipment designed according to unique plans or drawings that requires special construction.

Customer-centric A decision-making approach that emphasizes a course of action's impact on customers prior to its implementation.

Cycle menu A menu in which the food items rotate according to a planned schedule.

Damages Payments made to compensate another for harm, loss or injury.

Day-part A segment of the day that represents a change in menu and customer response patterns; for example, the time during which breakfast or lunch menus are offered.

DBA An abbreviation of "doing business as."

Debt financing The borrowed money used to finance a new restaurant.

Debt service The annual amount that must be repaid to those who have lent money to a business.

Décor The decoration of a room and the arrangement of the objects in it.

Delegate The process of assigning authority (power) to subordinates to allow them to do the work that a higher-level manager would otherwise need to do.

Democratic A leadership approach in which employees are encouraged to participate in the decision-making process.

Demographic A distinctive characteristic of a group used to identify a target market.

Depreciation A cost allocation system that charges a portion of the original cost of equipment to specific accounting periods.

Desktop publishing system A personal computer and specific software used to create on-site, high-quality page layouts for menus.

Die-cut menu A menu that has been punched or cut into a special shape with a metal tool (die).

Direct interview questions Specific questions asked to learn factual information about job applicants.

Discrimination Unfair treatment to another person based on his or her religion, race, age, national origin, gender or the condition of pregnancy.

Distillation A process in the production of alcoholic beverages that's used to increase the amount of alcohol contained in the beverage.

Diversity Ethnic, socioeconomic and gender variety in a group, society or business.

Dividend The portion of its profits paid by a corporation to its shareholders.

Draft beer An unpasteurized beer product sold in kegs. Also known as "tap beer."

Dram shop laws A variety of state and local regulations specifying the rules that must be followed by those who hold licenses to sell alcohol.

Drive-through customers Restaurant guests who place and receive their take-away food orders without leaving their car.

Dry aged The storing of fresh meats in an environment of controlled temperature, humidity and airflow for up to six weeks.

Dry heat A cooking method in which the food to be cooked is exposed directly to heat or flame. Examples: broiling and frying.

Du jour menu A menu in which some or all food items are changed daily.

Duty of care A legal obligation that requires a specific type of conduct.

Edible food yield The useable amount of a food ingredient that can be prepared from a given purchase unit of that ingredient.

Edible portion (EP) The amount of a food item that can be served to guests after a product is cooked.

Embezzlement The crime of fraudulently taking the money or property of an employer.

Employee benefits Indirect financial compensation paid to attract and retain employees or to meet legal requirements. Some benefits are mandatory (Social Security taxes) while others are voluntary (paid time off).

Employee discipline Corrective actions uniformly applied and designed to encourage employees to follow established policies, rules and regulations.

Employee handbook A manual that explains employment policies relating to employment issues; compensation, including benefits; operating concerns; and legal and other requirements.

Employee turnover rate The number of employees who leave during a specific period of time. This is calculated by dividing the total number of employees who leave an organization by the total number of employees during a specific period of time.

Empower The act of allowing employees to make decisions within their areas of responsibility.

Entrée A food served as a meal's main course.

Entrepreneur A person who organizes and manages a private business, usually with considerable initiative and risk.

Equity funding The personal money used to finance a new restaurant.

Ergonomics Analysis and studies to better fit a job to the employee who does it and to reduce work-related musculoskeletal disorders.

Espresso Coffee produced by forcing hot water under high pressure through finely ground coffee, typically in very small volumes.

Ethics Concerns relating to what is right and wrong behavior when dealing with others.

Executive committee The restaurant's top-level decision makers, including managers with property-wide responsibilities and department heads responsible for specific functions.

Exit interview A meeting with a departing employee that is conducted to learn what can be done to improve the restaurant.

Extension The price of an item multiplied by the number of items purchased.

External recruiting Activities used to inform people who don't work for the restaurant that new staff members are needed to fill vacant positions.

Farm-to-fork A term used to describe the handling of food through the stages of growing, harvesting, storage, processing, packaging and preparation.

Fast-track employees Those who perform effectively in their existing position and who participate in a planned professional development program designed to quickly promote them.

Features Specific menu items and services that a restaurant offers for sale.

Fermentation The conversion of carbohydrates to alcohol and carbon dioxide using yeast or bacteria to initiate the conversion process.

Financial sustainability The situation in which a restaurant continues to operate because the owner's investment is generating an adequate return.

Fiscal year Any 365-day accounting period that does not begin on January 1.

Fixed assets Assets with a cost greater than an amount specified by the restaurant that will benefit the restaurant for more than one year in the future.

Fixed cost A cost that does not vary as revenue changes.

Food allergy An abnormal response to a food that has no known cure.

Foodborne illness Sickness that results from eating contaminated food.

Food cost percentage The percentage of food revenue used to purchase the food that generated the revenue.

Fortified wine A wine that has had a spirit added to it to increase its alcohol content.

Franchise A relationship through which a business is run using the same name and operating system of another business.

Franchise agreement The legal contract detailing the terms of the relationship between a franchisor and a franchisee.

Franchisee A person or business entity that buys a franchise.

Franchisor A person or business entity that sells a franchise.

Fraud The intentional use of a trick, deceit or other dishonest means to unlawfully take the property of another.

Free pour A manual system of making mixed drinks that relies upon the bartender to control the quantity of alcohol in the drink without the use of a portioning device.

Front-of-house staff Employees whose jobs put them in direct contact with guests.

Fruit The reproductive organ of a flowering plant. All species of flowering plants produce seeds (fruits) for reproduction.

Fusion cuisine Foods that blend the traditions of more than one cuisine.

Garbage Food waste that cannot be recycled.

General partnership A business structure consisting of two or more owners or entities that share in the profits and losses of a business.

Grapevine An informal channel of communication operating throughout a restaurant.

Green practices Activities that protect the environment and minimize damage to the planet that may result from the operation of restaurants.

Guest Any customer lawfully utilizing the services of a restaurant.

Guest check A written record of what a guest has ordered and the price the guest will be charged for the item(s)—prepared manually or generated electronically by a POS system.

Guest profile The personal characteristics of the guests who would be attracted to a restaurant.

Harassment Threatening and illegal verbal, physical or visual conduct.

Hazards Microorganisms, chemicals and physical objects that can contaminate food.

Hazard analysis critical control points (HACCP) A practical system using proper food-handling procedures along with monitoring and record keeping to help ensure that food is safe for consumption.

Head The foam that accumulates on the top of a properly poured beer or ale.

Hostile environment The presence of a verbally, physically or visually offensive workplace.

Hourly wage Money paid to an employee for work performed during a one-hour time period.

House-brand liquor Alcoholic beverages sold by generic type rather than by brand.

In balance The concept that the amount of money owed by guests is received from guests.

Income before income taxes The "bottom line" of an income statement.

Income statement A summary of the restaurant's profitability that details revenues generated, costs incurred and profits or losses realized during a specific accounting period; also called an income and expense statement or a profit and loss statement (P&L).

Incremental sales Sales that are in addition to, not a replacement of, existing sales.

Incremental sales Sales increases beyond a benchmark of current sales.

Internal recruiting The use of existing employees to help fill position vacancies. Current employees may be promoted from within to fill vacant positions, or they may refer friends, neighbors and others to the property.

Ingredient file A computerized record with information about each ingredient purchased, including purchase unit size and cost, issue unit size and cost and recipe unit size and cost.

Intranet A network consisting of computers for a single restaurant.

Inventory The list of the food and beverages used in a restaurant and the amount of those items currently on hand.

Inventory turnover rate The speed with which food or beverage inventory is turned into revenue within a specific time period.

Investment The money that an owner has spent to start and run the business.

IQF An acronym that stands for "individually quick frozen."

Irradiation The use of x-rays for the purpose of preserving foods.

Job description A list of the tasks that must be performed by a person working in a specific position.

Job offer An invitation to the most qualified job applicant that outlines the terms and conditions under which employment is offered.

Joint liability Co-responsibility to repay all of an obligation.

Jurisdiction The geographic area over which a legal authority extends.

Labor cost control forecast An estimate of the revenue to be generated or the number of guests to be served for a specific period that will be used to schedule employees.

Labor cost percentage The ratio of labor costs incurred in a specific accounting period relative to the revenue dollars generated in that same accounting period, computed as: cost of labor (÷) revenue = labor cost percentage.

Labor dollars per guest A labor productivity measure that does not vary based on menu prices; computed as total labor dollars (÷) number guests served = labor dollars per guest.

Laissez-faire A leadership approach that minimizes directing employees and, instead, maximizes the delegation of tasks and results to affected staff members.

Law of supply and demand Economic beliefs about the supply of an item and its price relative to its demand. Sometimes, as the price of an item increases, demand for that item decreases (and vice versa).

Layout A sketch often drawn to scale showing the relationship of work stations to each other.

Lease An arrangement that allows a restaurant to use items such as land, buildings or equipment without purchasing them.

Lessee A person or organization that leases property from another.

Lessor A person or organization that leases property to another.

Leverage The use of borrowed money to fund an investment.

Liability A debt that is owed and must be repaid.

Light-emitting diode A semi-conductor that emits visible light when an electric current passes through it.

Limited liability company (LLC) A form of corporation created under state law rather than federal law.

Limited partnership A form of partnership similar to a general partnership except that in addition to one or more general partners (GPs), there is one or more limited partners (LPs).

Liquid asset Assets (something of value) that are cash or that can easily be converted into cash.

Liquidity The ability of a restaurant to pay its short-term (current) bills.

Liquor license A state-authorized permit that allows the holder of the license (the licensee) to sell alcoholic beverages in accordance with state, local and federal law. Sometimes called a liquor permit.

Low-proximity exhaust system A ventilation system for kitchen equipment with a low minimum exhaust (cubic feet per minute) requirement.

Make or buy analysis The process of deciding whether all or part of a menu item should be prepared on-site or purchased as a convenience food.

Market form Different ways that food products can be purchased. Examples: whole chickens, fresh bone-in chicken breasts or skinless, boneless and frozen chicken breast portions.

Marketing Activities designed to attract and expand a restaurant's target market.

Marketing plan A calendar of specific activities designed to the meet the restaurant's revenue goals.

Mark-up factor An objective menu pricing method that considers an item's fair "share" of all costs and desired profit.

Mash A mixture of grain, malt and water used to produce beverage whiskey.

Menu A term meaning "detailed list." In common restaurant industry usage, a menu is 1) the items offered for sale and 2) the way the items offered for sale are made known to guests.

Menu category A group of similar menu items, such as entrées or salads.

Menu engineering An evaluation method that attempts to maximize the sale of a menu's most popular and profitable items.

Menu item file A computerized record with information about each menu item's sales as recorded by the restaurant's point-of-sale (POS) system.

Menu layout A term relating to the placement of menu item categories on the menu.

Menu rationalization A menu planning tactic that involves using the same main ingredient in several different menu items.

Merchandising Promoting selected menu items to encourage guests to select them.

Merchantable Fit for an intended use (in the case of food and beverages, "fit" for human consumption).

Microbrewery A brewery that produces limited amounts of specialized beers.

Minimum wage The least amount of money employers covered by the FLSA or state law may pay their employees.

Mission statement A planning tool that broadly identifies what a restaurant wants to accomplish and how it intends to do it.

Mixed cost A cost that contains both fixed and variable components.

Mixed drink A drink made by combining a spirit with water, fruit juice or another alcoholic or nonalcoholic beverage. Also known as a cocktail.

Mixology The practice and study of alcoholic beverage drink production.

Moist heat A cooking method in which food is cooked by extended exposure to steam or hot liquids. Examples: stewing and braising.

Mollusks Shellfish with soft, unsegmented bodies and no internal skeleton. Examples include conch, clams and oysters.

Moment of truth An instance of interaction between a customer and a business that gives the customer an opportunity to form or change his or her impression about the business.

Morale Workers' feelings about their employers, workplace and other aspects of their job.

Motivate The act of providing an employee with a reason to do something.

Mystery shoppers Persons retained by the restaurant to pose as guests and to observe and report any service, food quality, cleanliness, sales security, or other problems that are observed.

Nonalcoholic (NA) beer Beer with an alcohol content less than 0.5%.

National Restaurant Association (NRA) A professional trade and lobbying group representing nearly 400,000 restaurant locations.

Negative variance An unfavorable difference between planned and actual operating results.

Negligent Guilty of the failure to exercise reasonable care.

Net operating income Operating income after operating expenses are deducted but before income taxes and interest are paid.

Noncommercial foodservice Food service operations that are not typically open to the general public. The goal of these units is to provide meals for a specially targeted audience in a cost-effective way. This segment is also commonly referred to as "nonprofit" or "institutional" food service.

No-show Employees who are scheduled to work but don't report for their assigned shift or notify their managers that they are not coming to work.

NSF Short for "nonsufficient funds." NSF checking accounts are those without sufficient funds to pay the full amount of the check.

NSF International An organization that develops voluntary standards for the manufacture and installation of food service equipment.

On-the-job training Individualized training in which an experienced and knowledgeable trainer teaches another employee how to perform necessary tasks in the workplace.

Open-ended interview questions Questions asked to learn about an applicant's opinions and attitudes.

Operating agreement The legal document outlining the manner in which an LLC is formed and how it will be managed.

Operating budget A financial plan that estimates revenues and expenses for a specific time period.

Organic foods Foods produced, processed and packaged without using chemicals, including antibiotics or growth hormones in animals and pesticides and fertilizers or radiation while growing fruits and vegetables.

Orientation The process of providing basic information about a restaurant that must be known by all staff members in every department.

Other assets The cost of the liquor license and deposits.

Over When the revenue collected is more than the sum of guest charges that are owed.

Overcharging The incidence of charging a guest more for a food or beverage product than its actual selling price.

Overtime The number of hours of work after which an employee must receive a premium pay rate, usually one and one-half times the hourly rate.

Oxidation The chemical reaction (and deterioration) that can occur when a substance is exposed to oxygen.

Pantry The work station in which servers pick up items including desserts and pre-made salads that have been portioned by production staff.

Par stock A predetermined amount of an inventory item that should be kept on hand at all times.

Partnership agreement A formal contract outlining the financial and operational arrangement agreed to by the co-owners of a business.

Pass-through equipment Refrigerated or hot food compartments separating two work areas that allow food to be placed by production personnel onto a shelf or cart on one side of a wall and then retrieved by serving personnel on the other side of the wall.

Payroll The total wages and salaries paid to employees.

Perpetual inventory system A process that records all products entering and being issued from storage so managers know, on an ongoing basis, the amount of product that should be in inventory.

Pesticide A chemical used to kill pests such as rodents or insects.

Physical inventory system A process used to determine the quantity and value of product inventory on hand at a specific point in time.

Plate cost The total of all per-serving costs for menu items included in a specific meal.

Point-of-sale equipment A computerized device used by servers and bartenders to record orders. The system tallies revenue, sales, and numerous other types of data; abbreviated "POS."

Position analysis A process to identify each task in a position and how it should be done.

Pre-check/post-check A system that matches the quantity and value of orders placed by servers to the number of items paid for by guests.

Positive variance A favorable difference between planned and actual operating results.

Prime costs The term used to categorize product (food and beverage) costs and labor costs; these are the largest expenses in most restaurants.

Prime real estate The areas on a menu most frequently viewed by guests, which should contain the items that menu planners most want to sell.

Pro forma A financial statement prepared on the basis of assumed future events and activities.

Produce Agricultural products, especially fresh fruits and vegetables, grown for human consumption.

Product yield percentage The ratio of a recipe-ready ingredient to its original purchase form.

Production forecast An estimate of the sales activity of future menu items.

Production loss The amount of a product's AP weight that is not servable; this may be due to loss from trimming (for example, removing fat and bones), processing or cooking.

Profit center A revenue-producing department within the restaurant.

Progressive discipline program A carefully planned series of corrective actions—each increasing in its severity—designed to encourage employees to follow established policies, rules and regulations.

Proof A measure of a beverage's alcohol content. The proof of an alcoholic beverage is equal to two times the amount of alcohol it contains.

Property and equipment The physical portion of the restaurant, including leasehold improvements and furniture, fixtures and equipment, less any accumulated depreciation.

Psychographic Any distinctive attribute of guests relating to personality, values, attitudes, interests or lifestyles.

Public accommodation A facility that provides eating, sleeping or entertainment services to the general public.

Public relations The active process of managing communications between an organization and those interested in the organization's activities. Also known as "PR."

Publicity Newsworthy information about a business that is distributed for free.

Purchase order (PO) A document that communicates to suppliers the quantities to be delivered and the prices to be paid by a restaurant for needed items.

Purchase specification A tool that details the product characteristics of a specific food or beverage item purchased for a restaurant. Also known as a "spec."

Purchase unit The unit weight, volume, or container size in which a product is purchased.

Quality assurance programs Those activities related to ensuring the attainment of high-quality restaurant products and services.

Quality grade Designation of an item's quality rank relative to established standards of excellence. For example, Grade A, Grade B, and so on.

Quid pro quo The asking or demanding of sexual favors *in exchange* for maintaining employment.

Range oven Food production equipment featuring electric or gas-fueled burners for a top cooking surface with an oven underneath.

Reasonable accommodation Any modification or adjustment to a job or the work environment that will enable a *qualified* person with a disability to participate in the application process or to perform essential job functions.

Reasonable care The amount of care a reasonably prudent person would use in a similar situation.

Recession A downturn in the economy that creates job losses, stock market decreases and uncertainty about the financial future.

Recipe conversion factor (RCF) A factor (number) used to adjust ingredients in a standardized recipe when the number of servings and/or serving size of a current recipe must be changed.

Recipe costing The process of determining the food cost per portion (serving) and total yield for a standardized recipe.

Recipe management software Written programs, procedures, instructions or rules relating to computer system operation that involves standardized recipes.

Recipe-ready The form of an ingredient when it's fully prepared to be added to a recipe.

Recruiting Searching for those who are interested in vacant positions.

Refuse Solid waste, including cardboard and glass that is not removed through the sewage system.

Remote printer An electronic unit in the cooks' line that prints food orders entered into point-of-sale (POS) equipment by service personnel.

Required shift labor The amount of labor and associated costs required to operate the restaurant for a specific shift regardless of revenue volume.

Resources The tactics and abilities that restaurant managers use to attain goals, including people, food and beverage products, time, and money.

Restaurateur The owner or operator of a restaurant.

Retained earnings The amount of profit that has not been withdrawn from the business.

Retention rate (employee) The number of employees who remain during a specific period of time divided by the number of employees who worked during that same period.

Return on investment (ROI) A ratio of profits achieved to money invested computed as: total revenue (÷) total labor hours used = revenue per labor hour.

Revenue The amount of money generated from the sale of food and beverage products.

Revenue collection The process of properly identifying and recording guest charges and collecting their payments.

Revenue per labor hour A measure of labor productivity.

Revenue recap sheet A document prepared daily that details the total revenue generated, type of payment received, cash on hand and appropriate deposit amounts for one day's sales.

RevPASH Stands for "revenue per available seat hour" and is a measurement designed to assess efficiency in using the seating capacity of a restaurant.

Roll out Introducing a new menu item on an existing menu.

S corporation (Subchapter S Corporation) A corporation that offers liability protection to its owners but is exempt from paying corporate taxes on its profits.

Salary Money paid to an employee for work performed as calculated on a weekly, monthly or annual basis.

Sanitizing Eliminating or reducing the number of microorganisms on a surface.

Sashimi A Japanese dish consisting of raw fish sliced and served alone.

Seat tax The contribution margin of a menu item or (in menu engineering) the weighted average contribution margin for all items sold during the period under study.

Selection The process by which job applicants are evaluated in order to assess their suitability for a position.

Service charge A guest charge added by management that's typically computed as a percentage of a guest's food and beverage expenditures and that is legally the property of the restaurant.

Serving cost The cost to produce one serving of a menu item when it's prepared according to the standardized recipe; another phrase for portion cost.

Sexual harassment Threatening and illegal verbal, physical or visual conduct of a sex-related nature (e.g., touching or making suggestive remarks or gestures.)

Shareholder An individual or other entity that owns one or more shares (portions) of a corporation. Also referred to as a "stockholder."

Shareholders' equity What remains after subtracting what the business shareholders (if a corporation) or owners (if not a corporation) owe to others (liabilities) from what the business owns (its assets).

Sheeting agent A chemical used in dish machines to help prevent water spotting and streaking on plates, flatware, and other items cleaned by the unit.

Short When the amount of money collected is less than the sum of guest charges that are owed.

Short staff Slang for a situation in which the ideal number of employees is unavailable for a specific work shift.

Shot A small (1- to 2-ounce) drink consisting only of a single spirit.

Signature menu item A food or beverage item that guests associate with a specific food service operation.

Significant variance A difference in dollars or percentage between planned and actual operating results that warrants further investigation.

Small Business Administration (SBA) A U.S. government agency that does not make loans but rather helps educate and prepare business owners to apply for loans through a financial institution or bank.

Sneeze guard A see-through barrier to protect foods on self-service counters from guests who might sneeze or cough on them.

Social media The use of web-based and mobile technologies to turn communication into interactive dialogue between a restaurant and its customers.

Sole proprietorship A form of business structure in which one individual owns, and frequently operates, the business.

Solvency ratio A comparison of a business's total assets to its total liabilities.

Source document A document that is an entry point for financial information into the restaurant's accounting system.

Source reduction The effort by product manufacturers to design and ship products to minimize waste resulting from a product's shipping and delivery.

Split shift A work schedule in which an employee works a specified number of hours, leaves the restaurant and returns later the same day to work a second shift.

Standardized recipe Instructions to produce a food or beverage item that help ensure that the restaurant's quality and quantity standards for the product are consistently met.

Standardized recipe file A computerized record containing recipes for the menu items produced including each recipe's ingredients, preparation method, yield, ingredient costs and each item's selling price and food cost percentage.

Start-up funding The money needed to open and sustain a restaurant until it becomes profitable.

Stock equipment Equipment manufactured in large quantities according to standard plans that is often available in dealer inventories or which can be quickly obtained from the manufacturer or distributor.

Stockout The situation that exists when food or beverage products required for production aren't available in storage.

Straight-line flow The concept that products move, to the extent possible, in a straight -line from receiving, storing, and issuing to pre-preparation, production, and service without the need for unproductive "back tracking."

Subordinate financing Financing that will be repaid after other financing debts are resolved.

Suggestive selling Encouraging diners to buy more, or to buy selected menu items, by emphasizing their availability to a restaurant's customers.

Sushi A Japanese dish consisting of cooked, vinegary rice commonly topped with other ingredients, such as vegetables, fish or other seafood, or put into rolls.

Sustainable fishing Fish harvesting methods that help ensure the long-term viability of a fish species.

Table menu A menu pricing plan in which all meal components are offered at a single price.

Table turn The number of times a dining room table is used during a dining period.

Tableside food preparation Food preparation in the dining room or at or near the guest's table.

Tap The mechanism used to dispense draft (tap) beer.

Target market A well-defined group of potential customers.

Task breakdown A position analysis tool that indicates precisely how each task identified in the task list should be accomplished.

Task list A position analysis tool that indicates all duties included within a position.

Temperature danger zone The temperature range of 41°F (5°C) to 135°F (57C°) in which harmful germs multiply quickly.

Texture A description of how a food feels that is an important factor in food quality.

Third-party harassment Harassment of a business's employee by someone other than that business's paid employees (e.g., harassment by a customer, vendor or service provider).

Tip Money voluntarily given to a server by a guest for appreciation of good service.

Total assets The combined value of the restaurant's assets.

Toxin A poisonous chemical produced by germs or other living things.

Trainee An employee learning about a specific task or skill.

Trainer A qualified individual who teaches another employee about a specific task or skill in the workplace and how to do it.

Training The process of developing an employee's knowledge and skills to improve job performance.

Training lesson The information and methods used to present one session in a training plan.

Training plan An overview of the content and sequence of a training program.

Transfer An adjustment to the "cost of goods sold" that increases or decreases food or beverage costs to better match product costs with the revenue generated by the product's sale.

Inventory turnover rate The speed with which food or beverage inventory is turned into revenue within a specific time period

Umami A term that describes a savory, brothy or meaty taste.

Undercharging The incidence of charging a guest a lower amount for a food or beverage product than its actual selling price

Value A concept addressing the relationship between selling price and quality.

Variable cost A cost that changes in direct proportion to revenue.

Variance The difference between planned and actual operating results.

Vegetable Any herbaceous (nonwoody) plant whose leaves, stems, roots, tubers, seeds or flowers are eaten for food.

Venture capitalist A person or organization that invests in a business venture by providing capital for start-up or expansion. Venture capitalists typically seek higher rates of return or ownership than they would receive in more traditional investments.

Vintage Wine grown from grapes in one vineyard during one growing season.

Void The removal of a sale from a revenue total after the sale amount has been added to the revenue total.

Wait list A document or software program that contains the names of guests who have arrived at a restaurant but haven't yet been escorted to their tables.

Walk The act of a purchasing products in a restaurant and then leaving without paying for them.

Wet aged The process of storing vacuum-packed meats under refrigeration for up to six weeks.

Wine and food pairings The concept that some wines go better with specific foods and that a wine should be selected *after* the food item to be served with it has been chosen.

Wine list The total number and kinds of wines sold in a restaurant as well as their price per bottle, carafe or glass. Also known as a "wine menu."

Workstation An area with necessary equipment in which closely related work activities are done by employees working in similar positions.

Yield The number of servings and the size of each serving produced when a standardized recipe is followed.

Yield test A carefully controlled process to determine the amount (in weight or percentage) of a product that remains after it has been processed into its recipe-ready state.

Zero defects A goal of no deviation from standards; there are no times where production/service goals aren't met.

Zero tolerance A policy that takes seriously even the slightest violation of a policy prohibiting harassment.

INDEX

Note: Text in boxes is shown with a *b*; text in figures is shown with *f*